Social Media in Iran

Social Media in Iran

Politics and Society after 2009

Edited by

David M. Faris and Babak Rahimi

Cover photograph: "Lonely Modern Human" © Mahmoud Arefi Ghouchani

Published by State University of New York Press, Albany

For information, contact State University of New York Press, Albany, NY
www.sunypress.edu

Production, Jenn Bennett
Marketing, Kate R. Seburyamo

Library of Congress Cataloging-in-Publication Data

Social media in Iran : politics and society after 2009 / edited by David M. Faris and
  Babak Rahimi.
      pages cm
  Includes bibliographical references and index.
  ISBN 978-1-4384-5883-0 (hardcover : alk. paper)
  ISBN 978-1-4384-5882-3 (pbk. : alk. paper)
  ISBN 978-1-4384-5884-7 (e-book)
    1. Social media—Iran.   2. Social media—Political aspects—Iran.   3. Facebook
(Electronic resource)   I. Faris, David M.   II. Rahimi, Babak.

  HM1206.S65423 2015
  302.23'1—dc23   2015001354

10 9 8 7 6 5 4 3 2 1

Contents

PART III. CULTURE

Acknowledgments

The idea of this volume was initially conceived at a workshop titled "Facebook and Iran" at the Annenberg School for Communication, University of Pennsylvania, in winter of 2012. Some chapters in this book were originally presented as papers at the workshop, later updated, and have since been rewritten, but most of the contributors were invited to submit a study on an aspect of social media in its Iranian context. In soliciting contributions, we aimed at a wide empirical and theoretical spectrum. The papers in this study have been chosen not because they display a certain degree of unity in approach, but because they all represent an original study on the impact of the Internet on Iran and beyond. We hope that the present volume will contribute to the general knowledge on the role of social media in contemporary Iranian society and also examine some conceptual themes in the general study of society and information communication technologies.

In attempting to rise to this challenge, we owe much to the critical commentary, assistance, and support of numerous colleagues and friends. Our main thanks go to the Annenberg School for Communication, University of Pennsylvania, for providing us the opportunity to host the workshop. Special thanks to Professor Monroe Price, director of the Center for Global Communication Studies (CGCS), whose commitment and generosity to this volume is matched only by his outstanding scholarly contribution to the field of media and society. This volume also benefited from the insights and support of Briar Smith, associate director of CGCS at Annenberg School for Communication at the University of Pennsylvania, who provided us with much assistance, including organizing the workshop and introducing us to some of the contributors. During the duration of the workshop and beyond, we benefited from the advice, assistance, and support of Kevin Anderson, Drew Cahan, Mahmood Enayat, Libby Morgan, Laura Schwartz-Henderson, and Mehdi Yahyanejad. We thank them for their help at the workshop and after.

We would like to express our gratitude to Nadine Wassef, who took the time to review and provide critical commentary on some chapters in the volume. We wish to acknowledge the assistance of Krittika Patil, who helped locate numerous sources for the volume. Thanks also to the anonymous reviewers for the State University of New York Press for their thoughtful comments, which improved the arguments of the chapters. We also thank the individual contributors to this volume for their hard work and patience during the editorial process. Finally, we are grateful to Said Arjomand, who played an instrumental role in the publication of this volume. In particular, we express our gratitude to the State University of New York Press for providing a venue to publish works written mostly by emerging young scholars, whose unique perspectives, we believe, can have an impact on how scholars approach the relationship between media technology and society.

The system of transliteration used here is loosely based on the *International Journal of Middle East Studies*. Vowels that appear in transliteration approximate modern Persian pronunciation. For the sake of simplicity for the general audience, we have avoided the use of diacritical marks and technical terms.

David M. Faris,
2014 Chicago

Babak Rahimi,
2014 San Diego

Introduction

David M. Faris and Babak Rahimi

What has been the effect of the diffusion of social media technologies in the Islamic Republic of Iran? Do applications like Facebook, Flickr, and Vine undermine the grip of the country's authoritarian elite, or does Iran's strategy of creating a system of increasing censorship and surveillance effectively prevent the kind of online organization that threatened regimes across the region during the events of the Arab Spring? To answer this question properly requires a multidisciplinary effort, one that seeks answers beyond elite political struggles that are visible to nearly all observers, and that seeks to situate the study of social media in the particular cultural, social, political, religious, and generational contexts of the Islamic Republic, a country whose place in Western public discourse nearly always exceeds granular knowledge about its people, internal dynamics, and structures. It requires us to see social change and dissent in arenas beyond high politics and to understand Iran not as a closed system of political inputs flowing from top to bottom, but as an arena for digital contestation in venues as diverse as popular films, lifestyle blogs, and social networking sites, and around issues that go far beyond the political structures of the state to include gender, sexual orientation, ethnicity, and religion. In this volume, we have brought together a diverse group of scholars with specialized knowledge about the use of social media in Iran in all of its many applications and fields. This is because one of the most persistent problems in seeking to study the impact of the Internet on authoritarian societies is the cordoning off of knowledge in various disciplines from one another. What should be a strength—that sociologists, anthropologists, communications specialists, and political scientists are all working on what is effectively the same set of

1

problems—becomes a glaring weakness, because most institutional processes reward mastery of one's own discipline only. This volume is thus not just an attempt to understand the role of social media in Iran but also, significantly, an attempt to bridge disciplinary boundaries and to bring the knowledge of different fields to bear on a discrete question.

Social Media and Networked (Counter)publics

Before we proceed to a discussion of Iran and the chapters in this volume, it would be worthwhile to quickly review the state of scholarly knowledge about social media more generally. It is important to note that the study of social media across many disciplines has produced a body of knowledge that would be impossible to summarize in a short chapter, and that our tour here represents merely a smattering of what we see as the most relevant ideas to come out of this field. Over the past ten years, a consensus has emerged across a number of different disciplines that networks and network analysis are key to understanding the function and purpose of social media. Crucial insights from mathematics strongly suggested that the Internet is governed by what are known as "power laws"[1]—meaning that a small number of websites get an extraordinary amount of traffic, while the rest—the "long tail" coined by *Wired* editor Chris Anderson—get only a few hits a day, if that. As Hindman argued, this has significant implications for our understanding of the Internet's dynamics.[2] The United States was perhaps the first country to see the impact of pioneering bloggers on political discourse, where bloggers weighed in on political matters and often clashed with journalists over what to cover and how to cover it.[3] While it may be that everyone has a voice in cyberspace, it is not true that every voice is equally amplified. As time goes on, first-movers and elites become increasingly entrenched, and while it is not impossible to break through these barriers, it does mean that the Internet should not be seen as a flat, equal space but rather as riven by dynamics of stratification, wealth, education, and gender, much like the real world.

The use of social media in authoritarian regimes has generally been studied through one of two lenses—either that of collective action or that of enabling dissent or the formation of what Fraser dubbed "counterpublics."[4] For theorists of collective action, even in democratic states, social media sometimes helps to resolve common dilemmas of participation such as high opportunity costs, the linking of geographically diffuse individuals with common interests,[5] and problems of information scarcity. Scholars generally perceive the difficulties of collective action in authoritarian countries as stemming from a set of interrelated problems, not unlike those in states where free expression is protected but more acute and deeper. First, citizens in authoritarian countries frequently have few legitimate opportunities to express their dissatisfaction with the government, the treatment of groups or individuals, social trends, or public policy more generally. Moreover, it is rarely just that the opportunity for self-expression is not there, but rather that the state will use citizens to report on one another, creating a climate of pervasive fear and mistrust in which individuals will rarely feel secure enough to express their "real" feelings about public issues. Timur Kuran famously dubbed these feelings "private information" that the state feels compelled to control, lest citizens discover that their dissatisfaction is shared widely.[6] Typically the only way to reveal these feelings, prior to the diffusion of the Internet, was through grassroots organizing and protest—both incredibly dangerous activities for individuals to undertake in states where repressive apparatuses are typically wielded with little compunction.

With social media, however, individuals are encouraged by the very nature and structure of the platforms to share as much information as possible with others—whether that information is public, as with most Twitter accounts, or semi-public, as it is on Facebook and its local competitors. The cumulative results of this revelation of previously private information, as we saw in the Egyptian uprising of January 2011,[7] can be an information (or informational) cascade—a widespread, seemingly sudden shift in beliefs, attitudes, or behaviors in a single direction.[8] For large-scale collective actions in authoritarian societies, individuals are much more likely to act if a substantial number of individuals in their social networks do so as well. In the Egyptian case, for example, hundreds of thousands of Egyptians had pledged before January 25, 2011, to protest, which in turn likely altered the willingness of many more individuals to join them.[9] The substantial role of social media in the Egyptian uprising in particular has been the subject of a number of supportive scholarly inquiries.[10] At the same time, authoritarian regimes have become increasingly aware of the threat posed by digital technologies and have responded with everything from violence against activists to the creation of elaborate architectures of control and surveillance. While shutting down Internet access is a tactic pursued particularly by authoritarian regimes during moments of crisis,[11] the toolkit of authoritarian regimes has expanded substantially in recent years. Iran in particular has aggressively pursued total mastery of its digital public sphere.

The default public nature of many social media applications can also influence protest intentionally or unintentionally. Bimber, Flanigin, and

Stohl referred to the intentional consequences as "communality." As they argued, "*Communality* refers to the public good that is derived from successfully collecting, storing and sharing such information resources among members of some public."[12] But these kinds of activities require a good deal of intentionality, and the authors identify a category of public goods that they subsume under the idea of "second-order communality." According to Bimber, "The communal information good now results from largely *un*coordinated efforts."[13] Such activities might include posting to a message board or contributing to a database or store of knowledge. Crucially, the authors argue that many social media activities effectively render collective action theory irrelevant, since they routinely make private-to-public actions (like signing an e-petition) more or less costless to the participant. These points could prove to be crucial in a country like Iran, where participation in (public) collective action might be fraught with danger, and where more ambiguous forms of participation and communality might have similar effects with substantially reduced risks. Furthermore, research from other milieus suggests that enlisting citizens in low-cost online action may increase their likelihood of participating in later, increased high-cost actions, through what is known as the "ladder of engagement.[14]

Seen in this way, social media refers not just to sites such as (micro) blogging, wikis, mashups, video or photo/image-sharing platforms but to a complex set of social practices associated with applications that operate in networked ways. Equally significant is the concept of "social" in "social media," which integrally underlines a participatory force, an interactive vibrancy with a distinct form of mediated experience for the users as potentially both audiences and producers. Social media technologies thus entail processes of sociability, irrespective of their quality or trajectory, together with how they are perceived and used in shifting contexts. While it remains unclear, as Matthew Allen has argued, how new and revolutionary its applications are, the novelty of social media can be identified as a new set of social practices, ranging from usability, participation, convergence, or design, which may or may not entail political implications.[15] Popularized by its users—in particular free software and open source advocates such as Tim O'Reilly, the founder of publishing house O'Reilly Media, who also popularized the term "Web 2.0"—social media involves complex ways in which people understand or frame their applicability for a "rich user experience."[16] Through discourses such as "user-generated content" or "platform," social media carries an implicit reference to an openness paradigm, inclusive and free to all. The rhetoric about social media, in many ways, can be recognized as part of its repertoire of social practices.

Whether social media technologies, however, give relative tactical advantage to activists or their government opponents is a question that has been the subject of robust scholarly debate. A phenomenon that has been dubbed "slacktivism," many critics contend that digital forms of protest and mobilization are less effective than their grassroots, offline counterparts.[17] Some scholars have challenged the particular importance of social media in the Arab Spring,[18] but the broader debate concerns whether better-funded and better-equipped states will ultimately use digital technologies to impose stricter and more effective forms of surveillance on their populations.[19] Certainly efforts by the embattled regimes of Bashar al-Assad in Syria[20] and Vladimir Putin in Russia, as well as the Chinese government's substantial efforts, suggest that determined regimes can either build parallel networks of supporters on social media or use the state's power and authority to interfere with the ability of anyone to productively use the technologies to challenge state policy.

But the conception of the Internet as a public sphere has also received pushback.[21] The most prominent figure from this view is the German social philosopher Jürgen Habermas. In his seminal 1962 book, *The Structural Transformation of the Public Sphere*, Habermas demonstrated that the public sphere is a discursive space where critical debates by individuals influence political action based on rational deliberation.[22] However, as Habermas has argued, digital communication practices, with the Internet as its most popular representative, do not "automatically" lead to the growth of the public sphere.[23] This is so since the Internet, as a multidirectional communicative domain, cannot produce a set of focused politically central questions for public action, often leading to fragmented "likeminded" associations online. While the new media technology has enabled more people to access diverse information, the messy communicative sphere of the Internet, described by Habermas as "digital noise," lacks coherency and inclusivity. The Internet is not a reflexive but a confused mode of communication.[24]

There is also the aspect of political economy. From a practical standpoint, MacKinnon also cautions that the Internet as a free public space requires robust cooperation between national governments, and that corporations have often violated privacy rights.[25] Youmans and York argue that "privatized goals of platform owners and developers can conflict with their use as tools for civil society and popular mobilization."[26] Activists who rely on such commercial applications may see their needs and interests subsumed either to financial exigency or state power. Theorists, meanwhile, have accused enthusiasts of digital communication of "ignoring the real (read material) constraints that both enable and prevent it."[27] While some observers claim that the Internet is "at the forefront of the evolving public sphere,"[28] others are skeptical of the depth and deliberative quality of conversations taking place online. Or, as Mark West argues, the Internet has "no more and no less potential to serve as a deliberative component in a public sphere than do other communication media."[29]

Yet while acknowledging the limitations of digital public spheres, the chapters in this volume certainly lend credence to the idea that democratic deliberation, mobilization, and advocacy can take place even under extraordinarily intense limitations imposed by an authoritarian regime.[30] This is so since the Internet involves some form of creative action. To various degrees, when users participate in creating the media content that they consume, and accordingly distribute and share, they also shape a more inclusive space of interaction, regardless of situational and structural limitations.

However, the Internet's effect on authoritarian societies goes, therefore, well beyond the headline-grabbing events of large protests and government-toppling. It is also the stuff of dissent-making, contentious politics, and everyday rebellion against enforced orthodoxies. It is also not just about using the technology, but living with it as an embedded feature of nightly/daily life.

In a significant way, connectivity remains a key feature of Internet practice. The Internet makes it possible for groups living in diaspora to maintain ties more closely and routinely with those living in homelands—and even to have significant impact on discourses, strategies, and actions back home.[31] In many countries, marginalized groups and individuals have been able to form "counterpublics" in order to rectify their exclusion from the public sphere. For countries like Iran, where substantial numbers of ethnic Iranians live abroad, social media technologies have a clear utility for uniting activists and dissenters in diasporic communities in the West with citizens in Iran. It has also given people from marginalized communities—women, gays, religious minorities, among others—the opportunity to comment on public affairs, to form groups and networks, and to press their demands on the state.

Outline of the Volume

With the aim to sketch out the shifting contours of a social media landscape, this volume provides an overview of the ways in which Iranians based in various localities build complex relations that reshape their lived environments and, accordingly, give rise to new possibilities for networked action.

We offer a collection of empirical and theoretical studies that underline the complexity and diversity of actions in which social media technologies have a multidimensional presence. While changes of socially mediated action in diverse settings is analyzed from various disciplinary perspectives, the authors demonstrate the need to recognize social media as a dynamic process (hence the book's title) that results from participatory interactions that arise from human agency. Such a frame of analysis, involving an understanding of audiences as content creators who operate along lines that are flexible and fluid, underlines what the French cultural theorist Pierre Lévy defines as "collective intelligence"—that is, distributed social intelligence that is perpetually generating the extent of human interaction.[32]

The book's fourteen chapters, though not comprehensive in ambition, focus on three key theoretical perspectives. First, as in-depth accounts of the complex dimensions of the Internet's penetration in everyday life, the chapters collectively evaluate social media in the context of globalizing communication practices seen in changing geopolitical settings. In a significant way, they look at how both state and nonstate actors, including diasporic communities, creatively and contentiously engage with social media processes to communicate, disseminate, and consume information for diverse purposes. Second, the chapters explore the increasing role of the Internet in the way individuals interact to build networked communities online with offline implications. The case of the 2009 Green Movement provides one among many other examples of how Iranians based both inside Iran and abroad blur the lines between information, networked communication, and collective solidarity. Third, the chapters reflect an interdisciplinary perspective to rethink the relationship between communication and society, and the intricate ways that convergence of media is making significant transformations in various spheres of life in a country like Iran.

Our focus on Iran is not meant to exoticize a unique Middle East case study, but to critically examine the social media landscape of a so-called "developing" country, undergoing major changes in the broader context of global communication processes. The view adopted is that contemporary Iran is far more multifaceted and interconnected in consequence to transnational processes that entail shifting relations between normative structures and mediated affects, between identity and politics, between self and reality. While regional specialists may find studies on specific themes useful, the aim of this volume is to provide broad narratives of actor-based conceptions of media technology, an approach that focuses on the experiential and social networking processes of digital practices in the information era, extended beyond cultural specificities. Technosocial analysis of contemporary Iran thus recognizes the role of agency in the technological context within which social change takes place in contentious ways. Such analysis advances a set of perspectives that essentially understand technology and society in terms of mutually shaping processes.[33]

These perspectives are studied within a three-part framework of society, politics, and culture, though with some degree of overlap. Part I of the volume looks at societal processes. The section begins with an essay on social capital and the Iranian social media. In this study, Jari Eloranta, Hossein Kermani, and Babak Rahimi argue that emerging social media such as Facebook are providing new social networking opportunities and alternative collective interactive domains for Iranians of diverse backgrounds, based in different localities, to build social capital, defined in their study as the dense network of social relations built around conceptions and practices of trust and support. Yet social media as a "many-to-many interactive" medium is a multilayered and permeable form of computer-mediated communication, and accordingly, its impact on offline domains of Iranian life or beyond is ambiguous and multidirectional.

In Chapter 2, Elham Gheytanchi expands on the gender dimension of social media with a focus on how gender relations and identities undergo change in popular sites such as blogs and Facebook. As Gheytanchi shows, social media is providing a distinct sphere of cooperation between diasporic communities and women inside Iran to build alternative network ties and defy state norms of gender relations and identities in everyday offline domains. Social media sites such as Facebook are not just places for social interaction but contested spaces where normative discourses such as motherhood and womanhood are rearticulated through national and transnational ties.

The discussion of the role of social media in the empowerment of marginalized groups is continued in Chapters 3 and 4, in which Abouzar Nasirzadeh and Kobra Elahifar offer in-depth analysis, backed by empirical evidence, about the ways in which gay and disabled Iranians use social media to express and make themselves visible to local and global publics. In his study, Nasirzadeh argues that online sites are carving out experimental spaces where gay Iranian men form new relations and construct alternative images of self in a positive light, thus challenging "heteronormativity." Increasing Internet penetration and growing civic engagement of the diasporic homosexual community have enabled Iran-based gay communities to become more visible, though more research is required to better understand diverse activities of gay Iranians, particularly among the lesbian community online.

Elahifar's essay focuses on another marginal community, disabled Iranians, which is subject to social exclusion primarily due to normative conceptions of the body rather than sexuality. In her study, Elahifar shows how disabled Iranian men and women based in Iran use social media, in particular blogs, to make themselves present as active individual members of contemporary Iranian society. She argues that through blogging practices disabled Iranians employ the individualized notion of "voice" to insert themselves online and forge new identities and practices of visibility for social recognition offline. Both Nasirzadeh's and Elahifar's works confirm the argument advanced by Zizi Papacharissi that activities that were once significant in the public domain are increasingly performed in the private sphere, where connections link "the personal with the political, and the self to the polity and society."[34] The private sphere exerts power within the frame of digital practices of public life.

In Chapter 5, the first chapter of Part II, on politics, Marcus Michaelsen offers an account of the role of the Internet in the reformist period (1997–2005). He focuses on the reformist journalists who identified the new medium as an alternative to print media, which by the late period of Mohammad Khatami's presidency had increasingly come under pressure by the conservative-dominated judiciary and state security apparatus. According to Michaelsen, prior to the 2009 elections, reformist Iranians, as some of the most politically active members of the Iranian society, had already developed vibrant online "counterpublics" that not only affirmed a new dissident political identity, but also challenged state ideology and bolstered offline civic support for reform. By the early 2000s, such vibrant publics had become active on the blogosphere, the topic of Chapter 6. In their essay on Persian blogs, Arash Falasiri and Nazanin Ghanavizi continue the discussion on dissident (online) publics and argue that blogs, as distinct social media sites, have provided a new public sphere for self-expression and, more important, for "the formation of public opinion." Following Hannah Arendt's notion of the public sphere as a site of political action and discussion, Falasiri and Ghanavizi argue that the Internet provides an alternative dialogical forum for political activism, in which even state actors are involved to promote state interests and compete with dissidents.

The use of social media for political mobilization is the focus of Mohammad Sadeghi Esfahlani's contribution in Chapter 7. Sadeghi Esfahlani provides a theoretically rich study of how Facebook was used by the Green Movement, a protest movement that emerged after allegations of electoral fraud in the June 2009 presidential elections in Iran. As an activist and also the founder of Mir-Hossein Mousavi's official Facebook site,

Sadeghi Esfahlani advances a unique argument that social media shapes social capital, following the sociological work of Mark Granovetter, through the bridging of diverse clusters of "weak ties" to build cooperative action and bring about change in politics.[35] Through framing practices, social networks construct collective action and contentious identities that, in turn, empower social movements to reshape political reality. Toward the end of his chapter, Sadeghi Esfahlani draws attention to his personal online activism. He shows how the Facebook site he designed for Mousavi's camp, while residing outside of Iran, facilitated the organization of rallies for electoral campaign, mobilization of street protests after the elections, and circulation and consumption of alternative news that would be censored by Iran state media or not made available by Western media.

In Chapter 8, Reza Masoudi Nejad offers an alternative discussion on the role of social media in the postelection protests. While his essay studies the close relationship between Web 2.0 and the geography of postelection protests, it argues that "the trans-local network of the Iranian diaspora" played a far more important role than social media. Defining the Green Movement in terms of "trans-spatial" fields of activism, Masoudi Nejad looks closely at the Iranian diasporic communities around the globe, and underscores how social media played merely a communication channel rather than a defining role for the diasporic communities to connect with Iran and influence the "geography of protests." At the heart of the 2009 Green Movement was the kind of collective action that primarily operated through trans-spatial domains of interaction, with social media playing only a part in the process. Politics on social media became meaningful only through concrete social interaction, in which the diasporic communities played a far greater role than often assumed.

In chapter 9, Babak Rahimi and Nima Rassooli move away from the online formation of political dissidents to the contentious politics of internal struggles and competitions within Persian-language social media domains. The chapter focuses on the popular collective blog site Balatarin and addresses the way political idealism can become undermined as a result of exclusionary practices through the intervention of gatekeepers and contentious politics. Despite its original ambitions to provide a free platform for all Iranians to voice opinion and create an online democratic forum, in the postelection period Balatarin evolved into an increasingly exclusionary site where opposition activists could interact for social and political purposes. Politics in its everyday contentious reality also prevails in social media.

Chapters 10 and 11 turn our attention to the Internet's communication networks and state power. David Faris's chapter provides a comparative study between Egypt and Iran and offers an overview of the online contentious politics and, correspondingly, reactions from the state to control dissent. While social media did contribute to Egyptian and Iranian social movements, it did so, Faris argues, in dissimilar structural ways and in different political contexts with divergent consequences. He provides a typology of state reaction in terms of (1) response regimes—regimes that imprison or persecute online activists, (2) control regimes—regimes that impose regulative measures such as filtering over the Internet, and finally, (3) cordon regimes—regimes that construct a "parallel set of social media and information sites" in order to defuse the impact of dissident sites. According to Faris, the Mubarak-era state in Egypt was a response regime, and therefore less creative in its reaction to the protesters and use of social media, while Iran represents a type of cordon regime that successfully and creatively stifled dissidents through social media.

In Chapter 11, Niki Akhavan further analyzes the uses of social media by state power. Since 2009, the Islamic Republic has engaged in policies and strategies that employ social media as a way to challenge a perceived cultural invasion to undermine its legitimacy. With the rhetorical charge of a brewing a "soft war," the Iranian state has sought to control the Internet by proactively producing pro-government material online, information that can ultimately bolster the legitimacy of the state. Akhavan's analysis focuses on the official rhetoric of values, purity of national culture, and "content production" for sanctified information with the aim to manufacture consensus in favor of state control over online domains. Though the rhetoric and practice of "soft war" has decreased since 2011, Akhavan underlines the significant role of state media policy to manage the ways in which Iranians engage with the social media for various purposes.

Chapter 12, the final chapter in Part II, serves as a transition to Part III, which comprises Chapters 13 and 14. In all three chapters, however, the authors map the relationship between cultural practices and the use of social media as a distinct digital technology. Taking the cultural dimension as their main frame of analysis, the authors in their studies also acknowledge the political potential of a new communication process in the context of Iranian sociopolitical life.

In Chapter 12, Samira Rajabi shows the multifaceted political dimensions involved in the online practices revolving around the death of Neda Agha-Soltan in the post-2009 elections. She argues that the death of Neda was redefined in the memorial practices of a rich online culture of symbols and visuals of a noble death, depicted through a fallen female body. In many ways, social media served as a political site of remembrance where cultural identity, based on national and transnational ties, could be reimagined in cultural memory. Remediation of Neda's martyrdom image through Facebook, YouTube, and other social media sites, in a sense played a critical role in reframing Iranian national identity through the trauma of the 2009 postelection crisis.

In Chapter 13, Michelle Langford, a film and media theorist, looks at Iranian cinema as a contested cultural site, where filmmakers have defined and defied boundaries of censorship and expression in creative ways. The emergence of social media on the Iranian cultural scene in the 2000s, particularly since the 2009 elections, has introduced a new vibrancy in audience and producer relations. Following Henry Jenkins, an American media scholar, Langford discusses cinema and media convergence processes as the merging of media technologies as a result of digitization and computer networking. In this dynamic media landscape, Langford addresses the increasing interdependence of old and new media as a way to resist media regulations beyond state institutions, and toward new engagements with civic activism for both Iranian and global audiences. What has emerged in the process is an increased potential for interactivity and participatory practices for creating and sharing content marked by changes in the relationship between existing audiences, genres, and technologies with global significance.

Jafar Panahi's *This Is Not a Film* (2011), Langford argues, exemplifies a new form of cinematic experience that articulates political discontent in practices and visuals of the everyday Internet culture, as it also deliberately employs media convergence in its narrative and structural strategy. In many creative ways, *This Is Not a Film* blurs the boundaries between old and new media and reconstructs an alternative mediated landscape of contentious character. Likewise, in Chapter 14, the book's final chapter, Staci Gem Scheiwiller also identifies creative processes. She shows that the digitization of the Iranian avant-garde in various social media platforms is less about subversive activities against the Islamic Republic and more about challenging the art market and gallery establishments in Iran and beyond. Following Walter Benjamin's critical theory of media art, Scheiwiller's study of online Iranian aesthetic practices provides an account of social media as an alternative platform that could potentially liberate art from elitism and institutional constraints.

The main theme running through this book is that social media, despite its limitations, foregrounds distinct forms of social dynamics that link human action with new technologies. While all the chapters in this volume address the theme of inclusion and expressivity in some ways, they offer only a glimpse into the vast and fast-paced social media cultures of Iran and beyond. Numerous other social media spheres of interaction yet remain to be studied, in particularly religion and the way it is negotiated through technology in everyday life. However, we hope that this volume, which contains contributions primarily from an emerging group of young scholars who have done innovative empirical and theoretical research on social media, can pave the path toward new understandings of local, regional, and global communication processes in the new age of digital media.

Notes

1. Duncan Watts, *Six Degrees: The Science of a Connected Age* (New York: W.W. Norton, 2003); Albert-Laszlo Barabasi, *Linked: How Everything Is Connected to Everything Else and What It Means for Business, Society, and Everyday Life* (New York: Penguin Books, 2003).

2. Matthew Hindman, *The Myth of Digital Democracy* (Princeton, NJ: Princeton University Press, 2008).

3. Scott Rosenberg, *Say Everything: How Blogging Began, What It's Becoming, and Why It Matters* (New York: Broadway Books, 2010).

4. Nancy Fraser, "Rethinking the Public Sphere: A Contribution to the Critique of Actually Existing Democracies," in *Habermas and the Public Sphere,* ed. Craig Calhoun (Cambridge: MIT Press, 1992): 109–142.

5. Clay Shirkey, *Here Comes Everybody: The Power of Organizing without Organizations* (New York: Penguin, 2008).

6. Timur Kuran, "Now Out of Never: The Element of Surprise in the East European Revolution of 1989," *World Politics* 44.1 (October 1991): 7–48.

7. David Faris, *Dissent and Revolution in a Digital Age: Social Media, Blogging and Activism in Egypt* (London: I. B. Tauris, 2013).

8. Sushi Bikchandani, David Hirshleifer, and Ivo Welch, "A Theory of Fads, Fashion, Custom and Cultural Change as Informational Cascades," *Journal of Political Economy* 100.5 (1992): 991–1026.

9. Faris, *Dissent and Revolution in a Digital Age.*

10. Sahar Khamis and Katherine Vaughn, "Cyberactivism in the Egyptian Revolution: How Civic Engagement and Citizen Journalism Tilted the Balance," *Arab Media and Society* 13 (Summer 2011): http://www.arabmediasociety.com/?article=769; Zeynep Tufekci and Christopher Wilson, "Social Media and the Decision to Participate in Political Protest: Observations from Tahrir Square," *Journal of Communication* 62.2 (April 2012): 363–379; Merlyna Lim, "Clicks, Cabs and Coffee Houses: Social Media and Oppositional Movements in Egypt, 2004–2011," *Journal of Communication* 62.2 (April 2012): 231–248; David Faris and Patrick Meier, "Digital Activism in Authoritarian Countries," in *The Routledge Participatory Cultures Handbook,* eds. Aaron Delwiche and Jennifer Jacobs Henderson (Routledge: New York, 2012): 195–205; Philip N. Howard and Muzammil M. Hussain, "The

Role of Digital Media," *Journal of Democracy* 22.3 (2011): 35–36; Christopher Wilson and Alexandra Dunn, "Digital Media in the Egyptian Revolution: Descriptive Analysis from the Tahrir Datasets," *International Journal of Communication* 5 (2011): 1248–1272; Sean Aday, Henry Farrell, Marc Lynch, John Sides, and Deen Freelon, "Blogs and Bullets II: New Media and Conflict after the Arab Spring," *United States Institute of Peace* (2012): 1–24.

11. Philip N. Howard, Sheetal D. Agarwal, and Muzammil N. Hussain, "When Do States Disconnect Their Digital Networks? Regime Responses to the Political Uses of Social Media," *Communication Review* 14.3 (2011): 216–232; 226.

12. Bruce Bimber, Andrew J. Flanigin, and Cynthia Stohl, "Reconceptualizing Collective Action in the Contemporary Media Environment," *Communication Theory* 15.4 (November 2005): 365–388. See also Marc Lynch, *The Arab Uprisings: The Unfinished Revolutions of the New Middle East* (Washington, DC: Public Affairs, 2012).

13. Bimber et al., "Reconceptualizing Collective Action in the Contemporary Media Environment," 372.

14. David Karpf, "Online Political Mobilization from the Advocacy Group's Perspective," *Policy and the Internet* 2.4 (December 2010): 7–41.

15. Matthew Allen, "What Was Web 2.0? Versions and the Politics of Internet History," *New Media and Society* 15.2 (2012): 260–275. For other critiques of social media, see Trebor Scholz, "Market Ideology and the Myths of Web 2.0," *First Monday* 13.3 (2008), n.p., and Christian Fuchs, *Internet and Society: Social Theory in the Information Age* (New York: Routledge, 2008).

16. For a definition of Web 2.0 by O'Reilly, see Tim O'Reilly, "Web 2.0: Compact Definition," http://radar.oreilly.com/archives/2005/10/web_20_compact_definition.html (accessed December 15, 2014).

17. Malcom Gladwell, "Small Change: Why the Revolution Will Not Be Tweeted," *The New Yorker*, October 4, 2010, 42.

18. Gadi Wolfsfeld, "Social Media and the Arab Spring: Politics Comes First," *The International Journal of Press/Politics* 18.2 (2013): 115–137.

19. For the most comprehensive iteration of this thinking, see Evgeny Morozov's *The Net Delusion: The Dark Side of Internet Freedom* (New York: Public Affairs, 2012).

20. William Lafi Youmans and Jillian York, "Social Media and the Activist Toolkit: User Agreements, Corporate Interests, and the Information Infrastructure of Modern Social Movements," *Journal of Communication* 62.2 (2012): 315–329.

21. Nancy Fraser, "Transnationalizing the Public Sphere: On the Legitimacy and Efficacy of Public Opinion in a Post-Westphalian World," *Theory, Culture & Society* 24.4 (2007): 7–30.

22. Jürgen Habermas, *The Structural Transformation of the Public Sphere* (Cambridge: MIT Press, 1989).

23. See Habermas's interview by Markus Schwering, "Internet and the Public Sphere: What the Web Can't Do," July 24, 2014, www.resetdoc.org. For a broader analysis of Habermas's theory of the public sphere in the information age, see Pieter

Boeder, "Habermas' Heritage: The Future of the Public Sphere in the Network Society," *First Monday* 10.9 (September 2005): http://firstmonday.org/ojs/index.php/fm/article/view/1280/1200 (accessed December 16, 2014).

24. For a comprehensive examination of critical literature on the Internet's public sphere, see Lincoln Dahlberg, "Rethinking the Fragmentation of the Cyberpublic: From Consensus to Contestation." *New Media and Society* 9.5 (2007): 827–847.

25. Rebecca MacKinnon, *Consent of the Networked: The Worldwide Struggle for Internet Freedom* (New York: Basic Books, 2012).

26. York and Youmans, "Social Media and the Activist Toolkit," 316.

27. Elisabeth Chaves, "The Internet as a Global Platform? Grounding the Magically Levitating Public Sphere," *New Political Science* 32.1 (March 2010): 25.

28. Peter Dahlgren, "The Internet, Public Spheres and Political Communication," *Political Communication* 22 (2005): 158.

29. Mark West, "Is the Internet an Emerging Public Sphere?" *Journal of Mass Media Ethics* 28.3 (2013): 155–159; 158.

30. See, in particular, Chapter 6 for a more articulated conception of the Internet and the public sphere by the contributing authors.

31. Jennifer Brinkerhoff, *Digital Diasporas: Identity and Transnational Engagement* (Cambridge: Cambridge University Press, 2009).

32. Pierre Lévy, *Collective Intelligence: Mankind's Emerging World in Cyberspace,* trans. Robert Bononno (New York: Plenum, 1997), 13. See Chapter 13 for a more elaborate discussion on "collective intelligence."

33. See Donald MacKenzie and Judy Wajcman, eds., *The Social Shaping of Technology,* 2nd ed. (Buckingham, England, and Philadelphia: Open University Press, 1999).

34. Zizi Papacharissi, *A Private Sphere: Democracy in a Digital Age* (Cambridge: Polity, 2010), 164.

35. See Mark Granovetter, "The Strength of Weak Ties," *American Journal of Sociology* 78.6 (1973): 1360–1380.

Part I

SOCIETAL

Chapter 1

Facebook Iran

Social Capital and the Iranian Social Media

Jari Eloranta, Hossein Kermani, and Babak Rahimi

In broad terms, social capital is a complex set of connections based on the resources of support and reciprocity that shape, what the late Charles Tilly called, "networks of trust."[1] The ways people interact and, accordingly, build to acquire resources, play a central role in the way trust and support is produced between diverse people, either through bonding based on internal relations, or "bridging" based on external relations (i.e., creating new connections with people outside of their known networks).[2] Such bonds identify a dense network of relations that encourage participation in voluntary organizations and civic activism that play an integral role in realization of the common good.[3] Yet social ties also include the element of risk or mistakes by members of an association, practices of persecution by rulers, as well as contentious politics of rumors and conspiracy discourses that can make a network unreliable or untrustworthy. Among these failures is the element of public apathy, caused by surplus work or leisure time, with the potential to fragment community and weaken civic engagement.

In his influential work, *Bowling Alone: The Collapse and Revival of American Community*, Robert Putnam lamented the decline of social capital in the American public life, primarily because he considered information and entertainment technologies, such as television, to function in facilitating citizens to become passive, mere consuming subjects. Since active associations and the degree of collective norms gained from civic participation indicate

19

the extent of social capital, the rise of television has introduced a level of disconnect, especially among young Americans, that entails an erosion of civic engagement and trust. *Bowling Alone* contemplated a society consisting of solitary individual activities rather than collective participation through civic associations.[4] While civic and voluntary associations promote collective trust, in particular through face-to-face interaction, "passive" entertainment practices lower group solidarity and enhance fragmentation.

But contrary to Putnam's study on television's negative impact as detrimental to civic life, numerous other studies have also shown how information technologies, in particular digital media, can in fact supplement or enhance social capital by creating new modes of communication, sets of relations, and civic norms of involvement.[5] With their distinct many-to-many communication features and reduced costs of usability, new technologies like the Internet can facilitate accessibility and increase in circulation of information for togetherness and solidarity, though its degree of social force remains contingent on specific contexts. The element of accessibility and enhanced circulation and communication implies that the Internet can make social action more efficient.[6] As an embedded everyday aspect of social practice, Internet technology presents a complex set of communicative practices that include ways to arrange, organize, and reconfigure experiences on both individual and collective levels.

It is at the collective level, the social networks encompassing diverse people and activities, where social capital operates in the form of civic engagement. Despite the fact that many users engage in personal activities that can add up to considerable time spent surfing, chatting, or shopping online, as an inexpensive communication technology (even in many so-called developing countries) the Internet provides collective venues for support and social engagement, especially pertinent for politics in its dissident form. Such collective venues are described by Manuel Castells as "mass self-communication," a horizontal form of communication that challenges hierarchical structures in the form of "counter-power."[7] The Internet disrupts, and in doing so decentralizes managerial authority in organizations. It also comprises the formation of informal ties and an increase in "weak ties," allowing for new forms of economic and political contestation.[8]

Decentralization in its digital form in certain algorithmic contexts, however, could also produce a passive domain of closed privacy, in which norms of social performance, as shown by Eli Pariser, become filtered into a personalized social networking space, a subjective realm where politics is undermined as a collective and a dialogical space of interaction between competing views and interests.[9] Zygmunt Bauman sees such a process in terms of increased privatization of cultural life with the convergence of identity and consumption that undermine political participation and civic ties for political participation.[10] There is an ambivalent feature with the Internet as a form of communication that could both undermine and produce social capital. The key is to understand which networks individuals and groups construct, and through which formal and informal ties social capital is produced in sustaining civic and social movements in a global context.

As a case study, the following discussion examines how social media as social technology can generate trust and social support for coordinated activity in the context of Iranian social life. Although not all Iranian activities on the Internet are social, the rise of social media in the context of the development of the Internet in Iran since the 1990s has led to new ways for Iranians to connect, exchange, and build new associations and collectivities in the postrevolutionary period. The networking aspects of the Iranian social media can be associated with informal ties identified in the form of primarily casual publics that take shape in lived contexts of informal shared environments. Such causal or informal ties are influential in encouraging online discussions, information sharing, news dissemination, and mobilization of collective action through ubiquity of access, despite censorship limitations imposed by the Iranian state over the Internet. These networked publics can be identified as complex clusters and cleavages of informal associations, interconnected in a variety of ways through popular social media sites such as Facebook, popular in Iran, mostly among the younger generation.[11]

This chapter is therefore an analysis of emergent social networks that identify the larger Iranian social media online. While relying on research produced by Iran-based scholars, mostly unknown to Western academics, the study also provides a synthesis of empirical-based studies on Iranian online networks that are unavailable to non-Persian speaking scholars. The following discussion does not claim to be comprehensive but offers an analytical descriptive account of how sociability takes form on social media sites such as Facebook. In terms of definitions, by "Iranian online social media" we are referring to many-to-many interactive computer-mediated forms of communication through which Iranians of diverse backgrounds—in terms of class, ethnic, gender, race and sexuality, and based both in national and transnational localities—participate to circulate, exchange, share, (re)mix, and consume information, images, affects, and imaginaries of identities and sociability.[12] The notion of "FacebookIran" implies the multiplicity of human affects and cognitive processes that underline the associations among intersecting networks, as well as cultural practices that turn resources into social capital.

In doing so, the Iranian Internet users *as* social actors build social capital, despite Internet surveillance and other filtering measures implemented by the state. Infrastructural and regulative practices can influence the distribution of resources and connections, but the effect of bonds shaped through Internet networks, however limited they might be in terms of pervasiveness, can produce effective resources through weak ties—that is, primarily among a network of loosely associated actors. In a significant way, while the formation of trust as social capital is not essentially linked to Internet regulation, political turmoil such as street protests could dramatically affect the degree and shape of connectivity in digital space with offline consequences.[13]

In this study, we focus on Facebook as a distinct social media network, built on the concept and practice of "friendship" connections. Iranian Facebook users, we argue, build relations with others through informal and weak ties that enhance social capital on various levels of digital connectivity. Although the impact of such social building, especially on offline domains, can vary based on gender, class, and other social factors, on Facebook the newly formed distant ties hold meaning for connections in terms of resources formed through sharing information that delineate new network publics specific to Iranian users of diverse backgrounds.

Divided into three parts, this study begins with a brief theoretical discussion of networks and social capital. The second section offers a sociohistorical account of social networks, and by extension social capital, in modern Iran. The study finally turns to empirical studies conducted by Iran-based scholars on social media and particularly Facebook as a way to expand on various social media processes in building trust and social solidarity formation, mostly through weak ties shaped online.

Conceptualizing Social Capital

The concept of social capital is not new, nor is it undisputed.[14] Sociologists in different forms and contexts have used the term during the 20th century, perhaps most explicitly by Pierre Bourdieu, for whom resources were typically tied to a network and access to economic resources was offered by social capital.[15] Francis Fukuyama has focused on the inseparable spheres of culture and economy to show how the cooperative dimension of social capital can promote civic actions in ways that ultimately bolster democratic rule.[16] James Coleman, one of the key figures in the development of social capital as a concept, has emphasized the links between human and social capital, the importance of education in changing societies, as well as social structure and individuals' functions within that structure.[17] In recent decades, especially since the rise of new democracies in Eastern Europe with the collapse of the Soviet Union and its sphere of influence, the concept has become much more widely applied among different fields in the social sciences and the humanities.

The most famous recent scholar of social capital is the aforementioned Putnam, who has argued that social capital is found in the various networks that permeate people's lives; he also distinguished between bridging (occurring among heterogeneous people and groups) and bonding (occurring among like-minded people and groups) forms of social capital. Putnam maintained that high levels of social capital correlate with lower crime rates and lead to higher levels of "happiness." In a "civil society" (or "civic community"), individuals feel a greater sense of contentment, which can be eroded by increased secularism, greater amounts of time dedicated to watching TV, fewer communal activities, and lower political participation rates.[18]

Putnam's version of social capital, and the concept itself, has been criticized from many different angles, as noted earlier. Some have objected to his emphasis on religious organizations, others to the causes and effects of political participation.[19] While the critique is in itself interesting up to a point, the uses of social capital in different fields of science are arguably more useful. Social capital is, for example, often linked to the development and formation of democracy, as well as social and political crises. For the most part, modern democracies tend to be more complicated and based on a variety of organizations other than voluntary associations.[20] Meanwhile, a number of studies have focused on analyzing different kinds of ethnic and social communities, and how social capital can be fostered in smaller groups via shared values and social constructs.[21]

Social capital is typically thought to arise from functioning with a network, and to increase exponentially through the interactivity of network processes.[22] Norms and information flows are the keys to a well-functioning network, which can serve as a conduit for spreading and building social capital. Moreover, a dense or close-knitted network can maintain and reproduce social capital collectively.[23] How much can social capital and the adjoining networks help us understand how civic involvement is realized in ways that contribute to political change?

First, we must acknowledge that getting data on the spreading of social networks and social capital is difficult in the Iranian case, and it is hard to come up with credible proxy data on social capital in general. One could look for data on leisure time and/or happiness in Iran or trust on Facebook, as this study tries to show, but typically data on the quality of life and social networks in Iran in recent years are sparse at best.[24] Usually any studies on the quality of life built on trust and reciprocity pertain to certain specific groups, such as cancer survivors, and lack the kind of data one would need to analyze the networks quantitatively, which would offer some further possibilities for the analysis.[25] The following section provides a brief account of the historical roots of social capital formation in Iran, and later we attempt to analyze some empirical data to be able to gauge the impact of social capital in the Iranian social media, with a focus on Facebook.

Social Capital of Social Networks in Iran (Offline)

The modern origins of Iranian networks, with their distinct Perso-Shiʿi identity, can be traced back to the construction of the new Isfahan under the Safavids (1501–1722) in the late sixteenth and early seventeenth centuries. The formation of new urban spaces in Isfahan unleashed the institutionalization of new civic associations with close connection to military-building with the promotion of new imperial cultural practices such as the camel sacrifice rituals initiated by the Safavid state under Shah Abbas I (1587–1629).[26] The proliferation of newly designed public spaces of conviviality, exchange, and self-cultivation such as markets (*bazaar*), coffeehouses (*qahvekhwaneh*), travel lodges (*caravanserai*), public baths (*hammam*), schools (*madrasah*), squares (*maydan*), and sports clubs (*zurkhwaneh*), along with the promotion of ritual practices such as commemorative rituals of Muharram, overlapped with the consolidation of socioprofessional groups, guilds, *futuvvat* (chivalry) associations, and religious circles devoted to Shiʿi Islam in its distinct Iranian manifestation since the Safavid period.[27]

From the seventeenth to the early eighteenth centuries, at least until the collapse of the Safavid Empire, the connection between urban spaces and civic associations was marked by the institutionalization of Shiʿism under Safavid rule. As Shiʿi Islam became increasingly fused with ancient Persian motifs of ethical and social conduct, along with traditions of folklore, art, poetry, and dramatic practices, mostly manifest in the mourning rituals of Muharram, a moral relation of trust consolidated that distinctively revolved around new urban centers. While Iran saw an era of economic and cultural growth during the Zand period (1750–1794) in the eighteenth century, the Qajar dynasty (1795–1925) marked a period in Iranian history when the clerical class, bazaar, and guilds formed a nexus of both formal and informal ties with impacts in the realms of discursive practices, ethical and kinship ties, and cultures of sociability.[28]

The bazaar served as one of the most significant network associations that included the intersections of various actors who shared symbolic ideals, affects, tastes, and styles of behavior in shaping a distinct market public.[29] The social capital of the bazaar combined the education and interpersonal relations of individuals who would be self-governed and connected through shared values, norms, and even kinship ties. Under the Qajars, the bazaar also served as a civic institutional arrangement that mediated the space between the state and society. Despite the Pahlavi modernization (1925–1979) that included the gradual consolidation of monarchy under a centralized state and an emphasis on economic growth through education, industrialization, urbanization, and cultural capital, the bazaar, as a civic market institution, continued to play a critical role in influencing the Iranian civil society. The eruption of the Islamic Revolution in 1979 can be partly credited to the active civic engagement of the bazaar network in the bolstering of the emerging militant clerics led by Ayatollah Ruhollah Khomeini, who maintained close ties with the bazaar while in exile in Iraq and, later, France.

The postrevolutionary period, beginning with the Iran–Iraq war (1980–1988), was a watershed moment for the Iranian civil society. With a revolutionary state seeking to consolidate power, many civic associations were either co-opted or marginalized into mere nonexistence. The most important were art and intellectual associations such as circles of directors, poets, and writers, which had grown in size and had become visible in the years prior to the revolution. With the end of the war in 1988 and the death of Khomeini in 1989, the landscape of Iranian civil life changed. In particular, Iranian economic and social life underwent important structural adjustments under Hashemi Rafsanjani's presidency (1989–1997). With the unleashing of new economic and technological developments, by the mid-1990s the postwar population, mostly under the age of thirty, shaped a new set of social networks with the growth of the educational sectors and the expansion of largely consumerist urban spaces. While familial and neighborhood ties in urban households continued to provide, in what Susan Bastani has described in her empirical research of middle-class Tehrani life, a basis for "social support," a new social network of middle-class young Iranians emerged to redefine the Iranian public life.[30] The younger networks combined both weak and strong ties that brought Iranians together either in leisurely interactive spaces of urban life or contentious political sites, especially during elections, over reform, which began with the presidency of reformist Mohammad Khatami in 1997.

The most significant addition to the existing networks was the introduction of the Internet, along with other information technologies such as cellphone and satellite broadcasting, to Iranian social life in the mid-1990s. While originally a luxury good, the Internet served as an emerging form of communication for unofficial cultural practices and expression of political views by primarily young Iranians in the educational sector. But the new media also facilitated the greater visibility of a new kind of social capital, namely trust networks built through horizontal associations and participatory practices such as online journalism and blogging—as shown in Chapters 5 and 6.[31] By the early 2000s, the Internet had strengthened the significance of weak ties as a network experience for cultural and civic participation within a contentious political context charged with tensions between reformist and conservative factional politics. With the consolidation of conservative politics under the presidency of Mahmoud Ahmadinejad in 2005, a key development in the growth of Internet developed with increasing popular involvement of the youth and other segments of Iranian population in the blogosphere and, later, in social media domains. When Facebook entered the Iranian Internet landscape in 2007, Iranians had already built up increasing social capital in diverse social spheres of the Internet. Facebook marked a new development in the new media landscape, as it opened a new site of interaction for various forms of social ties to take shape and spread.

Social Network Sites in the Iranian Cyberspace

The assessment of Iranian social networking sites involves the study of complex dimensions. For the most part, networking on social media is about new forms of social relations, new ways of connecting, and new ways of managing and creating cultural, economic, and political life. But the study also involves the renewal of close interpersonal relationships, some of which would include familial forms of ties that preexist life in the social media domains. Social media serve as interactive media sites through which affects, ideas, information, and visuals are exchanged, shared, played, and (re)produced. As self-generative content sites, they comprise users who connect with close friends and newly gained distant friends, acquaintances and family, lost friends, and old foes. Hence, social media activities in a range of platforms do not follow a distinct pattern or strategy, and this ultimately makes the task of producing a comprehensive study of social media a truly intractable project.

The following account focuses only on Iranian Facebook users and provides an analysis based on the limited data available on the subject. Two other difficulties also need to be addressed in studying the Iranian social media landscape on the domestic level. First, most Iranians are active on social media sites that are filtered or blocked by Internet Service Providers that are in turn monitored by the state. The difficulty of accessing popular sites for social networking shifts according to the changing censorship regime espoused by the state. Along with the presence of proxies and Virtual Private Networks, primarily prohibited by the state, it is considerably difficult to produce accurate statistical data about the percentage of Iranian Internet users based in Iran.

Second, it is even more difficult to accurately measure the number of Iranian Facebook users, especially since one user could have multiple accounts under various profiles. There is still a dearth of ethnographic studies with a focus on the internal dynamics of Iranian social media, largely because of the lack of researchers in various fields of humanities and social sciences. Other difficulties are due to an absence of sophisticated analytical-conceptual frameworks for studying social media specific to the Iranian context, and the typology of usage of diverse and changing social media sites. For example, we lack empirical evidence as to why Iranians preferred, especially between 2006 and 2008, Orkut.com over Myspace, or if their reasons for using Yahoo! 360° differ from joining LinkedIn or Facebook. In light of these methodological and theoretical challenges, the ensuing discussion offers a glimpse into a complex world of social media where an emergent digital culture is fused with the growing popularity of social networking. What follows, however, does not pretend to be a systematic study of the Iranian social media and its capacity to produce or supplement social capital.

Historically speaking, four major social networking sites have been identified as part of the Iranian social media, namely Orkut, Cloob.com, Yahoo! 360°, and Facebook. While in the late 1990s and early 2000s some online activity took place on the social networking site of SixDegrees.com, the launch of Orkut in autumn 2004 dramatically changed the Iranian Internet landscape. According to Masoud Kowsari, by the mid-2000s, while the popularity of blogs was also on the rise, Iranian users attained the third highest participation rate on Orkut.[32] Most Orkut users comprised the younger segment of the Iranian population. The Iranian government, meanwhile, continued to filter and block numerous sites, and by February 2004 Orkut was shut down and accessible only through proxies.

The next popular social networking site was Cloob.com. Though Cloob.com was launched in December 2004, many users did not turn to the site until Orkut was filtered. By 2006, Cloob.com gradually lost its popularity to other social networking sites, which began to redefine the Iranian social media life. Yahoo! 360° became the most popular site some time in 2006. Many former Orkut and Cloob.com users, including a younger generation of Internet users, joined Yahoo! 360°, making the site one of the most popular sites for both personal communication and social interaction. But Yahoo! 360° was closed down by Yahoo in 2009, and the sudden change introduced a new dynamic, as it coincided with the growing global popularity of Facebook.

Although available outside of Iran since 2006, many Iranian users turned to Facebook later, especially as the 2009 presidential campaign heated up electoral competition with the use of more creative ways to do advertisement and propagation. As Mohammad Sadeghi Esfahlani's study (Chapter 7) also shows, during the 2009 elections Facebook facilitated the coordination and dissemination of information and alternative news for opposition groups challenging the electoral results. On the day of elections, June 12, 2009, Facebook was filtered, and many used proxies or VPNs in order to use the highly popular site.

The demographic study of Iranian social media users is limited to a few studies on Orkut and Facebook. The Iran-based researcher, Kowsari, for example, in his 2007 study presented data on Orkut, which is worth mentioning here.[33] According to Kowsari's online survey, which is, of course, not representative of other social media sites, eight key points could be drawn based on the available data. With regards to age, about 54 percent of the Iranian users on Orkut were between ages seventeen and twenty-two. In terms of gender, 37.5 percent of the Iranian users were men, thus the majority were women. Most Iranians on Orkut were single (74.1 percent), while only 12.1 percent were married. Most users (78.1 percent) joined Orkut to find new friends, while the ratio of the circle of friends of a regular user was about 13 percent. Most of the users (60.7 percent), with 34.6 percent based in Tehran, had no affiliation with a political group. The type of activities they engaged in on Orkut mostly revolved around cultural activities such as art and literature (20.5 percent), entertainment (11.9 percent), and sex (6.2 percent).[34] Though scant in analysis and featuring conceptual limitations, this online survey illustrated that many Iranians on Orkut were young, unmarried women, and mostly interested in culture activities, entertainment, and finding a new network of friends.[35]

The online demographics of Facebook users differ from users of Orkut. According to a preliminary study by Majid Kashani and Somayih Zarih in 2010, the rate of Facebook penetration in Tehran was 12.3 percent, and the age of users was between twenty and twenty-four years old.[36] According to their study, 8.3 percent of Iranian Facebook users, mostly men, joined this site due to personal contact with friends, and 90 percent used real names and photos for their profile.[37] Based on this survey, 64 percent of Iranian users trusted their friends' information posted on Facebook.[38] In another important study, Rassooli and Moradi (1391, 63–65) listed the most significant reasons why users join Facebook, such as for entertainment or as a hobby (33.8 percent), social acceptance (30.8 percent), sharing of private and public information (22.8 percent), and, finally, scientific purposes (7.7 percent).[39] Moradi and Rassooli also noted that the filtering of the Internet does not have a significant impact on the users' ability to be active on Facebook.[40] The most important reasons for joining Facebook are for sharing information, connecting with friends, finding new friends, and discussing political and social matters for entertainment purposes.[41]

The most important aspect of social media appears to be recreational and, more important, to find or maintain a network of friends. Ali Asghar Kia and Yonis Norimurad Abadai, for example, have conducted surveys on Iranian students who use Facebook and have noted that the sample group increased their circle of friends by 60 percent after joining the social networking site.[42] In the same study, they also examined the interactive culture of Facebook and noted that 21.7 percent of the users liked their friends' posts, 12.9 percent of them shared photos, 12.9 percent of the respondents updated their status, 6.6 percent of the users wrote a memorandum, and 15.2 posted comments. In percentage terms, 13.1 percent of the Facebook users viewed their friends' posts and, finally, only less than 5 percent of the users searched for news.[43] The survey also indicated that the most important reason Iranians joined Facebook was to share information (39.1 percent), while others underscored the free domain of interaction (34.6 percent), in addition to the free flow of information within the social networking site (13.1 percent).[44] Connectivity on both strong and weak ties appears to be have been the most significant feature of the Facebook domain.

The above preliminary data shows the extent to which social media are about building social networks through the sharing of personal or public information. The practice of sharing signifies the aggregate of potential resources within which social connections are claimed. The element of friendship, which of course has many dimensions and practical contexts, plays a key role as well. Many Facebook users seek to maintain circles of friendships or make new connections in a networked environment, thus highlighting the fluid role strong-ties, face-to-face interactions play in reconfiguring intimacy and friendship on social media. Yet the feature of increased new friendships identify a bridging practice that enable individuals to risk building trust by crossing over into external linkages with possible transnational dimensions.

Social Capital and Iranians on Facebook

In her 2012 study, grounded in Putnam's theoretical approach, Mahin Shaykh Ansari explored the development of social capital in the context of Iranian Facebook sites.[45] She showed that the process of social capital building on Facebook is much stronger than for non-Facebook users. In her study, Shaykh Ansari was also able to identify a positive correlation between bridging and maintaining social capital in the intensity of Facebook activities. Shaykh Ansari's research illustrates how Facebook reinforces weak ties more than strong relations, though the latter continues to maintain a presence online.

Shaykh Ansari's research is a significant indicator that Iranian Facebook users tend to feel confident about the relationships they maintain or build online. This sense of assurance has a positive correlation with increased activity on Facebook, although the sense of trust built online differs from offline in experience and form. The users in the study also acknowledged that Facebook expanded their relations with others, especially in finding new friends, but not necessarily in reinforcing old friendship ties. Moreover, most respondents indicated that Facebook helped them find old friends, indicating how the activity of finding friends can also involve reconnecting with ex-friends as now new friends.[46] Facebook also played a role in the way users reconnected with members of their own family, after years of estrangement, hence underlining a bonding rather than bridging dimension. Furthermore, Sheikh Ansari's research indicated that Facebook users usually discussed with their friends issues such as ongoing social or political events, with a number of sites devoted to discussions that revolve around digital communication in the form of commentary posts, replies to other commentaries, and the popular practice of liking a comment or a photo posted and shared with others on the "wall" of a Facebook profile.

In his 2012 study, Hossein Kermani has also examined patterns of social capital building on Facebook with a focus on Iran-based users on the social media site.[47] His study assessed the level of network intensity and forms of connectivity of Facebook users, such as "likes," comments, posts, tags, and especially trust algorithms.[48] The results emphasize how the level of connectivity is closely linked with how trust is shaped through friendship networks. Equally important are factors such as education and gender, which carry a positive correlation with social capital on Facebook, though it remains difficult to identify the role of age and generational relations in this context. Education and gender also influence the level of social capital produced on Facebook in ways that correlate with civic participation offline. This dynamic underlines how education tied with gender identity can play a key role in the way trust and support networks are created, with age playing the most likely role in the process. The main reason for this correlation can be partly linked with the informational structure of Facebook that allows educated women, for example, to engage with subversive expressions and seek the Internet as an alternative platform for connection and communication. In addition, this correlation also highlights a possible intimacy dynamic as connections are made beyond the local-based resources through loosely knit relations that make resources more available for civic-related activities.

Several key themes can be identified in Kermani's Facebook study, namely between Facebook connections and social capital. In terms of identity, most users posted their real names (95.1 percent) and their actual photos (92.9 percent).[49] As for sharing practice, users tended to feel confident in circulating their personal information, except their personal photos and videos.[50] Trust, which is a key feature of our discussion, tended to play a key role in the ways users connected and interacted with each other on Facebook and, accordingly, shared personal information on a daily basis with friends, particularly newly found friends.[51] This feature is critical as bonds were shaped across time and space, and yet trustworthiness of Facebook friendships appeared to be also influenced by the privacy option settings, which Facebook provides.[52] In terms of offline connections, the face-to-face interactions of Facebook users comprised less than 50 percent, which means that most friendship networks were shaped online.[53] This point illustrates and underscores the emergence of new types of friendship built in the virtual landscape, where Facebook networks are typically shaped by an awareness of risk through intimate interactions beyond face-to-face encounters. The element of making friends perhaps explains why familial connections, which comprise only 14.6 percent of users' list of friends, play a less predominant role in ways social capital is constructed on Facebook.[54]

Support also plays a key role in the context of social capital building on Facebook. For example, nearly half (48.7 percent) of Iranian Facebook users sought assistance from friends on the site, showing the potential for social mobilization for personal or even collective purposes.[55] Also, in terms of types of activities on the site, the Iranian Facebookers frequently used the "like" feature and also tended to share posts rather than generating new content.[56] The friendship network studied in this survey was limited to those who know each other, both online and offline. This means that users rarely accepted friend requests from unknown individuals, hence bolstering trust among the immediate and distant relations with both bridging and bonding elements. This study also shows that the propensity for sending friend requests to strangers is low. In a significant way, the users make decisions to gain new friends based on the information available on the profile of the person they seek to become friends with, most likely connected via another friend or an acquaintance on the site. Users usually accept friend requests from those who have a picture or have more than five mutual friends, which illustrates the importance of visual intimacy for support among Facebook users. This feature also highlights the density of networks that overlap in close connection with friendship bonds in an online–offline dynamic context.[57] The level of interactivity through Facebook then mainly lies in connections made in loosely knit and geographically diffused settings. However, the element of preexisting relations in the form of strong ties in Facebook socializing also help us to understand how participants negotiate trust through weak ties.

The most significant finding in the above study was the aggregated level of trust and support needed in creating a dynamic environment on Facebook, where individuals can connect with others in their intended audience network. Regular posting of personal information and other private data generate new ties. While such bonds, many of which bridged across external links, might not necessarily lead to civic engagement offline or online, they can certainly provide resources for individuals to find support and encouragement in diverse and dispersed social networks. Likewise, Facebook users and other social media activists develop relations through loosely connected networks with clusters and disparate ties, building networks of support through what Alex Lambert calls "performances of connections" in bounded publics, wherein intimacy and connections are performed and sustained.[58] From various groups providing support and medical services to Iran (as a result of U.S.-led sanctions), to individuals with disabilities based in Iran blogging or using social networks for self-expressions, new forms of social capital are constantly being built online, with varied degrees of impact on life in the offline world. Through this process, online social media foster new understandings and practices of commitment for social engagement from the interpersonal to the international and transnational.

Conclusion

Although the Internet and other emerging media technologies do not alone produce trust and network support in digital space, social media continues to provide openings in ways individuals create new ties and engage in civic engagement of social networking at both the local and transnational levels.[59] Overall, social media involve the potential of simultaneous performance of trust and connectivity in the formation of what Alex Lambert calls— especially in reference to Facebook—"dialogical spaces," where social action takes place in the form of reflexive and interpretive interactivity.[60] In such dialogical spaces, the social media processes set new frameworks that enable various networking activities in "bridging" social capital, illuminating how connections are made in loosely bonded and geographically diffuse ways.

This study was an attempt to show how the Iranian social media, as a result of becoming increasingly embedded in everyday life, facilitate active participation in public life by building new friendship networks, support groups, charity projects, and political associations. Social media is a public domain of diverse practices. Two critical points can be emphasized here: (1) increasing activities on social media sites such as Orkut and Facebook have given way to an enhanced sense of trust and social support, though the causal relation between social media activity, for various purposes, and social capital building for civic involvement is hardly straightforward; and (2) though form and depth of trust that is built online may differ from the offline, the use of social media could serve as a way to access and engage with a wider range of network associations. While social media practices vary on regional and sociocultural contexts, the Iranian case underscores the growing presence of social and civic activism in making connections and building trust with complex impacts on the offline world. Such dynamic presence equally, and at times more effectively, accompanies other unofficial and official forms of communication, ranging from rumors and passive practices to state propaganda activities, all of which can undercut trust and social capital.

In considering this complex social media landscape, we are left with an ambiguity. First, the interplay between online and offline activities appear hardly straightforward, making social capital even more ambiguous in its formation process. For example, as with any technology, generational gaps persist in the use and application of Internet discourses. Moreover, with the Internet as a personalized space, the public life of the Internet could become splintered in personalized lock-ins without a vision of politics. As Putnam has argued: "The Internet may be part of a solution to our civic problem, or it may exacerbate it."[61] Second, there is also the ambiguity of correlation between the so-called online and offline worlds, which could also affect the way social capital is sustained in everyday life. The way social capital is maintained or reproduced at the bazaar, for example, may not necessarily correlate with the way social capital is built through a social media site devoted to an Iranian audience for e-commerce activities. Still, such sites might reinforce a support network, or create an alternative network hub, for, for example, Iranian carpet designers at the bazaar and carpet producers around the world.

Media technologies such as the Internet and its various applications are inherently social technologies, so their impact is as multilayered and porous as social life offline. It is precisely because of the element of social frenzy caused by lived interaction that social capital building on social media is hardly an unambiguous process. Social capital is about collaboration in the pursuit of (usually) common objectives; yet it is vulnerable to the defects of consumerism, privatization, and varied stratification in the new technological era. The case of Iranian Facebook opens up new ways to think about such ambiguities that defines living in the connected world of technological modernities.

Notes

1. See Charles Tilly, *Trust and Rule* (Cambridge and New York: Cambridge University Press, 2005).

2. Michael Woolcock, "Social Capital and Economic Development: Towards a Theoretical Synthesis and Policy Framework," *Theory and Society* 27 (1998): 151–208.

3. Robert D. Putnam, *Making Democracy Work: Civic Traditions in Modern Italy* (Princeton, NJ: Princeton University Press, 1993). See also Robert D. Putnam, "Bowling Alone: America's Declining Social Capital," *Journal of Democracy* 6 (1995): 65–78.

4. Robert D. Putnam, "The Prosperous Community: Social Capital and Public Life," *The American Prospect* 13 (Spring 1993): 35–42.

5. For critiques of Putnam's famous study, see Kenneth Newton, "Mass Media Effects: Mobilization or Media Malaise?" *British Journal of Political Science* 27 (1999): 577–599; P. Norris, "Does Television Erode Social Capital? A Reply to Putnam," *PS: Political Science and Politics* 29 (1996): 474–480; E. M. Uslaner, "Social Capital, Television, and the 'Mean World': Trust, Optimism, and Civic Participation," *Political Psychology* 19 (1998): 441–467. For a study of how the Internet promotes social capital, see Lee Rainie and Barry Wellman, *Networked: The New Social Operating System* (Cambridge, MA, and London: MIT Press, 2012), especially 255–274.

6. See T. Pénard and N. Poussing, "Internet Use and Social Capital: The Strength of Virtual Ties," *Journal of Economic* Issues 44.3 (2010): 569–595.

7. Manuel Castells, "Communication, Power, and Counter-Power in the Network Society," *International Journal of Communication* 1 (2007): 238–266.

8. David Karpf, "Understanding Blogspace," *Journal of Information Technology and Politics* 5.4 (December 2008): 369–395.

9. Eli Pariser, *The Filter Bubble: What the Internet Is Hiding from You* (New York: Penguin, 2011).

10. Zygmunt Bauman, *Wasted Lives: Modernity and Its Outcasts* (London: Polity Press, 2003).

11. For a classic account of "weak ties," see Mark Granovetter, "The Strength of Weak Ties," *American Journal of Sociology* 78 (1973): 1360–1380.

12. By "Iranian online social media," we do not refer to a closed and essentially national entity defined by a fixed, regionally bounded territorial space. In fact, a more in-depth study would show how online practices may be increasingly destabilizing concepts and notions of national identity, as shown by Niki Akhavan in her study of the cultural politics of the Internet in Iran. The aspect of Diaspora and transnational movements also adds to the complexity of the notion of "Iranian online social media," which would also require a separate study. See Niki Akhavan, *Electronic Iran: The Cultural Politics of an Online Evolution* (New Brunswick and London: Rutgers University Press, 2013), 13–34.

13. An irony of online political activism is that it tends to increase under the most intense political circumstances, during which the state expands surveillance and censorship efforts both in offline and online domains. The paradox can be partly explained with the element of risk, which is critical to any social movement that challenges the political status quo at times of crisis or erosion of state legitimacy, as was the case in postelection Iran in 2009 or the Arab Spring in 2011.

14. For a study on contested aspects of the concept of social capital, see Wilfred Dolfsma and Charlie Dannreuther, "Subjects and Boundaries: Contesting Social Capital–Based Policies," *Journal of Economic Issues* 37 (2003): 405–413.

15. A good overview of the origins of the term can be found in A. Portes, "Social Capital: Its Origins and Applications in Modern Sociology," *Annual Review of Sociology* 24.1 (1998): 1–24. See also Eric L. Lesser, ed., *Knowledge and Social Capital* (Boston: Butterworth-Heinemann, 2000), 43–67.

16. See Francis Fukuyama, *Trust: The Social Virtues and the Creation of Prosperity* (New York: Free Press, 1995).

17. J. S. Coleman, "Social Capital in the Creation of Human Capital," *American Journal of Sociology* (1988): 95–120; V. Gillies and R. Edwards, "A Qualitative Analysis of Parenting and Social Capital: Comparing the Work of Coleman and Bourdieu," *Qualitative Sociology Review* 2.2 (2006): 42–60.

18. Robert D. Putnam, *Bowling Alone: The Collapse and Revival of American Community* (New York: Simon and Schuster, 2000).

19. See, for example, C. Boggs, "Social Capital and Political Fantasy: Robert Putnam's Bowling Alone," *Theory and Society* 30.2 (2001): 281–297; T. Schuller, S. Baron, and J. Field, "Social Capital: A Review and Critique," *Social Capital: Critical Perspectives* (2000): 1–38; B. Edwards and M. W. Foley, "Civil Society and Social Capital beyond Putnam," *American Behavioral Scientist* 42.1 (1998): 124–139.

20. K. Newton, "Social Capital and Democracy," *American Behavioral Scientist* 40.5 (1997): 575–586.

21. See, for example, C. Bjornskov, "The Multiple Facets of Social Capital," *European Journal of Political Economy* 22.1 (2006): 22–40; J. Temple, "Initial Conditions, Social Capital, and Growth in Africa," *Journal of African Economies* 7.3 (1998): 309–347; M. Lindström, "Ethnic Differences in Social Participation and Social Capital in Malmö, Sweden: A Population-Based Study," *Social Science & Medicine* 60.7 (2006): 1527–1546; Christian Welzel, Ronald F. Inglehart, and Franziska Deutsch, "Social Capital, Voluntary Associations, and Collective Action: Which Aspects of Social Capital Have the Greatest 'Civic' Payoff?" *Journal of Civil Society* 1.2 (2005): 121–146. For an application in management, see, for example, P. S. Adler and S. W. Kwon, "Social Capital: Prospects for a New Concept," *Academy of Management Review* 27.1 (2002): 17–40; in business history, see J. Eloranta, J. Ojala, and H. Valtonen, "Quantitative Methods in Business History: An Impossible Equation?" *Management & Organizational History* 5.1 (2010): 79–107.

22. Manuel Castells, *The Rise of the Network Society,* vol. 1 (Oxford: Blackwell, 1996); see also M. Acevedo, "Network Capital: An Expression of Social Capital in the Network Society," *The Journal of Community Informatics* 3.2 (2007): http://www.cijournal.net/index.php/ciej/article/viewArticle/267/317 (accessed November 11, 2014); Manuel Acevedo, "Network Cooperation: Development Cooperation in the Network Society," *International Journal of Information Communication Technologies and Human Development* (IJICTHD) 1.1 (2009): 1–21.

23. N. Lin, "Building a Network Theory of Social Capital," *Connections* 22.1 (1999): 28–51.

24. See Amir Abbas Momenan, Maryam Delshad, Parvin Mirmiran, Arash Ghanbarian, and Fereydon Azizi, "Leisure Time Physical Activity and Its Determinants among Adults in Tehran: Tehran Lipid and Glucose Study," *International Journal of Preventive Medicine* 2.4 (October–December 2011): 243–251. Cf. A. J. Oswald, "Happiness and Economic Performance," *The Economic Journal* 107.445 (1997): 1815–1831. See also G. N. Saraji and H. Dargahi, "Study of Quality of Work Life (QWL)" *Iranian Journal of Public Health* 35.4 (2006): 8–14.

25. See, for example, M. Rambod and F. Rafii, "Perceived Social Support and Quality of Life in Iranian Hemodialysis Patients," *Journal of Nursing Scholarship,* 42.3 (2010): 242–249. On data available for analysis in the North American context, see P. Paxton, "Is Social Capital Declining in the United States? A Multiple Indicator Assessment 1," *American Journal of Sociology* 105.1 (1999): 88–127, and L. Keele, "Social Capital and the Dynamics of Trust in Government," *American Journal of Political Science* 51.2 (2007): 241–254.

26. Babak Rahimi, "The Rebound Theater State: The Politics of the Safavid Camel Sacrifice Rituals, 1598–1695 C.E.," *International Journal of Iranian Studies* 3 (2004): 451–478.

27. See Babak Rahimi, *Theater State and the Formation of the Early Modern Public Sphere in Iran: Studies on Safavid Muharram Rituals, 1590–1641 CE* (Leiden and Boston: Brill, 2012), and Masoud Kamali, *Revolutionary Iran: Civil Society and*

State in the Modernization Process (Aldershot and Brookfield: Ashgate, 1998). For a study of new urbanization patterns in the new Isfahan, see Susan Babaie, *Isfahan and Its Palaces: Statecraft, Shi'ism, and the Architecture of Conviviality in Early Modern Iran* (Edinburgh: Edinburgh University Press, 2008).

28. For a study on the formation of Iranian civil society in the Qajar period, see Kamali, *Revolutionary Iran*. It is important to note that such nexus of both formal and informal ties was not exclusive to the three associations. There were also secular intellectuals, women's organizations, and ethnic minority groups, among others, who also shaped and, at times, competed in early Iranian civil society.

29. See Arang Keshavarzian, *Bazaar and State in Iran: The Politics of the Tehran Marketplace* (Cambridge: Cambridge University Press, 2007).

30. See Susan Bastani, "Middle Class Community in Tehran: Social Networks, Social Support and Marital Relationship," PhD dissertation, Toronto, University of Toronto, 2001.

31. See Chapters 5 and 6 in this volume.

32. See Masoud Kowsari, *Jahan-e farhang-e karbaran-e Irani Orkut* (Tehran: Vezarat-e Farhang va Ershad Eslami, Pajoheshgha-he farhang, honar va ertebatat, 1386 [2007]).

33. Ibid.

34. Ibid., 111–113.

35. Sex and sexuality also play a role, which the survey might not have explored due to cultural or legal limitations in doing research in Iran.

36. See Majid Kashani and Somayih Zarih, "Motaleay-e jameyat shenakht-e shabakehay-e ejtima-ye-e majazi ba takid bar karbaran Facebook dar Iran," *Ulum-e Ejtemae-ye* 56 (1391/2012): 78–84. According to Internetworldstats.com in 2013, the Facebook user population in Iran was 46.7 percent.

37. Ibid., 83–84.

38. Ibid.

39. Mohammad Reza Rassooli and Maryam Moradi, "Avamil-e moasir bar towlid-e muhtava dar shabakiha-ye ejtemai," *Ulum-e Ejtemae-ye* 56 (1391/2012): 57–66, especially 63–65. The study did not indicate the geographical base of the Iranians whose answers to questions were examined.

40. Ibid., 65.

41. Ibid.

42. Ali Asghar Kia and Yonis Nori Murad Abadai, "Avamal-e murtabet ba gherayish-e daneshjoyan bi shabake-ye ejtema-ye 'Facebook': Barresi-ye tatbighi-yeh daneshjoyan-e Iran va America," *Motaleat-e Farhang-Ertebatat* 13.17 (1391/2012): 181–212, especially 203–207.

43. Ibid.

44. Ibid.

45. Mahin Shaykh Ansari, "Tahlil-e rabeti-ye hambastegi karbari dar shabake-ye ejtemai-ye Facebook va sarmay-i ejtemai," PhD dissertation, Tehran, University of Tehran, 2013.

46. The element of transnationalism is mostly evident in connection with the way users find friends residing abroad.

47. The sample of Facebook users in Kermani's study consists of students at Tehran-based universities, including the University of Tehran, University of Shahid Beheshti, Sanati Sharif, and Sanati Amir Kabir. The sample is representative of the larger Iranian population of Facebook users who are young and mostly university educated. See Hossein Kermani, "Sanjesh-e sarmay-e ejtema-e dar shabakehay-e ejtemai va majazi," PhD dissertation, Tehran, University of Tehran, 2012, 29–35.

48. Kermani's study on social capital is limited to cyberspace and does not examine precisely how online relations can be translated or overlapped with offline bonds developed among friends, family, classmates, or neighborhoods, although some preliminary analysis is articulated in the study.

49. Ibid., 66.

50. This practice shows how sharing personal information such as announcements of events like birthdays or educational background information involves less concern about privacy than personal pictures and films. The role gender might play in this distinct practice of privacy on Facebook, as Iranian women tend to be more selective, and hence more private, is displayed in the types of photos they post and share on Facebook. See Kermani, "Sanjesh-e sarmay-e ejtema-e dar shabakehay e ejtemai va majazi," 114.

51. Ibid.

52. The capacity of the privacy setting option to shape trust on Facebook also appears evident in a study conducted by the Iran Media Program at the Annenberg School for Communication, University of Pennsylvania. See *Liking Facebook in Tehran: Social Networking in Iran,* 2013, http://www.iranmediaresearch.org/en/research/download/1609 (accessed November 11, 2013).

53. Ibid., 66.

54. Ibid., 67.

55. Ibid., 68.

56. The percentages of Facebook activities range as follow: like (8.4 percent), commenting (4.1 percent), sharing commentaries or photos (3.6 percent), receiving invitations to events (3.5 percent), sending friend requests (2.3 percent), receiving private messages (2.3 percent), sending private messages (1.8 percent), tagging (1.2 percent), receiving friend requests (0.5 percent), and, finally, creating events (0.4 percent). Kermani, "Sanjesh-e sarmay-e ejtema-e dar shabakehay-e ejtemai va majazi," 114.

57. Ibid., 69.

58. See Alex Lambert, *Intimacy and Friendship on Facebook* (New York: Palgrave Macmillan, 2013).

59. As a convergent technology, the Internet can also involve spaces of addiction, obsession, and mistrust. For a study of online addiction among students and youth, as an example of social capital decay, see K. Ahmadi and A. Saghafi, "Psychosocial Profile of Iranian Adolescents' Internet Addiction," *Cyberpsychology,*

Behavior, and Social Networking (April 24, 2013): http://www.ncbi.nlm.nih.gov/ pubmed/23614793 (accessed July 19, 2013).

60. Lambert, *Intimacy and Friendship on Facebook*, 44.

61. Putnam, *Bowling Alone*, 170.

Chapter 2

Gender Roles in the
Social Media World of Iranian Women

Elham Gheytanchi

The Islamic state imposes strict boundaries of gender roles in the Iranian society. Since 1979, women's social and legal statuses have been defined by the Islamic state and the ruling clerics in sharp contrasts with that of men's. Women were barred from becoming judges, certain engineering majors were and remain closed to women in higher education, and women are barred from presidency in today's Iran. Vibrant grassroots women's movements have formed and persisted in Iran despite state regulations, but there have been many setbacks, and the legal system remains discriminatory against women of all socioeconomic, religious, and ethnic backgrounds. Iranian women's daily lives are filled with violations of Islamic mores regarding hijab workplace, legal injustice, and politics.[1] Gender roles, therefore, have remained the Achilles heels of the Islamic Republic. The Internet, specially Facebook and blogs, have become sites of contestation over the socially proper roles of women. Motherhood and women's rights activism are challenged and redefined in the virtual world of Iranian women more radically than they are in real life.

Two spheres of women's roles are defined by Islamic/Shia rules of engagement to safeguard the Islamic government. First, women's roles as mothers have been praised consistently by the ruling clerics in Iran since the revolution in 1979. Second, women's political and social activism was also praised by Ayatollah Khomeini. But women's active participation and interpretation of gender roles in these realms have challenged the parameters set by the clerics. The emergence of online sphere—blogs and Facebook pages—in recent years have allowed women of different backgrounds who could not have mobilized on the ground to meet online, share ideas, challenge the existing gender roles, and thereby pose an internal threat to the Islamic state.

A nuanced channel of communication and exchange of ideas regarding gender roles, motherhood and women's political and social activism have become social networking topics that were not possible a decade ago. This preliminary research shows that the virtual world—blogs, social networking sites such as Facebook, chat rooms, and the like—allows Iranian women to exchange ideas with their peers inside and outside of the country in horizontal ways that defy social norms and laws in the Iranian society.[2] Considering the restrictions on gender roles and Internet communication set by the Islamic state, women's access to the virtual world allows them to transgress state geographical as well as ideological boundaries.

Around the world, women publicly post and share their everyday life events and their views. Iranian women, politically active and vocal ones as well as "others," have also engaged in the virtual world. The mundane in countries such as Iran with a patriarchal structure and state that closely monitors the web does indeed lead to political statements. As noted by Van Doorn, "[the Internet] is made up of people who bring their everyday experiences to a realm where their actions mutually create a shared, temporal reality. It is important to keep in mind, then, that this 'reality' consists of discourses that originate from an embodied understanding of how our world works and who/what/how we can be to make our lives as livable as possible."[3] Iranian women who are limited in the public sphere by strict Islamic laws, hijab, and cultural mores create a temporal reality through the Internet in which they are free to roam around and express themselves in a liberated way. This is why their mere presence in cyberspace is a threat to the Islamic Republic of Iran and a reminder that women can and do transgress cultural and legal limitations imposed on them. Of course, there are also governmental sites that advocate the idea that the "authentic" Iranian Muslim woman is the one who is covered by black chador and closely follows Islamic guidelines.

Methodology

This research was carried out in 2011; the methodology is a mixture of the author's participation and observation as a women's rights activist, online ethnography, online interviews, and secondary sources. The sites under study were Facebook and blogs in Blogfa, using search keywords such as "zan" (women—which is, interestingly enough, censored occasionally inside Iran), "madar" (mother), "zananeh" (feminine), "jensiyat" (gender role), as well as phrases such as "Iranian women," "gender roles," and "women's roles." I analyzed and compared the contents of the websites for politically moti-vated Iranian women (Persian, German, and English) with blogs belonging to "ordinary" Iranian women inside Iran (Persian) who clearly stated their purpose is to discuss "motherly issues."[4]

Searching through Facebook pages and blogs written by Persian-speak-ing women, I have used a snowball online ethnography method as well as my own feminist activist's account of online ethnography.[5] I followed participants/bloggers and Facebook account holders as well as their friends and associates to provide a picture of gender roles in the virtual world. Although the results are by no means generalizable, it allows us to get an in-depth picture of a segment of Facebook users and bloggers who are women and write in Persian about motherhood and activism. This study traces the ways in which a randomly selected group of bloggers and Face-book members talk, think, interact, and exchange ideas about motherhood and the sociopolitical activism of Persian-speaking women in Iran and their counterparts in diaspora.

On this particular topic, qualitative methods seem to be most appro-priate because quantitative methods have these problems: (1) many use VPNs in Iran to access the Internet, (2) many profiles on Facebook are possibly pseudonyms, and (3) there are no official statistics available. In lieu of these deficiencies, I have conducted textual analysis of comments and posts regarding gender roles. My focus in this research is on two particular spheres: women as mothers without any publicly (read virtual) stated politi-cal inclination, and women as mothers of the young activists who were arrested, tortured, and/or killed in the aftermath of the 2009 presidential election in Iran. It should be noted that any study of Facebook is bound to be complicated and labor intensive. As Rieder notes, obtaining any macro view through Facebook is impossible due to its complicated web of networks and interaction spaces.[6]

A Note about Nonusers of
Facebook in the Context of Iranian Politics

Iranians have the habit of sharing books. This makes it hard to have statistics on book sales in Iran. The same is true about Facebook and blogs: non-users share information with users, which leads into multiplying the effects of Facebook and blogs in Iranian society in particular and the Persian-speaking diasporas community in general. In the blogosphere, Iranian women enjoy anonymity. On Facebook, women can choose to be anonymous or not and connect to each other in horizontal ways. Mothers and women's rights activists (obviously the two categories do overlap sometimes, but for analytical purposes the author keeps the two categories separate) tend to be more vocal in groups on Facebook because the forum allows like-minded women to connect to each other and sometimes results in gatherings of online and offline communities. These are gender-specific communities such as the ones formed around issues regarding motherhood and/or which elicit gender issues—from motherhood to the political rights of women. In fact, there is no distinction between political and personal because the mere presence of women (such as Facebook photos of women without veiling) defies Iranian state restrictions regarding women's proper clothing in public spaces and makes a political statement.

Considering the diaspora community of Iranian women connected via email listserves, as well as social networking sites and blogs, these virtual ties made through Facebook, for instance, will not disappear even if Facebook is banned in Iran, considering the vast use of VPNs such as TOR as well as satellite TVs and other forms of communication that have persistently proven to exist despite state censorship. In social movements, activists strive to find media coverage and broaden their audience pool. On Facebook this happens without much effort. Facebook has provided many instances of nonviolent civil disobedient acts to protest the status quo in Iran.

Why has Facebook been so popular in Iran since 2008? In many ways, Facebook allows horizontal relationships—built around people, not interests—to shape online content. Similar to attending a movie theater, activity on Facebook is a shared experience—in this case, for all those who are discontent with the status quo. Even for people who do not have access to the Internet, Facebook has become a part of their lives as we see its signs in political debates among dissidents. The ability to engage in discussions, exchange information, have access to news and information blocked by the state, and form campaigns online have created a wave of change among youth, women, and anyone interested or invested in social change.

The state authorities—that is, the ministry of intelligence and the ministry of ICT—have had a dubious relationship with social networking sites and blogs. During the presidential elections in 2009, state officials first allowed Facebook but later blocked it.[7] Many Internet experts think that the Iranian state is actively using the information on Facebook to gather intelligence, which is why it has not been blocked. The state and the people are playing a cat and mouse game with regard to web 2.0 and the Internet in general.[8]

Motherhood and the Women's Movement in Islamic Iran

In the first decade after the establishment of the Islamic Republic in 1979, women's roles were defined primarily by motherhood.[9] Ayatollah Khomeini praised mothers' roles during the eight-year war with Iraq. Women's active participation in the workforce and support line for soldiers was allowed only if women were fully veiled and complied with Islamic laws. Subsequently, many secular women fled the country and became active women's rights advocates outside of Iran.[10] The transnational ties were strengthened between women in general and women's rights activists—many of whom preferred to call themselves "social activists" rather than feminists—particularly through the emergence of emails (1990s), blogs (late 1990s), and social networking sites such as Facebook.

Independent and grassroots women's movement(s) gradually formed in the late 1980s as the Iran–Iraq war came to an end. The Iranian state has continuously contributed to the formation of state-funded Islamic feminism parallel to independent and grassroots feminist movements. Establishing GNGOs (government-backed NGOs) allow the Iranian state to save face and present GNGOs as the "real representative" of Iranian women.[11] The Internet, social networking sites, and blogs have provided the much-needed space for interaction and free exchange of ideas, strategies for action, campaigns, and nonviolent civil resistance. The choice for anonymity on the Internet allows women to express themselves more boldly.

Feminist Take on IT and FB

Feminist theory on IT and women's participation in the virtual world has not yet included the experience of non-Western women. Feminist scholars have demonstrated how the binary oppositions in Western culture, between culture and nature, reason and emotion, hard and soft, have privileged masculinity over femininity. The presence of women in cyberspace defies the cultural stereotype of women as technically incompetent or invisible in technical spheres. Gender is embedded in technology itself. Wajcman states that gender is integral to this sociotechnical process—that the materiality of technology affords or inhibits the doing of particular gender power relations. Women's identities, needs, and priorities are configured together with digital technologies. For all the diversity of feminist voices, feminist scholars share a concern with the hierarchical divisions marking relations between men and women.[12]

In their study on "networked identity performance" on the social network site Friendster, boyd and Heer explore the relation between identity and the online social network, examining how users simultaneously construct themselves and others on their profiles. They argue that the construction of a personal profile on a SNS is not an autonomous effort but the result of continuous interactions with one's online social environment. These conversational performances between SNS users change the profile "from being a static representation of self to a communicative body."[13] In this view, a SNS profile becomes a user's "digital body," which is collectively "written into being." This digital body, then, provides the social context for interactions in a space without physical infrastructure or a visible audience. Instead of respecting social norms due to other people's embodied presence, users have to create and interpret the semiotic resources (e.g., text, images, videos) that make up their profiles, which effectively constitute a digital infrastructure. These interactions dialogically produce a shared social reality through the distribution and interpretation of these artifacts.

Robert Shuter has pointed that computer-mediated communication, SNS, and mobile activities around the world show many signs of shared cultural elements. This finding allows us to consider a global culture of communication.[14] Although Persian blogs and Facebook pages of mothers appear to discuss local cultural norms and laws, these bloggers and Facebook users engage with their counterparts in the global South as well as with Western countries on topics related to motherhood and mothers' proper social status, power, and legal rights. While Iranian women's activity on the pages of Facebook shares many characteristics of a global communication culture in the forming, they also create shared digital bodies situated within Iranian culture and among their online social networks that (1) might oppose the realities of their lives on the ground, and (2), for women's rights activists, provide ample opportunity to mobilize, connect with peers across borders, and to a certain degree strategize. These two characteristics make the mere presence of Iranian women's rights activists and mothers on Facebook and blogs a threat to the Iranian political system—a modern theocratic political apparatus. In effect, by following the global culture within the social networks, Iranian women users of Facebook and Persian-speaking bloggers are the Achilles' heel of the Islamic Republic of Iran. The Achilles' heel here refers to women's roles and the extent of their agency within the Islamic guidelines in the age of global mass communication.

The Persian-speaking women who are avid users of Facebook or female bloggers who communicate in Persian on topics such as motherhood and political activism create and co-create digital identities that are bound to reshape gender relations. The effects of these bloggers and Facebook users writing about motherhood in its classic sense (mothering for toddlers and babies) as well as the Mourning Mothers of politically dissident youth reverberates through Iranian society as well as among perpetual waves of immigrants/refugees/political exiles who settle in their new homelands. A slow and incremental yet irreversible change in gender roles is taking place among Iranian women, especially as new immigrants/refugees/exiles come from all provinces of Iran following the Iranian state's crackdown of the Green Movement activists. The change in gender roles defies state mandates and is therefore threatening to the Iranian state, as explained below. Also, while many profiles on Facebook are real, I have encountered pseudonyms. Some Persian-speaking women from Iran as well as those in the diaspora want to connect with others and get their voice out, but choose to do so privately. This is because, in the Iranian context, *anything* women say on Facebook can be considered political.

Ethnographic Research: Motherhood and Activism in Iran

Despite the great success of the Islamic state in imposing Islamic laws on what is considered "the private realm," namely, family and particularly motherhood, some young mothers in Iran (mostly in urban cities and, in this research, in Tehran, Isfahan, Ahwaz, and Shiraz) challenge the Islamic laws and norms on the pages of Facebook and in their blogs. After a period of three months of conducting online ethnographic notes (September–December 2011), a pattern emerged: mothers in Iran via blogs and Facebook were/are discussing Western parental guidelines regarding respecting their children's views, empathy, discipline, and a less hierarchal parenting style that contrasts sharply with that preached on the state TV. One of the discussion threads and a pattern that developed during online interactions among mothers was that parenting has to involve respect for kids and allowing them to have a certain autonomy, thus refraining from orders based on religious beliefs.

A young Iranian mother writes in her blog on behalf of her four-year-old daughter about her chador and her spirited play during Ramadan, the holy month for Shia Muslims around the world.[15] She writes: "One night I went to Quran reading session and annoyed everyone by running around and having aunts and uncles chasing me around." In this post, the author is writing from the perspective of her daughter who is too young to respect religious spaces and is struggling with keeping her chador on her head. Although the mother is religious, she finds the religious mores regarding hijab for little girls unrealistic. Another young mother, in Ahwaz, writes openly about her Islamic views that are not in line with the state-imposed views.[16] She takes her child to various playgrounds in the city and talks about Disney movies such as *Shrek*. This young mother, who has fasted the whole month of Ramadan while watching state TV programs, writes about her daughter's adventures in Kermanshah and Tehran and posts pictures of her daughter (without veiling) watching Western children's movies.[17] She wants her daughter to see the Western movies banned by the state TV and defies the state-imposed restriction; she is both a devoted Muslim as well as a consumer of Western media.

Young mothers are also present on Facebook, in groups forming around common interests, such as swimming in Dubai.[18] Because the relationships are centered on common interests, young mothers freely participate in online discussions, adding comments and questions. Sometimes these online discussions on their Facebook pages lead them to uncharted territories, such as mothers discussing how to best raise their children in Iran and in Israel (the two countries have not had diplomatic relations in thirty-five years). Ziba, a mother in Iran who is active on Facebook, quotes child development specialists in Israel and the United States on how to raise disciplined yet creative kids, while other moms freely comment on her blogpost.[19]

Many young mothers of toddlers and babies use the Internet to find resources, updated research, and practical tips on parenting. Many who want to freely exchange ideas about parenting participate in discussion under pseudonyms such as "Fatemeh Irani" or "Shamsi Irani" (the first names are the same as in their blogs, but they change their last names to a generic 'Irani' to hide their identities). Persian-speaking mothers of toddlers and babies also search the web for similar resources. It is this free and open exchange of ideas regarding parenting by law-abiding mothers who connect beyond state borders that forms a global culture of motherhood on the web. The topics discussed range from the emotional health of toddlers, disciplinary issues, academic testing, college preparation, and enrichment classes, to milk products and birthday party themes. The advent of global mass communication has allowed mothers from various socioeconomic, religious, and ethnic backgrounds to exchange ideas about what is best for their children.

The idea of women first and foremost as mothers has been an important ideological pillar of the Islamic Republic since its inception. This mom, however, writes about motherhood with a twist of laughter and jokes. She says:

> My friends tell me, "I wish you could write about more important things [than what your little one did everyday]." I tell them I am what I am, not a researcher, not a writer, just a mom who can only write about mundane things. Our conversations are funny and this is what I write about because I love my toddler because she makes fun of everything.[20]

The friends of the author then carry the conversation into Facebook, where there are more jokes about the presumably "exalted" status of mothers in contrast with their everyday struggles in Iran. A working mom writes about the challenges of work and motherhood in Iran.[21] A mother writes playfully about her little girl's adventures that do not always follow the Islamic guidelines, although her own extended family members are devout Muslims.[22] Long after this blogger's blog became inactive, her followers continued to discuss her topics on Facebook, such as discussions about what to expect from dads.[23] In general, they demand a more active role from fathers and publicly defy the role of a domesticated mother as propagated by state TV. An observant Muslim mother discusses alternative paths of motherhood in her blog.[24] She wants her children to see her as a working mother and get inspired. She does not abide by state TV's renditions about the "proper place" for mothers. An Ahwazi mother is a fan of Children's movies made in the United States and adores the American pop culture that is banned in the Islamic Republic of Iran.[25] A mother living in Tehran and her friends discuss politics while traveling to religious sites in Syria.[26] Some of the friends and fans of these bloggers are then active in such discussions on Facebook. These bloggers have carved out a space for themselves as mothers who work, have political opinions, and follow Western media, while claiming their Muslim identities in cyberspace.

Social and Political Activism by Women

During the uprising of 2009 over the widely assumed fraudulent results of the presidential elections, women's rights activists used Facebook to create a group of mothers called Mothers of Park Laleh (originally called The

Mourning Mothers of Iran), which remains active. These women's rights activists consisted of male and female activists in Iran, Europe, and the United States,[27] and were (and still are) communicating in Persian via email list-serves that have long been created and maintained by grassroots, transparent, and socially connected networks of activists. The main purpose of this group was to find the best, most efficient, and culturally sensitive strategy to mobilize mothers whose sons and/or daughters had disappeared or been imprisoned, tortured, or forced to appear in state-run TV shows to confess to "their crimes," namely, endangering national security. Many have since fled Iran and live as refugees in Turkey, Germany, France, and the United States. They demanded that Iranian authorities identify and prosecute those responsible for the loss, execution, or imprisonment of their sons and daughters. Members of the group in Iran were harassed by authorities, but the transnational ties they had made via Facebook and email lists allowed the group to withstand pressure and publicize the arrests.

The Mourning Mothers first started gathering in Park Laleh in Tehran, and later at other parks in major cities on Saturdays at 4:00 p.m. to commemorate the loss, disappearance, or execution of their adult children who had joined the public demonstrations by supporters of the Green Movement in the aftermath of the presidential election.[28] The Iranian security apparatus did not tolerate the Mourning Mothers' peaceful gatherings as the mothers started reaching out to international entities such as the United Nations.[29] Despite pressures to shut down their activities on the ground, activists used Facebook pages to stay connected and publicize their cause. The supporters on Facebook were varied: some had never been involved in any political campaign, and many would not have known about this issue if not for Facebook.

When this group was formed in the immediate aftermath of the 2009 elections, many like-minded Iranian-American feminists championed their cause and collaborated via active email lists with their counterparts in Iran. They were inspired by the "Mothers of the Plaza de Mayo" in Argentina,[30] "Mothers in Black" in Israel, and transnational feminist movements that emphasize peaceful conflict resolution without the involvement of military and state apparatus after the injustices done to their politically dissenting sons and daughters.[31] Like mothers in Uruguay and their expatriate counterparts around the world, the exiled mothers (those who fled Iran after or at the time of the 1979 revolution) showed their solidarity with mothers in Iran and joined the campaign.[32] Many of these exiled mothers later formed their own branch of Park Laleh Mothers in various cities in which they have taken refuge since the revolution. The Supporters of

Mothers of Park Laleh, Valley–LA created websites (http://www.parklaleh. blogspot.com; http://www.facebook.com/mourningmothersofIran?fref=ts; http://www.facebook.com/LalehMothersValley), while their counterparts in Iran formed online groups such as Mothers of Park Laleh/Iran (http://www. mpliran.org).[33] In contrast to the first group of bloggers and Facebook participants, the Mothers of Park Laleh are politically and explicitly vocal, and publically voice their opposition to the status quo in Iran.

The Islamic state in Iran, of course, actively propagates its own version of the "authentic" Iranian Muslim woman. The "virtual world" could also become a space of identity reproduction—the Islamic state version of what an authentic woman is—rather than a space of liberation or transgression. For instance, the Basiji (state-operated militia) women in Iran claim to be a grassroots women's movement that is safeguarding the real identity of Iranian women. Sazeman-e Basij Jame Iran (The Basiji Organization of the Iranian Society) claims to be continuing a long tradition of devout Muslim women who fought during the revolution and the eight-year war. There were and still are devout Muslim women who are steadfast followers of Imam Khomeini. Some fought alongside Sepah Pasdaran, and some joined the ranks of Basijis and formed their own women's faction inside the Basij. The Basiji women are young, devoted, and rigid in their perception of who is qualified in the ranks of "Iranian women."

One can only imagine what the state-backed women's groups can do with all the resources available to them. One example is that of Basiji women discussed at Tanin-e Yas (echo of Jasmin): http://www.tanineyas. ir. Women with black chadors, fighting the "bad hijabs" (those who do not adhere to the Islamic dress code), are the role models praised in the pages of this site. There are, here and there, also references to mundane "womanly" concerns such as how to keep your nails clean, how to be a good mother, and how to pray according to the latest fatwas from the religious authorities. The state-backed women's organizations as represented in Tanin-e Yas actively reproduce seemingly all-inclusive conceptions of the "ideal" women's identity that supposedly transgress class, ethnic, and tradition lines, thus creating a utopian community of women who have become "enlightened"—that is, devout Muslim women fighting the smallest signs of impurity in the society.

In contemporary Iranian society, there are ample resources for conservative women who have been "guided" to serve God along the lines of the Islamic tradition/state/Sepah/Basiji lines. The Basiji women funded by the umbrella organization of the Mostazafin (which works closely with the Iranian state apparatus) have created numerous software tools, such as

"Women in the Holy Defense," which are distributed widely in society. At the time of this chapter's writing, this software is in its second edition and can be found at http://golenarges6416.blogfa.com. The conservative women's organizations, such as Basiji women and other state-backed groups, announce that among the responsibilities of their members is fighting to repress "women's rights activists who have gone strayed by the West."[34] A thorough study of conservative, state-backed women's organizations and GNGOs (government-backed NGOs) is beyond the scope of this chapter. Let us suffice by saying that the virtual world does not always allow women—be they activists, mothers, or even conservative women—to transgress the state geographical and ideological boundaries.

Conclusion

This paper attempted to show the nuanced ways in which Iranian women as mothers—albeit, politically active mothers, such as the Mourning Mothers or bloggers who are mothers—have created a new public sphere via the Internet where they challenge the Islamic state's strict gender roles. As demonstrated by "My Stealthy Freedom" campaign that has recently been launched in which Iranian women post their photos without hijab to protest the compulsory veiling in Iran, mothers challenge one of the most important pillars of the Islamic Republic of Iran, namely the obedient, veiled, and devout Muslim woman whose most important duty is to be a mother.

The Iranian mothers of young children and babies as well as mourning mothers of Iran use the Internet to stay connected, mobilize, exchange ideas freely and openly, strategize, and plan their activities beyond Islamic state guidelines and restrictions. While the former group of mothers is loosely networked, and the latter group a social movement in the making, willingly or unintentionally these women defy Iranian religious codes and red lines. Further research can explore ways in which women become activists online and how they form transnational ties that lead them to become active agents of social change. Of course, the Internet is just a medium, but in the contemporary Iranian society, the Internet in general and social networking sites and blogs in particular have become tools for peaceful protest, a contestation of the moral and religious norms that the theocratic state promotes via its state-run mass media outlets.

Contrary to the naïve expectations of those who praise the liberating powers of the Internet, the virtual world is not a utopia for the Iranian women. As for women everywhere, the Iranian woman's presence in the blogosphere, social networking sites, and other forms of Internet communication is still grounded in their real life with all the state-imposed restrictions on their body (hijab), in the workplace as well as their in roles as mothers. Yet the sheer number of women engaging in blogging, social networking, and photosharing has led to an alternative virtual public sphere in which the Islamic rule of the state is constantly contested. The Islamic state and the hardliners in Iran are also present on the Internet and do try to police it, but women's voices have incrementally opened up spaces in the virtual world.

Notes

1. For recent grassroots movements regarding hijab, see My Stealthy Freedom campaign on Facebook (https://www.facebook.com/StealthyFreedom).

2. Masserat Amir-Ebrahimi's ethnographic work illustrates this point.

3. N. A. J. M. Van Doorn, "Digital Spaces, Material Traces: Investigating the Performance of Gender, Sexuality, and Embodiment on Internet Platforms That Feature User-Generated Content," PhD Diss., Amsterdam School of Communication Research, 2010, http://dare.uva.nl/document/2/72919, 52.

4. The politically motivated websites are http://www.mpliran.org; http://madaransolhdortmund.blogspot.com; and http://parklaleh.blogspot.com.The blogs written by Iranian women inside Iran (the authors identify their location in different cities in Iran including Tehran, Isfahan, Rasht, Shiraz, and Ahwaz) are at these locations: http://goodmorning.blogfa.com/9004.aspx; http://diba-parand.persianblog.ir/; http://somy1359.persianblog.ir/1389/1/; http://siavoshi.persianblog.ir/1389/11/; http://manopesari.persianblog.ir/; and http://fatemehzahrakocholo.blogfa.com/.

5. For more on this type of online ethnography, see Patricia Zavella, "Feminist Insider Dilemmas: Constructing Ethnic Identity with "Chicana" Informants," *Frontiers: A Journal of Women Studies* 13.3 (1993): 53–76.

6. See http://thepoliticsofsystems.net for Bernhard Rieder's comments on Facebook studies.

7. For an updated report on filtering in Iran, see http://www.smallmedia.org.uk/sites/default/files/u8/iiipjune.pdf.

8. Shanthi Kalathil and Taylor C. Boas, *Open Networks, Closed Regimes: The Impact of the Internet on Authoritarian Rule* (Washington, DC: Carnegie Endowment for International Peace, 2003).

9. Not surprisingly, Saeed Jalili, one of the eight presidential candidates in the 2013 elections, has stated that women's role is primarily defined by their role as mothers. See http://www.bloomberg.com/news/2013-05-30/iran-candidate-jalili-says-women-s-rights-are-as-mothers.html.

10. Halleh Esfandiari, *Reconstructed Lives: Women and Iran's Islamic* Revolution (Washington, DC: The Woodrow Wilson Press, 1997).

11. GNGO, or governmental NGO, refers to an NGO created by a governmental entity to do work in support of, or in furtherance of, the state's interests and aims. Shirin Ebadi has repeatedly stated that GNGOs threaten the work and integrity of NGOs in Iran. In the last section of this article, published at Rooz online on May 12, 2010 (titled "From Banning to exit the country to parallel institution making strategies" and found at http://www.roozonline.com/persian/news/newsitem/article/-69fa8f1d75.html), Shirin Ebadi warns about a government's strategy to destroy old longstanding civil institutions in Iran by making parallel governmental institutions and thereby attempting to render the former institutions ineffective.

12. Judy Wajcman, "Feminist Theories of Technology," *Cambridge Journal of Economics* (2009): http://wiki.medialab-prado.es/images/4/4b/Wajcman_Feminist_theories_of_technology.pdf, 8.

13. danah boyd and Jeffrey Heer, "Profiles as Conversation: Networked Identity Performance on Friendster," *Proceedings of the Hawai'i International Conference on System Sciences* (HICSS-39), Persistent Conversation Track; Kauai, Hawai'i, IEEE Computer Society, January 4–7, 2006, 8.

14. Robert Shuter, "Intercultural New Media Studies: The Next Frontier in Intercultural Communication," *Journal of Intercultural Communication* 41.3 (2012): 219–237.

15. http://fatemehzahrakocholo.blogfa.com/post-65.aspx

16. http://youna.persianblog.ir

17. http://www.parmida85.blogfa.com

18. https://www.facebook.com/pages/Absolute-Swimming-Academy/241284869241768

19. Her Facebook page exists under a pseudonym and is frequently updated and changed.

20. http://goodmorning.blogfa.com/9004.aspx

21. http://diba-parand.persianblog.ir

22. http://somy1359.persianblog.ir/1389/1

23. http://siavoshi.persianblog.ir/1389/11

24. http://manopesari.persianblog.ir

25. http://youna.persianblog.ir

26. http://fatemehzahrakocholo.blogfa.com

27. The author has been an active participant in this group since its inception.

28. Here is the author's short call to action in Iranian.com (run by diasporic Iranian activists): http://iranian.com/main/blog/elham-gheytanchi/join-us-saturdays-park.html

29. Here is the text of what a number of activists drafted in Los Angeles on September 20, 2009 (obtained by the author). Petition to: UN Secretary General, Mr. Ban Ki-moon "From Banning to exit the country to parallel institution making strategies: We, the supporters of "The Committee of Mourning Mothers of Iran," call upon the UN Secretary General, Mr. Ban Ki-moon, to immediately send a delegate to Iran in order to investigate, identify, and prosecute those responsible

for imprisonment and torture of our children during and after the June 2009 presidential election. The Mournful Mothers of Iran have no access to international authorities to plea for justice. Hereby, we call upon the UN secretary general, Mr. Ban Ki-moon, to take action addressing the violation of human rights in Iran. We, the supporters of The Committee of Mourning Mothers of Iran, call upon UN Secretary General Mr. Ban Ki-moon to immediately send a delegate to Iran to investigate, identify, and prosecute those responsible for the imprisonment, disappearance, and killing of our children.

30. The supporters of Mourning Mothers in Los Angeles wrote this letter on February 11, 2002:

با درود به شما مادران پلازا د مایا که استواری ، حق طلبی و آزادیخواهی تان طی سی و سه سال اخیر بزرگترین درس مقاومت و شهامت برای بسیاری ر هروانی بوده که شما را از الگو های خود در مبارزات غیر خشونت آمیز علیه دیکتاتوری قرار داده اند.

مادران عزادار ایران نیز به جهانیان ثابت کرده اند که علیر غم همه فشار ها، تهدید ها و دستگیریهای پی در پی ، با دلهایی زجر کشیده ولی همچنان پر صلابت، بزرگترین پرچم داران دفاع از حقوق بشر در ایران را تشکیل می دهند. اینک آنان مادران تمام وطن به شمار می آیند و با خواستار شدن توقف اعدامها و آزادی تمامی زندانیان عقیدتی و سیاسی، برای دادخواهی در سرزمین خود به پا خواسته اند.

در شرایطی که علیر غم ادعاهای کذب نماینده جمهوری اسلامی در کنفرانس ژنو، هر گونه دفاع از حقوق بشر در ایران، و حتی امضای دادخواست برای برابری حقوق زن و مرد جرمی سنگین محسوب می شود، مادران عزادار ایران همچنان در تلاشند در خفقان بار ترین وضعیت فریاد داد خواهی خود را سر دهند.

اینجاست که حامیان آنان در خارج از کشور وظیفه بسیار سنگینی بر دوش خود احساس می کنند تا به درستی منعکس کننده صدای آن مادران و زنان حق طلب ایران بوده فریاد های خاموش آنان را به گو ش جهانیان برسانند. حمایت مبارزینی چون شما نه تنها موجب دلگرمی آن مادران بلکه ضرورتی محض برای برقراری عدالت در جهان به هم تنیده امروز به شمار می آید.

با آرزوی دنیایی صلح آمیز تر و عادلانه تر

حامیان مادران عزادار ایران در لوس آنجلس ،
سانفرانسیسکو و ساکر امنتو

"Warmest regards to the Mothers of Plaza de Mayo, whose courage during the past thirty years has been an inspiration to all activists engaged in nonviolent struggles. We, the supporters of the Mourning Mothers of Iran, have received your statement in support of your counterparts in Iran. We are grateful for your acknowledgment and continued support.

"The Mourning Mothers of Iran have shown incredible resilience in the face of violent suppression, threats, and continuing arrests. Mourning the loss of their children in the aftermath of the fraudulent presidential election on June 12, 2009, all mothers who have mourned the loss of their children involved in nonviolent struggles have gathered to champion for human rights in Iran. These mothers have risen up to the state authorities and have rightfully demanded a permanent halt to execution of political prisoners as well as identification and persecution of those responsible for killings.

"We, the supporters of the Mourning Mothers of Iran feel obliged to support them in their plight and echo their voices. Under the current situation in Iran, where no dissent is tolerated and the authorities lie about gross human rights violations in the country, your support is heartening and indeed vital.

"May we have a peaceful and just world.

"The Supporters of Mourning Mothers of Iran in Los Angeles, San Francisco, and Sacramento."

31. Elahe Amani, "Mourning Mothers of Iran Stand with Activists Mothers Worldwide," http://womennewsnetwork.net/2009/10/08/mourning-mothers-iran-stand-with-activist-mothers-worldwide.

32. See Gabriella Fried-Amivilia, "Remembering Trauma in Society: Forced Disappearance and Familial Transmissions after Uruguay's Era of State Terror (1973–2001)," in *Sociology of Memory: Papers from the Spectrum*, ed. Noel Packard (Newcastle upon Tyne: Cambridge Scholars Publishing, 2009), 135–159.

33. Here is the latest plight of Mothers of Park Laleh reflected in Amnesty International: http://www.amnesty.org/en/library/info/MDE13/031/2013/en.

34. In this article, at http://www.defapress.ir/Fa/News/20188, "Fixing the Hijab and Chastity Problem Depends on Unity among Government Officials" (5th of khordad 1393; May 26, 2014), Minoo Aslani, the representative of Basiji women, talks about the need to guide the strayed young women who are not keeping the Islamic hijab into the righteous Islamic path of life. She states that young women are the victims of a Western attack on Islamic values and she counts the humanities and social sciences divisions in the universities responsible for this social problem in the Islamic country of Iran since these topics are essentially Western and have no relevance to Islamic guidelines. Aslani also holds satellite TV programs responsible for showing anti-Islamic values to young Iranian women and thereby destroying the unit of family in the Islamic country of Iran.

Chapter 3

The Role of Social Media in the Lives of Gay Iranians

Abouzar Nasirzadeh

Same-sex relationships are often treated in a highly negative fashion in gender-segregated societies such as Iran.[1] Within Iran, topics dealing with sexuality are generally taboo, and there are various laws that make same-sex sexual contact illegal and punishable with extremely harsh sanctions, including the death penalty.[2] These sanctions as well as the general taboo surrounding talking about sexuality marginalize people who desire same-sex relationships and make them highly invisible as they do not fit in the societal heteronormative norms. Indeed, in 2007, during a speech at Columbia University, the Iranian president, Mahmoud Ahmadinejad, denied the existence of homosexuals in Iran by stating, "In Iran, we don't have homosexuals, like in your country. We don't have that in our country. In Iran, we do not have this phenomenon. I don't know who's told you that we have it."[3] Such pronouncements are not uncommon among prominent figures such as religious personalities and state leaders within Iran and the broader Middle East. In addition to denying that gay people exist in their countries, political and religious figures in the region often claim that homosexuality is a Western phenomenon being imported into their countries.[4]

Yet, in recent years, there has been an increasingly visible number of individuals identifying as "gay" in these countries.[5] This growing visibility of gay individuals has coincided with greater Internet penetration in Iran and a growing diasporic Iranian homosexual community in the West who are either immigrants or refugees from Iran or the Western-born sons and daughters of recent immigrants from there.[6] This chapter will provide an overview of the dynamics that have led to the emergence of Iranian people who identify as "gay" and the online spaces that these individuals use. As will be shown, these online spaces have been instrumental in the emergence of the nascent modern Iranian gay community in which gay individuals meet each other, arrange dates or sexual encounters, get useful information for their day-to-day life, and engage in activism by constructing culturally sensitive gay-friendly narratives, which is playing an instrumental role in making gay people in Iran more visible in a limited manner, at least to other Iranian Internet users. Moreover, as it will be shown, while the expressed identities of these individuals are not much different from their Western gay counterparts, social media has provided a space to experiment with the localization of Western gay identities, away from the violence of the Islamic regime in Iran, in dialogue with the diasporic Iranian communities in the Western world.

The first part of this chapter discusses the methodology employed in gathering data on social media and mention a few caveats as well as shortcomings in the research methodology employed in this study. The next section introduces readers to the general dynamics of same-sex desires in Iran by providing a brief account of the historical evolution of same-sex desires in the Iranian context from the nineteenth century to the current era, with special attention to the transformative role of the Internet on how Iranians with same-sex desires express their identities and relate to each other. The chapter then analyzes the growing role of social media in Iran in shaping gay identities in Iran. The chapter ends with a few conclusions focusing on the problems associated with the proliferation of online activity among the Iranian gay people and the exclusions that this trend has created among the Iranians who have same-sex desires. The author will suggest a few avenues for further research in social media and gay interactions in Iran and the broader Middle East.

Research Methodology

This research relies on a mixture of primary and secondary sources. There are a limited number of secondary sources that deal with the subject of homosexuality in Iran, which are augmented with primary sources in this research. In terms of primary sources, the research was conducted on social media networks popular among Iranians, including Facebook, Balatarin,[7] Twitter, Blogfa, BlogSpot, WordPress, Blogger, and YouTube. To find gay users or content on these platforms, search keywords such as "hamjensgara" (gay in Persian), "degarbashan jensi" (queer in Persian), "gay Iran/Persian," and "queer Iran/Persian" were used, which identified many gay Iranian users and content. Looking through the users' Facebook friends, YouTube subscribers,[8] Twitter followers/following, and the Blog rolls in the period between 2011 and 2012, the investigator was able to identify an extensive network of gay Iranian users who utilized social media platforms for arranging dates, making friends, and online activism. Moreover, the investigator looked at various gay dating sites, including gay.com, adam4adam.com, manjam.com, dudesnude.com, and gaydar.com to find out if these platforms are used by Iranian gay individuals and to what extent.

In the course of this research, using the publicly available information, 213 Iranian users were identified on Facebook as gay.[9] One hundred and ninety Iranian blogs were identified as having primarily homosexual content. On YouTube, two channels served as an online platform for disseminating gay content with countless videos on gay Iranian issues. On Twitter, the investigator had difficulty identifying gay Iranian users due to the format of the site, which made it difficult to mine the site for useful data.

Though attempts were made to engage some of these users to arrange interviews, especially on Facebook, the investigator was only able to meaningfully engage with a minority of Iranian gay users. The respondents comprised of eleven individuals who all resided in Iran. All respondents have been promised total anonymity, and the study will use pseudonyms to refer to them in the course of this chapter. The respondents, all males, were a mixture of university students and professionals between the ages of twenty-one and thirty-eight who resided in various cities in Iran, including Tehran, Isfahan, Yazd, Sari, Rasht, Shiraz, Hamedan, and Tabriz.[10] The respondents were asked about the history of online gay activities in Iran, the types of gay online activities that transpire on social media, and the underlying reasons that they used social media. Some of these respondents provided invaluable data for this study, which complemented the secondary sources used in this study.

This research methodology has its shortcomings as it mostly identified individuals who already have relatively open gay online profiles. As a result, the study is unable to draw valid and reliable conclusions in terms of the percentages of the Iranian gay individuals who utilize social media. Moreover, the researcher could not reach places where private Iranian online gay activities transpired, such as MSN Messenger, Google Hangout, or Skype, and relied only on data that could be publicly gathered from easily accessible sources online. Furthermore, the overwhelming majority of online activity that was observed involved gay males; lesbians were generally absent in all of the online spaces that were studied by the author.

Iran and the Emergence of the Nascent Modern Gay Community

The emergence of the nascent modern Iranian gay population and growing repression of homosexuality in Iran are inextricably linked to the broader developments in the modern history of Iran and the way it encountered modernity.[11] In that sense, previously, same-sex desires had occupied an ambiguous position within the Iranian society, and same-sex relations, especially those with intergenerational character, were widespread.[12] Indeed, much Iranian poetry contained strong elements of homoeroticism.[13] During the eighteenth and nineteenth centuries, the growing contacts of Iran with the notions of enlightenment began to alter social relations in Iran extensively. Thus, Iranian elites, many of whom had been educated in France, Belgium, and elsewhere in Europe, mimicked what they perceived as modernity in terms of gender and sexuality and pushed for repudiation of public manifestations of same-sex sexuality, whether in the form of pederasty or adult homosexuality.[14] This resulted in the erasure of the memories of the historical instances of same-sex love among Iranian elites, which was disseminated among the lower classes through the education system as well as popular media.[15] With this erasure, in 1979, when the Iranian revolution occurred, Islamic revolutionaries repudiated homosexuality as a form of Western immorality pushed upon Iran by the Shah and his colonial masters.[16] In line with that, Iranian revolutionaries engaged in a reign of terror in which an estimated 100 to 200 individuals accused of engaging in homosexual activities were executed in 1981 and 1982 alone.[17] Under the penal code adopted by the Islamic Republic government in Iran (Islamic Penal Code Articles 108–134), the active and the passive partner in same-sex penetration are to be put to death.[18] Nonpenetrative sexual activities are punished by flogging.[19]

Despite the great success of Islamic revolutionaries in pushing same-sex sexuality out of the public sphere through the adoption of an extremely harsh penal code, by the end of the 1990s there was a growing homosexual community in Iran, mostly in larger metropolitan centers such as Tehran and Isfahan.[20] What was remarkable about these individuals was that they literally identified themselves by using the English word "gay." Being "gay" was not only an important part of their identity, but for some it was the main marker of their identity and not just merely a sexual practice. Many of these individuals are young and very well versed in the sexual politics of the Western world.

The emergence of the nascent modern Iranian gay community has come about due to a variety of factors. The increasing opening of social spaces in Iran and the growing Iranian queer diasporic community who have acted as intermediaries in transmitting ideas with regards to Western conceptions of gay identities back home have played important roles.[21] In addition, a growing consumerist culture with its emphasis on individual expressionism in public spaces, which rejects the imposition of hegemonic identities by the Islamist government in Iran and defies Islamic legal restrictions, has been crucial to the emergence of gay Iranians.[22] While these factors have been instrumental, the most important factor that has facilitated these transformations among the Iranian gay youth has been the diffusion of Internet usage throughout Iran, which will be explored in detail below.

Internet and the History of Gay Online Activity in Iran

The widespread use of the Internet in Iran has provided the means for connectivity in new ways. Currently, Iran has the largest number of Internet users in the Middle East, with an estimated forty-two million users.[23] A poll conducted by the Iranian Student News Agency has found that Iranian "people trust the Internet more than any other media outlet, including domestic television and radio broadcasts."[24]

The origins of online activity among gay Iranians date back to the late 1990s. During that period, dial-up Internet slowly became more popular in Iran.[25] Using simple HTML codes, the first pages were made on Yahoo! Pages and were basic in design; the content was basic information about themselves and what they like in their potential partners. At the same time, Yahoo! chat rooms were also popular with Iranian gay individuals because it had rooms specifically for users located in Iran, and many gay individuals, especially from Tehran, used these rooms to find other individuals who wanted to talk to other people with same-sex desires.[26] As Saeed, a thirty-eight-year-old respondent from Tehran, mentioned, "My introduction to being 'gay' came as a twenty-five-year-old in 2000 in talking to others on Yahoo!'s Tehran chat room." Other than Yahoo! chat rooms, two respondents also mentioned that one of the earliest gay Iranian sites was *Gay Iran*, which is no longer online but was one of the first websites that dealt with the issue of homosexuality in Iran by providing information about what being gay meant.[27]

The spread of the Internet and its impact on collective action is generally seen in two very distinct lights in the literature on social movements. On the one hand, the Internet is seen as an effective democratizing force and the great equalizer, which expands freedoms and lower transaction costs of collective action. As Castells notes, "The Internet social networks . . . are spaces of autonomy largely beyond the control of governments and corporations."[28] This has reduced barriers for internal communication and organizing within social movements regardless of their size.[29] In doing so, individuals, communities, and social movements that were previously barred from participating in social and political discourse have found new ways to publicize their perspectives via the Internet.[30] People can better locate information and find like-minded people to form communities of interest.

On the other hand, other scholars believe that while the Internet makes communication easier, this type of virtual commination does not substitute for interpersonal networks and face-to-face communications.[31] Virtual communities, in this view, are ephemeral and lack the strength of physical communities.[32] Moreover, the Internet enables users to selectively filter out information based on their preconceived preferences and only access material that they already agree with in a manner that was not possible in the traditional media. For gay individuals in Iran, online communities are indeed not a substitute for the strength of physical communities, as online communities tend to lack the strength of intimate friendships or their hierarchical power base. These facets enable social movements offline to effectively organize for collective action, which may bring societal change and transformation in the lives of gay Iranians.

Yet, despite these limitations, the Internet has been an invaluable tool in facilitating gay Iranians to get connected in Iran. The Internet has provided a safe place for homosexuals to associate with each other that would have otherwise been difficult, if not impossible.[33] Indeed, all of the respondents who were engaged with as part of this study credited the Internet for preventing, or at the very least mitigating, the intense feelings of loneliness and isolation that they feel as a result of being gay in Iran. As Reza, a twenty-two-year-old university student from Isfahan, who identifies as gay online, mentioned in a Facebook chat, "I wouldn't have any social life had it not been for the Internet. I wouldn't know anyone, and I would be just alone by myself."

Second, the growing Internet penetration allows for getting information about a variety of subjects, including sexuality online and, more important, it affords people with same-sex desires the tools to bypass extensive restrictions imposed by authorities and form a nascent community, albeit a largely virtual one.[34] As Michel Foucault states, "Where there is power, there is resistance."[35] The Internet, thus, provides a venue for resistance to official discourse around homosexuality as foreign and un-Iranian by enabling Iranian gay social entrepreneurs to articulate competing narratives that portray homosexuality as consistent with Iranian values. These narratives and the various types of usage of the Internet will be discussed in more detail below.

Typology of Gay Iranian Internet Users

Gay Iranian Internet users use the Internet for a variety of purposes, but three general types of users emerge in terms of their general patterns of Internet use: socializers, information disseminators, and bridge makers. Socializers are characterized by the apolitical nature of their use of Internet. They form the substantial majority of Iranian gay Internet users. Socializers generally use the Internet only as a space to find friends or intimate partners on social media platforms like Facebook or gay dating sites. These individuals are simply seeking to end their isolation while searching for people like them and do not have an overt agenda in favor of transformative politics or reform of Iranian laws.

Information disseminators are those whose primary use of the platforms is to provide useful guidance on a variety of subjects, ranging from how to avoid conscription to applying for asylum in the Western world, for fellow gay Iranians. This group is not mutually exclusive to socializers or bridge makers and generally provides a social service toward educating fellow gay individuals on subjects of mutual concern that would otherwise be lacking.

Finally, bridge makers are generally middle-upper-class and educated individuals with strong linkages to the Western world. They are often engaged in activism under the relative safety and anonymity afforded by the Internet. These individuals generally speak English and are well versed in the history of sexual struggles in the Western world and the way gay rights there were advanced. They are also most concerned about the questions of sexual identity and articulating a localized and authentically Iranian gay identity. Bridge makers are the conduits through which Western notions of gay identity politics are localized within the Iranian setting. Each of these clusters is discussed in more detail in the following three sections of the chapter.

In Search of "BF" Online: Friendship, Dating, and Hook-ups

Social media play an integral role in the intimate interactions between gay individuals in Iran, without which many would have no way of finding others like them or even knowing that others like them exist. As Fereydoon, a twenty-four-year-old engineer from Tehran, mentioned: "Life is very difficult as a gay person in Iran. Actually, it is impossible, but I thank God so many times that we at least have Facebook to talk to others like myself. I don't even know what to do without Facebook, and I don't know what people did before Facebook."

Essentially, given the legal restrictions and societal obstacles that prevent gay Iranians from meeting each other offline leads to social media becoming the primary medium through which they can form a nascent community, albeit a limited one with little evident physical manifestation beyond the relatively safe boundaries of the Internet. This nascent community exists on websites such as Facebook and Man Jam, where users seek friendship, partnership, and hook-ups. It is a community of shared interest, which allows for self-expression outside of the confines of the cultural and religious mores that are enforced by the Islamic authorities in Iran. This is a parallel community that is not policed as closely as a physical one given the anonymity that it affords to its users (though that may be changing with the more intrusive surveillance tools deployed by authorities).

Yet, in facilitating online interactions on these sites and allowing for self-expression in a less policed environment, the Internet has also disciplined the manner in which gay individuals behave vis-à-vis each other and the language that they deploy in their interactions. Indeed, much of the language deployed in establishing intimate relationships is borrowed directly from English phrases, and attempts at hook-ups online are identical to those that unfold on comparable Western websites and apps.[36] The Internet, thus, shapes the social interactions of its participants while allowing them room for self-expression.[37]

Among the social media that were studied as part of the research, two platforms appeared to be most popular for socializers in terms of finding dates as well as intimacy. First was Facebook. Though Facebook is banned in Iran, many Iranians maintain an online profile on this platform.[38] On Facebook, a variety of strategies are used to find dates and intimacy. Some strategies are more conventional, including sending private messages or engaging in chats with other users who may be gay. Another less popular but extremely bold strategy involves setting up alternative profiles on Facebook as open pages and posting pictures of themselves, which results in other users leaving their cellphone numbers to be text messaged by the user to arrange for sexual encounters.[39] Where previously people desiring same-sex sexual encounters had to frequent public locations such as parks, they can now use social media to facilitate such encounters.

Surprisingly, the second platform that has been effectively used for dating is Western gay dating websites that are also heavily popular among Iranian gay people. The gay dating site Man Jam was by far the most popular among such gay dating sites. A search through the site for users who reside in Iran returned a staggering 14,711 unique users.[40] For comparison, other gay dating sites ranged between 20 and 150 users, with many users having been inactive for many months.[41]

Many users on Man Jam were quite open in terms of posting their personal information, including actual photos of themselves, despite a variety of social as well as legal risks involved in doing so. Inquiring about this boldness and whether the risks are significant, Fereydoon once again chimed in: "Obviously there are risks involved in finding boyfriends and people for sex online, but what do you expect us to do?" In fact, there are a variety of risks in online dating in Iran. Human Rights Watch has documented these risks by interviewing various gay informants in Iran.[42] It found instances of entrapment in which operatives from the Basij (Iranian militia) have posed as potential suitors for the unsuspecting users of Facebook and gay dating sites and have lured these individuals to meeting points at which point they have been arrested.[43] While some have been charged with morality crimes, others have reported being raped or blackmailed by the militia men and silenced by threats of legal action or outing them to their families. Overall, while enabling the mass participation by even the most vulnerable sections of the society, such as gay people in Iran, Facebook and other social media have disciplined the manner in which gay individuals interact with each other and have produced gay bodies that look no different from Western gay individuals.

Conscription, HIV/AIDS, Immigration: Social Media as a Source of Subversive Information

Social media, and the Internet in general, allow for participatory culture in a way that enables users to generate content, disseminate it widely, and consume this content at a rapid pace.[44] Online spaces have become sites of subversive knowledge where dissemination of information about a variety of issues that gay individuals face in their day-to-day lives occurs. This information dissemination ranges from how to have safe sex to, more commonly, how to deal with conscription as a gay person and how to file a refugee application.[45] In doing so, information disseminators create knowledge on how to interact with the state and society, thus actively using the Internet to assert individual identity and frustrate the state's attempts to produce a fully heteronormative society (a society based on the tenets of traditional Shi'ism, which has been ongoing since the 1979 revolution).

On the online activities of LGBT people in Iran, the NGO Small Media covers the activities of information disseminators in detail. Indeed, as they have found, a blog called Our Little Dictatorship,[46] authored by a gay Iranian, provides a thirteen-page PDF file with detailed instructions on how to get an exemption from military service.[47] The guide even includes suggestions on which psychiatrists are trustworthy for obtaining the necessary medical certificates for obtaining the discharge from the compulsory military service.

Other sources, such as the Iranian Railroad for Queer Refugees, provide detailed guidelines on how to obtain refugee status in accordance with United Nations guidelines, as well as a step-by-step process to coming to Western countries.[48] The guide provides contacts for the United Nations' UNHCR in Turkey and India, where Iranian gay people commonly head to apply for status as a protected person, and goes into detail regarding timelines, required documents, and how to receive legal assistance for applying for refugee status in Western countries such as Canada. Overall, in this way, social media in general and blogs in particular have allowed Iranian gays to access information that would otherwise not be available to them and provide venues for sites of subversive information on interacting with state and society. This information, of course, is in direct contradiction with the predominant social norms and mores.

The Virtual Coming Out: Cultural and Political Activism

Another aspect of social media activity among Iranian gay individuals is cultural and political activism, which is restricted to a select group of active Iranian social media users—that is, the bridge makers. Four major media in gay activism online that are used by bridge makers are weblogs, Internet magazines (e-zines), Facebook, and Balatarin. The small number of Iranian gay individuals who responded to questions as part of this research identified *5pesar* as the most important and popular gay blog. This weblog collects content written by gay bloggers and disseminates it, making this site an important portal in Iranian gay activist networks. Beyond weblogs, various e-zines are available with *Neda*—previously published as *Cheraq* and *Delkadeh*—being the most prominent among the gay-oriented Iranian publications.[49] *Neda* is published in a PDF format and is distributed via Facebook, websites, and email to subscribers.[50] On Facebook, various pages have been created that are geared toward publicizing gay rights, which will be discussed in more detail below.

Overall, activism in the online Iranian gay community unfolds in three major ways among the bridge makers. First, and most important, the primary focus of bridge makers in their activism is narrative formation and construction of Farsi alternatives to the broadly used Western words that are used by gay Iranians in their everyday language.[51] This tactic is to rationalize, normalize, and localize gay identity to the Iranians with same-sex desires. E-zines are the primary vehicle in the process of constructing culturally appropriate gay narratives. Some 70 percent of articles in the *Neda* e-zine deal with arguments for inclusion of gays and lesbians as full Iranian citizens. A theme that runs through all the articles is summed up in an editorial in the August 2009 issue of *Neda*: "What is not in dispute is that gay rights are human rights." Some of the articles in the e-zines are translations of Western queer political literature, such as queer theory, or scientific studies about homosexuality, such as broad discussions of the Kinsey scale. A significant part of these articles deals with Islam and homosexual-friendly interpretations of the Quran, generally drawing on the all-knowing nature of God to point out that homosexuality has its place in God's plans, and that the condemnation of homosexuals by Islamic authorities is wrong. A March 2009 article entitled "A Homosexual: I Have Rights" laments the hostility of religions to homosexuality while asserting that homosexuality is not an illness:

> The Islamic jurisprudence states that God is all-knowing. Even Satan has a part in his plans according to them. So why are religions so against homosexuality? We are told that God loves all his creations, so why are we under attack?[52]

Importantly, a significant number of these articles include historical accounts of the existence of homosexuality in Iran, such as by highlighting the vast amount of Iranian homoerotic poetry, thereby attempting to portray Iranian queers as authentic Iranians and showing continuity between historical instances of same-sex relations and current expressions of homosexuality. An open letter by an Iranian lesbian in the January 2009 issue of *Neda* illustrates the general thrust of these articles:

Will there be a day that Iranian queer people be fully accepted in the Iranian culture? Is Molana (a famous Iranian poet) not enough reason for them? Do those people who enjoy his poems know that he was a homosexual? Why is homosexuality the forbidden love? Why?[53]

Another author echoes these points in an article in the October 2010 issue of *Neda*. This article provides an overview of famous homosexuals in Iranian history and criticizes then-president Mahmoud Ahmadinejad for his denial of the existence of homosexuals in his speech at Columbia University:

I don't think the idiotic and illiterate president has any knowledge of Iran [and] famous Iranian [poets] such as Attar, Saadi, Hafez, Molavi, Hami, Obeid Zakani, and Iraj Miraza whose same-sex desires and attractions are ever-present and hard to deny in their work.[54]

The primary target audience of bridge makers is their fellows with same-sex desires in Iran. Their attempts are essentially about making sense of their existence and the repression they experience. They do so by importing ready-made Western gay identity politics frameworks and localizing them to produce narratives that make sense to an Iranian audience.[55]

As part of these attempts to localize the gay experience, a broad trend has emerged that seeks to infuse the Farsi language with new words, which are intended to articulate the gay experience in a positive light. To that end, a new project called Degar Vajeh (alternative word) has been initiated, which is acting as a word mill and a dictionary for gay individuals in Iran. New words such as *degarbashan jensi* (queer), *hamjans garaa* (a positive term to refer to homosexuality, which denotes homosexual as a sexual orientation), and *degarbash setizi* (homophobia) have been introduced to localize the Iranian gay experience, given that most Iranian gays currently use English words to refer to themselves and to describe their most intimate interactions with each other.[56] In this sense, social media have simultaneously acted as the disciplining power that has shaped Iranian gay identities in the mold of their Western counterparts, while also affording these same people safe spaces to engage in experiments to produce a "more Iranian" gay identity.

A second, less-developed aspect of activism for gay Iranians is focused on increasing visibility of gay Iranians among the Iranian community and humanizing gay individuals, given that homosexuality is viewed by many Iranians as either a Western phenomenon, an immoral behavior that needs to be punished, or a pathological behavior in need of medical treatment. As Jamshid, a twenty-seven-year-old resident of Iran who did not disclose his location, explains, ". . . the problem is that people don't know we exist. When you ask them what is a gay person? They just think we are bunch of lustful individuals who only want sex. They don't think we have emotions or want friends or go to cinema or talk to each other like normal people."[57]

To that end, various strategies have been adopted. One has been to stage a virtual "coming out" to raise awareness about the plight of gay Iranians and draw attention to the difficulties facing them in their everyday lives. A Facebook page called "We are everywhere" set up by a group of Iranian gay, lesbian, and transsexual people posted various videos of gay individuals discussing their plight.[58] One of the individuals who posted a video on this page mentions, "As a gay person, my biggest problem in Iran is that I cannot be my real self. I always have to play a role. I always have to suppress my own existence and part of my identity and hide myself in fear from the society and potential problems that I might face."[59] The page also features photos of the unfurling of the rainbow flag and flying rainbow balloons at various locations inside Iran, seeking to emphasize that gay individuals live everywhere in Iran.

Another strategy has been to designate July 27 (the first day of the Iranian month of Mordad) as the day of sexual minorities in Iran and attempting to publicize this day heavily on Facebook to gain recognition among Iranians on social media. Iranian queer diasporic advocacy networks such as the Toronto-based Iranian Queer Organization (IRQO) are intricately involved in publicizing this day through their YouTube and Facebook pages. Furthermore, online award ceremonies have been organized to draw attention and extend gratitude to Iranian individuals who have spoken out or acted in favor of defending gay rights. To this end, the Sepas award is given to such individuals as part of publicizing gay rights and gaining recognition for gay individuals. Emotional appeals have also been a central tenet of attempts to increase visibility and generate support for the gay rights movements. The photos of the executions of two alleged gay teenagers in Mashhad in 2005 were widely circulated by the Iranian Queer Organization and Iranian Railroad for Queer Refugees, with slogans such as "Help save an Iranian queer refugee's life."[60]

Finally, bridge makers on social media have also sought to combat overt homophobia online, though not as systemically as the first two aspects of their activism. *Spesar blog* opens with an explanation of homophobia and why it is harmful.[61] As Kamran, a twenty-seven-year-old writer in Yazd, mentioned: "Once in a while I see a story about gay people, and then in the comments section, you see a lot of homophobic comments from users, and sometimes I spend time arguing with them. We need to speak to educate people who lack proper information about us, and these [online] places are one of the places to start doing that." Overall, the broad thrust of the work of bridge makers has been attempts to rationalize and legitimize the existence of gay Iranians to themselves, along with devising strategies to develop visibility within the broader Iranian and international community by highlighting the plight of gay Iranians.

Conclusion

From the very origin of the Internet, the Iranian gay community has depended heavily on online platforms for visibility. Social media have allowed for a limited degree of visibility of homosexuals among themselves and the broader Iranian online community. Moreover, social media and the Internet are primarily where gay individuals meet, make friends, and arrange sexual encounters inside Iran. In addition, the social media is where social as well as political activism is occurring in the form of narrative formation, at a safe distance from the repressive government apparatus. This has resulted in the localization of universal discourses on sexuality and the drawing of attention to the plight of gay individuals in Iran. Gay Iranians have also been able to forge their identities by experimenting with fusing Western conceptions of sexuality with the norms and language of Iranian culture. Overall, the Internet has played a crucial role in creating the means for the existence of queer activist networks.

By way of conclusion I would like to offer some final thoughts on the efficacy of online activism and the virtual nature of the Iranian gay community, as well as some suggestions for further research. It is difficult to accurately assess the successes and failures of online gay Iranian activism within the broader Iranian society given the difficulties in conducting surveys of Iranians inside Iran on this topic. What is clear is that the advocacy for gay rights has been successful to some extent within the Iranian diasporic community in the West, where the notion of gay rights, at least among young university students, is treated increasingly as a legitimate concern.[62] Indeed, this is evident in the emergence of diasporic-based media such as Radio Zamaneh, which includes gay programming as well as covering events publicizing gay rights that have taken place at the University of Toronto and other universities in the West. These events have drawn a large cadre of students of Iranian origin.[63]

While this research has provided an overview of the type of activities that are undertaken by gay Iranians on social media, a number of areas need further research. In the course of research, the author came across many instances of homophobia on social media where gay rights were portrayed as being unworthy of support; in some cases, gay individuals were portrayed as un-Iranian, effeminate, rapists, or pedophiles. What are the homophobic trends online?[64] Is homophobia growing or diminishing? To what extent are homophobic outbursts among online users of social media similar to those in the West? Are Iranian homophobic outbursts mimicking those of the Western world, or is there something unique about them?

Moreover, this research did not find much evidence of lesbian online activity, which raises the question of how and where lesbians are meeting in Iran.[65] This question is crucial in light of the importance of social media in the everyday lives of gay males in Iran. If the Internet does not serve a similar role for lesbians, then what are the tools they use to meet each other? To what extent is the Internet and social media gendered places among Iranians? Finally, comparative research among various locales that have repressive laws against people with same-sex desires would be beneficial in further exploring to what extent social media shape conceptions of identity that lead individuals to identify as "gay."

Notes

1. I would like to thank Katarzyna Korycki, who worked on two previous papers on the topic of homosexuality in Iran with me, and Professor David Rayside, for encouraging me to undertake this research project.

2. Currently, the Middle East, Iran, Saudi Arabia, Yemen, and Sudan uphold the death penalty for those convicted of engaging in sodomy.

3. *Pink News,* "Ahmadinejad's Gay Comments Lost in Translation," October, 30, 2010. http://www.pinknews.co.uk/news/articles/2005-5566.html/ (accessed October 20, 2012).

4. For example, Ayatollah Ali Meshkini, in 2000, "criticized the German Green Party for being pro-homosexual," while Ayatollah Ebrahim Amini, in 2002, claimed that "gay and lesbian marriages reflect a weakness of Western culture."

5. Janet Afary, *Sexual Politics of Modern Iran* (Cambridge: Cambridge University Press, 2009), 327.

6. Ibid., 336. These individuals regularly march in gay pride parades in locations such as Toronto under the Iranian flag.

7. Balatarin allows for sharing interesting links between users and has consistently been one of the most used social network platforms in Iran. In effect, Balatarin is similar to Digg or Redit and has been cited as the second most-frequently used website in Iran according to topmedia.ir, which is run by the Islamic Republic and does not include foreign sites such as Facebook or Twitter in its rankings.

8. YouTube has since changed this functionality and made subscriber information private since February 2012, which means it is now nearly impossible to identify users who subscribe to various other users, groups, or channels on YouTube.

9. It should be noted that these are only open profiles that could be accessed. A Facebook survey set up by a gay Iranian user received responses from 983 users from inside Iran who identified themselves as gay.

10. The diversity of the location of the locales was noteworthy because it shows that identifying as "gay" is not happening only in mega cities such as Tehran and that there is a much broader trend in the country.

11. For a more in-depth study of the impact of Iran's encounter with modernity on sexuality in Iran, please see Katarzyna Korycki and Abouzar Nasirzadeh, "Desire Recast: Production of Gay Identities in Iran," *Journal of Gender Studies* (2014). doi: 10.1080/09589236.2014.889599. Also see Afsaneh Najmabadi, *Women with Mustaches and Men without Beards: Gender and Sexual Anxieties of Iranian Modernity* (Berkeley: University of California Press, 2005).

12. Najmabadi, *Women with Mustaches and Men without Beards,* 154.

13. Korycki and Nasirzadeh, "Desire Recast," 5.

14. Ibid; Najmabadi, *Women with Mustaches and Men without Beards,* 235.

15. Janet Afary and Kevin Anderson, *Foucault and the Iranian Revolution: Gender and the Seductions of Islamism* (Chicago: University of Chicago Press, 2005), 155.

16. Ibid.

17. Helene Kafi, "Tehran, Dangerous Love," in *Sexuality and Eroticism among Males in Moslem Societies,* ed. Arno Shmitt and Jehoda Sofer (New York: Haworth Press, 1992), 67.

18. The Islamic Penal Code of Iran can be found at http://mehr.org/Islamic_Penal_Code_of_Iran.pdf.

19. It should be noted that the Iranian government adopted a revised penal code earlier in 2012. The treatment of homosexuality generally remains the same under the revised codes with the exception of glaring omissions regarding execution of lesbians, which raises question on whether this is intended to give judges more leeway in handing out death sentences to individuals accused of homosexuality. Please see Radio Zamaneh's analysis of the new penal code (in Farsi) at http://www.radiozamaneh.com/society/degarbash?page=1.

20. Afary, *Sexual Politics of Modern Iran,* 352.

21. Korycki and Nasirzadeh, "Desire Recast," 11.

22. Shahram Khosravi, *Young and Defiant in Tehran* (Philadelphia: University of Pennsylvania Press, 2008).

23. Internet World Stats, "Internet Users in the Middle East 2012," http://www.Internetworldstats.com/stats5.htm (accessed October 11, 2012).

24. OpenNet Initiative, "Internet Filtering in Iran in 2004–2005: A Country Study," https://opennet.net/studies/iran (accessed October 1, 2012).

25. Small Media, "LGBT Republic of Iran: An Online Reality?" http://smallmediafoundation.com/files/LGBTRepublicofIran.pdf, 50 (accessed September 29, 2012).

26. Yahoo! announced the closure of Yahoo! chat rooms in December 2012. These chat rooms had been available since 1998.

27. *Small Media,* "LGBT Republic of Iran," 50. Unfortunately, the investigator was unable to locate any parts of this site stored anywhere on the Internet, such as Google cache, which could have determined the content of the site more accurately.

28. Manuel Castells, *Networks of Outrage and Hope: Social Movements in the Internet Age* (Cambridge: Polity Press, 2012), 2.

29. Bruce Bimber, Andrew Flanagin, and Cynthia Stohl, "Reconceptualizing Collective Action in the Contemporary Media Environment," *Communication Theory* 15.4 (January 2006): 365–388.

30. Arthur Lupia and Gisela Sin, "Which Public Goods Are Endangered? How Evolving Communication Technologies Affect the Logic of Collective Action," *Public Choice* 117.3–4 (2003): 315–331.

31. Doug McAdam, "Conceptual Origins, Current Problems, Future Directions," in *Comparative Perspectives on Social Movements: Political Opportunities, Mobilizing Structures, and Cultural Framings,* ed. Doug McAdam, Jackie McCarthy, and Mayer Zald (New York: Cambridge University Press, 1996).

32. Amitai Etzioni and Oren Etzioni, "Face-to-Face and Computer-Mediated Communities: A Comparative Analysis," *The Information Society* 15.14 (October–December 1999): 241–248.

33. Korycki and Nasirzadeh, "Desire Recast," 11.

34. Iran currently has one of the most restrictive Internet censorship regimes in the world, with some experts believing it is second only to China in the intrusiveness and comprehensiveness of its censorship. Please see OpenNet Initiative's report on Iran available at http://opennet.net/sites/opennet.net/files/ONI_Iran_2009.pdf.

35. Michel Foucault, *The History of Sexuality, Volume 1: An Introduction* (New York: Knopf Doubleday, 1990).

36. Words used to describe their sexual position include top, bottom, versatile, and bareback (sex without a condom) are directly taken from English, which shows a great level awareness of the gay culture outside of Iran in the West. See Korycki and Nasirzadeh, "Desire Recast."

37. John A. Bargh and Katelyn Y. A. McKenna, "The Internet and Social Life," *Annual Review of Psychology* 55 (February 2004): 573–590.

38. No official statistics are available for how many Facebook profiles are from Iran, but a cursory search of Facebook indicates a significant number of Facebook users are Iranian.

39. It should be noted that these activities are in clear violation of Facebook terms of use and conditions.

40. The author was unable to interview any users of this site or know of others using this site.

41. It is noteworthy that Man Jam is the only gay dating and hook-up site that has not been banned in Iran. Iranian gay rights activist Arsham Parsi has consistently warned about the dangers of Man Jam, which in his view is used by the Islamic government of Iran to identify and entrap gay individuals in Iran. It should be noted, however, that he does not offer much in terms of evidence to back up this claim except for an account from one of his acquaintances in Iran who was arrested by the Iranian government, as well as pointing out that Man Jam is the only gay dating site that escapes government sanctions. Other websites with gay content have all been banned and filtered by the Iranian web censorship regime.

42. Human Rights Watch, *We Are a Buried Generation: Discrimination and Violence against Sexual Minorities in Iran* (New York: Human Rights Watch, 2010).

43. Ibid., 58. Also see Katarzyna Korycki and Abouzar Nasirzadeh, "Homophobia as a Tool of Statecraft: Iran and Its Queers," in *Global Homophobia,* ed. Meredith Weiss and Michael Bosia (Urbana: University of Illinois Press, 2013).

44. Henry Jenkins, Ravi Purushotma, Katherine Clinton, Margaret Weigel, and Alice J. Robison, "Confronting the Challenges of Participatory Culture: Media Education for the 21st Century," http://www.newmedialiteracies.org/wp-content/uploads/pdfs/NMLWhitePaper.pdf (accessed June 15, 2014).

45. *Small Media,* "LGBT Republic of Iran," 41.

46. Please see http://littledictatorship.wordpress.com.

47. Ibid., 42. In a contradictory stance, the Iranian government allows discharge and exemptions for soldiers who have "mental illnesses," which include homosexuality.

48. Please see (in Farsi) http://persian.irqr.net/?page_id=10.

49. To see this publication and download it in PDF format, please visit http://www.nedamagazine.net.

50. The life of e-zines tends to be relatively short, and e-zines continuously end publication only to be replaced by new e-zines.

51. Korycki and Nasirzadeh, "Desire Recast," 13.

52. Parsa, "A Homosexual: I Have Rights," *Neda* 1.3 (March 2009): 14. http://www.nedamagazine.net/03/parsa.htm.

53. "From Me to You: Letters from Iranian Queer," *Neda* 1.1 (January 2009): 33. http://www.nedamagazine.net/01/manto.htm.

54. Omid Sepehrza, "Don't Homosexuals Have Permission to Be Alive?," *Neda* 2.22 (October 2010): 36, http://www.nedamagazine.net/22/omid.htm.

55. Korycki and Nasirzadeh, "Desire Recast."

56. Words such as "koni" and "hamjens baaz" that have traditionally been used to describe and refer to people who have same-sex desires—especially those referring to the passive partner during sexual intercourse—are extremely negative and degrading. Please see Korycki and Nasirzadeh, "Desire Recast," for more on this.

57. A report by *Small Media* found that many gay Iranians were actually glad that Ahmadinejad talked about their nonexistence, as it raised awareness about the plight of gay individuals in Iran. For the report, see http://smallmediafoundation. com/files/LGBTRepublicofIran.pdf.

58. Please see the Facebook page at http://www.facebook.com/WeAreEvery Where17.

59. Saeed Kamali Dehghan, "We Are Everywhere: Gay and Lesbian Iranians Come Out on Facebook," *The Guardian*, September 13, 2011. http://www.guard-ian.co.uk/world/2011/sep/11/gay-iranians-facebook-defiance (accessed October 2, 2012).

60. Mahmoud Asgari and Ayaz Marhoni were two teenagers who were hanged in 2006 in the city of Mashhad. British LGBT groups such as Outrage! alleged that they were executed for consensual sex, while others argue that the reason for the executions was the rape of a minor. Please see http://ilga.org/ilga/en/article/688.

61. Please see http://5pesar.wordpress.com/homophobia.

62. For a broader discussion of acceptance of gay rights as a legitimate concern in diasporic Muslim communities, please see David Rayside, "Muslim American Communities' Response to Queer Visibility," *Contemporary Islam* 5.2 (2010): 109–134.

63. See video of an event like this at http://www.youtube.com/watch?v=i UDV0Nf_j50.

64. For some preliminary research on this trend, please see Katarzyna Korycki and Abouzar Nasirzadeh, "Homophobia as a Tool of Statecraft: Iran and Its Queers," in *Global Homophobia*, ed. Meredith Weiss and Michael Bosia (Urbana: University of Illinois Press, 2013).

65. The *Small Media* report "LGBT Republic of Iran" draws attention to this fact and speculates it has to do with gender roles and the greater difficulties that women generally have in Iran. See http://smallmediafoundation.com/files/LGB-TRepublicofIran.pdf, 79.

Chapter 4

Disabled Iranians on Social Media

Reflections on the Empowering Experiences of the Iranian PWDs in the Blogosphere

Kobra Elahifar

According to the Statistical Center of Iran (SCI), three million people with disabilities (PWDs) reside in Iran as of 2005.[1] By 2012, only 4,700 of the disabled, a mere fraction of the total population, came under the protection of the State Welfare Organization.[2] Equally important are the young people, which comprise 450,000 of the disabled population, all under twenty-five years of age.[3] According to Majid Mohammadi, a professor at Tavaana E-Learning Institute for Iranian Civil Society, the official figure might not give the full picture, estimating that the disabled population might be in fact larger than twelve million total.[4] Similar estimates remain problematic since no feedback from the SCI has been available to this date. Other problems also pertain to the available data, particularly in terms of types and causes of disabilities. Overall, the problem is not just statistical uncertainty, but also the methods used to gather information in a country where disability continues to be stigmatized and members of the disabled population marginalized.[5]

The dearth of information about the living conditions of the disabled population, spread across Iranian society, underlines the need for a qualitative study. With a qualitative approach we can have a better understanding of how disabled Iranians think, desire, and strive in various public spheres of everyday life. A qualitative approach would inform us about the challenging issues related to identity politics in postrevolutionary Iran. This approach will also highlight the ways in which disabled people have carved out individual and group identities, as agents seeking recognition and social inclusion.

Normalcy, as the dominant ideology in the modern era, excludes disabled bodies.[6] It serves to reproduce economic privilege for educated white heterosexual men with normal bodies,[7] and denies the rights of bodies with impairment. Since the disability movement began in 1981, PWD advocates in developed countries have made several efforts to promote the disabled as an identity group. PWD advocates support the disabled population's active participation in social and economic life. In Iran, the bill in support of disabled rights passed in 2004, and following this legal development the number of nongovernmental organizations has also flourished. Though it was passed during the late Reformist era (1996–2005), the sixteen-article bill came into full practice when president Khatami gave extensive support to the civil rights of minority groups. Included among the legal benefits for PWDs were rights such as accessibility to public goods, formal education, and a conducive, nonviolent environment for disabled people. Access to the information and communication technologies (ICTs) was also declared as one of the mottos of disabled activists in 2006's World Disability Day.[8] This was the case because information was meant for all segments of the population, including the disabled.

The main purpose of this chapter is to examine what opportunities ICTs provide to disabled Iranians. It also examines whether ICT use enhances PWDs' social inclusion as individuals as well as their identity group formation. The digital divide literature gives a large amount of attention to minority groups' access to ICTs. The situated context in which marginalized groups use ICTs is another focus of this literature.[9] The major theme in this chapter is to study how blogs are used within the disabled community and its scope and capacity as a social medium.

One of the issues that the State Welfare Organization in Iran faces is PWDs' self-perception of disability.[10] The general attitude toward impairments in Iran gives way to an inappropriate representation of their life-worlds. This chapter is an effort to provide further understanding of the way disabled individuals and/or community renegotiate their identity through the use of blogs. The questions this chapter reflects on are: What narratives do people with disabilities provide about their blogging practices to present their individual identity as a person with disability? Do they view these narratives as influential in their social inclusion, and ultimate empowerment either in the virtual or real worlds as individuals with disabilities? The chapter provides a phenomenological perspective to the disability narratives around blogging experiences in Iran.

Social Inclusion and ICT Use in Everyday Life

Social exclusion is a multidimensional phenomenon constituted by individual, socioeconomical, political, institutional, and organizational aspects to problematize.[11] A person with disability, who has been excluded as an individual, will also become excluded from other domains of social life. The aim of social inclusion is to reverse the process of exclusion to integrate the disadvantaged social groups back to everyday life domains. The literature addresses the systemic problems with social inclusion. Phipps, for example, examines disability through the lens of neglected human potential.[12] The literature in domesticity or ICT use in everyday life builds on the human potential to seek social inclusion.[13]

Spilker and Sørenson argue that computers are no longer about "programming, systems, controlling and calculating," but that they are "a gateway for communication and cultural activities."[14] This is particularly true with the rise of new media and "home activism" in recent years in Iran and the Arab countries. Hynes et al. argue that as a result of a conceptual shift in the relation between technology use and other variables (e.g., gender and age) larger groups of users, particularly groups that have been so far excluded from the social participation (e.g., the elderly and women), may use the Internet in their everyday life in ways that are meaningful to them.[15]

This view of ICT use makes it impossible to imagine that an individual's Internet use, as a virtual space, is separate from the real world where most of their everyday activities take place. An individual's Internet use, in return, was an experience realized through different social, interpersonal, economic, and civic domains of everyday life. The concept of "virtual togetherness" hints at the kind of relationship between the virtual and real worlds and explains that activities that take place in these two spheres affect each other.[16] Blogs are an important form of ICT to study in the context of Iran because immediately after their launch they became alternative media for a range of activities, including online journals and political and social activism. In 2001, Hossein Derakhshan created the first Persian blogging template, and many young Iranian bloggers started their own blogs afterward. Blogs are powerful networking tools that allow for building social connections within virtual and/or social circles.[17]

PWDs' Blogging Practices and Social Networking

Blogs, as influential social networking media, rose to public attention after the events of 9/11 and the Iraq War in March 2003, when citizens in the region became activists and bloggers as a result. Easy and convenient use of XML and hyperlink options resulted in the expansion of blogging, and blog use as a tool for exposing one's opinions, self-presentation, and social interaction.[18] Blogs became a medium that for the first time in history allowed for the grassroots to be heard. There has been an upsurge in using blogs as daily journals, as well as news filtering blogs.

Mitra calls blogger's lives "a synthetic congruence of the real and the virtual."[19] Mitra points out that when individuals decide to create a blog page their voice enters cyberspace, where the traditional limitations of real life have no place. Blog readers are able to become part of the discourse formed around these blogs, and to start developing a sense of belonging to the blogs built around these discourses. The interviews with bloggers throughout the research were aimed at exploring this aspect of blogging. In other words, the research focused on those disability narratives and blogging practices that connect the experiences in the social world to experiences in the virtual world. The interviews further our understanding of the ways that Iranians with disabilities in the study carved out imagined communities of like-minded people, and came out of isolation.

People with Disabilities:
Individual and Societal Empowerment in Cyberspace

People with disabilities' perception of their bodies can cause communication problems (e.g., aggressive behavior that is rooted in low self-esteem) in their social encounters with others that can result in their isolation from social circles.[20] To avoid social stigma, people with visible impairments tend to "pass" and/or "cover" their defect in public; in this sense, passing and/or covering are associated with low self-esteem and identity issues.[21] In his observational work *Stigma*, Goffman describes covering and passing in terms of mechanisms to overcome stigma in people suffering from split identities.

People with physical defects tend to have problems identifying with individuals that have the same physical defects. Instead they displayed a tendency to identify with "normal" body types, often unsuccessfully, as normal people accept them as different in their groups.

A person with a visible defect encounters identity issues as a result of the denial of belonging to a group of people with similar impairments and partial acceptance in the group that they identify themselves with. Recent developments through the disability movement tend to look at the dominant identity issue among the disabled. They valorize disability as an identity group and use the term "people with disability" (PWD) in reference to their call for a unified identity among the disabled. They also advocate for social inclusion and active participation of PWDs in social life.

Empowerment is key in positive recognition of one's group identity and social inclusion. The empowerment process involves parties' encouragement to take action and mobilize their internal motives to fulfill tasks and feel accomplishment. It falls into two categories: individual and societal empowerment.[22] At the individual level, empowerment is the power to gain control over one's life and the belief that one can reach his or her goals.[23] At the community level, empowerment is the sense of dependency, as in belonging to a community and having control over the community and its structures.[24]

The characteristics that indicate that a person has reached individual empowerment include a sense of power to control one's life and reach goals;[25] taking positive social roles;[26] having access to information; a sense of power to change others' images about one's abilities and capacities; making efforts to promote one's self-image, and, finally, a sense of power to make decisions for oneself.[27] The characteristics indicative of a society reaching empowerment are participation in and dependence on a community to bring positive change; a sense of control over the community and the power to help the community reach its values and goals;[28] a sense of awareness about the needs and problems of the community;[29] and efforts to improve the community or the lives of its members.[30] Minor social groups had growing access to the Internet as a medium for self-presentation. Ameli observes weblogs as the space that curates one's "identity needs; it changes the geopolitics of human relations, makes the realities of the real world tangible and helps grasp them better."[31]

The mass media in Iran does not represent the Iranian disability communities as empowered social groups whose individual members embrace "disability" as their unified group identity. This lack of media representation of the Iranian disabled speaks to social construction of the disabled as nondominant social groups that are less visible in the social context or within social circumstances. Blog pages are accessible to anyone around the world, and from an intercultural perspective, blogs can be a beneficial medium in terms of social management of muted groups.[32] They can serve to elevate the representation of nondominant social groups. This makes a good case to ask whether active Iranian bloggers view blogging as a practice to create an imagined community that represents disabled Iranians. If not, how their narratives reconstruct disability as an identity construct. This question is in alignment with the critiques of social media as a tool for empowerment.[33] These critiques point out how marginal identities' Internet use can be oppressive, and a manifestation of further marginalization and institutional oppression toward minority groups.[34] The study aligns with other research in this vein,[35] and is designed to flesh out possible themes of self-presentation and empowerment in interviews with active disabled bloggers to enable critical reflection on the forgoing discussion.

Method of Study

In this study, I used qualitative methods to conduct the research. Qualitative research seeks to "preserve and analyze the situated form, content and experience of social action."[36] Theoretically, qualitative studies are applicable to the extent they enable researchers to stretch their imaginations in order to create and validate claims about the data they have generated.[37] From the exiting techniques applied in qualitative research methods, respondent interviews seemed the most practical. The purpose of this research technique is to "elicit open-ended responses."[38] I designed the research around the following queries about disabled peoples' blogging practices:

- Do individuals discuss their disabilities in their blogs?
- Do they practice relationship building and networking with other individuals and groups through the blog?
- Does blogging help individuals establish some level of power and control in their virtual or real relationships?

People with a disability who had regularly updated blogs were selected for the study in the initial round of interviews. Snowball sampling techniques were used to find additional participants. To start the search for research participants, my thesis advisor, Mehdi Montazerghaem, a communication scholar with research expertise in issues related to the media representation of social groups, introduced me to the Baavar Organization. Baavar is an active nongovernmental organization in Tehran involved in activities that enhance civil engagement for people with disabilities. The goal of the organization is to be inclusive and involve as many able-bodied members as disabled-bodied members in its organization of events and programs. In Baavar, I was introduced to Maani, an active blogger and member of Baavar who introduced me to other disabled bloggers in and out of Baavar.

It took three weeks to search their blogs and blog rolls and come up with a list of bloggers best suited to the selection criterion of this study. I made a list of twenty-five bloggers, five of which blogged regularly about disability issues in the community. The rest of the bloggers maintained personal blogs featuring outlines about their everyday lives, personal thoughts, and concerns. Another two weeks was spent sending out invitations to bloggers' profile emails, and awaiting their approval for participation. The participant invitation received a good deal of attention on the part of the bloggers, and most participants expressed their personal and professional interests in the research. Three bloggers turned down the invitation because of severe disability, lack of convenient access, or the lack of an available caregiver to come along for the interview.

Fifteen individual interviews were conducted. Each blogger was contacted and interviewed at most twice. In case the interviewee could not make it for a second interview, interviews were conducted via telephone, email, or chatroom. The interviews were held between January 4 and March 12, 2010. The interviewees' ages ranged from twenty-six to forty-two. Given the high rate of disabilities due to road accidents in Iran (10 percent), the research was designed to represent participants with disabilities caused during road trips. The research aims were explained to the bloggers during the first phase of data collection. Interviews were carried out only after both parties reached agreement about the terms of the research.

In the Name of Community Outreach: "We Have a Share in Being Isolated!"

Bloggers described the practice of blogging as helpful in getting in touch with other disabled users.[39] They saw blogging as a medium to maintain health-related information, as well as a self-help window to gain life skills to manage disability in everyday life. Accessibility remained a major difficulty and a huge hurdle against "community needs." Discussions repeated themselves around the question of how blogs are to be put to the best possible use for the disabled community. In other words, blogs were seen as self-help guides that provided a comprehensive tour to the world of disability—all that a disabled person must cope with and go through in its everyday life routine, such as getting dressed, dining, bathing, and traveling.

The bloggers refused to bring up problems that the community faced within the society at large. This theme came out as bloggers idolized their efforts for community outreach, refusing to politically question their stance toward the isolation that they reinforced in their blogging practices. For example, Mohammad Reza, age thirty-seven, believed in the impact of his social services in the online world and assessed it as a more vital practice than a criticism of the community. Still, his own conversation represented his social exclusion in the real world, and was infused with social exclusion narratives:

> [A] good place to at least have my own medium for the disabled. You can't imagine from which places I've [been able to] get in touch with [others] via my blog. From Sistan . . . Germany and Canada!

Reza juxtaposes Sistan—a province at the far end of southwest Iran, where there is lack of sufficient resources for economic growth and development—with Germany and Canada to convey the impact of his services to the Iranian disabled community. After all, from a social exclusion perspective, his words resonated with the multiple dimensions in which a person with disability is excluded from society. Reza believed that he had revealed his real identity in order to gain credit and render social services to benefit the community he was in touch with.

This self-professed aspect of isolation from society revealed itself further in my dialogue with the writer of a blog called "Disability is No Sentence!" about her decision to refuse marriage to an able-bodied person after consulting with other disabled individuals in the virtual community:

> Their advice really helped me through the marriage I was about to make. I needed terribly to go and see a family consultant to see what my condition, as a woman with disability, might cause when I marry a man without disability. Or perhaps to talk it over with some friends, aside from all the advice my parents gave me . . . you need it, especially people like us. And I couldn't, for I first needed a consultant whose office was convenient to walk into! I was restrained, and my friends with disability, whom I had met on the net, they helped me with *their experience*.

The blogger had chosen to stay celibate and refused marrying the able-bodied fiancé. She believed her friends' advice helped her with the decision to stay single until she met a disabled partner. Did *"their experience"* reveal the truth about a community that viewed itself through the socially isolating lens of the society? Did her communal experience convince her to choose to stay isolated, and thus reproduced the normalcy ideology? Did *her experience* seem helpful because it reified the ableist views of society toward disability? Maani, a twenty-seven-year-old blogger who was also an active member of Baavar, brought this issue up while speaking of his own blogging experience. He was expressive about the dominating ableist views that further isolated the disabled individually and communally:

> My personal interest is that a certain criticism should start emerging within the disabled communities. I mean we should get to learn that we have a share in being isolated from the larger society, simply because we isolate ourselves and find it hard to get out. I've once or twice tried it myself on my own blog. But each time have been stopped by my co-workers at our NGO. They said I was affecting the NGO's relations with other disability NGOs, where as I was speaking through my own blog, it's my place for free-minded speech; it was my vision, being expressed in my personal blog! It had nothing to do with others! But I was hushed.

Due to structural barriers to the public sphere in Iran, one can argue whether minority communities reproduce the same structural boundaries against practicing discourse in the virtual world. I would say that isolation is rooted in the reproduction of the repressed cultural identity of the disabled bodied individual within the disabled community. It stems from an ableist ideology, which is a function of the instrumental rationality of modernized Iran.

The bloggers in my study believed that once they revealed their real identities they had the responsibility to render services to their community—a community that viewed isolation through a fatalistic lens. They had denied their right to freely discuss the novelty of living in a diverse society. The fact is that the virtual world cannot be a separate social reality from the real world—it actually moves in parallel with the everyday life of people.[40] I would argue this in terms of the weak growth in critical rationality as an arguably difficult social problem in Iran. Thus the extent that individuals seek the "better argument" in the virtual world is tightly connected to the ethics of argumentation as grown and practiced in the real world.[41]

After All, She Didn't Like "to Only Reach Disabled Readers": Writing Disability and Blending In

Bloggers claimed that they mentioned their disabilities in their personal accounts in situations when they believed they were addressing readers without physical disabilities,[42] such as this entry by the thirty-one-year-old writer of a blog called "The Tears and the Laughs":

> I scarcely write about my disability. . . . I never liked only reaching disabled readers in my [online] journaling. I'm really against being excluded and or being seen or portrayed as different. I always wanted to make friends with everyone not just the disabled, so I'm doing the same in my blog.

This strikingly recurrent theme in the bloggers' experiences was also observed in their struggles with questions such as, How to reveal their disability? How much of it to reveal? Where in their daily blogging was disability *an issue* to reveal? What made it fun to read them? Many of the bloggers had dilemmas in making up their minds about whether to reveal their identity as a disabled bodied person—that is, writing disability. Targeting disabled identity to a nondisabled readership juxtaposed the wish to "get out of isolation" and blend in.

Blending in was recurrently juxtaposed with narrations about accessibility issues that bloggers recounted as a rare chance to "go out for fun" and hang out. The bloggers viewed their blogs as a space to present their everyday life, and it was centered on flashing momentary images of themselves and their lives for the sake of interacting with a nondisabled readership. They indicated that blending in required presenting *all* aspects of their lives; disability was just one part of the panorama they sketched for self-presentation.

The other noticeable element in what I came to call "blending-in narratives" was the story behind the bloggers' views of *their greatest achievement* in terms of blending in through their blogging, such as shown in this entry by a twenty-six-year-old who called her blog "The Girl Who Walked With Her Brain":

I can't go out and watch what people do, what difficulties they've got, just as I do. I don't have a way out except for the Internet. I can go out perhaps once or twice a month at most, but I can use the Internet two to three hours a day or even more. And I can get in touch with those I feel like. It's great.

Bloggers observed that most people without disabilities observed their disability rather than the person they were. The bloggers pitched this observation to the Television and Radio Broadcasting Center of the Islamic Republic of Iran (IRIB), also publicly known as *Seda-O Sima,* explaining that the focus of IRIB programming was to represent PWDs' achievements and barriers in terms of their successes in sports and educational competition or their challenges as burdens to the healthcare system. In contrast to such "dominant" stories of "achievement despite pain" and "burden due to lack," the bloggers believed that they were highlighting what society *didn't see*: the story of an ordinary woman or man's life in which disability does not play a fatal or determining part.

I would question whether the bloggers' stories of "achievement through strategy" were "the greatest" despite the fact that they are commensurate with hyperpersonal (HP) theory.[43] I agree with HP theory, though with a healthy dose of reservation, that blogs seem to have enabled a selective self-presentation on the part of the users and that it gives users opportunities to present themselves more freely and positively.[44] However, I would argue that the bloggers in their narrations explained that they relied on strategic blend-in narratives; that is, they tended to narrate their disability only in ways that they knew would gain them acceptance in the eyes of the nondisabled reader. In this respect, they promoted the disablist ideology that dominates in society.

We can argue that the bloggers in the study reduced the potentially negative aspects of disability to the able-bodied eye, and thus presented other more positive aspects of their lives. Still, as online relationship literature suggests, most of the online friendships that the bloggers made through blogging were to compensate for a lack of social encounters in daily life. Blending-in narratives did not prove to be successful as long as they recaptured the ableist notion of disability as a split identity that can succeed only in conditions defined as "normal" in society. The repressive dimension of the bloggers' blending-in narratives captured their effort to meet with new people, pass time, and entertain themselves, but escaped the normative underlying of the stories that pointed to dilemmas regarding whether to "reveal it or to not" and the strategies regarding *how* to reveal it.

Relationship Expansion and Real-World Outings:
Equity and Gendered Disability Talk

A contentious theme in the study of disabled bodied blogging experience has remained the differences in online relationships between disabled men and women bloggers. The theme involved further study on gender and connectivity patterns among disabled individuals. The talk about freedom to "access/hang out" was uniquely gendered in my interviews. All the disabled men in the study, regardless of the severity of their disability, believed that their online friendships had extended over to the real world, and that they had had face-to-face encounters. It was not the same case with the disabled women in this study. As "The Tears and the Laughs" blogger suggested,

> Um . . . I've never devoted any time to that. Other bloggers do. They go to parks or cafés together. And the main reason has been my disability. It's too difficult to coordinate it . . . and to go together with them. For us disabled people, it is way too hard. So they're virtual friends, but no more than that.

For the disabled women in this study, gendered disability talk was a revealing theme, as far as friendship development outside the online world was concerned.

Relationship Depth and Reciprocity in the Online World:
"A Feeling Quite Different . . ."

For this study I have adopted Altman and Taylor's investigation on interpersonal intimacy to understand the expansion of online relationship in the blogging experience of the disabled group. Blogging has increased dependence, intimacy (depth of relationship), reciprocity, and a variety of ways of getting connected (expansion of relationship) among the disabled bloggers under study.[45] The relations under study, primarily created online, confirm McKenna and Bargh's social compensation hypothesis[46] rather than Valkenberg and Peter's "the rich become richer" hypothesis.[47] The former contends that the Internet is particularly useful for introverted people, whereas the latter advances the point that extroverted adults use the Internet to develop their communication skills. As the bloggers largely use the Internet and blogging as a practice to come out of isolation, get to know new people, and have a good time, the findings support the compensation hypothesis.

As Cunningham and Barbee have shown, the perception of "having access to support" has an effect on emotional adaptation, and on satisfaction with relationships.[48] Bloggers have a perception of access to support in the times they need it most. This is best articulated by a twenty-three-year-old blogger:

> I sometimes check my blog page five or six times a day. And whenever I see that my friends have come and read me, well this has a feeling quite different from the intimacies or friendships out in the real world.

Although this blogger draws a clear distinction between the intimacy felt between offline friendships and support through his blog, it is clear that his blog serves as an access point for social support.

Individual Empowerment

I sought blogging practices that challenged the delimiting forces reflected in the interviews. These blogging practices included:

- writing practices (including mental and physical aspects of such practice);

- interpersonal communication (commenting, sending/receiving emails, chatting, face-to-face encounters);

- search for information and seeking entertainment (recreation, educational/medical/healthcare information).

Three themes on individual empowerment were elicited, including "the power to make change," "the power to access needed information," and "the acquisition of a positive role as a blogger." The other two themes— "enriched social life" and "expanded world views"—reflected the empowering experiences at the social level.

The disabled bloggers found blogging a convenient technology to gain power and change aspects of their individual life and to obtain control over them. Blogging helped with finding a venue to vent all the problems and difficulties they had faced through their disability. This use was especially widespread among those who had been left disabled through accidents. Blogging also enabled bloggers to be more selective and precise about what subjects they chose to write about and how to present it, as suggested in this entry written by a blogger with a spinal cord injury:

> I think a lot over whatever I want to post about. I read it a number of times, edit it, and edit it again. This helps me better understand my thoughts and ideas and to adopt them in dealing with my own life . . . it's a good practice, since it first helps change the blogger's behavior themselves.

For those bloggers who had difficulty holding a pen, using the keyboard to type was a phenomenal change in life.

After a bad fall, the owner of the blog "My Pinkie" had to spend most of his time in bed. As he describes:

> I was in such a bad physical condition that I couldn't even push a button on the keyboard. As time passed, by practicing I could finally use my pinkie finger to type. I started enjoying it because this is the only way I can keep in touch with people out of this room.

Blogging also introduced the chance for the bloggers to feel that they were socially present and involved; this was due to the online connectedness of being online.

> Due to my physical problem, I have little presence in the society. Though I'm working and this helps me to be active but as for my pass time . . . well, not that. It's my way to find friends. I can't go to cinema, or go to a park and talk to the fellow sitting next to me, but I can have fun and know about out there right in front of my PC.

As these two examples clearly demonstrate, blogs become a means for my participants to build on their social connectedness in ways that had not been possible for them in the past.

Gendered disability also revealed differences between disabled men and women who used the Internet to search for and gather information. While men with disabilities searched for technical and educational information that had something to do with their profession, women largely used the Internet to provide or seek consultation or get information on know-how or practical skills in the domestic domain. The twenty-six-year-old male blogger "Always Too Lonely" explains:

> All I need, from program codes to learning English, all the questions that I could not find an answer to, all but all. Blogs have been really useful; you should spend a whole lot of money to get them sometimes.

Like other women bloggers in this study, the blogger with the blog titled "The Girl Who Walked with Her Brain" enjoyed a variety of online socializing get-togethers:

> I found a circle of friends with disabilities. We shared the same experience and I always was curious how they would have reacted in such or such situation that I found myself in.

Blogs serve as an expressive space to gain a positive social role as bloggers within the disabled network. It provides them with a place to feel that they are more visible in a network of nondisabled bloggers and readers.

Being a blogger was considered something positive for those who managed and owned one, and also for those who used blogs to reach out to their community. "The Girl Who Walked with Her Brain" blogger explains:

> There were those among my readers who would've never known a person with disability, now they do! I've presented new ideas and issues about the disabled. Most people think a person who uses a wheelchair is different, you know. But I've shown them that I do live like they do, perhaps I'm slower in getting my stuff done, same difference.

As this example demonstrates, many of the bloggers in this study saw their activities as being positive not just for themselves but also for the wider society.

Social Empowerment

Focusing on the key concepts of social participation, two major themes emerge from the interviews. Tagged as "enriched social life," this theme was about how blogging has been a useful tool to meet like-minded people, learn more about people's needs, share experience with others, and receive and give social support in different times (such as in cases of a physical difficulty or in disability management). All these had reinforced the sense of social participation among bloggers, as shown in this entry by a twenty-seven-year-old writer who called his blog "Disability Is Not a Sentence":

> When people like us, who have physical problems, start blog-ging, they gradually find people who think and feel like them. Of course you always have those against you, but as time goes by, they go away, and more interesting is that you write about your problem but you receive ten other problems like that. You come to learn that you were not alone.

Writing about their problems created a feedback mechanism of social sup-port, which helped some participants realize they were not alone. This made me interested in knowing how online communities formed around disability blogs and how they sparked discussions.

Nancy Baym shows that every single virtual community has its own particular characteristics; each community in the virtual world has distinct and special norms that bring the users together.[49] Drawing on this, two sorts of communities were found existing around the studied blogs: those having fun and those bolstering social support. Neither of the two communities had set goals to discuss seriously the issues concerning identity and disability. The kind of community that the disabled have carved out is, for the most part, apolitical. As far as embracing disability as an identity, they avoided it because it reinforced that they were inferior and marginal in society. The community seemed unwilling or unable to develop a political critique of the way they had internalized "disability as defect."

"The Girl Who Walked with Her Brain" blogger advances this view by taking a critical stance toward the disabled virtual community one would risk being excluded from. She explained:

> You simply can't say your ideas openly; firstly they never listen to you, secondly they get hurt and you are no longer part of them.

Online presence, however, had an empowering effect in the sense that it helped expand the worldviews of people with disabilities, as Maani indicates here:

Sometimes, there are people who criticize you and your thoughts, or they simply swear at you. Most people get hurt and their friendship ends. But blogging has helped me to look at one issue from different aspects. It's a great tool in this term.

The dynamics of empowerment and oppression that are created through this virtual community are complex and likely not experienced in exactly the same way by each member.

Conclusion

In this chapter I have examined the blogging practices of Iranians living with disabilities. My aim was to interpret these practices in terms of the difficulties and challenges these disabled Iranians encounter in everyday life, and their effort to voice them through an alternative medium of expression. I further engaged in a critical analysis of the empowering themes in the bloggers' experiences. The bloggers in this study regarded their blogging practices as insufficient in either voicing or refuting the ableist views that were dominant in the disabled communities about living in a diverse society as a person with disability. The narratives in this study support this suppressed and disempowering aspect of the blogging experience. The bloggers admitted that the disabled community in the online world disqualified people with disabilities and tended to promote the ableist narratives about disability in their society.

If the bloggers envisage that they were giving service to their online community, they preferred to use their real identity for more effective services. Such bloggers were reluctant to expose the disabled population to criticism about exclusions and acceptance in fear of generating a feud in the online world, in the same way that occurs in the real world. This might point out how precarious the position of the disabled is in the public sphere and within the broader Iranian society. It might also explain how such perspectives have spread into the disabled communities online.

In spite of all the claims regarding the democratic space that the Internet appears to provide, this study found no proof of that in the disabled online community as a minor social group with an unacknowledged political identity. On the other hand, women with disability in this study claim that they refused face-to-face encounters because of major setbacks that their disability provoked in their everyday lives. This can be explained in terms of the politics of gendered disability, reflected in the interviews with the disabled women in this study. Females with disability are more vulnerable in society than are disabled men, and measures should be taken to empower them through inclusionary initiatives.[50] As UN-sponsored Article Six of the International Convention of the Rights of People with Disability advocates, women and girls with disabilities face double discrimination as being both disabled and women. As this study shows, women and younger girls with disability feel more limited in the context of social interactions. As a result, this study further highlights the role of ICT in the empowerment and socialization of disabled women and girls.

All the bloggers in the above study viewed blogging either as a leisure-time activity or a place to receive and provide social support; yet, despite the democratic features associated with cyberspace in the literature, these online communities did not provide the participants of this study with a space to discuss or criticize the disabled society and the rigid prejudices against the exclusion of people with disability from the rest of society. This might be argued in further studies in order to highlight the marginal role disability activism plays in Iranian society, as far as the identity rights of people with disability is concerned.

Blogs are used as tools to connect and share with one's community. Future studies should focus on the possible uses of social-networking sites, and of sharing tools in the everyday lives of people with disabilities. Potential uses of new media for social inclusion, empowerment of people with disabilities, and receiving online social support in society demands further study. This study has implications for the capacities of user-generated content, particularly in societies in which accessibility remains a ubiquitous problem in the everyday lives of people with disabilities.

Notes

1. Montazerghaem Mehdi and Kobra Elahifar, "Bloggers with Disabilities: Individual and Empowering Experiences in Blogosphere," *Social Welfare Quarterly* 12.47 (2013): 319–355.

2. Islamic Republic News Agency, "Four Thousand Accessible Automobiles Transferred to the Ministry of Work and Social Service," http://www.irna.ir/fa/News/80646760/ (accessed May 8, 2013).

3. Montazerghaem and Elahifar, "Bloggers with Disabilities."

4. Majid Mohammadi, "The Iranian Disabled Legal Struggle," *Radio Farda,* May 27, 2010, http://www.radiofarda.com/content/f35_Disability_Rights_Com/2036120.html (accessed June 7, 2010).

5. Ibid.

6. For more on this, see David J. Lenard, *Enforcing Normalcy: Disability, Deafness, and the Body* (London: Verso, 1995).

7. Rosemarie Garland-Thompson, "Feminist Disability Studies," *Signs* 30.2 (2005): 1557–1587.

8. *United Nations, Disabilities: A Guide to Adaptation and Effective Implementation of the International Covenant of the Rights of People with Disabilities*, trans. Abolhassan Faghih, Nazmdeh Kazem and Hamrangi Yousefi, Mohammadtaghi (Tehran: State Welfare Organization, 2007).

9. Bharat Mehra, Cecilia Merkel and Bishop, Ann Peterson, "The Internet for Empowerment of Minority and Marginalized Users," *New Media and Society* 6.6 (2004): 781–802.

10. Behzad Jaghatayee, "The Condition of People with Disability in Iran," Rahman NGO, rahman.org. 2007, rahman.org.ir/sportal/.../uploads/Dr.%20Joghataee%2001.pdf. (accessed June 7, 2010).

11. Floya Antias, "The Concept of 'Social Division' and Theorizing Social Stratification: Looking at Class and Ethnicities," *Sociology* 35.4 (2001): 835–854; Jo Beall and Laure-Hélène Piron, "DFID Social Exclusion Review," *Overseas Development Institute* (London: The London School of Economics and Political Sciences, May 2005), http://dspace.cigilibrary.org/jspui/bitstream/123456789/22869/1/DFID%20Social%20Exclusion%20Review.pdf?1 (accessed June 7, 2010); Daniel Béland, "The Social Exclusion Discourse: Ideas and Policy Change," *Policy and Politics* 35.1 (2007): 123; Tania Burchardt, Julian LeGrand and Pichaud, David, "Social Exclusion in Britain 1991–1995," *Social Policy & Administration* 33.3 (1999): 227; Claire Curran, Tania Burchardt, Martin Knapp, David McDaid and Li, Bingqin, "Challenges in Multidisciplinary Systematic Reviewing: A Study on Social Exclusion and Mental Policy," *Social Policy and Administration* 41.3 (2007): 289; Torlid Hammer, "Transitions and Mobility in the Youth Labor Market," TIY workshop (Oslo: NOVA, 2000); Graham J. Room, "Social Exclusion, Solidarity, and the Challenge of Globalization," *International Journal of Social Welfare* 8.3 (1999): 166; Linda Phipps, "New Communications Technologies: A Conduit for Social Inclusion," *Information, Communication, and Society* 3.1 (2000): 39; Nicolas Pleace, "Single Homelessness as Social Exclusion: The Unique and the Extreme," *Social Policy and Administration* 32.1 (1998): 46–59.

12. Phipps, "New Communications Technologies."

13. Merete Lie and Knut Holtan Sørenson, *Making Technology Our Own: Domesticating Technology into Everyday Life* (Oslo: Scandinavian University Press, 1996).

14. Hendrik Storstein Spilker and Knut Holtan Sørenson, "A Room of One's Own or a Home for Sharing," *New Media and Society* 2 (2000): 265.

15. Deirdre Hynes, Tarja Tiainen and Emma-Reetta, Koivunen, *Articulating ICT Use Narratives in Everyday Life* (Manchester: Ideas Publishing Group, 2006).

16. Maria Bakardjieva, "Virtual Togetherness: An Everyday-Life Perspective," *Media, Culture, and Society* 25.3 (2003): 291.

17. Guillaume Thevenot, "Blogging as a Social Media," *Tourism and Hospitality Research* 7.3–4 (2007): 287.

18. Robert Godwin-Jones, "Emerging Technologies: Blogs and Wikis, Environments for Online Collaboration," *Language Learning and Technology* 7.2 (2003): 12.

19. Ananda Mitra, "Using Blogs to Create Cybernetic Space, Convergence," *The International Journal of Research into New Media Technologies* 4.4 (2008): 459.

20. Ali Eslaminassab, *A Clinical Approach to the Psychology of the Disabled and Disabled War Veterans* (Tehran: Safi Ali Shahi Publications, 1994).

21. Erving Goffman, *Stigma: Notes on the Management of Spoiled Identity* (New York: Simon and Schuster, 1963).

22. Mann Hyung Hur, "Empowerment in Terms of Theoretical Perspectives: Exploring a Typology of Process and Components across Disciplines," *Journal of Community Psychology* (2006): 523.

23. Lee H. Staples, "Power Ideas about Empowerment," *Administration in Social Work* 14.2 (1990): 29.

24. Ibid.

25. Ibid.

26. Barbara Bryant Solomon, *Black Empowerment: Social Work in Oppressed Communities* (New York: Columbia University Press, 1976).

27. Judi Chamberlain, "A Working Definition of Empowerment," *Psychiatric Rehabilitation Journal* 20:46 (1994): 44.

28. Hur, "Empowerment in Terms of Theoretical Perspectives."

29. Julian Rappaport, "Terms of Empowerment/Exemplars of Prevention: Toward a Theory of Community Psychology," *American Journal of Community Psychology* 15 (1987): 121.

30. Marc A. Zimmerman, "Empowerment Theory: Psychological, Organizational, and Community Levels of Analysis," in *Handbook of Community Psychology,* ed. Julian Rappaport and Edward Seidman, 43 (New York: Spring Press, 2000).

31. Said Reza Ameli, "Web Log: House of Identity and Imagining Personhood," *Hamshahrionline,* September 4, 2006. http://hamshahrionline.ir/details/3233 (accessed June 4, 2010).

32. Ibid.

33. Gerard Goggin and Christopher Newell, *Digital Disability: The Social Construction of Disability in New Media* (Lanham: Rowman & Littlefield, 2003), 129–145.

34. Lee Raine and Barry Wellman, *Networked: The New Social Operating System* (Boston: MIT, 2014); Goggin and Newell, Digital Disability.

35. Assa Gardelli, "ICT as a Tool for Empowerment with People with Disabilities," *From Violence to Caring: Gendered and Sexualized Violence as the Challenge on the Life Span* (Oulu, Finland: Kasvatustieteiden tiedekunnan elektronisia julkaisuja 8, 2008), 193; Azy Barak and Yael Sadovsky, "Internet Use and Personal Empowerment of Hearing-Impaired Adolescents," *Computers in Human Behavior* 24.5 (2008): 1802; Dorothe Durieux, *ICT and Social Inclusion in the Everyday*

Life of Less Able People (Liege and Amsterdam: University of Liege and ASCOR, 2003); Sylvia Söderström, "Offline Social Ties and Online Use of Computers: A Study of Disabled Youth and Their Use of ICT Advance," *New Media & Society* 11.5 (2009): 709.

36. Thomas R. Lindlof and Bryan C. Taylor, *Qualitative Communication Research Methods* (London: SAGE, 2002): 18.

37. Pertti Alasuutari, "Theorizing in Qualitative Research: A Cultural Studies Perspective," *Qualitative Inquiry* 24 (1996): 371.

38. Lindlof and Taylor, *Qualitative Communication Research Methods,* 178.

39. The opening quotation to this section is from 2009 interview transcripts with blogger Maani, twenty-seven.

40. Mehra et al., "The Internet for Empowerment of Minority and Marginalized Users"; Mitra, "Using Blogs to Create Cybernetic Space, Convergence."

41. Nick Crossley and John Michael Roberts, *After Habermas: New Perspectives on the Public Sphere* (Oxford: Blackwell, 2004).

42. The opening quotation to this section is from 2009 interview transcripts with "The Tears and Laughs" blogger.

43. HP Theory attributes two main features to computer-based communication, and one is that communication cues an asynchronous nature of CMC. See Joseph B. Walther, "Computer-Mediated Communication: Impersonal, Interpersonal, and Hyper-Personal Interaction," *Communication Research* 23.1 (1996): 3–43.

44. Joseph B. Walther and Judee K. Burgoon, "Relational Communication in Computer-Mediated Interaction," *Human Communication Research* 19.1 (1992): 50–88.

45. Irwin Altman and Dalmas A. Taylor, *Social Penetration: The Development of Interpersonal Relationship* (New York: Holt, Rinehart, and Winston, 1973).

46. Katelyn Y. A. McKenna and Bargh, John A., "Plan 9 from Cyberspace: The Implications of the Internet for Personality and Social Psychology," *Personality and Social Psychology Review* 4.1 (2000): 57–75.

47. Patti M. Valkenberg and Jochen Peter, "Pre-Adolescents' and Adolescents' Online Communication and Their Closeness to Friends," *Developmental Psychology* 43.2 (2007a): 267.

48. Michael R. Cunningham and Anita P. Barbee, "Social Support," in *Close Relationship,* ed. Clyde Hendrik and Susan S. Hendrik, 273–285 (Thousand Oaks, CA: Sage, 2000).

49. Nancy Baym, "The Emergence of On-Line Community," in *Cyber-Society 2.0: Revisiting Computer-Mediated Communication and Community,* ed. Steve G. Jones, 35–68 (Thousand Oaks, CA: Sage, 1998).

50. Virginia Kallians and Phyllis Rubenfeld, "Disabled Women and Reproductive Rights," *Disability and Society* 12.2 (1997): 203.

Part II

POLITICS

Chapter 5

The Politics of Online Journalism in Iran

Marcus Michaelsen

On November 10, 2006, about a month before the municipal elections in Iran, news websites close to the political reformists published a list with possible candidates running for the Tehran city council. The list had also been distributed to journalists of similar political orientation who posted it on their blogs engaging fellow bloggers in a lively debate on the qualification of the candidates and, more important, the question whether one was to participate in the vote or not. More than a year after the surprising election of President Mahmoud Ahmadinejad had stirred up the political scene of the Islamic Republic, the reformists and their adherents were still seeking strategies to express their opposition to the new hardline government. Websites and blogs were the main forum for these deliberations.

About a year later, in September 2007, judicial authorities ordered the closure of the website *Baztab* (Reflection) at the insistence of Ahmadinejad's government. The website did not belong to the reformist media, usually the target of Internet filtering and censorship, but it was close to former Revolutionary Guard commander Mohsen Rezai, the secretary of the Expediency Council, a key institution in the regime. Among a growing number of online news media, *Baztab* had attained a leading position by divulging background information on alleged high-profile corruption cases and by attacking the performance of the president. The government of Ahmadinejad, under increasing pressure from conservative critics, tried to silence one of the most disturbing voices and closed down *Baztab*'s offices. It was only a brief success: the website soon reopened with similar makeup and content under the name *Tabnak* (Shining).

Both episodes hint at the significance that the entire spectrum of Iran's political class attached to communicating news and information on the Internet. Well before the use of social media by the Green Movement, protesting the controversial presidential elections in summer 2009, attracted worldwide attention and led Western media to speculate about a "Twitter Revolution," a lively landscape of news websites and blogs had already developed in Iran. In fact, the role that digital communication networks came to play for articulating resistance and informing on the course of the protests cannot be fully understood without taking into consideration the previous evolution of Iranian online media. With the rise to power of the conservative hardliners and increasing state pressure on civil society, the Internet became an essential platform for the reform movement in the years after 2000. Journalists and intellectuals published online; student and women's rights activists retreated on the Internet in order to preserve their networks and information exchange. Yet the authoritarian forces recognized the advantages of online media, too. News websites attached to various groups and personalities of the power elite emerged. This trend intensified particularly when internal rivalries broke out among the conservative and hardline factions after they had pushed their common opponents, the reformists, out of the institutions.

This chapter retraces the development and the political role of Iranian online media before the election crisis of 2009—an event that can unquestionably be considered as a rupture both for the history of the Islamic Republic and that of journalism in Iran.[1] The years between 2001 and 2008 were marked by a growing popularity of Internet use in Iran, particularly in the capital and the larger cities. The overall estimated penetration rate during that period grew from 1.5 percent to 10.2 percent of the population.[2] In parallel, the Iranian state built up its own approach to domesticate the Internet through an increasingly sophisticated system of control and censorship while at the same time seeking to exploit the technology's potential for economic and political purposes.[3]

From a political point of view, that period corresponded to a process of authoritarian rigidification. The push coming from the reform movement for more social and political liberties during the presidency of Mohammad Khatami (1997–2005) produced a conservative backlash that strengthened the pivotal position of Supreme Leader Ali Khamenei. Consequently, a new generation of hardliners closely affiliated to the Revolutionary Guards and the security establishment rose to power. Elected in 2005, President Ahmadinejad also hailed from the "Principalists," as this political current named itself, but his willful style of exercising office soon triggered new factional rivalries. The reformists, for their part, underwent a phase of reorientation after being pushed to the political sidelines. Ultimately, they supported the candidacy of former prime minister Mir-Hossein Mousavi, a moderate political retiree remembered for his managerial expertise and closeness to Khomeini, in the presidential elections of 2009.[4]

It was during these years of intense political contestation that websites and blogs acquired their significance as means of political expression. In a media environment characterized by strong state control, the Internet opened up new and highly appreciated communication channels. While television and radio were closely tied to the power circles around the Supreme Leader, the press had always been a battleground for competing visions within the political elite of the Islamic Republic. Print publications, however, were not only vulnerable to censorship but also required certain economic resources and infrastructure. As a result, websites and blogs became flexible and inexpensive alternatives to publish political news and opinions. Blogs in particular helped form a more participatory and interactive way of producing and circulating information, anticipating the qualities of later social media networks.

As this chapter shows, online media supported the emergence of an information landscape with remarkable diversity in political views and widespread transnational bonds. A case study of a reformist website at the time of the municipal elections in 2006 will demonstrate how the reformists as political challengers to the hardline government used online media to carve out counterpublics where they not only deliberated on their political strategy and collective identity but also sought to defy dominant political views and reach out to supporters. Analyzing the corresponding debate on the municipal elections among a network of bloggers, I underline the role that journalists played as transmitters of information and ideas in the blogosphere. The communication spheres that the Internet opened up in Iran, however, did not remain free from state influence. In addition to the authorities' continuous efforts to censor and control Internet use, members of the power elite created their own online media to be actively present on the Internet. My observations of conservative and hardline websites will illustrate how these publications exposed and intensified rivalries among the "Principalist" factions.

Media and Political Contests

In his examination of the media's role in political conflicts, Wolfsfeld argues that media are "part of a larger and more significant contest among political antagonists for political control."[5] Political opponents thus compete on a structural as well as on a cultural level when seeking to gain access to the media and to shape the meanings ascribed to media content. In this competition, dominant state actors have clear advantages since political status, financial and organizational resources are central factors determining media access. As political conflicts are an expression of competing visions of reality, political antagonists, at the same time, try to enforce interpretations of events that support their political aims. Social movement theory analyzes this process of creating media frames as an essential strategy of collective actors challenging established norms and power structures without having access to the institutions of political decision making. Accordingly, social movement actors "select some aspects of a perceived reality and make them more salient in a communicating text, in such a way as to promote a particular problem definition, causal interpretation, moral evaluation and/or treatment recommendation for the item described."[6]

The opportunity to put forward certain media frames may rise out of unanticipated events. In winter 2005, for instance, air pollution in Tehran reached such high levels that public life in large parts of the city became unbearable. The Iranian reformists used this incident for their first public critique of newly elected President Ahmadinejad, who had been de facto responsible for traffic planning in his previous post as the mayor of Tehran. In another example, in the protests of summer 2009, the shooting of Neda Agha-Soltan and the use of the Internet to distribute images and videos of her death provided the Green Movement with a powerful symbol of worldwide resonation, representing the struggle of nonviolent young protesters against a repressive state. In general, however, framing is a constant process that movements undertake to strengthen internal cohesion and mobilize support. Consequently, movement actors are considered "as signifying agents actively engaged in the production and maintenance of meaning for constituents, antagonists, and bystanders or observers."[7] In their capacity as professional public interpreters of reality, intellectuals and journalists play a key role in the creation of frames. Even if not directly engaged in a movement's struggle, they can act either as innovators, bringing up new ideas and spurring debates, or as allies, supporting the cause of a movement with factual knowledge and intellectual reputation.[8] In the case of Iran's reform movement, for example, religious intellectuals initially pushed the boundaries of public discourse on the role of Islamist ideology as the source of state legitimacy so that sociopolitical actors striving for a more open and participatory system gained new maneuvering space.[9]

Of course, authoritarian regimes command multiple levers to manage media access and content in order to prevent dissenting views from being publicized. In addition to implementing censorship, coercion, and legal frameworks, these regimes use the means of public communication to legitimize their hold to power and propagate a particular worldview. The combination of restrictive measures and active involvement has also been observed as a typical method of authoritarian rulers who seek to expand their power over online media.[10] Nevertheless, the media are rarely forced into a quasi-totalitarian alignment. Varying degrees of state control over the media as well as elite factionalism allow for the emergence of diverging political views.[11] This is particularly relevant for Iran's Islamic Republic, a system described as "fragmented authoritarianism," in which different factions of the revolutionary elite have always been engaged in a vivid, at times fierce, competition without ever actually questioning the political order.[12]

In addition to the effects of elite fragmentation that may offer political challengers the opportunity to access the media and propel oppositional positions, the exclusion of certain social groups from public debate can also result in the formation of alternative discursive spheres. According to Fraser, these "counterpublics" comprise a dual orientation: "On the one hand, they function as spaces of withdrawal and regroupment; on the other hand, they also function as bases and training grounds for agitational activities directed towards wider publics."[13] Iranian blogs have actually been described as a space for refuge and identity formation for marginalized social groups such as women or youth who currently face the restrictions of ideological norms and traditional values.[14] It is thus important to extend these observations into the realm of concrete political debates in order to analyze to what extent online media have opened up a new field of contestation among actors involved in the larger conflict about the future trajectory of the Islamic Republic.

Emerging Online Media

Journalism in Iran has always been closely linked to the political development of the country. Due to the absence of established political parties, print media frequently became mouthpieces of political factions and groups, propagating political visions and agitating the public for support. As a result, the shorter periods of relative freedom in Iranian modern history went along with a flourishing of various publications. Conversely, the press had to bear the consequences of its political entanglements when autocratic rule was reinforced again.[15] This pattern seemed to repeat again when, at the end of the 1990s, the policies of the reformist president Mohammad Khatami resulted in a relaxation of state control over the press. Print publications grew both in quantity and quality as the increasing number of newspapers and magazines offered room for a greater variety of topics and opinions. An emerging generation of writers pressed into offices and posts of new publications, mostly reformist, and enthusiastically began to engage in journalism. The success of the press and that of the reformist government were closely intertwined: while the administration provided breathing space for the foundation of new papers, journalists promoted Khatami's discourse on reform, participation, and civil society.[16] While mobilizing public opinion in favor of the reformists, the press became "the vehicle through which differentiated opinions were made public, not merely as a means to inform but also as a claim to power."[17] Unsurprisingly, conservative retaliation first and foremost targeted the press. In spring 2000, the judiciary closed down sixteen newspapers in one sweeping strike. In the following years more than one hundred publications were forbidden, and hundreds of journalists lost their jobs.[18]

The clampdown on the press overlapped with a period of significant Internet expansion. A former head of the press department in the ministry of culture, a journalist himself, therefore saw a direct relationship between the closure of newspapers and the emergence of numerous news websites in these years.[19] In order to avoid censorship, journalists began publishing their articles on the Internet. Primarily the young generation perceived the openness of online media as an attractive alternative to the political restrictions on print publications. For the political reformists who had neglected the setup of organizational structures and mostly relied on appealing to public opinion, websites opened up an essential channel to address supporters. Editorial teams close to the progressive wing of the reformists and groups like the Participation Front (*Mosharekat*) and the "Warriors of the Islamic Revolution" (*Mojahedin-e Enqelab-e Eslami*) moved online to compensate for the censored newspapers.

During their first years, reformist websites such as *Emrouz* and *Rouydad* worked unrestrained from Internet censorship in parallel to remaining print media. After 2002, blogs added another possibility of publication for journalists that many other Iranians embraced rapidly and in great numbers.[20] Particular political occasions, such as elections, produced additional websites dealing with information related to the event. Prior to the municipal elections of 2006, for instance, an editorial team led by Mohammad Qowchani, chief editor of the daily *Shargh* that had been closed only a few weeks before, started the website *Shahr-e Farda* (City of Tomorrow), which distributed news on the reformist campaign. The website *Baharestan*, named after the square opposite the Iranian parliament in Tehran, fulfilled the same purpose in the run-up to the legislative elections of March 2008. An initiative of young reform supporters for a renewed candidature of ex-president Khatami in the 2009 presidential elections was equally sparked off by a few websites and later became one of the driving forces in Mousavi's campaign.[21] The team of the second reformist candidate Mehdi Karroubi even tried to relate to Barack Obama's success in the 2008 United States elections by titling their new website *Tagheer* (Change).[22]

In general, these news websites functioned as a kind of online newspaper or magazine updated on a regular basis depending on the material available. Small editorial teams would aggregate articles of external contributors and sources. Due to limited resources, the design and format of the websites remained rudimentary. Some publications had subsections organized by topics, but often all articles appeared on one central page. Regular authors were listed on a sidebar with their photo and most recent article. The background of these contributors as well as links to other websites or blogs gave insight into the "informational universe" of each website and easily revealed its political affiliation.

Voices from Outside

On the Internet, the first reform websites joined a number of online media published by the Iranian Diaspora. Due to the rapid proliferation of Internet use in Europe and North America, as well as the keen interest of Iranian migrants to connect with each other and their land of origin, the exile websites appeared even before the first online publications from within Iran. A pioneer among these publications was the information portal *Gooya,* established in 1998 by Belgian Farshad Bayan. Initially, *Gooya* started as a collection of web addresses linking to all kinds of Internet publications dealing with Iran. Later, the separate section *Gooyanews* tried to respond to a growing interest in exchanging news and information online. With restricted editorial resources, the website had to rely mostly on voluntary contributions and re-publications of Iranian newspaper articles. Nevertheless, it developed into a popular forum bringing together various authors.[23] Another example of a successful publication from exile was the online newspaper *Rooz,* founded in May 2005 by a group of Iranian journalists who had left the country during the crackdown on the press in the preceding years. Scattered over different countries, the editors collaborated through the Internet and kept close relations to political and civil society circles inside

Iran. Published daily with a focus on internal affairs and human rights, *Rooz* gained a reputation as a credible news source so that even conservative parliamentarians accorded interviews. The filtering of the website for the Iranian public in early 2006, however, reduced the number of readers. Fearing judicial persecution, journalists contributing from inside Iran had to use pseudonyms. Yet *Rooz* continued its publication, trusting readers' motivation to circumvent the filters.[24]

These early examples highlight the transnational disposition of Iranian online publications—a feature to be enhanced significantly by social media networks in the years to follow. The Internet linked members of a widespread exile community to each other and to a public in Iran. It gave exiled journalists and intellectuals the opportunity to participate in debates within Iran. The significance of online publications from outside the country varied according to changing restrictions on the media in Iran. While the early websites published by Iranian exiles certainly stimulated the development of online media in the country, they apparently lost impact with the increasing number and popularity of news websites produced in Iran. This changed again after Ahmadinejad's access to power in 2005 when the tightening Internet censorship and persecution of journalists and bloggers in Iran created a renewed demand for media operating outside the reach of the authorities. More journalists left the country in search of new opportunities in journalism. Western media institutions such as the BBC and Radio Free Europe, producing Farsi programs and websites with considerable budgets, absorbed part of these exiles.[25] The repression against the Green Movement in 2009 that was followed by another wave of political émigrés has also brought about a number of new independent Iranian online media working outside the country.

Reform Activism Online

Among the first reformist online publications, the website *Emrouz* (Today) was launched in response to the clampdown on the press after 2000. As early as May 2003, some Iranian Internet providers started blocking access to the website before it was entirely blocked in summer 2004 at the behest of Tehran prosecutor Saeed Mortazavi, a notorious persecutor of journalists and the reformist press. Iranian bloggers reacted to the closure by changing the title of their blogs to *Emrouz* for one day, attracting even the attention of foreign media.[26] At the same time, Mortazavi oversaw the arrest of a dozen authors and technicians working for *Emrouz* and other reformist online media who had been accused by the hardline newspaper *Keyhan* as being part of a "spider's web"—a secret global network allegedly supported by the CIA to destroy the political and moral foundations of the Islamic Republic. A number of detainees were pressured to publically confess and repent their crimes.[27] The so-called "bloggers' file" shed light on the importance that hardliners in the judiciary and the intelligence accorded to the activities of a few online critics whose writings had, after all, limited outreach.

These restrictions notwithstanding, *Emrouz* continued its publication. The responsible editor, Mostafa Tajzadeh, a former vice-minister of the Interior in Khatami's government, claimed that it was important to maintain presence on the Internet and that the website helped to distribute information to reform supporters, even though readers had to circumvent filters for accessing the content.[28] An analysis of the website's articles of November 2006 showed how *Emrouz* perpetuated the discourse of the reformists more than a year after Ahmadinejad's election and a few weeks until the municipal elections provided a first occasion to challenge his government.[29] Compared to other news websites of different political affiliation, the website published a high quantity of articles, probably to compensate for the reformists' blocked access to other media. With restricted editorial resources, however, *Emrouz* was not able to produce much of its content. Accordingly, most of the articles were selected from other blogs and websites or republished print media items. The way in which the articles were chosen and assembled thus shaped the discourse that the website sought to promote. A significant number of articles, for example, highlighted the failure of Ahmadinejad's economic policy that increasingly attracted criticism at the time. But three weeks before the municipal elections, the domestic political scene was of course the central topic on *Emrouz*.

The website approached the municipal elections through two main strings of narrative that in a way ran contrary to each other. On the one hand, the website followed the formation of a reformist coalition for the Tehran city council. The final list of candidates was supported by all groups within the reformist camp and included former technocrats of the Khatami government with a rather pragmatic approach. The articles on the website closely observed the negotiations for the coalition and particularly stressed the agreement with Mehdi Karroubi, the former speaker of the parliament who had angrily parted ways with other reformists after they failed to support his candidacy in the 2005 presidential elections. The focus on the accord as well as on the managerial experience of the candidates aimed at overcoming the reformists' central flaws in the 2005 election: the incapacity to agree on a single candidate and the neglect of economic anxieties in the lower classes of the population. This presentation of the reformist coalition contrasted, on the other hand, with the website's spotlight on the difficulties of the conservatives to agree on a common list of candidates. Due to the refusal of Ahmadinejad's overconfident followers to compromise with other Principalist groups, the camp ultimately broke up into multiple lists. In detail *Emrouz* reproduced the contradicting statements of conservative politicians who were partly still expressing optimism on a possible agreement, partly already revealing anger as to the hard-nosed stand of the president's camp.

Presenting opponents as power hungry and incapable while underlining their own pragmatic and consensual approach, the website obviously employed a common communication strategy of election campaigns. This political competition, however, was played out under authoritarian rules. The reformists were in the role of inferior challengers to the conservative and hardline factions, who controlled all institutions overseeing the electoral process as well as the mass media. The reformists' discourse, as relayed by one of their central websites, thus revealed a framing that is characteristic for contestants of the status quo. A significant group of articles, for instance, dealt with the disqualifications of reformist candidates, the restricted access to state broadcasting, the censorship of the press, and the risk of election fraud within Ahmadinejad's ministry of the Interior. Highlighting the unequal conditions in the elections, these reports transmitted a sense of injustice that aimed at reinforcing solidarity and determination among the reformists in their position as political challengers and conferred a sort of moral legitimacy to their actions.

Another important set of articles on the website discussed the significance of the municipal elections from both a strategic and symbolic point of view. Some reformist authors saw the elections as an opportunity to halt the hardliners' rise to power and to break their hold on the state, at least at the lowest institutional level. Others elaborated on the importance of the elections as a means for political participation and the decentralization of state power. Even if conditions for fair elections were not entirely met, it was argued, the reformists needed to participate in order to strengthen the republican components of the Constitution. Underscored by certain urgency, this line of argumentation led to a clear recommendation: the only solution against further authoritarian undermining of the political system was gradual change within the institutions. Such framing of the political situation not only refuted confrontational strategies such as election boycott or civil disobedience brought forward by more radical opponents of the regime, but also confirmed the reformists' approach of pursuing democratization within the framework of the Islamic Republic.

The entire discourse that the website transmitted reflected the reformists' efforts to position themselves as a credible force of opposition to the government as well as a political movement for reform and democratic change. *Emrouz* and similar online media served for creating counterpublics in which the reformists questioned dominant positions, debated strategies, and negotiated their collective identity. The frames dissected in the analysis not only sought to promote a particular diagnosis of the political issues at hand and possible solutions but also to strengthen the internal cohesion of the movement and motivate supporters. In order to assess how this discourse of the political reformists resonated within the environment of the movement I will now turn to an analysis of the corresponding debate on the municipal elections among a network of bloggers.

Debating in the Blogosphere

The blog debate on the municipal elections was kicked off about a month before the actual vote after a few known bloggers posted a list of possible reformist candidates for the Tehran city council. An author of the group blog *Hanouz*, for instance, invited readers to comment on the candidates and to send in links to all blog entries dealing with the elections.[30] In the ensuing discussion, this blogger, a journalist, not only wrote the highest number of articles but at times also took on the role of moderator, connecting and commenting contributions. Altogether, ninety-eight bloggers were identified as taking part in the exchange by writing an entry and linking it to other participants.[31] Among the seventeen bloggers who posted five or more blog texts on the topic, eleven were journalists or had at least a journalistic background. Also, seven of these active bloggers were closely affiliated to the progressive wing of the reformists in the Participation Front, and seven others were openly sympathetic to the reform movement. Such clustering of bloggers with similar backgrounds and political orientation is a typical feature of blogospheres worldwide. From the four poles that Kelly and Etling identify in their mapping of the Iranian blogosphere, the debate on the municipal elections and its participants clearly fell into the "secular/reformist pole" that exhibits a "substantial recognition of particular high-profile bloggers" and a "structure of links among bloggers [that] forms a single large neighborhood."[32]

The course of the debate reflected the journalistic orientation of the participants who often reacted and linked to news published on other news websites or in newspapers. At the same time, these journalist bloggers shared information they had collected professionally and that they now discussed in more detail and with a personal perspective in the blogs. In fact, some Iranian journalists described blogs as an additional and less restricted publication channel that complemented their work in the press.[33] In the election debate, a journalist reporting for a reformist newspaper, for example, in her blog discussed the eligibility of candidates for the Tehran city council based on her encounters with the representatives and observations of their work. Her motivation was to incite readers to participate in the elections and to vote for the most apt candidates without necessarily following a particular political orientation.[34] Due to their professional experience, journalist bloggers possessed the necessary skills to quickly aggregate and interpret information for their readers. By influencing and intensifying the debate, these bloggers played the role of opinion leaders who transmitted ideas and arguments from other information circuits and the media into the more personalized exchanges of the blogosphere. Yet the impact of even the more influential blogs was limited. According to one of the authors, the group blog *Hanouz* reached about six hundred readers per day.[35] Other bloggers claimed that in exceptional cases, such as when a news website referred to one blog entry, consultations could rise up to two thousand per day. In this sense, one of the active participants in the debate described his motivation for blogging not in trying to reach a larger public, but rather in contributing to a process of opinion building within a network of journalists, students, and other educated readers interested in politics.[36]

Since blogging as a genre generally encourages the expression of personal opinions, the issue of election participation or abstention was the central topic in the entire debate. Bloggers who contributed only a single entry posted it most of the time on the day before the election and used it to inform readers whether they would vote. Most of the bloggers supported voting—an observation that underlined, again, the homogeneity of the network but that may also have been caused by the political frustration of abstainers who possibly showed no interest in contributing to the debate. The rare proponents of election boycott among the bloggers were either disillusioned by the restrictions of the political system or presented their decision as a form of opposition. Those favoring participation clearly sought to motivate readers to vote and used a rationale similar to the one analyzed in the discourse of the website *Emrouz*. The elections were thus depicted as a rare chance to have a say in politics, as a democratic means to strengthen the elected institutions, as a strategic step to curtail the power of the hardliners, and as a possibility to select the politicians who would be making the decisions on development in the municipalities. Although in the majority adherents of the reform movement, the bloggers did not defend reformist policies per se but used the debate for critically reassessing the achievements and failures of Khatami's government. Overall, the exchange among the bloggers resulted in an intense and at times controversial debate. Key participants repeatedly urged others to preserve a rational discussion and to tolerate diverging views. A day before the vote, one of the active bloggers addressed both the advocates of election participation and the adherents of boycott on a conciliatory note: "Don't forget that we on both sides struggle for a better future of Iran. Our common dream is that the country will be free and independent from those bonds that the authoritarian powers tie day by day tighter around Iran."[37]

The analysis of the debate showed that blogs in fact provided space for the development of counterpublics. Here, journalists found a platform to exercise their skills of argumentation and analysis in a way that was not possible in the printed press. The fact that the bloggers mostly addressed possible reformist supporters and boycotters but never those who might vote conservative underlines the introversive nature of these counterpublics. In a phase of authoritarian rigidification, blogs gave refuge to the adherents of reform and political change in order to negotiate identities and discuss potential strategies. The loose networks of blogs bred the political culture of critical debate and civic engagement that was to become a central characteristic of the Green movement. Imprisonment and judicial persecution of bloggers nevertheless underlined the fact that these counterpublics formed under the restrictions of an authoritarian state keen to preserve control over public discourse.

Principalist Online Media

In response to the mushrooming reformist online media, conservative and hardline groups of Iran's political elite started publishing different news websites, too. The decline of the reformist government and the consolidation of conservative power had actually triggered intense competition among the forces defending authoritarian state power and ideological values of the revolution. In the 2005 elections, three Principalist candidates ran for the presidency, each representing a different segment of the conservative camp. After the victory of Ahmadinejad, these fissures, running along the lines of political and economic interests but also generational, sociocultural, and ideological differences, deepened significantly.[38] Although conservatives and hardliners had no need to compensate for censored media access, the Internet opened up an additional possibility to communicate political messages directed against both reformist opponents and intrafactional rivals.[39]

Early conservative websites resembled what an Iranian journalist called "bulletins"—newsletters spreading rumors against political adversaries. Publications titled *Yek Khabar* (A Message) or, rather programmatically, *Efsha* (Disclosure) sought to tarnish the reputation of reformist politicians who served at the time in the parliament and government.[40] Another website apparently tried to capitalize on the popularity of *Gooya*'s Internet portal by providing links to conservative online publications with an identical design and the title *Gooyaa*. Such publications, however, were unable to gain a stable community of readers and had only momentary effects. From 2002 onward, a series of more professional news websites, linked to different groups and figures among the Iranian conservatives, began to emerge.

The website *Baztab*, mentioned in the introductory paragraph, turned into one of the most successful and controversial conservative online news sources after its establishment in 2002. Newspapers and even the state television quoted *Baztab*'s reports. Already under Khatami's government, *Baztab* paid with temporary blockages of its site for criticizing the nuclear negotiations team under Hasan Rowhani, a pragmatic conservative who then held the post of the Security Council's secretary.[41] During Ahmadinejad's first tenure, *Baztab*, for instance, questioned the benefits of the president's trip to Latin America and attacked him for watching a dance performance of unveiled women at the opening ceremony of the 2006 Asian Games in Doha. To justify the closure of *Baztab* in September 2007, authorities stated that the editors had exaggerated the probability of an Israeli or U.S. military strike against Iran. The website had actually warned of possible harm that Ahmadinejad's provocative attitude on the international stage might cause. But with Western pressure over the nuclear program mounting, the impression of diverging opinions within the political elite represented a sensible issue. The attempt to silence *Baztab* revealed how much influence on public opinion the government attributed to the website.[42]

Other members of the Principalist current also used websites to channel their discontent with the government. Linked to Ahmad Tavakkoli, an influential parliamentarian, the news website *Alef* investigated the falsified PhD certificate of Ahmadinejad's minister of the Interior, Ali Kordan, who was then impeached by the Majles in a spectacular session. Websites such as *Fararow, Shafaf,* and *Asr-e Iran* supported the position of the Tehran mayor,

Mohammad Baqer Qalibaf, a former Revolutionary Guard commander and bitter rival of the president.

On the government's side, *Raja News* became a central mouthpiece for Ahmadinejad's associates. The website *Nowsazi* (Modernization), notorious for slander against political opponents, published the writings of Fatemeh Rajabi, wife of government spokesman Gholam-Hussayn Elham, who had glorified Ahmadinejad in a book titled *Miracle of the Third Millennium* and attacked former president Khatami as a proponent of a "pleasure-seeking aristocratic Islam." In autumn 2008, *Nowsazi* accused the grandson of Ayatollah Khomeini of leading a luxurious life in Tehran's privileged North. Hassan Khomeini had apparently angered the hardliners when he criticized the growing political influence of Revolutionary Guard members as clear deviance from his grandfather's ideas. In the ensuing dispute, Ayatollah Tavasolli, a close associate of the Islamic Republic's late founder, died of a stroke while fervently defending Khomeini's family in a speech.[43]

The online news agency Fars News became a source often cited as "semi-official" in Western media. Founded in 2002, Fars had a conservative stand but later tilted towards the hardliners in the Revolutionary Guards and the security apparatus.[44] During the election crisis of 2009, Fars played a key role in perpetuating the narrative of a "Velvet revolution" that was allegedly being directed against the Islamic Republic. In several cases, the website's staff had privileged access to forced confessions of political prisoners. Fars also reported extensively on the show trials of August 2009.[45]

The Internet's advantages of flexibility, low cost, and easy accessibility made news websites an attractive medium for political groups in the conservative elite. The number of such online media augmented in parallel to the intensified rivalries among the Principalists. Distributing rumors or divulging background information became a strategic tool in the competition between the president's camp and his critics in the parliament and other regime institutions. In Iran's factionalized political landscape, with its shifting alliances and complex battles, online media allowed for a quick, and often anonymous, distribution of news that could possibly harm adversaries and strengthen one's own position. Thus the websites not only perpetuated historical patterns of the politicized press in Iran but also exposed conflicts within the elite that leading conservative figures, not least the Supreme Leader himself, sought to minimize. Reformist journalists dissected with great interest the diverging positions in the Principalist online media and thus further intensified the rivalries. Moreover, as the analysis of the website *Emrouz* has shown, the disclosure of the fissures between the pro-state factions actually stimulated the reformist opposition to challenge the government.

Conclusion

This chapter has shown that the phase of intense political conflict that accompanied the failure of the reformist government and the concurrent authoritarian rigidification of Iran's political system in the years up to 2009 equally found an expression in online journalism. After the conservative elite around Supreme Leader Khamenei restricted the reform movement's access to the means of public communication, websites and blogs became a platform for the formation of counterpublics, which allowed for internal deliberations as well as an externally directed transmission of alternative views. The outreach of these online media, of course, was restricted both by state censorship and the sociostructural factors shaping the Iranian online public. It has been outlined that the online media of the reform movement by and large addressed educated and politically engaged sections of the middle class. Nonetheless, within these publics online media allowed for intense exchanges of information and opinion involving parts of the exile community. At the same time, however, the chapter has demonstrated that the power of the authoritarian state also permeated the Internets communication spheres. On the one hand, state influence manifested itself through the impact of censorship, surveillance, and the persecution of online dissidents, and, on the other hand, through the discursive "occupation" of online space by various news media tied to conservative and hardline groups. Exploiting the new media's qualities, the Iranian Principalists found on the Internet an additional and flexible channel to access public discourse and propagate their interpretations of reality in order to strengthen their political positions. The different news websites thus exposed and occasionally even fueled the rivalries among the conservative factions. This, however, did not lead unavoidably to political instability. In the Islamic Republic, factional competition within the margins of the system, stemming from the hybrid nature of the constitutional setup and overlapping institutions, has actually for long helped to accommodate diverging ambitions of the political elite as well as sociocultural developments. By fulfilling the communication needs of both the challengers and the defenders of the status quo, online media merely added an additional dimension to these multilayered conflicts. As the different political forces discovered and shaped the means of online expression according to their requirements during the first decade of the 2000s, digital media in Iran took on a contentious character, and the Internet opened up an "agonistic space of interaction."[46] The practices in the handling of the digital media that all political actors acquired in that phase would be put to use with further intensity in the moment of crisis during the election protests of 2009.

Notes

1. Ali M. Ansari, *Crisis of Authority: Iran's 2009 Presidential Elections* (London: Royal Institute of International Affairs, 2010); Marcus Michaelsen, ed., *Election Fallout: Iran's Exiled Journalists on Their Struggle for Democratic Change* (Berlin: Hans Schiler Verlag, 2011).

2. Figures as given by the International Telecommunications Union. Statistics on Internet use in Iran are often inaccurate and contradictory. The Statistical Centre of Iran, for instance, publishes far more conservative estimates on Internet use than the Ministry of Information and Communication Technology.

3. Babak Rahimi, "The Politics of the Internet in Iran," in *Media, Culture, and Society in Iran: Living with Globalization and the Islamic State,* ed. Mehdi Semati (London, New York: Routledge, 2008), 37–56; OpenNet Initiative, "Internet Filtering in Iran," 2009, http://opennet.net/sites/opennet.net/files/ONI_Iran_2009.pdf; OpenNet Initiative, "After the Green Movement: Internet Controls in Iran 2009–2012," 2013, www.opennet.net/iranreport2013.

4. Anoushiravan Ehteshami and Mahjoob Zweiri, *Iran and the Rise of Its Neoconservatives: The Politics of Tehran's Silent Revolution* (London, New York: I. B. Tauris, 2007); Said Amir Arjomand, *After Khomeini: Iran under His Successors* (New York: Oxford University Press, 2009).

5. Gadi Wolfsfeld, *Media and Political Conflict: News from the Middle East* (Cambridge, New York: Cambridge University Press, 1997), 3.

6. Robert M. Entman, "Framing: Toward Clarification of a Fractured Paradigm," *Journal of Communication* 43 (1993): 51–58; 52.

7. Robert D. Benford and David A. Snow, "Framing Processes and Social Movements: An Overview and Assessment," *Annual Review of Sociology* 26 (2000): 611–639; 613.

8. Rosanne Rutten and Michiel Baud, "Concluding Remarks: Framing Protest in Asia, Africa, and Latin America," in *Popular Intellectuals and Social Movements: Framing Protest in Asia, Africa, and Latin America,* ed. Rosanne Rutten and Michiel Baud (Amsterdam: International Review of Social History, 2004), supplement, 197–217.

9. Abbas Kazemi, *Jamehshenasi rowshanfekri-ye dini dar Iran* (Sociology of Religious Intellectualism in Iran) (Tehran: Tarh-e Now, 2004), 162.

10. Shanthi Kalathil and Taylor C. Boas, *Open Networks, Closed Regimes: The Impact of the Internet on Authoritarian Rule* (Washington, DC: Carnegie Endowment for International Peace, 2003); Evgeny Morozov, *The Net Delusion: How Not to Liberate the World* (London: Allen Lane, 2011).

11. Kai Hafez, "Globalization, Regionalization, and Democratization: The Interaction of Three Paradigms in the Field of Mass Communication," in *Democratizing Global Media,* ed. Robert A. Hackett and Yuezhi Zhao (London, New York: Rowman & Littlefield, 2005), 145–161.

12. Arang Keshavarzian, "Contestation without Democracy: Elite Fragmentation in Iran," in *Authoritarianism in the Middle East: Regimes and Resistance,* ed.

Marsha P. Posusney and Michelle P. Angrist (Boulder: Lynne Rienner, 2005), 63–88; Houchang E. Chehabi, "The Political Regime of the Islamic Republic of Iran in Comparative Perspective," *Government and Opposition* 36.1 (2001): 48–70; see also Mehdi Moslem, *Factional Politics in Post-Khomeini Iran* (Syracuse, NY: Syracuse University Press, 2002).

13. Nancy Fraser, "Rethinking the Public Sphere: A Contribution to the Critique of Actually Existing Democracy," *Social Text* 25.26 (1990): 56–80, 68.

14. Masserat Amir-Ebrahimi, "Weblogistan: The Emergence of a New Public Sphere in Iran," in *Publics, Politics, and Participation: Locating the Public Sphere in the Middle East and North Africa,* ed. Seteney Shami (New York: Social Science Research Council, 2009), 325–358; Annabelle Sreberny and Gholam Khiabany, *Blogistan: The Internet and Politics in Iran* (London, New York: I. B. Tauris, 2010).

15. Hossein Shahidi, *Journalism in Iran: From Mission to Profession* (London, New York: Routledge, 2007). The periods of freedom for the press include the years around the Constitutional Revolution at the beginning of the twentieth century, the interregnum after the abdication of Reza Shah (1941–1953), and the months after the fall of the monarchy in February 1979.

16. Gholam Khiabany and Annabelle Sreberny, "The Iranian Press and the Continuing Struggle over Civil Society 1998–2000," *Gazette* 6 (2001): 203–223; 215.

17. Farideh Farhi, "Improvising in Public: Transgressive Politics of the Reform Press in Postrevolutionary Iran," in *Intellectual Trends in Twentieth-Century Iran: A Critical Survey,* ed. Negin Nabavi (Gainesville: University Press of Florida, 2003), 147–179; 151.

18. Hamidreza Jalaeipour, *Dowlat-e penhan: Barresi-ye jamehshenakhti ava-mel-e tahdidkonandeh-ye jonbeshe eslahat* (The Hidden State: A Sociological Analysis of the Elements Menacing the Reform Movement) (Tehran: Tarh-e Now, 2000); Reza Veisi, "From 'Guerrilla Journalism' in Tehran to Exile Journalism in Prague," in *Election Fallout: Iran's Exiled Journalists on Their Struggle for Democratic Change,* ed. Marcus Michaelsen (Berlin: Hans Schiler, 2011), 174–189.

19. Interview, Tehran, May 3, 2005.

20. Sreberny and Khiabany, *Blogistan.*

21. Arash Ghafouri, "Setad 88: Iran's Greatest Campaign in Support of Mir-Hossein," in *Election Fallout: Iran's Exiled Journalists on their Struggle for Democratic Change,* ed. Marcus Michaelsen (Berlin: Hans Schiler Verlag, 2011), 50–61.

22. All these websites are no longer accessible.

23. "Khabarnameh gooya, soal-ha va javab-ha" (News Magazine Gooya: Questions and Answers), *Gooyanews,* July 15, 2005; "Daramad-ha hazineh-ha ra mipoushanand: Goft-o-gou ba Farshad Bayan" (The Returns Cover the Costs: A Conversation with Farshad Bayan), BBC Persian, March 12, 2004. Among the authors of Gooyanews were Abolhassan Banisadr, the first Iranian president after the revolution, now living in France; Akbar Ganji, an investigative reporter and dissident; and Masoud Behnood, a prominent journalist who had left Iran in 2002.

24. Interview (by email) with Hossein Bastani, editor of *Rooz*, October 20, 2007.

25. Mehdi Khalaji, *Through the Veil: The Role of Broadcasting in U.S. Public Diplomacy toward Iranians* (Washington, DC: The Washington Institute for Near East Policy, 2007); Paul Cochrane, "BBC Persian Television Launches," *Arab Media & Society* (Spring 2009): http://www.arabmediasociety.com/?article=716.

26. This was an initiative of the "godfather of Iranian blogs," Hossein Derakhshan, who had promoted blogging in Iran from September 2001 onward. Taking origin in a loosely connected grassroots network of bloggers and then spiralling up to the content of international media, the initiative anticipated the patterns of later social media campaigns for defending freedom of expression online, although on a smaller scale. See: "Shekast-e Mortazavi: doshanbeh hameh Emrouz khahim boud" (Defeating Mortazavi: Monday We Will Be All Emrouz), blog Sar-Darbir Khodam, September 13, 2004.

27. "Khaneh-ye ankabut" (The Spider's Web), Keyhan, September 29, 2004. The editorial's argumentation resembled the accusations that were brought forward against reformist politicians, intellectuals, and journalists during the show trials of August 2009 and the suppression of the election protests. Allegations published in the hardline newspaper *Keyhan* have often preceded procedures of the judiciary and the intelligence against all kinds of dissidents on the grounds outlined in the editorials. See also Iran Human Rights Documentation Center, "Ctrl+Alt+Delete: Iran's Response to the Internet," New Haven, 2009, http://www.iranhrdc.org/english/publications/reports/3157-ctrl-alt-delete-iran-039-s-response-to-the-internet.html; Iran Human Rights Documentation Center, "Forced Confessions: Targeting Iran's Cyber-Journalists," New Haven, 2009, http://www.iranhrdc.org/english/publications/reports/3159-forced-confessions-targeting-iran-s-cyber-journalists.html. Accusing critics to be part of a "fifth column," working against the established political order, and forcing them into confessions is a recurrent pattern in Iranian politics. See Ervand Abrahamian, *Tortured Confessions: Prisons and Public Recantations in Modern Iran* (Berkeley: University of California Press, 1999).

28. Interview with Mostafa Tajzadeh, Tehran, November 13, 2008. After the elections crisis of 2009, the website lost its archives when it had to change host and web address.

29. For a qualitative content analysis, all 331 articles that appeared on the website in the week of November 26 to December 3, 2006, were first assorted into thematic categories (e.g., economy, foreign affairs, media, domestic politics, etc.). By way of content abstraction, a total of 131 articles dealing with the elections were then further dissected into subcategories (e.g., significance of the elections, negotiations for a reform coalition, conservative disputes, etc.). A critical-interpretive analysis of key texts finally carved out central ideas and patterns of argumentation, which were clustered again according to particular frames.

30. "Fehrest-e eslahtaleban dar entekhabat-e showra-ha va chand nokteh-ye digar" (The Reformists' List for the Municipal Elections and Some Other Points), blog *Hanouz*, November 11, 2006.

31. Similar to the content analysis of the website *Emrouz*, the blogs were analyzed with a qualitative and critical-interpretive approach: starting from a few central blogs featured on *Emrouz*, a network of participants was identified through the links and comments in the blog entries. The texts were then broken down to topics and lines of argumentation. The background of the active bloggers was reconstructed from the information available on the blogs (only a few wrote under pseudonyms), and some of them were later interviewed.

32. John Kelly and Bruce Etling, *Mapping Iran's Online Public: Politics and Culture in the Persian Blogosphere* (Cambridge: Harvard University, Berkman Center for Internet and Society, 2008), 20.

33. Interviews with five bloggers, Tehran, November 9 and 14, 2008.

34. Interview, Tehran, November 9, 2008, and five blog entries in Herfeh and Khabarnegar between November 13 and December 8, 2006.

35. Interview, Tehran, November 14, 2008.

36. Interview, Tehran, November 14, 2008.

37. "Farda-ye entekhab" (Tomorrow's Choice), blog Daftarcheh-ye Mokhateb, December 14, 2006.

38. Ali Gheissari and Kaveh-Cyrus Sanandaji, "New Conservative Politics and Electoral Behavior in Iran," in *Contemporary Iran: Economy, Society, Politics,* ed. Ali Gheissari (New York: Oxford University Press, 2009), 275–298; Arjomand, *After Khomeini.*

39. Of course the websites had also the purpose to propagate political positions in society. The editor of the moderate conservative website *Arya News,* for instance, described the Internet as a bridge to the youth helping to carry the idea of the Islamic Republic into the next generation. Interview, Tehran, November 19, 2008.

40. Interview with a blogger and journalist in the newspaper *Kargozaran,* Tehran, November 7, 2008.

41. Hassan Rowhani initiated the publication of a news website, titled *Aftab* (Sun), in order to defend the approach of his negotiation team. Before the presidential elections of 2005, *Aftab* became a more complete news website and supported the candidacy of Hashemi Rafsanjani.

42. "Goft-o-gou ba masoulin-e Baztab" (A Conversation with the People in Charge of Baztab), *Gooyanews,* March 6, 2005; "Baztab, az aghaz ta polomb" (Baztab: From the Beginning until the Closure), Baztab, September 20, 2007; "Tahaqoq arezou-haye riyasat jomhouri va polomb-e daftar-e Baztab" (The Realization of the President's Dreams and the Closure of Baztab's Office), Baztab, September 22, 2007.

43. "Az sekteh-ye Ayatollah Tavasolli ta geriyeh-ye Hashemi" (From Ayatollah Tavasolli's Stroke to the Tears of Hashemi), *Rooz,* February 17, 2008.

44. "Fars, khabargozari mored ta'id-e nezam" (Fars, a News Agency Recognized by the System), *Rooz,* July 14, 2008; "Rasaneh-ye bartar-e jomhouri-ye eslami tavassot nezamiyan edareh mishevad" (The Elite Medium of the Islamic Republic Run by Militaries), *Rooz,* October 26, 2009.

45. Iran Human Rights Documentation Center, "Violent Aftermath: The 2009 Election and Repression of Dissent in Iran," New Haven, 2010, http://www.iranhrdc.org/english/publications/reports/3161-violent-aftermath-the-2009-election-and-suppression-of-dissent-in-iran.html.

46. Babak Rahimi, "The Agonistic Social Media: Cyberspace in the Formation of Dissent and Consolidation of State Power in Postelection Iran," *The Communication Review* 14 (2011): 158–178.

Chapter 6

The Persian Blogosphere in Dissent

Arash Falasiri and Nazanin Ghanavizi

"In solitude a dialogue always arises, because even in solitude there are always two."

—Hannah Arendt, *Denktagebuch*

On June 15, 2009, more than four million people took to the streets of Tehran to protest the June 12th presidential election results, perceived by many as rigged. This was the largest demonstration after the 1979 Islamic revolution, and the Internet, as an emerging public sphere, played a critical role in the street demonstrations that ultimately questioned the legitimacy of the Islamic Republic. Since 2009, the online sphere, blogging in particular, has played an important role for Iranians to express their views, thereby linking the Internet with democratic politics and the privileges of democratic speech and inclusion. The interesting aspect is the ways in which the Internet has contributed to a public space as a forum for more democratic deliberation in comparison with what is possible in the Iranian physical sphere. Certainly, if a government ensures space for its citizens to access a range of media outlets, discussions and communications can take the place of more democratic political forms. But democracy is only achieved when people know their rights and have sufficient capacity to understand and debate their common needs and interests. The distinct history and shape of the Internet in Iran, in many ways, provides an example through which we can consider the associations among blogs, free speech and protest, and the new salience of the Internet in relation to public reasoning and social protest.

This chapter focuses on the role of new media in improving public reasoning in countries where people have limited opportunities for publicly sharing and publishing their sociopolitical views. While there are discussions surrounding the idea of the Internet as a public sphere, we argue that, at least for a country like Iran, the Internet and blogging in particular have contributed greatly to the formation of public opinion.[1] In order to develop this argument, we address the case of the Iranian presidential election because it amply demonstrates the ways Iranians stood up for their civil rights and enhanced the prospect for democratic rule. While there is much debate about the democratic credentials of the Internet, the case of Iran underlines that the democratic credentials are highly context dependent. In other words, rather than generalizing the role of Internet in bringing about democracy, we will study how in the case of Iran it can open the path toward a democratic public sphere.

Internet as Public Sphere

One of the underpinning questions in the political discourse is the creation of a collective identity, a "we" to which an appeal can be made when faced with the problem of deciding between alternative courses of action. This sense of plurality emerges only in the public realm and requires a mutual understanding of society's needs and interests by its citizens. In this respect, modern political theory benefits from ideas of public sphere and the political to analyze how these concepts work in today's politics. The political for Hannah Arendt is a specific sphere of life that emerges only in the public realm. She argues that the public realm should be conceived as separate from both the private and the social. Rather, it is the public that is home to the political. It is merely in the realm of the political that men appear before one another in a way that underscores the individuality of each while also affirming their shared world.[2] For Arendt, action is "the only activity that goes on directly between men without the intermediary of things or matter, corresponds to the human condition of plurality, to the fact that men, not Man, live on the earth and inhabit the world. While all aspects of the human condition are somehow related to politics, this plurality is specifically the condition of all political life."[3] Arendt asserts that action is only possible in the political and not in any other realms of human life.[4] She stresses the importance of public sphere and explains with the following:

The emergence of society from the shadowy interior of the household into the light of the public sphere, has not only blurred the old borderline between private and political, it has also changed almost beyond recognition the meaning of the two terms and their significance for the life of the individual and the citizen. Not only would we not agree with the Greeks that a life spent in the privacy of "one's own" (idion), outside the world of the common, is "idiotic" by definition, or with the Romans to whom privacy offered but a temporary refuge from the business of the res publica; we call private today a sphere of intimacy whose beginnings we may be able to trace back to late Roman, though hardly to any period of Greek antiquity, but whose peculiar manifoldness and variety were certainly unknown to any period prior to the modern age.[5]

For Arendt, the public sphere ensures the autonomy of the political for citizen action.

The public sphere is composed of two dimensions that are interrelated though drastically different. The first is the *space of appearance*, a space of political freedom and equality that emerges only when members of society act in concert through the medium of speech and persuasion. The second is the *common world*, which is conceived as a shared and public world of human artifacts, institutions and settings that distinguishes us from nature and provides a permanent condition for our activities. Arendt considers both dimensions crucial for the practice of citizenship: space of appearance provides the necessary spaces for emergence and growth of citizenship, and the common world provides a stable background from which public spheres of action and deliberation may emerge. Arendt suggests that the condition for citizenship in the modern world depends on both the improvement of a common, shared world and the creation of numerous spaces of appearance in which individuals can reveal their identities and establish relations of solidarity. Identity construction is a continuous process of negotiation in which actors articulate cultural and political concepts.

Carl Schmitt is another theorist who emphasizes the importance of the political realm. He argues that the condition for a political community's existence is a group of people who are willing to engage in political life by distinguishing themselves from outsiders. He maintains that a completely de-politicized world would only encourage human beings to enhance consumption and amuse themselves with modern entertainment. It would reduce politics to a value-neutral technique for the provision of material amenities. Consequently, individuals would not have values to give life meaning beyond the satisfaction of private desires.[6]

Jürgen Habermas argues that public spaces constitute an aspect of civil society by providing citizens with opportunities to form critical reasoning skills, which promote free speech and other democratic rights. This element of civil society is also predominantly seen as contrary to hegemonic interests. Mark Poster states that the Habermasian public sphere "is formed within civil society that fosters resistance to formal institutes of the state."[7] In the modern world, other forms, including media, that arguably isolate citizens from each other rather than bringing them together, have largely replaced the classic forms of public space. However, the same degree of isolation is not applicable to all modes of modern media. If television and radio diminish critical reasoning by their unidirectional dissemination of news and information, the Internet, at least in part and in potential, provides users with spaces for interaction that may support the formation of critical reasoning. Although Habermas does not consider the Internet as such a public space, he suggests that "the symbolic structures of every lifeworld are reproduced through three processes: cultural tradition, social integration, and socialization," and such symbolic structures can certainly be deployed to consider the relations between the Internet and the public sphere.[8]

Theorists like Downey and Fenton argue that the public sphere cannot be considered a public media arena, but rather a series of overlapping spaces for the dissemination, diffusion, and deliberation of information.[9] Mitzi Waltz also argues that the Internet is such a space because it connects its users to websites and discussion groups, which provide them various webs of information.[10] The cyber public sphere, as a plural sphere, provides its users with a broad range of publics, which expose them to greater social diversity.

The Internet allows mobility from one public to another easy, fast, and cheap for its users, and this inclusion improves the propensity of participants to engage in discussions in different publics. It also satisfies the need for multiple public spaces through which participants can engage in different publics that are convergent to their interests. It matters too that no participant in online discussion is restricted to only one interest, one community, or one public; the potential to focus on different interests further encourages engagement with multiple publics. Another important factor that helps to improve engagement in cyber publics is the absence of any physical dimensions in personal interaction. In other words, while participants may not actively participate in certain offline publics due to social, political, economic, or spatial restrictions, they might participate online more freely, encouraged by the openness that anonymity allows, the degree to which social placement by appearance and demeanor is limited online, and cheap rates for communication over great distances.

The Blogosphere

In light of suppression of speech and tight state control of the press and other broadcast media industries over the last three decades in Iran, blogging in recent years has provided Iranians with a unique opportunity to express themselves. Although one of the crucial issues in "Internet Studies" is consideration of the limitations of Internet access and the skills needed for both Internet use and blogging, in the Iranian case these limitations are slight compared to the tight control of other forms of media in relation to the articulation of individual and community interests.

ISPs opened for business in Iran in 1994, establishing organized systems providing Internet connection. After just one decade, in its March 2004 report, TCI claimed that there were 684 active ISPs serving five million Internet users in 331 cities in Iran.[11] The Internet access that ISPs were offering was appreciated in varying ways by almost all sectors of society. Business people, students, academics, intellectuals, and everyday people soon started to include the Internet in their daily lives. One of the most dramatic and visible signs of this inclusion was the integration of computer skills into widespread systems already in place for learning English. The high speed of the Internet in Iran at the time of its inception, together with its low price, were key factors underpinning its popularity. In Iran, blogging reached a high popularity in 2004, the year that is also called "the year of blogs" throughout the world.[12] At this point, the number of Internet users in Iran grew at an extraordinary pace, with an average annual rate of approximately 48 percent, increasing from under one million Internet users in 2005 to around twenty-three million in 2008.[13]

Crucial factors affecting Iranians' appreciation of these new technologies are the nation's fairly high rate of literacy—77 percent—and high education levels. As university students, members of Iran's youth population were provided with Internet access and personal email addresses at their universities. Free participation in online chat rooms in university computer labs proved a strong starting point for the rise in the number of computer-literate, educated young people. This particular demographic also has a high unemployment rate due to economic problems including U.S. sanctions and Iran's limited political and economic relationships with developed countries.

In consequence, the Internet boom period in Iran was increasingly led by an educated and computer-literate young generation with considerable time to engage with platforms to express and communicate, not the least of which was their growing criticism of the social, political, and economic failures of the Iranian government. Another crucial point contributing to escalating Internet use in Iran, one which also stems from the higher education rate, is the fact that many Iranian university students who were not originally from the big cities returned to their home towns after completing education.[14] Most of these graduates, who had become accustomed to using the Internet during their student days, made efforts to remain connected. They introduced the people of their communities, including in the rural areas, to the possibilities of the Internet.

As has been observed in many other countries, the Internet provided Iranians of various backgrounds, including those residing outside of the country, with an opportunity to express their political views free from numerous restrictions that hindered their activities in "real" or offline life. Today, Iranians around the world participate in this virtual public space as a way to find broader scope for discussion and receive audience for in expressing their ideas. Given that public conflict and even debate between the reformists and conservatives has always been suppressed by the Islamic state, a repressive history that predates the revolution, the relative difficulty in censoring the Internet continues to add immense value and opportunity to the political lives of every day Iranians.

The first Iranians to participate in such online debate were the journalists and writers, who began writing about issues that they could not discuss in other public media forums, at times not even at private gatherings. In 2002, while still working in more traditional media industries within Iran, pro-reformist journalists such as Omid Memarian and Roozbeh Mirebrahimi, who were writing for *Hayat-e-No* and *Etemad* at that time, were among the first writers to participate in the Iranian blogosphere. Then emerged the blogs. Former journalist Hossein Derakhshan largely popularized Iranian blogging in November 2001, when he published using the free site blogger.com on how to blog in Persian.[15] Within a few months, the first free blog service, PersianBlog.ir, appeared, initiated by three young engineers in Tehran. In less than a year, it had more than one hundred thousand blogs in Persian.[16] Similar services followed, including BlogFa, Mihanblog, Blogsky, and Parsiblog, all started in 2004. The rapid growth of blogging came as no surprise to its founders. Derakhshan discussed the reasons behind the popularity of blogging in his Interview with *Wired* Magazine in 2003:

> The blogs show that [Iranians] are carrying new values and pro-
> moting new lifestyles. Older generations try to hide their personal
> feelings and opinions from others. Individuality, self-expression
> and tolerance are new values which are quite obvious through
> a quick study of the content of Persian weblogs.[17]

By using blogs anonymously, journalists, writers, and intellectuals began to share ideas with the general public. Today, bloggers challenge the strategies of the state in the most strident way possible. They even question the legitimacy of the Islamic Republic itself. In a country where the state does not tolerate dissent in any form and reformist newspapers are banned one after the other, journalists and intellectuals increasingly opt to write blogs.

Iranians use the blogosphere to communicate, deliberate, and exchange ideas on a variety of concepts related to their daily and political lives. This is the form of deliberation on matters of common concern that both Jürgen Habermas and Chantal Mouffe address in that these exchanges invite others to participate in the formation of public opinion. Mouffe and Ernesto Laclau concur that public opinion is not objectively there to be found.[18] Rather, it is something that should be constructed through articulation. While it is not expected that all members of the online public will make useful claims, through free access to debate and the formation of public opinion, they can participate in the political articulations that overcome state hegemony by making alternative forms of common sense available.

Iranian online activities, especially blogging, have enhanced the public's ability to question the ideologies imposed on them by the Iranian state. While journalists, intellectuals, and experts challenge the current attitudes of the state as well as representing different cultural, social, economical, and political events around the country, a deliberative process is possible precisely because there is also a considerable number of bloggers supporting the state. Moreover, the standard format of the blog inevitably invites audiences to participate. Understanding the significance of these practices is not just a matter of measuring Internet access and Internet literacy. Everyone who reads blogs and online news and discussions becomes an agent within the blogosphere, with the opportunity to participate in the circulation of these discussions online and within a broader community of family and friends.

The most significant role of the blogosphere is the promotion of public awareness in ways that could have the potential to overcome state-based hegemony and propaganda. The circulation of voices and ideas on blogs is comparable not only to the mobile gatherings of Iranian taxi passengers, but also to Habermas's portrayal of eighteenth-century coffee houses. In *Transformation of the Public Sphere*, Habermas argues that this was a novel form of association in which private individuals entered into an enjoyable, exploratory companionship, free from the observance of rigid political ties.[19] Drawing on Habermas, Harry Boyte and Kathryn Stoff Hogg highlight the importance of private social actors articulating ideas and news to the formation of public opinion, suggesting that "released from old unities, the new solidarity of private persons has to constitute itself as a public fashioned out of information and opinions."[20] In the process of public opinion formation, the ease with which blogs can be authored anonymously, under pseudonyms, or even with invented or multiple identities, can empower diverse forms of expression, normally restricted in other contexts. The fact that readers can also respond in selectively public identities means that these deliberations can take place in a more general or common voice, hence underscoring the formation of a civic environment that citizens inhabit.

A study of the events during the 2009 presidential election period in Iran shows how the online media, and blogging practices in particular, raised political awareness and promoted collective action for civic change. The postelection period, which saw millions of Iranians taking the streets of Iran's cities, was not only a shock to the Iranian regime but also to the international community. For the first time in more than thirty years after the revolution, Iranians reacted to the political system of the Islamic Republic in very contentious ways. The protestors, many from the younger segment of the population, emerged to show their dissatisfaction with the regime in an organized manner. The question that eventually emerged afterward was how and when the protestors organized action in light of the tight state control over the public sphere? With police presence in major public spaces, it would not have been easy to take to the streets in an organized manner just hours after the results of the presidential election were revealed. In the classical form of revolutionary uprisings, not enough time was available to organize such a huge crowd across the country. However, for those who had followed Iranian online sphere, the answer was clear.

Since the early 2000s, the online sphere, and blogging in particular, has become important to Iranians as a contentious site, wherein self-expression occurs, thereby linking the Internet with democratic politics and the privileges of democratic speech and inclusion. Early in 2004, the growing popularity of the Internet and the rise of blogging encouraged Iranians to discuss various aspects of their sociopolitical life. In this respect, what the 2009 postelection protests revealed was a consequence of years in active deliberation in the emerging Internet domains as a new public sphere. Dur-

ing the presidential campaign, the number of blogs grew, and Iranians started sharing and discussing campaign news from both sides. The transnational
nature of the online sphere meant that discussions and news of the Iranian
campaigns by bloggers and their blogs, along with other online venues,
transcended geographical boundaries, a transnational process that inspired
large numbers of expatriate Iranians to participate in the election as well.

Ahmadinejad's victory shocked the Iranian public. Many took to the
streets in protest, concerned that the election had been rigged. Iran's defeated
presidential candidate, Mir-Hossein Mousavi, called for demonstrations on
his website. Within minutes, with the help of link-sharing websites hosted
by Iranians residing outside of the country, many Iranians were made aware
of the planned protests. The thousands of protestors who showed up to
demonstrate did so despite the fact that the rallies were organized extremely
quickly online, a process that had a tremendous outcome for Internet activism in Iran. Given that the Internet was Mousavi's only outlet, since the
old media was under the control of the state, the circulation of announcements for popular protest was thus conducted almost solely online. Once
released online, the call for action would then circulate by word of mouth
and mobile text messages.

The reaction from the state was a repressive one. The Basij, the vol-
unteer militia force, swept the streets and arrested protestors. The majority
of international journalists were expelled from the country at the beginning
of this conflict, and the rest were forced to leave in the following days.
Official Iranian media did not make mention of the demonstrations and
police violence, and President Mahmoud Ahmadinejad even claimed that
the people in the streets were there to celebrate his success. At this stage,
something extraordinary started to develop for the first time. In the post-
election media reportage vacuum, citizen journalism emerged as a norm in
the form of political contestation with the manifestation of a visual critical
discourse against state power. With the inability to provide media reports
on the events, citizen journalism confirmed Lynda Lee Kaid's and Christina
Holtz-Bacha's definition of which underscored "a move toward openness of
information; horizontal structure of news gathering and news telling; blurred
lines between content production and use; and diffused accountability based
more on reputation and meaning than on structural system hierarchies."[21]
While many Iranians were quite active online before the election and during the presidential campaign, at this crucial juncture blogs and online
sites became the only reliable source for international media, seeking information about the developments in the protest activities. With high levels
of telecommunication activity in Iran, especially among the large number

of Iranians who own mobile phones, it became commonplace for citizens to document the unfolding events. This recorded information was then broadcast online. From June 16 onward, all street-demonstrations, including activities of police and militias, and also declarations by reformist leaders, were recorded and distributed to the international community as vlogging (video blogging) became popular. A crucial result of this activity was citizen documentation of events and critical commentaries that they promoted through the circulation of photos and videos. This gave credibility to blog discussions of unfolding events in Iran during the first days after the election, which provided international media with credible and visual sources, and also a public sphere of critical thinking amid the street-level protests.

When the state realized the extent of the Internet's social impact, the attempt to control the information flow became evident. While a grassroots blog movement developed in the postelection period, the state reacted by creating a budget for online activity, a process that involved the employment of members of the Revolutionary Guards and the Basij to blog daily and promote pro-regime ideologies and hardliners like Ahmadinejad. They also monitored and reported developments in the Iranian blogosphere, a practice that could be identified as surveillance blogging. During this time, approximately five million websites, social networks such as Facebook, and blogs were filtered, and many dissident bloggers were imprisoned. The war between the state's sophisticated information filter against Iranians and non-Iranians trying to cross that filter wages on.

Since 2009, the popularity of blogging has decreased. Through state-filtering practices, arrests, torture, and even the execution of dissident bloggers, the form and nature of blogging has changed among Iranians. While a large number of students, activists, and intellectuals used to update their blogs on a weekly basis, there are considerable numbers of blogs that have not been updated for months. Yet a broad question remains to be answered: Has the passion of bloggers for online dialogue faltered due to political repression? Are Iranian bloggers afraid of self-expression?

To be sure, one dimension could be explained in terms of threats that some activist bloggers have faced from state repression, especially since 2009. In the aftermath of elections, when the state suppressed the street protests, the number of active blogs also began to fall. While Internet speed has decreased, making it harder and more time-consuming to post a blog entry, so has the ability to blog on a daily basis.

However, the main reason for the apparent decline of blogging practices can be found in the effect of social networks as a new platform for self-expression and critical discourse. More and more Iranians have turned to social networks such as Facebook and Twitter. And while Twitter was an effective tool to post rapid-fire updates on the situation on the ground during the protests, it did not sufficiently replace blogging. The character limit precluded most of the discussion and in-depth criticism that had given the blogosphere its strength. The number of Iranians in the country joining Facebook increased dramatically after the 2009 incidents, in spite of the government's intermittent blocks of the site. For many, Facebook became an important tool for finding their favorite writers and bloggers and tracking their activity. Like the blogosphere, Facebook has enabled its users to discuss daily matters and have a dialogue with others. Like the blogosphere, Facebook also provides its Iranian users with a forum for democratic discussion. In some ways, social media proved preferable to the blogosphere as a tool to efficiently and securely coordinate action among like-minded users.

Consequently, many bloggers opted to use Facebook in lieu of private blogs. For example, Touka Neyestani, a famous Iranian cartoonist and popular blogger, chose Facebook for the better control it provided him over who can read and comment on his posts. Another reason bloggers have migrated to Facebook is security. The Islamic regime's cyber agents can more easily hack and alter private blogs as opposed to Facebook pages. Indeed, the past few years have witnessed the growing threat of government cyber attacks. For many Iranian bloggers, Facebook is a more secure option. Facebook also made it easier for bloggers and users to efficiently connect with like-users through public fan pages. It also allows users to enlarge their networks through link sharing, which was previously achieved through separate websites such as Balatarin.com and Gooya.com. Facebook provided Iranians with numerous online facilities on one page. This is particularly important when one keeps in mind the low Internet speed. Thus, Facebook, as a single website with multiple purposes, has made it much easier and faster to read news, post blogs, and socialize.

As much as it has affected Iranians' lives politically, the Internet has also had significant impact on the state by intervening in the organization of news media. From the beginning, the state viewed the Internet as an arena for modernization; the problem, however, lies in an authoritarian state's inability to fully restrict the Internet's openness. With the increasing popularity of dissident websites, blogs, and social networks such as Facebook, the state became concerned that its political ideology had become undermined in the Persian cyberspace. Recognizing the popularity of the personal websites of dissident figures like Ayatollah Hossein-Ali Montazeri,[22] many state figures, including the Supreme Leader and former president, Ahmadinejad, established personal websites to disseminate opinions, publications, and memoirs in favor of state power.[23] Just as the government ran satellite channels in many languages, such as Press TV, to promote a friendlier picture of the regime, so it began to launch news websites targeting a global audience. In December 2012, Ayatollah Khamenei joined Facebook, which came as a shock to many Iranian users. This was an indicator of Facebook's popularity in the Iranian public sphere, which it seems the state has come to realize as well.

Although the first public access in Iran, as in other countries, belonged to an academic space, the strategic potential of the Internet as a tool for public diplomacy was not overlooked. Antony Loewenstein explains: "Developed within the university system, the Internet was initially promoted by the regime as a way to prove the country's technological prowess in the years that followed the Iran–Iraq war."[24] Thus unlike many other electronic devices, such as video players and satellite television networks, the Internet was generally received as of possible use to the state and was thus acceptable to Islamic Iran.

In fact, one of the state's major attempts to manage media was the engagement with cyberspace. The Islamic Republic News Agency (IRNA) was pioneering in its contribution to the online sphere in 1996. On March 23, 1997, it opened its own website and wowed its audience with the range of news provided online.[25] Shortly after, many conservative newspapers (such as *Kayhan* and *Iran*) launched their own websites.[26] Other newspapers soon followed suit, publishing news daily online. Fars News, a government news agency linked to the Revolutionary Guards, is an example of the state's attempt to distort news on Iran. The website actively spreads censored, pro-regime news in Farsi, English, Arabic, and Turkish. Websites such as these have become another tool for the government to control the flow and content of information. A recent example is the coverage of Asghar Farhadi's speech after his film *A Separation* won an Oscar. While Farhadi had dedicated the prize to the "peace loving people of Iran," Fars News published it as a dedication to "a peace loving people whose only demand is having a peaceful nuclear power." This was on the website for about two hours, only to be removed after significant outrage was expressed on the site's commentary section.[27]

What is clear to all those who follow Iranian politics online, as well as the politics of the online world, the power struggle continues over the Internet, as Iranians increasingly pursue their political activities in the digital sphere. The passion among Iranians for exchanging ideas is alive and well, and, given the events of June 2009, so is the faith in the outcome of deliberation that can be convened through Internet access.

Notes

1. James Bohman, "Expanding Dialogue: The Internet, the Public Sphere, and Prospects for Transnational Democracy," *The Sociological Review*, v.52, (2004): 131–155.

2. Hannah Arendt, *The Human Condition* (Chicago: University of Chicago Press, 1958), 57.

3. Ibid., 7.

4. Ibid., 178.

5. Ibid., 38.

6. Carl Schmitt, *The Concept of the Political* (Chicago: University of Chicago Press, 2007), 35, 57–58.

7. Mark Poster, *Information Please: Culture and Politics in the Age of Digital Machines* (Durham, NC: Duke University Press, 2006), 63.

8. Jürgen Habermas, *The Theory of Communicative Action* (Boston: Beacon Press, 1984), 102.

9. John Downey and Natalie Fenton, "New Media, Counter Publicity, and the Public Sphere," *New Media and Society* 5.2 (2003): 185–202.

10. Mitzi Waltz, *Alternative and Activist Media* (Edinburgh: Edinburgh University Press, 2005), 89.

11. See "Middle East Internet Users," http://www.Internetworldstats.com/stats5.htm#me; Telecommunication Company of Iran, "TCI at a Glance," http://www.tci.ir/eng.asp?sm=0&page=18&code=1 (accessed June 16, 2008).

12. Axel Bruns and Joanne Jacobs, *Uses of Blogs* (New York: Peter Lang, 2006).

13. Internet World Stats available at: http://www.Internetworldstats.com/stats.htm.

14. Babak Rahimi, "The Politics of the Internet in Iran," in *Media, Culture and Society in Iran: Living with Globalization and the Islamic State*, ed. Mehdi Semati (London: Routledge, 2008), 41.

15. In early September 2001 the first Persian blog was published by Salman Jariri. Hossein Derakhshan published his in late September of the same year. Derakhshan published his manual on writing blogs in Persian in response to his readers' requests.

16. Dan Gillmor, *We the Media: Grassroots Journalism by the People, for the People* (Sebastopol: O'Reilly, 2004), 141.

17. Michelle Delio, "Blogs Opening Iranian Society?" July 21, 2009. http://www.wired.com/culture/lifestyle/news/2003/05/58976?currentPage=all (accessed August 13, 2012).

18. Ernesto Laclau and Chantal Mouffe, *Hegemony and Socialist Strategy: Towards a Radical Democratic Politics* (London: Verso, 1985).

19. Alessa Johns, *Women's Utopias of the Eighteenth Century* (Urbana: University of Illinois Press, 2003), 17.

20. Harry C. Boyte and Kathryn Stoff Hogg, *Doing Politics: An Owner's Manual for Public Life* (Minneapolis: Project Public Life, University of Minnesota, 1992), 343.

21. Lynda Lee Kaid and Christina Holtz-Bacha, *Encyclopedia of Political Communication* (Thousand Oaks, CA: Sage, 2008), 1: 105.

22. Ayatollah Hossein-Ali Montazeri was a dissident cleric, formerly a deputy to Ayatollah Khomeini, who was exiled to his house in the religious city of Qom for criticizing the ideology of Velayat-e Faqih (Guardianship of Jurisprudence) and thus the very foundations of the Islamic state. His online publication of books, pamphlets, interviews, and memoirs in Persian, English, and French shocked Islamic conservatives.

23. See Ahmadinejad's blog (http://www.ahmadinejad.ir/) and Khamenei's blog (http://english.khamenei.ir/).

24. Antony Loewenstein, *The Blogging Revolution* (Carlton: Melbourne University Press, 2008), 35.

25. See Iran, IRNA, http://www5.irna.ir/ (accessed March 2012).

26. See Iran, *Kayhan* News website (www.kayhannews.com) and *Iran* website (www.iran.com).

27. http://english2.farsnews.com/farsnews.php The editor at Fars News removed the news on Farhadi two hours after publication due to the number of comments from readers indicating Fars News' article was not accurate.

Chapter 7

The Politics and Anti-Politics of Facebook in Context of the Iranian 2009 Presidential Elections and Beyond

Mohammad Sadeghi Esfahlani

The Iranian tenth presidential elections, held on June 12, 2009, have been among the most controversial elections in the history of the country. While Iran's hostile position toward the West after the 1979 revolution has ever since contributed to its isolation on the international stage, concerns over the Iranian nuclear program, particularly the progress in nuclear enrichment technology in the past decade, has pushed Iran into the center of international attention.

Just a day before the presidential elections in 2009, opposition candidate Mir-Hossein Mousavi, in an interview with Al Jazeera of the English news channel, openly announced that Iran would definitely engage in direct talks with the United States, thereby indicating a possible change in the course of Iran's foreign policy and thus in its future position in international politics.[1] At the time of his interview, Mousavi's campaign had developed into a "fast-cresting popular movement known as the Green Wave" within just a few weeks. However, the dispute over the rushed official results in favor of the incumbent president Ahmadinejad and the subsequent events surged the Green Wave into "a tsunami of protest that transfixed the world."[2]

About three months earlier, on January 19, 2009—the inauguration day of President Obama—I decided to register a Facebook page for Mousavi, whom I believed to be the most proficient opposition candidate and the most capable to successfully run against the incumbent president

Ahmadinejad. At that time, social media technology, and particularly the social networking site Facebook, had been celebrated for having transformed the power dynamics of politics in the U.S. presidential election 2008 by means of empowering grassroots and utilizing youth participation,[3] thereby paving the way for the first "social media president."[4] Later, in early 2011 and with the unfolding of the Arab Spring, the term "Facebook Revolution" was coined for uprisings that toppled authoritarian rulers in Tunisia and Egypt.[5] Considering the importance ascribed to the role of social media technology in facilitating these dynamics on an international level, and particularly in context of Middle Eastern politics, this chapter seeks to illuminate the role of Facebook in the events that led to the 2009 presidential elections and the subsequent events that transformed the campaign dynamics into a social movement.

For this purpose, a set of theoretical literature on the politics of technology, social networks, and social movements will be reviewed in order to generate propositions about the political implications of social media technology, particularly the political implications of social networking sites. These propositions will be compared to empirical evidence about the role of Facebook in the Iranian 2009 presidential elections and the subsequent events associated with the Iranian Green Movement; these evidences include a narrative of my personal observations as the founder and head administrator of Mousavi's Facebook campaign, substantiated by references to contemporary news articles of major Western news organizations about relevant events, demonstrations, and related videos posted on Facebook and YouTube, as well as Facebook statistics demonstrating virtual interactions with Mousavi's Facebook page. The goal of this comparison is to test the theoretical propositions against the relation between virtual interactions with Mousavi's Facebook page and actual demonstrations as well as other forms of collective action related to Mousavi's election campaign during the time leading to the elections and subsequent protests.

Technology and Politics in Literature

The notion of politics in a technological context originates from the critical perspective of Langdon Winner; in a critical study of the relationship between technology and society, Winner has introduced the idea of autonomous technologies—that is, technological developments that "outpace the capacity of individuals and social systems to adapt"[6]—as a significant new theme in contemporary political thought. In a later article, Winner has specified the notion of politics as "arrangements of power and authority in human associations as well as the activities that take place within those arrangements."[7]

In Winner's view, technologies are either "ways of building order in our world" or a "political phenomenon in their own right."[8] The most obvious example of such technologies is the atom bomb, which has been specified by Winner as an *inherently political artifact* possessing intractable lethal properties that require a particular pattern of power and authority: "a centralized, rigidly hierarchical chain of command closed to all influences that might make its workings unpredictable."[9] Inherently political artifacts thus induce such an authoritative pattern upon their respective sociopolitical context. Other examples discussed by Winner concern technologies that have a range of flexibility in their material form that enable certain social actors to influence their design and arrangement and inscribe them with features that would (re)produce specific patterns of power and authority in a given sociopolitical context. Bridge height in the urban planning of the early twentieth-century New York design, for instance, has been suggested to be a feature that excludes low-income social groups from accessing Long Island through public transportation. Furthermore, untested molding machines in a late nineteenth-century reaper manufacturing plant in Chicago have been argued to be a strategic bargain in the battle of the owner with the National Union of Iron Molders.[10]

However, the political qualities of technologies as discussed by Winner are inscribed features in the *context of design*, in "technical arrangements that precede the use of the things in question."[11] Political qualities evoked by the *context of use*, however, remain unexplored in this study. Thus Winner's perspective has been criticized and labeled as an "intentionalist" perspective in science, technology and sociological studies, in that technologies are considered to be carriers of the intention of privileged actors who in turn seek to arrange and rearrange power and authority toward their own favor.[12]

Social media technologies are a relatively recent phenomenon. As a subset of the Internet, the technological development of social media seems to be most influenced by demand factors, which acted as a pulling force upon markets that were saturated by technological innovations in the era of the "dot-com bubble." In a study about innovation theory paradigms from 1995, the latest trend in theorizing technological innovations has been described as the strategic paradigm with a focus on demand factors pulling technological innovations in saturated markets.[13] In order to discover the implications of the social media technology for the arrangements of power and authority, the following section will introduce the notion of social capital and the political economy of social networks and discuss their interrelation.

Social Media Technology, Social Capital, and Social Networks

The term *social media* has been coined along with the emergence of MySpace and Facebook in the early 2000s, and gained prominence as a result of the diffusion of high-speed Internet access. Social media has been defined as "a group of Internet-based applications that build on the ideological and technological foundations of Web 2.0 and allow the creation and exchange of user generated content (UGC)—various forms of media content that are publicly available and created by end-users."[14] Facebook has been categorized in social media research as a social networking site (SNS), a type of social media offering a high degree of self-representation and self-disclosure by allowing the revelation of personal information and relative control over other people's impressions about oneself; it also offers a medium degree of social presence and media richness, enhancing intimacy and synchronicity of social relations.[15]

In the most frequently cited article on social networking sites, boyd and Ellison have emphasized the uniqueness of SNSs to be enabling users to "articulate and make visible their social networks."[16] Another study argues that the key factor leading to Facebook's popularity is its core functionality of generating an inherently synchronous and dynamic social experience through its "news feed" function, thereby enhancing social relations.[17] Similarly, in a small-scale quantitative study, which investigated the relationship between the use of Facebook and the formation and maintenance of social capital through surveys, results indicated that while the use of the Internet alone did not predict the accumulation of social capital, "intensive use of Facebook did."[18] In particular, the "bridging" aspect of social capital—that is, the formation of loose connections referred to as "weak ties" in network studies—has been argued to be significantly facilitated through the use of Facebook.[19]

Bourdieu and Wacquant define the notion of social capital as "the sum of the resources, actual or virtual, that accrue to an individual or a group by virtue of possessing a durable network of more or less institutionalized relationships of mutual acquaintance and recognition."[20] In this definition, the notion of networks plays a pivotal role for the assembly of social capital, which is an accumulation of relationships between individuals and groups, a point that is also expanded in Chapter 1 of this volume. In the study of networks, the strength of weak ties has been conceptualized as the primary facilitator of novel information acting as a bridge between different clusters of a social network. Social structure that has the form of networks has been argued to affect economic outcomes beyond the influence of institutional structures, implying a political significance of social networks in the arrangements of power and authority.[21] Mark Granovetter argues that social networks facilitate a sense of trust that others in the network will "do the 'right' thing despite a clear balance of incentives to the contrary,"[22] by enhancing the flow of information and facilitating a system of reward and punishment deviating from institutionalized norms of the economy.

The most important influencing factors according to Granovetter are the strong ties that influence the network density—that is, the "unique paths along which information, ideas and influence can travel between any two nodes"[23]—and the weak ties through which novel and nonredundant information flows; whereas strong ties make a social network dense and cohesive, thereby fostering collective action, the strength of weak ties is a key property for facilitating the access to more novel information and allowing information to flow between isolated clusters.[24] Thus, the political property of Facebook—a social networking site that has been pulled by social demands throughout its technological development—seems to support the accumulation process of social capital. The literature suggests that Facebook would particularly facilitate the bridging aspect of social capital, thereby enabling different clusters of social networks to bridge, novel information to flow, and collective action to be facilitated outside of the institutional context of political authority.

Collective Action, Collective Identity, and New Social Movements

Collective action is a central theme in the study of social movements. Particularly, the process through which collective action is "framed" has been considered "a central dynamic in understanding the character and course of social movements." The notion of "framing" in this context has been understood by social movement scholars as "signifying work or meaning construction" and described as "an active, procedural phenomenon that implies agency and contention at the level of reality construction."[25]

The initial and core task in the framing process of collective action is "diagnostic framing"; this task involves reaching a consensus regarding the problem and its source. Thereupon, a solution is articulated through the "prognostic framing task" and the "motivational framing task," resembling a final "call to arms" for the exercise of collective action.[26] Another theme in the study of new social movements is collective identity and its construction process. Throughout this process, personal identities of movement participants have been argued to enhance with a collective aspect that includes "shared meanings" that become common through various "framing mechanisms."[27] The notion of collective identity has been employed in context of "new social movements" to account for the cultural process that is essential to the formation of shared meanings and interests beyond the concept of structural interest, such as in institutions and social classes.[28]

Collective identity has been characterized as a way of "transform[ing] the institutional political playing field."[29] From this perspective, when social networks enroll in a framing process toward becoming a social movement, the outcome of this process would be a collective identity that is recognized to have a power position in the political context, mainly acquired by strategies of symbolic association.[30] This part of the process has also been referred to as the "influence process" or the "sociopsychological process" of "identity amplification," which transforms the personal identities of movement participants.[31] This part is essential for the framing process of collective action, particularly for the prognostic and diagnostic framing tasks.

The framing process of a collective identity affects the ability of a social group—or a social network cluster—to recruit members and gain recognition.[32] However, "without structural factors that would expose the individual to participation opportunities and pull them into activity, the individual would remain inactive."[33] Similarly, a study about the influence of social interaction on political participation has provided evidence for the kinship of political participation and the amount of political discussion that occurs in social networks. The effect of informal interactions in social networks has been explicitly distinguished from the effects of formal interaction in social groups, and informal social interaction has been argued to influence political participation beyond the effects of formal groups.[34] Therefore, Facebook can be understood to provide an essential structural facilitation for accumulating social capital for an emerging collective identity and for linking it to collective action in new social movements.

Related studies and relevant theoretical literature as reviewed have emphasized the political implications of collective action in context of social movements. In addition to the framing process of a social movement, structural factors, particularly in social networks, can be expected to have a significant impact on the mobilization process of collective action. Facebook, the most prominent social networking site in the technological realm of social media, can be thus expected to support the accumulation of social capital for a collective identity, particularly by facilitating the bridging of social capital through reinforcing the strength of weak ties in social networks.

The structural facilitation provided by Facebook, therefore, can be expected to have empowering properties, particularly for grassroots and novel campaigns. Facebook would compensate the cohesion of social networks by providing additional paths for a synchronous flow of information between individuals. While such strong ties would also empower institutional relations, the flexible structure of social networks would benefit significantly from the strength of weak ties; supported by the bridging capacity of Facebook, weak ties empower social networks by facilitating the flow of novel information—particularly during the influence process of reaching a consensus with regards to the meanings related to the collective identity—in diagnostic and prognostic tasks. Furthermore, by exposing a wider range of individuals from different network clusters to opportunities for collective action, Facebook can be expected to facilitate framing tasks for mobilizing collective action, particularly outside of the institutional context.

In sum, Facebook seems to have rather displacing properties for established arrangements of power and authority, as captured in the notion of anti-politics in the title of this chapter; it seems to support the recognition of new collective identities and the mobilization of collective action by reinforcing social relations that are less established and institutionalized, thereby creating a sense of trust in collective action that contrasts with systems of reward and punishment established by the political authority or regime. In this light, the next section of this chapter will provide an analysis of my observations from the events related to the Iranian 2009 presidential elections, using the theoretical lens that has been developed throughout this section, and will compare the outcomes to the theoretical propositions. Besides a narrative based on my personal experience supported by a set of news article about the events, this section will also present a statistical sample of virtual interactions on Facebook and compare them to actual forms of collective action such as demonstrations, as recorded by mainstream international news media.

Observations

"The Green Movement, according to its foundational principles and origins and by means of utilizing social networks relies on the thought, comprehension and civic innovations of the Iranian people and believes that understanding goals such as justice and freedom can only be achieved once these creative forces flourish. Our campaign slogan, *Every Iranian is a camp[aign headquarters]* can now be changed to *Every Iranian is a movement.*"

—Mir-Hossein Mousavi, "Statement 18:
The Green Movement Charter," June 15, 2010

Looking back to January 2009, I was one of the many Iranians who were worried about the dystopian prospect of our country's future. Born in Iran, I immigrated to Germany and joined the rapidly growing community of emigrated Iranians. Despite the diffusion of Iranians across different continents and various countries, the dispersion of different network clusters and their dissenting opinions left many holes in the diaspora network of Iranians; a sense of collectivity for Iranians outside of the country was thus undermined by structural holes and the isolation of network clusters.

At that time, most of the talks about Iran in Western mainstream news media was about the country's president, Mahmoud Ahmadinejad; the collective Iranian identity, from this perspective, was mostly associated with his controversial and radical positions in international politics, which often captured the attention of Western media. Thus, the framing process of the Iranian identity as institutionalized by the established political authority in Iran has been unable to represent social networks of Iranians, especially those in diaspora. On the other hand, the lack of a significant political opposition due to decades of political cannibalism between political forces after the 1979 revolution left the institutional arrangement of power and authority in Iran—the framework of the "Islamic Republic"—in the last three decades practically unchallenged.

However, within the political regime of the Islamic Republic—which used to be a political party and the nucleus of the followers of Ayatollah Khomeini—there has been a division between conservative and moderate elements. The two eminent figures who represented these elements in the first decade after the revolution were Seyed Ali Khamenei on the conservative side—the current supreme leader of the Islamic Republic holding president office at that time—and Mousavi on the moderate side—the presidential candidate challenging Ahmadinejad in the 2009 presidential elections who was holding the office of Prime Minister back then. In a 1985 showdown between the conservative parliament led by President Khamenei and Prime Minister Mousavi, Ayatollah Khomeini—Supreme Leader since after the revolution at that time—intervened in favor of Mousavi and opposed his removal from office.[35] However, after the end of the Iran–Iraq war and the death of Ayatollah Khomeini in 1989, and when president Khamenei became his successor, Mousavi stepped down from political office and returned to art and cultural work primarily as the head of the Iranian Academy of the Arts.[36]

In the subsequent era of technocracy, President Rafsanjani's pragmatic approach for stability and economic reform led to the formation of a new "middle class." As a result, the civil society had a chance to respire, and the road was paved for the reform movement, which emerged with Khatami's victory in the 1997 presidential elections. Under President Khatami, civil society had a chance to institutionalize for the first time in the form of NGOs, grassroots and other social and political organizations, in addition to newspapers and magazines.[37] Consequently, public opinion became a politically significant power in the arrangement of power and authority throughout the era of reform under President Khatami.

This in turn led to the increase of popular expectations from the reform movement. However, when the reform movement later met with institutional impediments, the result was a general disappointment and the drawback of popular as well as intellectual support.[38] Hence, the road was paved for the populist approach of Mahmoud Ahmadinejad, who came from an ultraconservative background. In the Iranian presidential election of 2005, Ahmadinejad managed to oust a fractioned reformist camp on the back of the rural population in relative absence of middle-class participation and with the almost evident support of the supreme leader.[39] The election process, however, raised serious suspicions about fraud and systematic manipulation.[40]

Every Citizen Is a Campaign Headquarters: Decentralization and the Power of Social Media for Mousavi's Campaign

After having observed the impact of social media on the 2008 U.S. presidential elections and how this technology facilitated a profound change in the way campaign machineries work, I initiated a grassroots campaign on Facebook by registering a multilingual page for Mousavi and drafting an initial strategy less than two months prior to his official registration for candidacy on January 19, 2009. The main promising factor that drew my attention was not only Facebook's practicality in the distribution of campaign information and messages, but particularly its utility in offering a mechanism for the ongoing engagement of participants by exposing them to activities in a virtual environment. Studies about the role of social media in the U.S. 2008 presidential election indicated similar effects, particularly regarding the use of Facebook.[41]

When Mousavi officially announced his bid for presidency with an official statement issued on March 11, 2009, the Facebook page had about four hundred "supporters"—the type of interaction with the page of a political figure was framed as "support" by Facebook at the time.[42] This number was already well beyond the range of my personal friends list and network of acquaintances on Facebook. More than a month before, on February 2, Mousavi had already appointed Ghorban Behzadian Nejad as his chief strategist and Abolfazl Fateh as the head of the steering committee for the campaign's media planning.[43]

A few days after his official bid on March 16, 2009, the main campaign slogan was introduced in the Ghalam News—the main news website of his campaign administrated by Fateh—as "Every citizen is a campaign headquarters."[44] The main idea behind this slogan was described by Mousavi in a meeting with his campaign staff on March 28, as a decentralized concept for "steering and leading existing resources," particularly oriented toward reaching out to the "unknown layers of society" and empowering grassroots initiatives.[45] Throughout the month of April 2009, grassroots initiatives and small-scale innovative campaigns had a chance to spawn and spread among various layers of the society that had been previously isolated and disengaged with each other and with a character such as Mousavi. For instance, whereas the strategy of associating the campaign symbolically with the color green—representing shared religious and cultural meaning—had been suggested by local supporters in the religious city of Mashhad,[46] the Facebook campaign as a structural facilitation for activism had been initiated by myself, an Iranian student living in Germany.

Mousavi was considered a favorite candidate of both the pragmatic conservatives and moderate reformists[47] and thus still an insider of the Islamic Republic's political regime, especially by Iranians who lived abroad and in exile. However, his long-term detachment from the political power struggle and his focus on arts and cultural work, alongside his wife Dr. Zahra Rahnavard, provided him with special access to the attention of alienated groups and social networks. Together with his decentralized approach, clusters of supporters began to emerge and develop across a broad spectrum of Iranian society, including the social networks abroad.

When Mousavi officially registered as a candidate in the Interior Ministry of Iran on May 9, he further illuminated his approach and objectives in a remarkable speech. The following excerpt is the first paragraph of the main body of his statement after the introduction:

"I, Mir-Hossein Mousavi, a humble son of the Islamic Republic, have come to the scene because I found the current political, economic and cultural trends worrying. I have come to guard human dignity. I have come to defend [the] nation's right to know about the affairs of the country, and to be an advocate for free and clear circulation of information for the people, who are the masters of the government. I have come to guard the freedom of thought and speech and to be an advocate for the freedoms clearly stated in the constitution. I have come . . . to fulfill citizen's rights and to protect private boundaries. I have come to be a tool to restore Iranian power, dignity and identity."[48]

With a reference to the scholarly literature on social movements, as previously mentioned, this speech can be considered a significant task of diagnostic framing associated with the initial influence process of framing a collective identity. At that time, the number of supporters on Mousavi's Facebook page had grown to fifteen hundred, and when political institutions started to form official alliances, I conjoined with the IT department of the Executives of Construction Party—a pragmatist technocrat political party officially recognized by the political regime of the Islamic Republic of Iran and mostly affiliated with the so-called "era of construction" under President Rafsanjani.[49]

The sociopsychological influence process initiated by Mousavi to counter-frame—"Attempts to rebut, undermine or neutralize a person's or group's myths, versions of reality or interpretive framework have been referred to as counter-framing"[50]—a collective identity through his presidential campaign had started with framing the problem in his speech on May 9, 2009. However, a comprehensive manifestation of the prognostic frame was published as a book on June 9—a few days before election day and after Mousavi's last debate in the first-ever debate program for presidential candidates on national television—encompassing comprehensive cultural, social, economic, and political agendas of the government of *Omid* (Hope)[51]—as promised by Mousavi during the debate. This publication can be considered the result of an interactive process of consensus reaching over the campaigning period leading to election day, expedited by the technological capability of social media that facilitated the accumulation of social capital, the promotion of an emerging collective identity, as well as the formation of collective action by reinforcing ties of activism.

Whereas the campaign's decentralized approach supported grassroots initiatives and embraced diversity, social networking sites such as Facebook strengthened the weak ties in the networks and facilitated the bridging of various network clusters, allowing the "unknown layers of the society" to be exposed to activism and the diverse campaign network to remain nevertheless cohesive. As a result, a collective sense of trust as necessary for collective action began to reflect itself in massively attended campaign rallies that were initiated on a grassroots level significantly supported by social media, particularly Facebook.

One of the gatherings that was particularly supported by the social media campaign and Mousavi's Facebook page—by then recognized as the official Facebook page of the campaign, but one of many pages supporting Mousavi—took place on the anniversary of the election of President Khatami on May 23, 2009, in the packed twelve-thousand-seat stadium in Tehran, whereas Mousavi himself was attending another rally in the city of Isfahan.[52] The Iranian government, having realized the role of Facebook in mobilizing this event—particularly the role of Mousavi's page, with about fifty-five hundred supporters at the time—blocked access to its website on the same day.[53] However, since the use of anti-filtering software had become common after a decade of enforcing filtering policies,[54] virtual interactions with Mousavi's Facebook page, instead of declining, peaked following the filtering of Facebook, as shown in Figure 7.1.

The first form of street demonstrations emerged right after the first televised debate on June 5, 2009;[55] Ahmadinejad used this opportunity for broadcasting various accusations against prominent supporters of Mousavi while banking on political gamesmanship, whereas Mousavi refused to engage in the discourse that he was trying to impose on the debate by turning to the audience and highlighting the danger of such an attitude not only in a political context but, more importantly, on a sociocultural level. After this tense debate, supporters of both sides peacefully took to the streets, extending the discussion into a parade, whereas campaign competition was mixed with joy and hope on both sides.

Days later, when the government denied to issue permission for a gathering of Mousavi supporters in the one-hundred-twenty-thousand-seat Azadi stadium on June 9 at short notice, a call for a rally was initiated through Mousavi's Facebook page. With the help of text-messaging and social media, a nineteen-kilometer human chain was formed throughout Tehran in less than twenty-four hours, just a few days before the election.[56]

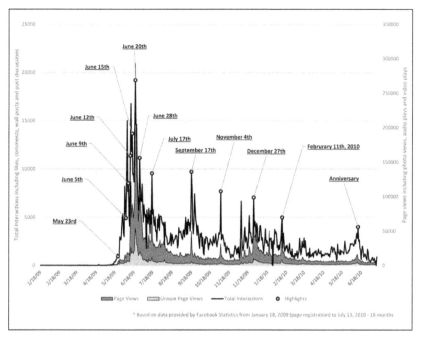

FIGURE 7.1. Virtual interactions with Mir-Hossein Mousavi's Facebook page (January 2009 to July 2010).

It was during this event that encounters with security forces first erupted.[57] According to the literature about the developments over the campaigning period, Mousavi's campaign developed into "a popular movement known as the Green Wave [which] picked up speed and carried Mousavi into an eagerly anticipated election day on June 12."[58] While prominent political figures—such as the former reformist president Khatami, as well as other social and political organizations—provided a sort of institutional support, the cohesion of the social networks that were supporting the campaign grew significantly with the help of the Internet and social media. For instance, while the number of supporters on Mousavi's Facebook (see Figure 7.2) had grown to nearly forty thousand, with virtual interactions at about thirteen thousand per day, large mailing lists, such as the central *88camp,* boasted nearly four-hundred-thousand subscribers.[59]

However, the greatest peak of both the number of supporters (Figure 7.2) and daily interactions (Figure 7.1) emerged about a week after election

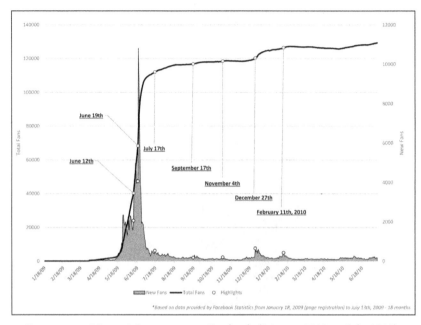

FIGURE 7.2. Mousavi Supporters on Facebook (January 2009 to July 2010).

day. After many complications reported by Mousavi's sentry committee for votes on the day of elections—such as the lack of enough ballots at many stations, the early closure of the election process, and the quick announcement of dubious results that showed stern linear developments in favor of Ahmadinejad—and the first raid on Mousavi's headquarters on the same day, he anticipated the spurious outcome by announcing that he "will not surrender to this dangerous charade."[60]

Furthermore, the early arrest of a wide range of journalists signified an anticipation of the ruling establishment for maintaining the arrangement of power and authority by keeping Ahmadinejad in office at any price, even the regime's democratic legitimacy.[61] This became obvious as the supreme leader in the first Friday prayer after the elections on June 19 attested the results, took side with the incumbent president, and warned Mousavi—who had just appealed to the Guardian Council in a formal letter that provided details about fraud in the election process[62]—and his supporters of a violent crackdown on demonstrators on the streets.[63]

Each Iranian Is a Medium: The Iranian Green Movement

One of the most significant events that stimulated the rushed and radical reaction of the supreme leader took place on June 15, 2009. Three days after the 2009 presidential elections, despite the anticipation of the ruling establishment—for example, by limiting access to the Internet and mobile text messaging and arresting reformist journalists, political figures, and influential activists—millions of Iranians, shocked by the election results, took to the famous Azadi (Freedom) Square in the greatest rally since the rallies leading up to the 1979 revolution.[64] This event most popularly marks the transition of the Green Wave—set in motion by Mousavi's campaign—to what has been referred to as the Iranian Green Movement, which emerged along with the core theme, "Where is my Vote?"[65]

Mousavi and Karroubi—the other reformist candidate in the 2009 elections—were supportive of this event, which went peacefully for the most part but was interrupted by incidents of violence leading to cases of injury and death.[66] After insisting on the annulment of this election in a meeting with the supreme leader, and after receiving his refusal, Mousavi called for a peaceful march, asking for official permission with a reference to the Iranian constitution. However, government officials quickly rejected this request, warning that the state police force would be called to duty in the event of a march.[67] After an intimidating speech by Ahmadinejad on June 14, in which he called the dissidents "dust and dirt," many spontaneous ideas for voicing protest erupted on social media.[68] One of these ideas, which I observed as the administrator of Mousavi's Facebook page, had proven highly effective during the 1979 revolution: chants of "Allahu-Akbar" (God is great) on rooftops by way of voicing protest.[69]

I picked up the idea of using this form of collective action, which could be exercised on the roofs of private homes at night for creating a collective sense of trust to participate in a public demonstration the following day. In an interview on the VOA satellite channel following the June 15 protest, I provided an argument for why this form of protest could be used for reinforcing a sense of solidarity without contradicting Islamic values, as claimed by authorities to be the main concern for issuing permissions.[70] However, the political establishment found itself in shock when Mostafa Ghanian was shot on the rooftop of his university home while chanting "Allahu-Akbar" and took indirect responsibility for his death when high officials later attended his memorial.[71] Nightly chants on rooftops kept occurring on subsequent nights, especially after Ayatollah Khamenei's speech on June 19.

Whereas the main motivational task of the Green Wave in context of presidential campaigning was aimed at bringing people to the polls to vote for Mousavi, the pivotal motivational task of the Iranian Green Movement was to protest the election results. However, the diagnostic task began to blur with the continuing irresponsibility of supervisory institutions about incidences of fraud. While the nightly chants continued on the rooftops, street demonstrations began to disperse and decentralize. Particularly after the supreme leader's open threat and the subsequent increase of violence, participating in public demonstrations was fraught with significant life-threatening risks. This effect was also reflected in the decline of virtual interactions with Mousavi's Facebook page after the peak on June 19.

After the death of Neda Agha-Soltan—a young woman who was shot in the chest and died in front of an amateur mobile camera—on the day after Khamenei's speech, Mousavi took a passive position when it came to the mobilization of rallies. However, through simple crowd-sourcing strategies, an interesting idea was suggested: to attend official demonstrations, which had been held by the regime since the 1979 Revolution in order to show its popularity, while holding up green symbols that were created and distributed throughout the electoral campaign. The promotion of this idea, together with posters of Ayatollah Khomeini—leader of the 1979 revolution—was picked up quickly and resulted in an unanticipated participation in the next rally.[72] In terms of virtual interaction with Mousavi's Facebook page, this event on June 28 marked the first peak since June 19. The further a resolution over the election results faded out, the more dynamic did the prognosis task become, and in this context Facebook played a key role in facilitating the process of reaching a prognostic consensus for the Iran Green Movement. Nevertheless, mobilizing efforts went well beyond the virtual realm; flyers were distributed in Tehran as well as graffiti and inscriptions on banknotes and, again, rooftop chants the night before the rally.

When the pragmatist Ayatollah Rafsanjani announced he would preach a Friday prayer on July 17, a hope for the resolution of the conflict once again began to revive. After his affiliates assured me that Rafsanjani was not going to turn his back on the Green Movement and Mousavi, I wrote an open letter to Mousavi inviting him on behalf of his supporters to attend the Friday prayers,[73] to which he responded positively.[74] Again, a scheme similar to the one utilized for the march on June 15 was used for the mobilization process building up to the rooftop chants on the night before the rally. Despite the massive attendance of this event by the Green Movement supporters, Rafsanjani's cautious criticism of the regime's handling of the situation and his proposed solutions, the political establishment kept refusing to accommodate any revisions.

While the Iranian Green Movement, relying on its decentralized organization, maintained another four months of street demonstrations, with the strategy of changing the symbolic content of demonstrations organized and promoted by the regime, Mousavi focused on steering the discourse that has been formed around the Iranian Green Movement. As reflected in his seventeen official statements, as well as in many unofficial interviews and speeches delivered in meetings with families of "martyrs" of the Iranian Green Movement, those injured and the political prisoners, he provided a guiding perspective on cultural issues, seeking to recapture the political problem of democracy at a cultural level.

While a discourse analysis of Mousavi's statements, notes, interviews, and speeches is an interesting subject of inquiry for further research, the focus here shall remain on the impact of Facebook in the political realm, particularly in context of the Iranian Green Movement. Between September and December 2009, several demonstrations that were considered strategic for showing the popularity of the political establishment were themed with Green symbols, indicating the emergence of a new collective identity. However, while hopes for a revision of the election results diminished, the dissolving of the initial prognostic frame paved the way for alternative framings in light of the intolerance of political establishment for a peaceful social movement and its demands. As a result, the revolutionary position demanding the immediate overthrow of the regime—mostly associated with radical Iranian political opposition groups in exile—began to disintegrate the cohesion of the Iranian Green Movement. It was at this stage that the anti-political properties of Facebook began to displace the arrangement of power and authority within the networks of the Iranian Green Movement.

On September 17, 2009, Qods day, for instance—traditionally a demonstration organized by the political establishment against Israel—was massively attended by Iranian Green Movement supporters with the theme of "Stop Violence" suggested on Mousavi's Facebook page. Just a few weeks earlier, cases of sexual violence against arrested demonstrators in custody had been revealed by the other reformist candidate, Mehdi Karroubi.[75] However, slogans such as "Not for Gaza, Not for Lebanon, I will give my life only for Iran," which were occasionally documented on this day, signified a deviation from the suggested theme.[76] Furthermore, occasional calls for an "Iranian Republic"[77] occurred during a demonstration celebrating the anniversary of the start of the hostage crisis on November 4, and chants of

"Death to Khamenei" erupted on the day of "Bloody Ashura" on December 27.[78] These chants reflected only a fraction of the discursive discrepancy that occurred on virtual networks—instances can be found in various comments on Facebook posts on Mousavi's page during that time. However, dispersed demonstration occurring on the day of Ashura—a main historic reference for the Shia concept of martyrdom—became a ground of serious confrontations between demonstrators and security forces, during which control over the city of Tehran was partially lost for some hours.[79]

However, a subsequent demonstration planned to be themed with Green Movement symbols on February 11, 2010—the most vital demonstration to the popularity of the regime held each year on the anniversary of the establishment of the Islamic Republic—became the first demonstration in which Green symbols had almost no appearance. While Mousavi in a special statement insisted on "attending the rally with the spirit of togetherness while maintaining our identity,"[80] the strategy that prevailed in social media was the "Trojan Horse" strategy—suggesting green symbols to be carried undercover for a collective showdown in order to avoid a systematic crackdown. However, the immense presence of security forces on this day, in addition to the previous exercise of violence by the regime, discouraged Green Movement supporters from taking the risk of exposing green symbols on this historic day.[81]

Subsequently, the only street demonstration of the Iranian Green Movement occurred about a year later, when Mousavi and Karroubi requested an official permission for a rally in support of the Arab Spring. Although an official permission for this event was denied by the political establishment, again with the help of social media, and particularly facilitated by Facebook, people took to the street on February 14, 2011. However, the political establishment, which had demonstrated its extreme intolerance toward the Iranian Green Movement by harassing Mousavi and Karroubi, placed Mousavi; his wife, Dr. Zahra Rahnavard; and Karroubi under House arrest, where they remain to this day.[82] With the exclusion of Mousavi and Karroubi from the discourse of the Iranian Green Movement and the further fraction of prognostic framing tasks, the discursive discrepancy deepened while a consensus seemed further out of sight. Accordingly, there has been no basis for any motivational task and, thus, there has been no evidence of collective action associated with the Iranian Green Movement over the following two years.

Facebook in this context reinforced this fractioning process by providing a highly interactive platform for the many alternative voices and opinions that were seeking to frame their own diagnosis, prognosis, and motivation for collective action. Because most of the alternative voices with a systematic presence on Facebook ever since reflected radical and dispirited tendencies, Facebook facilitated a polarization of the Iranian Green Movement into radical and melancholic positions and thereby undermined its cohesion. In light of this development, the Iranian Green Movement has been declared "dead" by its opponents—mostly officials and affiliates of the political establishment—and even by some of its proponents.[83] In light of these developments, how has Facebook been politically significant in rearranging power and authority in Iran? Can these developments be considered a dystopian realization of Mousavi's prospect of "every Iranian" becoming a "movement"?

Conclusion

"The Green Movement has been responsible for a wave of dialogue about important questions regarding our future. This event is incomparable to any other in our modern history."

—Mir-Hossein Mousavi, Statement 18:
The Green Movement Charter," June 15, 2010.

Without making reference to the theoretical literature on social movements, Mousavi seems to have realized the importance of the notion of collective identity. After a permission for a demonstration on June 15, 2010, was denied—the anniversary of the first Iranian Green Movement demonstration—Mousavi introduced the Charter for Strengthening the Collective Identity of the Green Movement, inviting all Iranians to contribute to its development.[84] This charter can be considered the result of Mousavi's focus on the sociopsychological process of framing, providing Iranian Green Movement participants with a cultural meta-framework.

Although the solutions suggested in this charter might have seemed arbitrary at first, the 2013 presidential elections in Iran, in which the moderate reformist Rowhani was elected president, indicated the effects of Mousavi's proposal. Prior to this charter, Mousavi—right after the events on the day of Bloody Aashura—had emphasized that a solution can only be approached through "allowing smaller rivers and springs of clear water into this great river, leading to a gradual change in conditions."[85] Gradually, this approach bore fruit in the 2013 presidential elections in which social media, again, played a key role in reaching a consensus within a divided social body of the reformist movement and the Iranian Green Movement.[86]

Furthermore, the demand for the release of Mousavi and Karrubi from House arrest emerged as a bold theme throughout Hassan Rowhani's campaign in social media, and prominent reformist figures such as the former president Khatami took key references to Mousavi when meeting the president-elect and discussing possible political resolution for the country.[87] As described in the observations, Facebook demonstrated political qualities by displacing the arrangement of power and political authority in the context of the 2009 presidential election. Initially, Facebook provided a reciprocal platform for the sociopsycological influence process of framing a collective identity by empowering "weak ties" and facilitating their strength for bridging social capital in flexible structure of social networks and reaching consensus with regards to the meaning of the collective identity. A virtual image of Mousavi on Facebook not only "densified" the virtual networks of supporters around the alternative presidential candidate, but also facilitated the weak ties and the reciprocal flow of novel information as well as the rapid bridging of many structural holes, especially in the virtual environment of Facebook. As a result, not only did the diffusion of campaign information become more efficient and outreaching, but the interactive environment in Facebook allowed individuals across various networks to be exposed to opportunities for campaign activism. Thus, Facebook facilitated the accumulation of social capital throughout the campaign era. Once enrolled in activism for Mousavi's campaign, each of the participating actors, like myself, can be considered "well placed to innovate" on a grassroots level to conduct framing tasks for collective action.[88]

When it came to the linking of collective identity to collective action after the 2009 presidential elections, Facebook facilitated the exposure of movement participants to collective action, but at the same time it undermined the cohesion of the movement by facilitating framing processes for alternative meanings and forms of collective action. However, despite its displacing properties for the arrangements of power and authority within the context of the Iranian Green Movement, Facebook seems to have rather displacing properties within the context of the overall establishment of political authority in Iran by facilitating emerging grassroots initiatives that lack institutional merits, such as authoritative supremacy and communicational infrastructure.

Therefore, it can be concluded that the political quality of Facebook would lie precisely in its anti-political properties. In context of political institutions that seek to establish their own frame of meanings and forms of collective action for the collective identity of Iranians, Facebook provided a platform for alternative meanings to frame, diffuse, and become the basis for a new collective identity for Iranians seeking a change in political arrangements. Once such a sense of collectivity had been established, it was only a matter of time until a form of collective action would be agreed on and exercised. When Rouhani positioned himself as a moderate reformist and practically aligned with Mousavi's suggestions for a political resolution, he could appeal to many participants in the Iranian Green Movement as well as a wide range of others on the political spectrum who were disaffected by the arrangements of power and authority during Ahmadinejad's presidency and who re-aligned to ultimately provide Rouhani with an "overwhelming popular victory."[89]

On this note, I would like to conclude with a quote from Mousavi taken from an interview during the aftermath of February 11, 2010; the quote captures in a nutshell the effect of social media on Iranian society:

> I still believe [in] the importance of the motto "Every citizen, one medium," along with increased usage of social networks to raise awareness. I believe that there is no alternative for such social networks. Although, I should add that the current difficult conditions [of the country] have also had some advantages alongside all the damage. Among them is the development of self-reliance and the expansion of the Green Movement to countless other social networks.
>
> In this regard, the use of virtual space was miraculous. [The web] has established itself as a stable and trustworthy structure that, in connecting people and networks, brings them together to collaborate. It is very similar to traditional bazaars where countless stores and booths of varying size are connected, along with mosques and teahouses, to produce an image of one coherent structure, despite the differences in every unit. What is interesting is that on one side of the bazaar you can have very different appetites, opinions, and capital flowing from the other sides, but this variety never constrains its totality or its concept of unity. Instead, [this variety] acts as a point of strength.[90]

Notes

1. "Iran Elections: Mousavi Speaks to Al Jazeera–11 Jun 09," YouTube video posted by "AlJazeeraEnglish," June 11, 2009, http://www.youtube.com/watch?v=qlYK2bRv9bg.

2. Ali Afshari and H. Graham Underwood, "The Green Wave," *Journal of Democracy* 20.2 (2009): 6, doi: 10.1353/jod.0.0124.

3. Matthew Fraser and Soumitra Dutta, "Barack Obama and the Facebook Election," *U.S. News & World Report,* November 19, 2008, http://www.usnews.com/opinion/articles/2008/11/19/barack-obama-and-the-facebook-election accessed June 15, 2013); Claire C. Miller, "How Obama's Internet Campaign Changed Politics," *New York Times Bits blog,* November 28, 2009, http://bits.blogs.nytimes.com/2008/11/07/how-obamas-internet-campaign-changed-politics/ (accessed June 15, 2013).

4. David Sarno, "Obama, the First Social Media President," *LA Times Technology blog,* November 18, 2009, http://latimesblogs.latimes.com/technology/2008/11/obama-the-first.html (accessed June 15, 2013).

5. Abigail Hauslohner, "Is Egypt About to Have a Facebook Revolution," *Time World,* January 24, 2011, http://www.time.com/time/world/article/0,8599,2044142,00.html (accessed June 15, 2013); Eunice Crook, "Tunisia: The Facebook Revolution," *British Council Voices,* February 11, 2011, http://blog.britishcouncil.org/2011/02/11/tunisia-the-facebook-revolution/ (accessed June 15, 2013).

6. Langdon Winner, *Autonomous Technology: Technics-out-of-Control as a Theme in Political Thought* (Cambridge: MIT Press, 1978): 3.

7. Langdon Winner, "Do Artifacts Have Politics?" *Daedalus* 109.1 (1980): 121–136; 123.

8. Ibid., 127.

9. Ibid., 131.

10. Ibid., 124–125.

11. Ibid., 125.

12. Roel Nahuis and Harro Van Lente, "Where Are the Politics? Perspectives on Democracy and Technology," *Science, Technology & Human Values* 33.5 (2008): 559–581.

13. Jon Sundbo, "Three Paradigms in Innovation Theory," *Science and Public Policy* 22.6 (1995): 399–410.

14. Andreas M. Kaplan and Michael Haenlein, "Users of the World, Unite! The Challenges and Opportunities of Social Media," *Business Horizons* 53.1 (2010): 61.

15. Ibid., 62.

16. danah m. boyd and Nicole B. Ellison, "Social Network Sites: Definition, History, and Scholarship," *Journal of Computer-Mediated Communication* 13 (2008) 210–230; 211.

17. Brady Robards, "Leaving MySpace, Joining Facebook: 'Growing Up' on Social Network Sites," *Continuum* 26.3 (2012): 391.

18. Nicole B. Ellison, Charles Steinfield, and Cliff Lampe, "The Benefits of Facebook 'Friends': Social Capital and College Students' Use of Online Social Network Sites," *Journal of Computer-Mediated Communication* 12.4 (2007): 1143–1168; 1164.

19. Ibid., 1162–1164.

20. Pierre Bourdieu and Loïc J. D. Wacquant, eds., *An Invitation to Reflexive Sociology* (Chicago: University of Chicago Press, 1992), 14.

21. Mark Granovetter, "The Impact of Social Structure on Economic Outcomes," *The Journal of Economic Perspectives* 19.1 (2005): 33–50.

22. Ibid., 33.

23. Ibid., 34.

24. Ibid.

25. Robert D. Benford and David A. Snow, "Framing Processes and Social Movements: An Overview and Assessment," *Annual Review of Sociology* (2000): 614.

26. Ibid., 615–618.

27. Ibid., 614–615.

28. Francesca Polletta and James M. Jasper, "Collective Identity and Social Movements," *Annual Review of Sociology* (2001): 283–305.

29. Ibid., 297.

30. Ibid.

31. Roger V. Gould, "Collective Action and Network Structure," *American Sociological Review* (1993): 185; Doug McAdam and Ronnelle Paulsen, "Specifying the Relationship between Social Ties and Activism," *American Journal of Sociology* (1993): 663; Polletta and Jasper, "Collective Identity and Social Movements," 296.

32. McAdam and Paulsen, "Specifying the Relationship between Social Ties and Activism," 663.

33. Ibid., 644.

34. Scott D. McClurg, "Social Networks and Political Participation: The Role of Social Interaction in Explaining Political Participation," *Political Research Quarterly* 56.4 (2003): 449–464.

35. Mohammad Sahimi, "The Political Evolution of Mousavi," PBS Frontline Tehranbureau, February 16, 2010, http://www.pbs.org/wgbh/pages/frontline/tehranbureau/2010/02/the-political-evolution-of-mousavi.html (accessed June 15, 2013).

36. Ibid.

37. Ghoncheh Tazmini, *Khatami's Iran: The Islamic Republic and the Turbulent Path to Reform* (London: I. B. Tauris 2009), 46.

38. Ibid., 135–146.

39. Mohammad Sahimi, "An Administration Plagued by Fraud and Corruption," PBS Frontline Tehranbureau, March 30, 2010, http://www.pbs.org/wgbh/pages/frontline/tehranbureau/2010/03/ahmadinejad-and-his-men-embodiments-of-fraud-and-corruption.html (accessed June 15, 2013).

40. Mohammad Sahimi, "New Evidence of Fraud in 2009 Election," PBS Frontline Tehran Bureau, August 11, 2010, http://www.pbs.org/wgbh/pages/frontline/tehranbureau/2010/08/new-evidence-of-fraud-in-2009-election.html (accessed June 15, 2013).

41. See Emily Metzgar and Albert Maruggi, "Social Media and the 2008 US Presidential Election," *Journal of New Communications Research* 4.1 (2009): 141–165; Sunil Wattal, David Schuff, Munir Mandviwalla, and Christine B. Williams,

"Web 2.0 and Politics: The 2008 US Presidential Election and an e-Politics Research Agenda," *MIS Quarterly* 34.4 (2010): 669–688.

42. "Mir-Hossein Mousavi announces bid for presidency [Persian]," *Fararu,* March 10, 2009, http://fararu.com/fa/news/21585/ (accessed June 15, 2013).

43. "Head of Mousavi Campaign Introduced [Persian]," Khabaronline, February 2, 2009, http://www.khabaronline.ir/detail/3178/ (accessed June 15, 2013).

44. "2009 election Calendar—'Every Citizen Is One Camp' Introduced as Mousavi's Official Campaign Slogan," Kaleme, March 16, 2012, http://www.kaleme.com/1391/12/26/klm-137122/ (accessed June 15, 2013).

45. "Mousavi: We Have Been Oblivious of the Underserved Population [Persian]," March 27, 2009, http://www.asriran.com/fa/pages/?cid=68299 (accessed June 15, 2013).

46. Najmeh Bozorgmehr, "Mousavi Rides a Green Wave," *Financial Times,* June 12, 2009, http://www.ft.com/intl/cms/s/0/4aef93a8-56c1-11de-9a1c-00144feabdc0.html#axzz2E3jE3V2d (accessed June 15, 2013).

47. Scott Macleod, "Top 10 Players in Iran's Power Struggle: Mir Hossein Mousavi," *Times Lists,* http://www.time.com/time/specials/packages/article/0,28804,1905910_1905908_1905892,00.html (accessed June 15, 2013).

48. "I, Mir Hossein Mousavi, the most humble child of the revolution, have come to the scene [Persian]," *Aftab News,* May 8, 2009, http://www.aftabnews.ir/vdcjmteo.uqeoizsffu.html (accessed June 15, 2013).

49. "The Executives of the Construction of Iran (ACI)," Princeton University Iran Data Portal, http://www.princeton.edu/irandataportal/parties/kargozaran/ (accessed June 15, 2013).

50. Benford and Snow, "Framing Processes and Social Movements," 617.

51. Mir Hossein Mousavi "The Agenda of Hope Administration for Better Future [Persian]," Presidential Campaign Manifesto, June 2009, http://www.4shared.com/account/document/EbUsEAgM/Ketabe_Dolate_omid.html (accessed June 15, 2013).

52. Aresu Eqbali, "Reformist Khatami Throws Weight behind Iran Ex-Premier," AFP, May 23, 2009, http://www.google.com/hostednews/afp/article/ALeqM5i--f28ybkPsaVznt84MsFVj06tew (accessed June 15, 2013).

53. "Iran Blocks Facebook ahead of Presidential Election," CNN, May 23, 2009, http://articles.cnn.com/2009-05-23/world/iran.elections.facebook_1_facebook-internet-access-financial-times?_s=PM:WORLD (accessed June 15, 2013).

54. Babak Rahimi and Elham Gheytanchi, "Iran's Reformists and Activists: Internet Exploiters," *Middle East Policy* 15.1 (2008): 46.

55. Nahid Siamdoust, "Iran's Presidential Debate: Will Ahmadinejad's Attacks Backfire?" *Time World,* June 5, 2009, http://www.time.com/time/world/article/0,8599,1902921,00.html (accessed June 15, 2013).

56. Thomas Erdbrink, "In Iran Election, Tradition Competes with Web," Washington Post, June 09, 2009, http://www.washingtonpost.com/wp-dyn/content/article/2009/06/08/AR2009060804090.html (accessed June 15, 2013).

57. Farnaz Fassihi, "Iranians Voice Discontent in Massive Street Rally," *Wall Street Journal,* June 10, 2009, http://online.wsj.com/article/SB124451146408496649.html.

58. Afshari and Graham Underwood, "The Green Wave," 6.

59. Ibid., 7.

60. Ian Black and Saeed K. Dehghan, "Riots Erupt in Tehran over 'Stolen' Election," *The Guardian,* June 13, 2009, http://www.guardian.co.uk/world/2009/jun/13/iran-mahmoud-ahmadinejad-riots-tehran-election (accessed June 15, 2013).

61. "Iran," Human Rights Watch World Report 2010, http://www.hrw.org/world-report-2010/iran (accessed June 15, 2013).

62. Ian Black and Saeed K. Dehghan, "Iran Elections: Mousavi Lodges Appeal against Ahmadinejad Victory," *The Guardian,* June 14, 2009, http://www.guardian.co.uk/world/2009/jun/14/iran-election-mousavi-appeal (accessed June 15, 2013).

63. "Iran's Leader: End Protests or Risk Bloodshed," *MSNBC News,* June 19, 2009, http://www.msnbc.msn.com/id/31440649/ (accessed June 15, 2013).

64. Nahid Siamdoust, "Iran's Presidential Debate: Will Ahmadinejad's Attacks Backfire?" *Time World,* June 5, 2009, http://www.time.com/time/world/article/0,8599,1902921,00.html (accessed June 15, 2013).

65. Leyla Ferani, "Iran Can No Longer Suppress Its Youth," The Telegraph, June 15, 2009, http://www.telegraph.co.uk/comment/personal-view/5543122/Iran-can-no-longer-suppress-its-youth.html (accessed June 15, 2013).

66. "Iran," Human Rights Watch World Report 2010, http://www.hrw.org/world-report-2010/iran (accessed June 15, 2013).

67. "Mousavi Calls for Rally on Monday [Persian]," *BBC Persian,* June 15 2009, http://www.bbc.co.uk/persian/iran/2009/06/090614_bd_ir88_mousavi_phone_statement.shtml (accessed June 15, 2013).

68. Robert Tait, "The Dust Revolution: How Mahmoud Ahmadinejad's Jibe Backfired," *The Guardian,* June 18, 2009, http://www.guardian.co.uk/world/2009/jun/18/iran-election-protests-mahmoud-ahmadinejad (accessed June 15, 2013).

69. "Allahu-Akbar" is one of the foundational slogans of Islam.

70. "The Latest from Iran: Demonstrations and an Appeal to the Guardian Council (15 June)," *EA World View,* June 15, 2009, http://enduringamerica.squarespace.com/june-2009/2009/6/15/the-latest-from-iran-demonstrations-and-an-appeal-to-the-gua.html (accessed June 15, 2013).

71. "Iran: Thousands Attend Memorial of Green Student Protester Mostafa Ghanian in Mashhad," June 19, 2010, http://www.payvand.com/news/10/jun/1176.html (accessed June 15, 2013).

72. Michael Slackman, "Iran Arrests Iranian Employees of British Embassy as Protests Return," *New York Times,* June 28, 2009, http://www.nytimes.com/2009/06/29/world/middleeast/29iran.html?r=0 (accessed June 15, 2013).

73. Borzou Daragahi, "After a Long Absence, Pro-Mousavi Cleric Rafsanjani to Lead Prayers," *LA Times,* July 13, 2009, http://articles.latimes.com/2009/jul/13/world/fg-iran13 (accessed June 15, 2013).

74. "Mousavi to Make Public Appearance," *BBC News,* July 16, 2009, http://news.bbc.co.uk/2/hi/middle_east/8153593.stm (accessed June 15, 2013).

75. "Written Evidence Submitted by Justice for Iran," Justice for Iran Report to the International Development Committee of the UK Parliament, May 20, 2013, http://www.publications.parliament.uk/pa/cm201314/cmselect/cmintdev/107/107vw33.htm (accessed June 15, 2013).

76. "17 Sept 2009—Tehran. No to Gaza, No to Lebanon, I Die for Iran," YouTube video, posted by "Irandoost09," September 18, 2009, http://www.youtube.com/watch?v=SSpG7EH6yrA (accessed June 15, 2013).

77. "Iran Tehran 4 Nov 09 People Chanting Independence Freedom Iranian Republic P54," YouTube video, posted by "Millionoillim," November 06, 2009, http://www.youtube.com/watch?v=Kx-DbgS0cLo (accessed June 15, 2013).

78. "'Death to Khamenei' Ashura Protests Dec 27," YouTube video, posted by "2009IranRevolution," December 27, 2009, http://www.youtube.com/watch?v=AKJcbP4i2jI (accessed June 15, 2013).

79. "IRAN: Even more footage, pictures from Ashura protests," LA Times Babylon & Beyond, December 27, 2009, http://latimesblogs.latimes.com/babylonbeyond/2009/12/iran-more-video-footage-from-protests-surface-2.html (accessed June 15, 2009).

80. Mir-Hossein Mousavi, "The Green Movement Is Standing Firm on Its Rightful Demands," Mir-Hossein Mousavi's Interview with Kaleme, translated and published in a Facebook note on his Facebook page, February 27, 2010, http://www.facebook.com/note.php?note_id=330992387605&id=45061919453 (accessed June 15, 2013).

81. Cameron Abadi, "Iran, Facebook, and the Limits of Online Activism," Foreign Policy, February 12, 2010, http://www.foreignpolicy.com/articles/2010/02/12/irans_failed_facebook_revolution (accessed June 15, 2013).

82. September 1, 2014, marked the 1,293rd day of their house arrest.

83. Bahman A. Diba, "Is the Green Movement of Iran Dead?" *Peyvand Iran News,* March 4, 2012, http://www.payvand.com/news/12/apr/1020.html (accessed June 15, 2013).

84. Mir-Hossein Mousavi, "Statement #18: The Green Charter," note published on Mousavi's Facebook page, June 15, 2010, http://www.facebook.com/note.php?note_id=400395637605.

85. Mir-Hossein Mousavi, "17th Statement: 'Ways Out of the Crisis,'" trans. Khordaad 88 blog, January 1, 2010, http://khordaad88.com/?p=925 (accessed June 15, 2013).

86. Suzanne Maloney, "Rouhani Goes to Isfahan: Why Iran's Elections May Yet Get Interesting," Brookings, June 4, 2013, http://www.brookings.edu/blogs/iran-at-saban/posts/2013/06/04-rouhani-in-isfahan; Saeed K. Dehghan, "Iran's President Signals Softer Line on Web Censorship and Islamic Dress Code," *The Guardian,* July 2, 2013, http://www.guardian.co.uk/world/2013/jul/02/iran-president-hassan-rouhani-progressive-views; Babak Movahedi, "Media Tools by Means of Which the

Victorious Candidate Won the Elections [Persian]," *Iranian Journalists*, July 1, 2013, http://khabarnegaran.info/article.php3?id_article=2129.

87. "Rouhani's View on the House Arrest of Mousavi & Karroubi w/ English subtitles," YouTube video, from a Q&A session at the Sharif University of Technology on May 13, 2013, posted by "RouhaniCampaign," May 29, 2013, http://www.youtube.com/watch?v=hYwM4Na1HIQ; Seyed Mohammad Khatami, "In the Recent Elections, the Reformist Approach for Change from within the Political Regime Has Won [Persian]," from a speech performed in a meeting with student from across Iran, transcript published by Khatami's official website on July 3, 2013, http://www.khatami.ir/fa/news/1188.html.

88. "The actor who sits astride structural holes in networks . . . is well placed to innovate." Granovetter, "The Impact of Social Structure on Economic Outcomes," 46.

89. Suzanne Maloney, "Why Rouhani Won—And Why Khamenei Let Him: The Ahmadinejad Era Comes to an Auspicious End," *Foreign Affairs*, June 16, 2013, http://www.foreignaffairs.com/articles/139511/suzanne-maloney/why-rouhani-won-and-why-khamenei-let-him.

90. Mir-Hossein Mousavi, "The Green Movement Is Standing Firm on Its Rightful Demands," Mir-Hossein Mousavi's Interview with Kaleme, translated and published in a Facebook note on his Facebook page, February 27, 2010, http://www.facebook.com/note.php?note_id=330992387605&id=45061919453 (accessed June 15, 2013).

Chapter 8

Trans-spatial Public Action

The Geography of Iranian Post-Election Protests in the Age of Web 2.0

Reza Masoudi Nejad

This chapter treats the geography of Iranian post-election protests (June 2009) in "public spaces" by focusing on the notions of diaspora and protest in the age of Web 2.0. The post-election protests, often called the Green Movement, were first described as the first "Twitter Revolution," but soon careful analyses showed that the role of Twitter was greatly exaggerated by the Western media.[1] While many of the protests also took place outside of the country from Dhaka, Berlin, London, and Washington DC, led by the Iranian diaspora communities, the Green protests were seamlessly connected to Iran. The relationship between diaspora and new communication technology (NCT) within the framework of globalization suggest that the protests were de-territorialized. This chapter, however, argues that the 2009 protests were a trans-spatial collective action. The trans-spatial protests, as collective action not limited to the national borders, was shaped as a result of juxtaposition of trans-local networks of Iranian diaspora communities with NCT. In many ways, the Green protests took form entirely different in a landscape in which conventional protests/revolutions (e.g., the 1979 Iranian revolution) have previously taken place.

The initial perception is that the post-election protests across borders were connected as a grand protest through the structure of Web 2.0; this is the basis of social networks (e.g., Facebook and Twitter) that equally

connects everyone-to-everyone and everywhere-to-everywhere. Dale Bough-
erty, co-founder of O'Reilly, coined the term "Web 2.0" in 2004 during
a brainstorming session; the idea was to articulate how the landscape of
the web has been metamorphosed by new applications and websites such
as Wiki, Google's AdSense, Napster, and YouTube.[2] Although Web 2.0 has
come under attack as a meaningless marketing jargon, the concept has
emerged to be understood in terms of interactive applications and websites
that allow users to collaborate as both audience and creators of content, in
contrast to conventional websites where people are merely viewers. Therefore
Web 2.0 can be an all people–centric web.[3] Web 2.0 appears to be one
of the structures through which the post-election protests had a base and
operated. However, my analysis of interviews in this study suggests that the
trans-local network of the Iranian diaspora played a greater role than Web
2.0 in constituting the geography of protests.

The following discussion is arranged in three main sections. The first
examines the Iranian diaspora. The second takes into account the role of
new technology in the protests by articulating the specific nature of the
recent protests as compared to Iranian protests in the nineteenth and twentieth centuries. The third section examines the interviewee accounts. The
interviewees were selected to typify the protest experiences and are gender
balanced. The people interviewed for this study participated in the protests
in either Iran or abroad, and some participated in protests in both Iran and
outside of the country. In light of limitations of space, this study does not
discuss all the interviews; rather the focus is on those who best articulate
the idea of trans-spatiality.

Diaspora in the Age of Globalization

The term "diaspora" is commonly used to describe Jewish communities
dispersed across the world. Until recently, in most dictionaries diaspora
has been both illustrated and defined in reference to the case of the Jews.[4]
However, since the 1980s, the term, as a noun, has been transforming into
a social science concept, leading to a diversification of the idea of "diaspora."
Brubaker suggests that such diversification resulted from the "dispersion of
the meaning of the term in semantic, conceptual, and disciplinary space";
he coined this condition "diaspora diaspora."[5]

Brah explains that "diaspora" means "dispersing from"; "hence the
word embodies a notion of a centre, a locus, a "home" from where the

dispersion occurs."[6] This is essentially a spatial description that illustrates a polar network centered at a homeland. However during the 1990s, scholars including Appadurai (1990), Cohen (1997), and Scholte (2000) suggested that globalization de-territorializes notions like diaspora. They articulate de-territorialization as the consequence of (1) the end of the national project, (2) international financial flows, (3) the rise of international corporations, (4) the presence of ever faster and cheaper transport, and (5) new communication technology. Under these circumstances, collective action has been increasingly established based on nonterritorial notions, such as feminism and gay rights, and supraterritorial notions such as environmental issues and global warming.[7] The Occupy movement is the most recent example of a collective action based on nonterritorial solidarity, as the worldwide movement addresses structural inequalities by targeting capitalism and global corporations. The movement is associated with neither countries nor nations, and is not limited to national borders.

Trans-locality is the spatial characteristic of the diasporic social network that exists and operates across and within state borders.[8] The social networks of diaspora communities are strongly influenced by the processes of globalization and new communication technology, bypassing some of the spatial divisions.[9] As just mentioned, although some initially suggested that the idea of diaspora is de-territorialized, many observations show that the experience of diaspora is not really de-territorialised.[10] The age of globalization and communication technology provides a condition in which de-territorialized solidarities emerge; however it does not mean all collective actions in this age are de-territorialized. We may see similarities between the Occupy movement and the Green Movement, as both were organized within and across borders and greatly benefit from the Internet. The Occupy movement is based on a nonterritorial and nonnational solidarity. In contrast, the Green Movement was a national movement intimately tied to Iran; thus it has a strong territorial component. Yet the Green Movement is manifested and practiced as a *trans-spatial* collective action.

I prefer to describe the Green Movement as a *trans-spatial* protest (not "trans-local" or "trans-territorial") as it implies a perceptual image of space rather than physical place, which trans-territorial refers to. As will be discussed here, participants conceive of the Green Movement based on a kind of cognitive map rather than a geographical map. Moreover, *trans-locality* has an established meaning in diaspora studies, describing the social network of diaspora communities, especially during the nineteenth and twentieth centuries. The concept aimed to articulate how diaspora communities interconnect different localities around the world, maintaining the interaction with their community through cultural, religious, and financial mediums.[11] In particular, trans-local studies consider the agency-oriented approach to show how "relatively powerless actors from the global periphery have been able to transform themselves into migrant entrepreneurs. In doing so they have become active participants in the global order."[12] However, the case of Iran differs from those described by *trans-locality* because in the age of seamless communications Iranians act globally to make change at home.

The aftermath of the 1979 revolution contributed to the worldwide growth of the Iranian diaspora population.[13] The Iranian diaspora community, however, does not only comprise those who were exiled on the eve of, or shortly after, the revolution. Iranians also left their homeland because of the Iran–Iraq war (1980s), and because of a new global era that can be called the age of immigration, when mass immigrations took place across the globe. Brah explains that following the collapse of the Soviet Union and major re-alignments in the world political order, "there has been a rapid increase in migrations across the globe since the 1980s. These mass movement[s] are taking place in all directions."[14]

Conventionally, migration takes place from a few places to a few places, but the notion of migration has changed, and now people move from many places to many other places. This has created "super-diversities," a situation coined by Vertovec, who aims to underline the complexities that surpass the conventional experiences and concepts of immigration. He explains that, globally, over the past two decades more people moved from more places to more places, creating increasingly complex social formations both in countries of origin and host countries.[15] Although Vertovec discusses this subject by addressing the case of the UK, Iranians have also vividly perceived the shift in the idea of migration. While in the past Iranians had mostly immigrated to western European and North American countries, there is now an Iranian community almost everywhere. It is astonishing to realize that the post-election protests took place in forty countries, dispersing the protest to about one-hundred-forty cities around the world, from Manila, Dhaka, and Haydarabad, to London, Washington DC, and Los Angeles.[16]

The Iranian diaspora community is characterized not only by geographical dispersion but also by sociopolitical dispersion. The community formed based on the phases of pre- and postglobalization migration patterns. After the 1979 revolution, the political exodus was comprised of those who were forced to the leave the country; hence they settled permanently in host countries and disconnected from the homeland. However, since the 1990s the majority of migrants have left the country by choice. These migrants have a hybrid status as they constantly travel between their host country and Iran.

The exiled opposition groups, such as SMKI[17] or the Monarchists, have mainly driven the political campaigns in the West against the authority of the Islamic Republic during the last three decades. These groups, disconnected from Iran, largely shaped Iranian activism in the diaspora. This status, however, has changed since the late 1990s, for two reasons. First, at that time a large number of Iranians left the homeland as a choice and maintained their connections to Iran. Second, there was a wave of reformist activists who left Iran when the conservatives in Iran harshly challenged the reform movement. While the presidency of Khatami in 1997 opened a window for change, the conservatives showed they would not let it happen. The Kooy incident (1999),[18] when the student protest against the closing of the Salam Newspaper was harshly suppressed, particularly signified that the Islamic Republic decided to derail the Reform Movement. A series of incidents from the serial killing of activists (revealed in 1998), the 2000 assassination of Hajarian, an influential reformist figure, and the shutting down of reformist newspapers (2000) all clearly exhibited that the conservatives were not going to let the change be realized. Throughout this period, reformist activists and journalists were widely arrested and charged. Consequently they—from Masoud Behnood, Mohsen Kadivar, and Akbar Kanji, to younger generations such as Ali Afshari and Omid Memarian—had no choice but to leave the country.

The Iranian diaspora shaped activism and civil society in Iran, especially during Khatami's reign.[19] However the immigration of reformist activists during the early 2000s has changed the landscape of Iranian diasporic activism. Reformists in diaspora may use more radical language to criticize the Islamic Republic; but their approach is much more connected to the sociopolitical realities of Iran and has had a major impact on changing the face of Iranian activism in the diaspora, an activism that used to be dominated by exiled opposition groups. This paradigm shift particularly manifested during the post-election protests outside of Iran; Iranians that I interviewed for this study commonly talked about how Monarchists and the SMKI were marginalized during the initial protests. This has been well identified by Dabashi, who argues that the supreme leader and expatriate opposition groups were the most important losers in the consequential events of the 2009 presidential election.[20]

New Communication Technology and Protest

The impact of new technologies on social and political movements is not a new subject; political movements have always benefited from the new technologies of their times. For example, we cannot think of the Tobacco Protest in Iran in 1891 without considering that the Ayatollah Mirza Hassan Shirazi's *fatwa* was telegraphed from Iraq to Iran. The *fatwa* mobilized people against the tobacco concession granted by the Shah of Iran to Britain; the concession signified the expanding domination of colonial power in the country. The *fatwa* sparked the protest, which forced the Shah to abolish the concession.

While most of the twentieth century was the mass media era, the second half of that century was the time of small media, such as the audio-cassette and photocopy machine. The classic example of using small media in a political movement is the use of audiocassettes by Ayatollah Khomeini to mobilize people against the Iranian monarchy while he was in exile during the late 1970s. Audiocassettes were cheaply duplicated and allowed the Ayatollah to reach a vast Iranian population of which only about 30 percent of adults were literate at that time.[21] Moreover, although mass media was under state control, the Ayatollah's statements were widely duplicated by photocopy machine.

The outcome of Iran's 2009 presidential election sparked massive street demonstrations in Tehran as well as protests all over the world. A media tsunami also ensued. According to the Project for Excellence in Journalism (PEJ) (2009), during the week of June 15 through 19, Iran was the subject of an astounding 98 percent of the links on Twitter.[22] BBC reporter Lyse Doucet explains in her lecture that "social media became virtually the only way people could see and be part of what was happening in Iran. She notes that at one point there were anywhere between two hundred and twenty-five hundred Twitter updates a minute."[23] In this circumstance, the U.S. State Department officially asked Twitter to postpone planned maintenance that would have disrupted daytime service to Iranians.[24] There was so much optimism about the role of Twitter that former U.S. Deputy National Security Advisor, Mark Pfeile, argued in favor of Twitter as a candidate for the Nobel Peace Prize.[25] However, it became clear that the role of Twitter in "mobilizing" people in Tehran was greatly exaggerated.[26] It is necessary to consider the fact that only handfuls of people were tweeting in English from Iran, and Twitter was overwhelmed with tweets posted from outside Iran. Weaver quotes Hamid Tehrani, the Persian editor of the blogging network Global Voices, who argues that "such hyperbole reveals more about [W]estern fantasies for new media than the reality in Iran."[27]

I interviewed Ali Abdi, who was in Tehran during the post-election protests; a few months later he left Iran to study in Budapest. He narrates that shortly after his arrival he gave a talk titled "The Green Movement

111 Days Later" at the university. When he asked audience members what they knew about the movement, one member replied, "Oh, yes, we heard of it—it was the first Twitter revolution." Ali said that he was astonished to hear that, as no one in Iran sees the event as being associated with Twitter (interviewed December 2012, over Skype while he was in New York City). As Solow-Niederman argues about the role of Twitter, "although it did not necessarily change the way that people mobilized within Iran, Twitter had a more global impact because it allowed citizens to publish information that helped win international support."[28]

While there was a great fascination about Twitter in the West, the Green Movement benefits from a range of new communication technology from text messaging (SMS) and email services to new social media technologies such as Facebook, YouTube, and satellite TVs. Average people became journalists by uploading video-clips, recorded by mobile phones, to YouTube. However they were still depending on satellite TVs to broadcast their reports back into Iran. Almost all interviewees in Tehran narrated that they only realized the scale of the first rally, in which they participated, when they came back home and watched the news via satellite TVs. In fact, new realizations about the scale of the protests helped to empower and motivate people to insist on their demands. One interviewee in Tehran argues that, without BBC Persian satellite TV reporting the events back to Iran, the movement would have been suppressed much sooner. Moreover, as online services and even SMS services were sometimes cut or limited in Iran, people had no choice but to use comparatively more low-tech ways of communication, such as email, to call for protests in Iran.

In two classic Iranian examples, communication technologies helped leaders to overcome the geographic distances and mobilize people across political borders. What particularly differentiates the recent protests from the two classic Iranian cases is the territory of protest. In the classic examples, the protests mainly occurred inside Iran.[29] In contrast, the recent post-election protests were a trans-spatial collective action, including Iranian communities dispersed worldwide. Seamless and instant connection to Iran particularly changed the way that Iranians in diaspora followed and engaged with the protests in Iran and other places.

The post-election protest occurred at the time when Web 2.0 technology began dominating the Internet. Although Web 2.0 sounds like a new version of the World Wide Web, it does not refer to an update to any technical specification, but rather to cumulative changes in the ways software developers and end-users use the web. A Web 2.0 site allows users to interact and collaborate with each other as creators of content, in contrast to conventional websites where people are viewers of content. Examples of Web 2.0–based social media are Facebook, Twitter, YouTube, and wikis. Following the post-election protest, "crowd-sourcing" became a new dictionary entry, signifying a new method of data accumulation and news provided by large numbers of people on a Web 2.0–based website.

Experiencing a Trans-spatial Protest

In this section mainly two interviews are discussed, but the accounts of other interviewees are also regarded. The two interviews were selected from a large number of interviews to address protest in the diaspora particularly. The first interviewee is with Farokh Negahdar, a well-known Iranian activist, who has lived in London since 1992. He describes himself not only as a leftist activist, but also as a professional political analyst. He was invited to appear on BBC Persian TV programs a couple of times every week before and after the 2009 presidential election. He engaged in organizing the post-election protests in London. I interviewed him in September of 2012. The second interviewee is named Maryam here (interviewed in October of 2012); she was an ordinary participant in the initial protests at the Iranian Embassy in London. However she explained that when the protests and slogans were radicalized she stopped joining the gatherings. Both interviews were semi-structured interviews; here only two topics from the interviews are explored: (1) discussions about media, and (2) how interviewees perceived the Iranian diaspora protests in different cities.

On the role of media, Farokh explained that:

> If the incidents after June 12, 2009, had happened 10 years before, it wouldn't have been like that. Technology had a very effective role, and that technology was mainly about [corporate] media; and I think the social media had a secondary, not primary role. Corporate media, large news firms like radio and TV, BBC and Radio Farda, have more impact compared to the social media. . . . The social media is not able to create an image, such as confirm that the election has been rigged. But corporate media connects to millions of audiences and has the authority to make a convincing statement. Nevertheless, social media is able to process that statement, modify it and even help to create such a perception. But I believe that the main player is [still] corporate media.

In contrast with Farokh, Ali Abdi argues that the Green Movement is not conceivable without Facebook and other social media (informal interview in New York, February 2013). While activists may have very diverse opinions about the role of media, the nonactivist interviewees have very similar ideas about media. Maryam explained how she followed the events and used media:

> I was really excited and frequently called my friends in Iran . . . I was calling to see what was up there. For news my main sources were Balatarin and Facebook, as they were frequently updated, so I could seamlessly follow the news. However Balatarin was not reliable . . . if I wanted to be sure about news, I was checking Gooya News. It was not frequently updated but was more reliable, as it seems someone acted as news editor. Facebook was really quick; so I got news mostly from Facebook both about Iran and here [London]. When you browsed Facebook, you see how things happened. . . . As everyone moving together, you were informed and at the same time, you were part of a group. You followed the news on Balatarin, but on Facebook you were part of the news. You could share actions with others, change your name, or share a clip, you were part of an event. . . . I was not in Tehran, but through Facebook, I knew they [her friends] were in Vanak, or Sadat Abad. As I knew where my friends were, if something happened [there], I could check how they were. . . . I was thinking, if I cannot go to Vanak Square, I can spread the call for Vanak Square. You felt like you were part of the event. Facebook was the only place that I could connect myself to my friends.
>
> But at the same time it was not a good feeling to watch the events in Iran while I was sitting here in a comfortable house. For example when a clip was spread that showed a riot police car running over someone, it was not a good feeling that you were sitting on your computer and having your tea, and feel like you were doing something. But at the same time we were with them in some way.
>
> Sometimes, when much of the communication mediums were blocked or disrupted [in Iran], I was emailing news and the call for gatherings to my friends in Iran. If they needed to be more careful, I [also] passed along analyses. I was doing that consciously, and sending messages to certain friends that I care

about, to inform and warn them, as some of them were too excited; they did not care if they died.

Interviewees both in Iran and abroad unsparingly talked about a hunger for news, to the degree that some of them even said they did not care about reliability of sources. The most striking point throughout interviews was that no one talked about Twitter, however Facebook and Balatarin[30] were the most mentioned Web 2.0–based websites.

Interviewees in Iran particularly used all media to inform themselves of the next move and to understand the scale of event that they perceived as participants. For example, Mina (a pseudonym) explains, "I only realized the scale of the first rally on the 25th of Khoradad when I arrived home and watched the news on Al-Jazeera. . . . [Therefore] every day after each event we ran to get home and see the full image of the event" (Interviewed in Berlin, May 2013). The narrative offered by interviewees show a convergence between old and new media (radio and TV against social media) as they simply talk about different media without emphasizing the differences. In Iran, even for young educated and middle-class interviewees who widely use social media, satellite TV channels remain an important source of news. This was partly because access to the Internet was easily filtered and limited, while it is very difficult to constantly jam satellite TV channels. Doucet explains that social networks and civil journalism were not only accepted as a source of news by large news corporations, but also news agencies and journalists used social media to reach their audiences.[31] In fact, when new and old media entwined, old media no longer functioned in conventional ways. For example, BBC Persian TV heavily relied on materials posted to YouTube, Facebook, and blogs during the aftermath of the 2009 election. Such a convergence is one of the reasons that interviewees did not distinguish between new media and old media.

Interviewees in Iran mainly talked about all communication technologies and media as a source of news. However as Maryam expressed, she used mediums from telephone calls to Facebook, not only to follow the news, but also to create a sense of engagement with the events in Iran. Regarding the protests at the Iranian embassy in London Farokh Negahdar explains:

The general atmosphere was like "we are with you"; participants wanted to send this message to their family, friends, and classmates in Iran. [The message was] if you are gathering in Iran for a cause, I haven't forgotten you; I am with you. It was an

emotional link between people here and there. I haven't seen
that those Greens were like "we want to show to the world the
brutality of the Islamic Republic." However the other groups
[Mojahedin and Monarchists] wanted to do that.

These accounts show that Iranian diaspora protests expanded the territory of the Green Movement into a worldwide phenomenon; this created
a landscape that connected Iranians in diaspora to the events in Iran.

I discussed the relationship between protests in different cities around
the world with Negahdar. He explained that the Iranian diaspora communities in different countries are not politically similar. He argued that
because of class discrimination, Germany is the host of leftist groups, Los
Angeles moved to the right, and Iranians in London are a mix of different
groups. He explained that while the protest in London was predominantly
a reformist event, this was not the case everywhere. He narrated:

> . . . If you were in Stockholm, there was no way to take the
> poster of Mousavi or Karroubi [to an event]. If you had the official
> Iranian flag, they would kick you out [of the gathering]. From
> day one, if your family was in the [streets] in Iran you followed
> them here in London; but they [Iranians in Stockholm] had no
> connection and presence in Iran. London was more Iranian than
> other places, as it was totally under the effect of what was hap-
> pening in Tehran. The second place was Paris and then Berlin.
> These three capitals have been more affected by events in Iran.

I asked, "What about other cities, like Washington?" He said, "I do not have
any ideas about Washington." I was surprised by his response and asked,
"Washington was not an important city for the protest, or you did not have
a connection with it? "I didn't have a good connection," he replied. Farokh
then mentioned that he was, however, well informed about the protests in
European cities. "We knew about decisions, news, and slogans in Paris,
Vienna, Berlin, Cologne, Stockholm, and Florence." How did you contact
each other? "It was Facebook, mainly Facebook. Each city has a Facebook
page, and [they] liked[32] each other." He added:

> The link between protests in different countries was not strong;
> they were all linked to Iran. . . . Let me explain why I believe
> that. We tried to run a friendship-tour by the embassy personnel,

instead of gathering at the embassy all the time; [we planned to] take a bus and go to Paris, arriving there on a day that they had a gathering. Then taking two buses and going to Cologne, arriving on a day that they had an event, then return to London via Brussels. I thought about it a lot, and made arrangements with friends that we had in different cities; but it did not go well, it was not actualized.

The connections were weak; now after three or four years that they exchanged ideas in Facebook groups and forums, knowing each other in depth, seeing hundreds of photos of each other, meeting face-to-face in some events, for example in the congress of Green Ambassadors, they got to know each other. There was no such connection at that time; it was only a name on Facebook. There was no desire to go to meet a Facebook ID. I know guys in Paris for over 20 years; I know who I am going to meet in Paris. But there was no such sense among the new generation. . . . For example, we meet just today and chat for a long time, and get to know each other. Such a relation can happen in the web, not in a day but in a year.

Maryam also talked about the events in different cities outside of Iran:

[I was following] those places that were on [my] Facebook, for example Toronto, as my friends were very active in Toronto. . . . U.S., I knew [about] again via Facebook, as some of my friends were there; I was following the news about the events in U.S. also as I was following Dabashi, Ganji and others. . . . In short, I was following the events through the network of my friends on Facebook, and in the U.S. because of Ganji and Dabashi. I was aware of events in Germany and Sweden as well, and I knew that as there were links in Gooya News.

I asked her, "Which city do you think was the most important city during that time and why?" "Probably America,"[33] she replied. I asked her which American city. She explained:

I don't know; America was more important because the events had better coverage; the news was spread both by Ganji and Dabashi; moreover, most of the bloggers were in the States at that time, those journalists who left Iran [were in the U.S.], like Ali Afshari. . . . I was following the events in London via

Facebook, and I was a part of it. Therefore I would say it was important as well. Farokh Negahdar was active and was here, and I followed his analyses; I followed Behnood a lot; [she paused] maybe I followed London a lot, especially Mohajerani, Farokh Negahdar and Behnood, all were here, I was following them seriously. . . . Perhaps London was more important [than other cities].

Talking about the relation between different cities, she explained:

They knew about each other; however, the source for all of them was supposed to be Iran. Iran was the source of motivation, all of the Green Wave groups in different countries had announced that we are moving in parallel with Iran, not less, not more; our demands were the demands of those who were in Iran. . . . All of these groups organized events at the same time but they did it at the same time with Iran. . . . [Personally] my attention obviously was directed at Tehran. . . . I followed the events in other cities but I was not emotionally involved with them.

These two accounts illustrate how the protests were practiced and per-ceived. It is highly interesting to understand how the sociopolitical network of individuals defines the geographical perception of the protesters. Even Farokh's perception has geographical limitations shaped by the network of his connections. The limit is not created by physical distance, but by the social and political distance between Iranian communities.

Facebook helped Maryam to closely follow and emotionally interact with places where her friends were during the protest. For her, London was much closer to Canada, U.S., and Tehran than France or Germany. In fact, in London she was more emotionally adjacent to Tehran than any other place. The perceptual and emotional closeness is not defined based on geographical proximity, but on a personal network that is geographically dispersed. The interviews show that the trans-local connection appears to be more important than real geography in shaping the perception and practice of the post-election protests. More importantly, although social media, such as Facebook, and communication technology create the possibility to be connected to everywhere, it is our sociopolitical connections that define the limits of our imagination.

Iranians in diaspora expanded the geography of protest, creating a space in which they associated themselves with the events in Iran. Interviews show that such a space connected everywhere to Iran, not everywhere to everywhere. Moreover, the trans-spatial protest was predominantly based on a network of one-way connections, not based on a network of interconnections. Although interviewees in Iran were somehow aware of protests worldwide, they did not much focus on the Iranian protests in the diaspora, even when I directly asked questions about them. In other words, they did not pay meaningful attention to the events abroad. I particularly discussed this subject with Ali[34] and Layla, who participated in the protests in Tehran and London. Ali lives in London and participated in protests in Tehran during his holiday; Layla lives in Tehran, and joined a gathering in London. While Ali and Layla have been directly engaged with the protest abroad, their narrations also focused on the events in Iran. For example, I directly asked Ali if he followed the news of protests in London while he was in Tehran. He said: "No, I didn't follow the events in London; I was at the heart of the events, and I didn't pay attention to inferior events" (Interviewed in October 2012 in London). The protests in the diaspora expanded the arena of protest to connect everywhere to Iran, and was not aimed at creating an interconnected system of protests.

Conclusion

The aim of this chapter was not to explore cyberactivism in the age of Web 2.0. Rather it articulated how protest and the perception of protest have changed in the age of seamless communication technology. The post-election event was new fangled not simply because of employing new technology to report events, but also in how it manifested as a trans-spatial collective action.

For the most part, the age of globalization and the Internet have immensely affected the network of diaspora communities and the way that they practice and perceive collective actions. The age has founded condition and offered facilities and structures without which the post-election protests would have manifested and functioned differently. In other words, the age of globalization and Web 2.0 instituted an infrastructure based on which the protests were manifested as a trans-spatial collective action. Web 2.0 offers an infrastructure to connect everyone to everyone and everywhere to everywhere.

However, interviewee accounts show that the configurations of trans-spatial protests were mainly based on connections made everywhere to Iran. There were connections between protests in cities around the world, but these connections did not have a major role in configuring the geography of the protest. Rather, the protests were strongly linked to Iran. Brah explains that "diaspora" refers to "dispersing from home," but trans-spatial protest implies a space that connects dispersed collective actions "back to home."[35] Web 2.0 technology and social media influenced the geography of protest, but the social network of the Iranian diaspora played a greater role in constituting the geography of protest. In conclusion, this study suggests that the geography of protest is not manifested through time or space, but through a trio of social, temporal, and spatial dimensions.

Notes

1. Matthew Weaver, "Iran's 'Twitter Revolution' Was Exaggerated, Says Editor," *The Guardian*, June 9, 2010, http://www.guardian.co.uk/world/2010/jun/09/iran-twitter-revolution-protests; Ethan Zuckerman, "International Reporting in the Age of Participatory Media." *Daedalus* 139.2 (2010): 66–75.

2. Tim O'Reilly, *What Is Web 2.0.* (Beijing, Cambridge, Farnham, Köln, Sebastopol, Tokyo: O'Reilly Media, 2009).

3. San Murugesan, "Understanding Web 2.0," *IT Professional* 9.4 (2007): 34–41.

4. Gabriel Sheffer, *Diaspora Politics: At Home Abroad* (New York: Cambridge University Press, 2006), 9; Kim Butler, "Defining Diaspora, Refining a Discourse," *Diaspora: A Journal of Transnational Studies* 10.2 (2001): 189.

5. Rogers Brubaker, "The 'diaspora' Diaspora," *Ethnic and Racial Studies* 28.1 (2005): 1.

6. Avtar Brah, *Cartographies of Diaspora: Contesting Identities* (London: Routledge, 1996), 181.

7. Jan Aart Scholte, *Globalization: A Critical Introduction* (Basingstoke: Palgrave, 2000), 160.

8. Jamse Busumtwi-Sam and Robert Anderson. "Trans-Local Diaspora and Development: A Concept and Research Note," Simon Fraser University, 2010, 4, http://www.sfu.ca/diasporas/research.htm.

9. Mark Graham and Shahram Khosravi, "Reordering Public and Private in Iranian Cyberspace: Identity, Politics, and Mobilization," *Identities* 9.2 (2002): 219–246.

10. Thomas Faist, *The Volume and Dynamics of International Migration and Transnational Social Spaces* (Oxford: Clarendon Press, 2010); Micheline Labelle and Franklin Midy, "Re-reading Citizenship and the Transnational Practices of Immigrants," *Journal of Ethnic and Migration Studies* 25.2 (1999): 213–232; Michael P. Smith and Luis Guarnizo, eds., *Transnationalism from Below* (New Brunswick: Transaction Publishers, 1998).

11. See, for example, Ulrike Freitag, Achim Von Oppen, and Elisabeth Boesen, *Translocality: The Study of Globalising Processes from a Southern Perspective* (Leiden; Boston: Brill, 2009).

12. Roger Ballard, "The Dynamics of Translocal and Transjurisdictional Networks: A Diasporic Perspective," *South Asian Diaspora* 1.2 (2009): 141–166. See also Katherine Brickell and Ayona Datta, *Translocal Geographies: Spaces, Places, Connections* (Ashgate, 2011), 3–23.

13. Mehdi Bozorgmehr, Mehdi, "From Iranian Studies to Studies of Iranians in the United States," *Iranian Studies* 31.1 (1998): 4–30.

14. Brah, *Cartographies of Diaspora,* 178.

15. See, especially, Steven Vertovec, "Super-Diversity and Its Implications," *Ethnic and Racial Studies* 30.6 (2007)): 1028–1044.

16. See "2009–2010 Iranian Election Protests," Wikipedia, the Free Encyclopedia, 2012, http://en.wikipedia.org/w/index.php?title=2009%E2%80%932010_Iranian_election_protests&oldid=523144897.

17. Sazeman-i Mojahedin-i Khalegh-i Iran.

18. Kooy is the dormitory of the University of Tehran.

19. Paola Rivetti, "The Role of the Iranian Diaspora in Shaping Iranian Activism," 2012, http://www.academia.edu/1800365/THE_ROLE_OF_THE_IRANIAN_DIASPORA_IN_SHAPING_IRANIAN_ACTIVISM; Paola Rivetti, "The Role of Diasporas in Establishing Transnational Activism: The Case of Iran," 2012, http://www.iranianalliances.org/?p=659&option=com_wordpress&Itemid=458.

20. Hamid Dabashi, *The Green Movement in Iran,* ed. Navid Nikzadfar (New Brunswick and London: Aldine Transaction, 2011), 60–64.

21. Majid Tehranian, "Iran: Communication, Alienation, Revolution," *Inter-Media* 7.2 (March 1979); Majid Tehranian, "Global Communication and International Relations: Changing Paradigms and Policies," *The International Journal of Peace Studies* 2.1 (1997): http://www.gmu.edu/programs/icar/ijps/vol2_1/cover2_1.htm; Annabelle Sreberny and Gholam Khiabany, *Small Media, Big Revolution: Communication, Culture, and the Iranian Revolution* (Minneapolis: University of Minnesota Press, 1994); Gladys D. Ganley, "Power to the People via Personal Electronic Media." *The Washington Quarterly* 14.2 (1991): 5–22.

22. Journalism.org., "PEJ New Media Index: June 15–19, 2009, Iran and the 'Twitter Revolution,'" Journalism.org Pew Research Center's Project for Excellence in Journalism, June 2009, http://www.journalism.org/index_report/iran_and_%E2%80%9Ctwitter_revolution%E2%80%9D.

23. Lyse Doucet, "#BreakingNews: Can TV Journalism Survive the Social Media Revolution?" presented at the RTS Huw Wheldon Lecture 2012, minute 15, http://www.bbc.co.uk/programmes/b01nd97f.

24. Ed Pilkington, "Evgeny Morozov: How Democracy Slipped through the Net," *The Guardian,* January 13, 2011, http://www.guardian.co.uk/technology/2011/jan/13/evgeny-morozov-the-net-delusion; Lev Grossman, "Iran Protests: Twitter, the Medium of the Movement," Time, June 17, 2009, http://www.time.com/time/world/article/0,8599,1905125,00.html.

25. Mark Pfeifle, "A Nobel Peace Prize for Twitter?" *Christian Science Monitor,* July 6, 2009, http://www.csmonitor.com/Commentary/Opinion/2009/0706/p09s02-coop.html.

26. See, for example, Christian Christensen, "Iran: Networked Dissent," *Le Monde Diplomatique,* July 2009, http://mondediplo.com/blogs/iran-networked-dissent; Weaver, "Iran's 'Twitter Revolution' Was Exaggerated, Says Editor"; Joel Schectman, "Iran's Twitter Revolution? Maybe Not Yet," *BusinessWeek: Technology,* June 17, 2009, http://www.businessweek.com/technology/content/jun2009/tc20090617_803990.htm.

27. Weaver, "Iran's 'Twitter Revolution' Was Exaggerated, Says Editor."

28. Alicia Grae Solow-Niederman, "The Power of 140 Characters? #IranElection and Social Movements in Web 2.0," *Intersect: The Stanford Journal of Science, Technology and Society* 3.1 (2010): 35.

29. For example, in the case of the 1979 Revolution, Iranian activists abroad were comprised mostly of a limited number of students in Europe and North America.

30. As discussed in Chapter 9, Balatarin (meaning the "highest") is a Farsi crowd-sourcing website in which registered users can post links to a webpage of their interest, which initially go to the "recently posted" page. Once a link collects enough positive votes, it is moved to the front page. In other words, it works as many other Web 2.0 websites do such as reddit, digg, and del.icio.us. Although the website is not a news website, it functioned as a news portal during post-election events.

31. Doucet, "#BreakingNews."

32. "Liking" a person or page is the way to link to and follow the person or group on Facebook.

33. She meant the United States of America.

34. The interviewee requested that his name be changed.

35. Brah, *Cartographies of Diaspora.*

Chapter 9

Balatarin

Gatekeepers and the Politics of a Persian Social Media Site

Babak Rahimi and Nima Rassooli

This chapter offers a study of the Persian social networking sites, with a focus on the popular social site, Balatarin. It shows how various online practices in emerging Persian social sites facilitate and also limit political activism in the broader context of transnational communication and market processes. Underlying the chapter is the general claim that all politics, including online politics, involves a contentious field of idealism and practice, and varied ways through which online political communities become products of historical circumstances and competing political persuasions.

Founded in 2006, the Persian social media site Balatarin is, as aptly described by its cofounder, Aziz Ashufteh, a kind of "news and content aggregator" that promotes dynamic interactivity between Persian-speaking users at both national and transnational levels. Balatarin serves as a distinct collective blog site with crowd-sourcing capacities that exemplify a transnational Persian language site in the form of an alternative platform for political discussion, circulation of information, and news. Yet the site has also involved exclusionary practices, a process that accelerated after the 2009 election unrest, when discussion on the site effectively became more regulated by administrators and users, primarily comprised of Green Movement activists who subscribed to Balatarin. In this light, despite the idealism of its founders, based outside of Iran, the element of gatekeeping has played a critical role in the origins and development of Balatarin as a news and content aggregator and, later, as a major website for political activism.

Emerging from the Web 2.0 dynamic social-networking environment in the mid-2000s, Balatarin represents a kind of emerging online forum that incorporates both inclusive and exclusionary political practices that underline political activism in connection with power relations.

The chapter is divided into two sections. The first (shorter) section focuses on the history of Persian social media in the context of postrevolutionary Iranian history. The second section is divided into three subsections. The first subsection offers a short history of the site from 2006 to 2007; the second subsection focuses on the period from 2007 to 2009, a pivotal time in the history of the site, when limitations of the website became apparent to its administrators. In 2008, administrators carried out a survey on the site, which revealed that users did not reflect the overall demographics of Iranian society. In 2007, the Ministry of Communications banned the site in Iran, hence underscoring the increasing political significance of Balatarin in the realm of online activism.[1] The third subsection focuses on the full-throttle politics of contention that exploded after 2009. In February 2009, pro-regime hackers stole the website's web domain, and the first signs of polarization among users began to brew when Green Movement activists dominated the site, accordingly stifling plurality of political activism on the most popular Persian social media site. What follows is an account of the challenges in the realization of the ideals of inclusivity and pluralism for one of the most popular Persian-language social media sites.

Landscape of the Persian Language Social Media

While in the mid-1990s the Internet emerged in the United States and, to a lesser extent, in Europe as a commercialized venture leading to the dot. com bubble in the late 1990s, Iranians first encountered the new technology in the form of an academic venture and, later, as an alternative space for civic activism and informal journalism.[2] In its earlier age, Internet sustained fantasies of free expression and political dissent, rousing excitement among activists and new technology enthusiasts alike.[3] Amid the conservative and reformist conflict, characteristic of the reformist period under Mohammad Khatami's presidency (1997–2005), the marker of such transition occurred first with the rise of a new generation of political activists and journalists who experimented with the launch of newly designed websites, though at times crude in conception, to display alternative news and express political views online, though not always with the intention of reaching a global audience.[4]

The second significant change occurred in the early 2000s with the rise of blogs as a new social platform for individual and collective expressions for a new, confident young generation of men and women activists who saw the 1997 elections as a democratic opening for political and social change. The growth of the Iranian blogosphere coincided, in this historical context, with the rise of a restless young population under the age of thirty, who began to shape a new culture of civic engagement in postrevolutionary era. The new youth was belligerent, subversive, and innovative in self-expression. The blogs, in many ways, served as an unofficial medium of expression for a younger generation of Iranians who, in the words of Nasrin Alavi, were experiencing a "changing consciousness" in participation and consumption of a transnational market economy and, specifically, a global youth culture, especially in the so-called developing world.[5]

In correlation with the proliferation of blogs in the early 2000s, Persian became a major feature of the social media landscape. The critical date in the emergence of Persian as a leading blogging discourse was marked with the arrival of the Unicode system, unifying character sets with a single encoding system, in November 2001. The introduction of such global software technology to the Iranian Internet market brought about a dramatic shift toward a new popular culture of Internet activities. With Hossein Derakhshan, an Iranian-Canadian journalist, posting the first weblog guide, Persian-language weblogs began to proliferate. This development in many ways overshadowed the proliferation of minority languages such as Azari, Baluchi, and Kurdish. Yet Persian became a sort of a transnational mode of communication for many Iranians, living in Iran or abroad, who sought to carve out spaces of national cultural expression in cyberspace.

The popularity of blogging practices overlapped with other global processes. In their study of the Iranian blogosphere, Annabelle Sreberny and Gholam Khiabany describe how the rise of blogs was directly connected with business models that opened the way for private capital to expand in the cultural industries.[6] During the era of expanding consumerism in the late Khatami period (2001–2005), the private sector emerged as a key actor in the growth of new media in Iran. PersianBlog, launched in June 2002, for instance, owned by the Iranian company Ariangostar, served as the first blog server to provide a discussion forum for various topics. Other blogs served as discussion forums for topics ranging from music to marriage and literature to politics.[7]

With the end of the Khatami presidency in the mid-2000s, when the reformist administration had completed the construction of a 56,000-kilometer network of high-speed fiber-optic cables, the Iranian blogger community began migration to social media sites such as Orkut, an online network community created by a Turkish software engineer, Orkut Büyük-kökten, in 2004 and owned by Google. With Orkut's popularity on the rise, by 2008 Iran's social media had entered a new stage of interconnectivity that increasingly began to revolve around sharing-connectivity sites such as Flickr, YouTube, and, by 2009, Twitter and Facebook.[8] While Western social media sites were filtered by the state, a new Internet culture linked through computer-mediated communication infrastructure had emerged with the vernacular language as the dominant means of discussion and interaction among Iranians living both in Iran and outside of the country.

Cloob, launched in 2004, is one of the earliest Persian-language sites. The social networking site, also known as the "Iranian Virtual Society," became popular after Orkut came under state censorship, and since the site operated in accordance with regime guidelines it gained popularity among computer users. Cloob combines networking and advertising, a common feature of the global socioelectronic commerce. Yet Cloob is also a site that includes links to state-sanctioned blog sites, banking and health services, online shopping, e-commerce, and numerous online news sites. A link on the site Cloob.com describes the self-regulative feature of the social media site this way: "What is certain is that the launching of Police Cloob is not about unwarranted limitations but in fact for respect and protection of the freedom of the users and providing a more pleasurable experience with the second life known as the virtual life."[9] Though such a self-regulative state-ment reflects the enhancement of censorship regulation over the Internet since 2001, the social site remains popular among users, in particular its popular chat rooms, which provide real-time and immersive online conver-sation forums in Persian.

Other government-sanctioned social-networking sites such as Afsaran. ir and Persigg.ir identify both the highly politicized and also the social char-acter of Persian-language sites, which combine various subjects and themes from political commentary to humor and recreational activities. Persigg. ir, for example, provides photo- and video-sharing services with the ethos that privileges the amateur user. Numerous other sites ranging from e-news, file-sharing, religious blogs, and search engines such as rismoon.com and electronic email servers such as maildata.ir represent varied types of govern-ment-approved Internet sites that provide services to Iranians based in Iran. Equally important is the rise of e-commerce and e-governance in Persian, which has been on the rise since 2006 with the increasing commercialization of the Iranian Internet. Online shopping sites such as Shahrvandonline.com and Shopkeeper.ir and online banking services by Bank of Sepah underscore a distinct Persianization of Iranian online activities, with a focus on public interaction through private or public institutions.

Meanwhile, many new social media sites, some designed and managed outside of Iran, represent emerging networking hubs, where users can post jokes, political statements, commentaries, links to news, and gossip, and share self-help guidelines or poetry. Sites such as Manmigam.com, for instance, serve as assemblage sites, bringing together some of the most popular blogs with the "hottest" online links about actors and other famous Iranians. Sites such as "Like bezan va bekhand" (Like and laugh) are popular satirical sites designed for social media such as Facebook, YouTube, Twitter, and Instagram, with a large young audience. Ashioon.com is another social-networking site for youth at large, while Shajar.ir targets the younger population with a religious orientation. With the growth of Facebook popularity in 2009, a number of Persian sites, some of them satirical, have emerged to reconfigure the Iranian social media around Facebook's concept of friendship networking practices through private or public messaging activities.[10] Iranfacebook.net is a site, for example, modeled after Facebook as a social-networking site with a design that is purportedly based on Iranian national culture—a nativist version of Facebook. As social media evolves, so do online activities that reshape informational networks defined by designers and users who participate in the larger market, society, and state settings.

In this complex dynamics of social media constellations and configurations, Balatarin has emerged as one of the most popular Persian-language sites since 2006. A site that gained popularity during the 2009 election turmoil, when many would receive and circulate news on the site, Balatarin has emerged as a quintessential Persian-language social-networking site to bring together both social and political news and views on an online platform. Yet it is precisely this social networking that highlights a contentious dynamic in terms of what can be included and excluded in the process of posting online. It is to this feature that we now turn.

The Case of Balatarin

Balatarin literally means "highest" in Persian. The record of seminal events in the history of Balatarin present here is a "living history" of a Persian language website. Guobin Yang argues that "the development of the Internet is like the development of a person or a society. One's past is always part of the present identity."[11] In many ways, the trajectory of the website has been shaped by the chaotic multi-interaction environment of the World

Wide Web where administrators, algorithms, users in Iran and the diaspora, cyber nationalists, the Iranian state, and other transnational forces clash and coexist.[12] But more than a clash spot for activists, Balatarin is also a site of contention over identity, language, and political idealism.

The Beginnings (2006–2007): Utopian Hopes

Web developers Aziz Ashufteh and Mehdi Yahyanejad cofounded Balatarin in August 2006. As business entrepreneurs in the United States and Norway, respectively, Ashufteh and Yahyanejad were deeply troubled by the gatekeeping occurring in the Iranian collective blogs. Collective blogs are a centralized network of bloggers under one umbrella site with an editor. These sites are updated regularly and have the potential to be a platform for diverse "arguments, opinions, and analysis."[13] The aim of these collective blogs, according to one blog editor, Darius Ashouri of malukut.org, is to function as an online equivalent to free and open discussion circles where respecting the right of "freedom of speech" and "pluralism" are the rules for being a member of a blog.[14] However, in contrast to Darius Ashouri's utopian vision of collective blogs, the cofounder of Balatarin, Ashufteh, believed editors of collective blogs had "dictatorial" control of their sites.[15] Gatekeeping was largely left to the whims of the editor. For instance, the collective blog Sobhana, edited by the "Blogfather," Derakshan, was criticized for being akin to "Hossein Derakshan's personal blog." He claims to have introduced Iranians to blogging in 2000 with a tutorial in Farsi on how to write a blog, and he was the most prominent face of the Iranian blogosphere. Derakshan used the blogosphere to promote his popularity and create a cult of personality around him. Though the collective blog claimed to be open to all to post, the sign-up process was limited, scheduled for once a month.[16]

Around the same time collective blogs were becoming popular, Web 2.0 sites also became popular on the World Wide Web. In 2005, Tim O'Reilly started the Web 2.0 conference in Silicon Valley. Tim O'Reilly argued dynamic social-networking environments brought the full democratic and market potential to the web.[17] Not so much the market aspect, but the democratic potential of Web 2.0 technology mesmerized the two cofounders of Balatarin. The site that got most attention from the cofounders was the Web 2.0 site Digg.com. According to Ashufteh, a Persian-language Digg would be the solution to the problem of arbitrary gatekeeping in collective blogs.[18] Digg.com is a social-networking news site that uses crowd-sourcing algorithms. Users post and vote on what posts are popular. The crowd-sourcing element of the site prevents arbitrary gatekeeping.

The Persian-language Digg.com appeared in 2006. Crowd-sourcing algorithms were used to create an environment where freedom of speech would be maximized in the Iranian blogosphere. The era of editorial gatekeepers of collective blogs ended, since on Balatarin the gatekeepers are algorithms and the anonymous registered users of the site. Balatarin users vote on the most popular content and news to appear on the site. Items with positive votes would be more visible than those with negative votes.[19] Crowd-sourcing algorithms were used to ensure diverse content on the website. There would be a trigger limit for the placement of different content. Political news and content would need forty positive votes to be promoted, while art and literature news and content would need fewer votes. A degree of personalization is visible on the site. For those users only interested in political, arts, or sports posts, there are category filters called "highlights" to look at specific content that meets their criteria.[20]

Not only did Ashufteh and Yahyanejad believe they found a solution to the gatekeeping problem with Web 2.0 media, they also believed they found a technological solution to limitations in Iranian civil society. Balatarin came to be seen as a way to creatively shape an alternative public sphere that would foster unprecedented dialogue, away from the watchful eye of the theocratic state. In particular, they believed Balatarin would be a powerful tool to foster an exchange of ideas and discourses between the rural and urban divide, the religious and nonreligious, men and women, the poor and the rich, and ethnic minorities and Persians. The differences in lifestyle and culture would be bridged. People of all political and ethnic persuasions would coexist in a pluralistic public sphere, which would strengthen Iranian civil society.[21] Such was the utopian aspiration of Balatarin.

The Realities (2007): Realizing the Limits

Six months after the launch of the website, Balatarin faced obstacles from the state. The Ministry of Information and Technology blocked access to the site on February 1, 2007. The official reason the Iranian government gave for blocking the site was a link posted on the site about the rumored death of Supreme Leader Ali Khamenei.[22] The decision to filter the site reflected the increasing trend to block sites during the Ahmadinejad administration. Much of the energy of the administrators of the site diverted from the lofty goals laid out in the preceding section to ensuring access to the site.[23] The administrators tried to launch other sites, such as Balatarin.info, but those attempts were futile as those sites were blocked as well. Users in Iran soon had to use proxies to visit the site. Popular anti-filtering software such as Tor and VPNs are examples of methods to bypass online censorship. The proxies Iran-based users used to circumvent filtering made it impossible to gather accurate web-trafficking statistics reflecting the actual demographics of the site, which is important to analyze the base of the site.[24]

Despite the roadblocks to surveying the website faced from government filtering, in 2008 administrators decided to do a survey on the site.[25] Using data from their surveys, Google analytics, and Alexa, figures were amassed.[26] Alexa showed that only 40 percent of the traffic on the site was from Iran. Such a statistic, however, is difficult to confirm. Iranian users had to use proxies to pose as users from random places, such as African countries, to visit Balatarin. Thus, the statistics were erroneous.[27] It turned out that 95 percent of users on the site were men. Though Ashufteh notes there were some prominent active female users on the site, and male users on the site were receptive to their posts, the gender gap on the site was too wide.[28] Most users were between the ages of twenty-three and thirty-five, urban, and had at least some higher education. It was revealed that there were populations of ethnic minorities using the site, including Afghanis, Azaris, Kurds, and Arabs. Since xenophobia toward ethnic minorities is prevalent both in Iran and among the diaspora, minority Balatarin posts, especially posts advocating autonomy or separatism for Kurds or Azaris, for instance, would receive negative votes.[29] The Persian-speaking majority then utilized negative votes to lower the placement of views advocated by ethnic minorities.

Later in its rise in popularity, it was revealed that the website had a long way to go to restructure Iranian public sphere. Not only did the user population of the site forge ahead with exclusionary politics that prevented Balatarin to achieve an idealized democratic forum for all Iranians, but the Iranian government also made access to the site more difficult through filtering and, hence, limiting the diversity of views and voices on the site. Yet the early obstacles that the site faced were minuscule compared to what was to come in 2009 during the postelection turmoil.[30] As Iranian politics became more polarized as a result of the 2009 elections, so did Balatarin, with administrators facing the most serious challenge to their vision of building democracy through Internet activism.

The Maelstrom (2009–Present): Site Goes Green

With the approach of the 2009 elections on June 12, Balatarin was hacked by pro-government online activists. As Saed Golkar documents, the Iranian regime created a cyber-army pro-government militia unit to attack sites they perceived to be antigovernment. The cyber basij movement stole Balatarin's web domain on February 3, 2009. The website was shut down for two weeks as servers were shut down. Fortunately, the administrative passwords weren't stolen, or else the security of the site would be breached permanently.[31] The justification the hackers gave in shutting the site down was that the pro-Palestinian posts during the Operation Cast Lead Operation in late 2008 were not getting many positive votes.[32] Instead of taking part in the Balatarin community to promote their views, pro-government hackers decided to sabotage the site. The attempts by government to sabotage the website backfired, as supporters of the site launched a campaign to support the return of the site, and traffic on the site increased as the 2009 Presidential elections approached.[33]

Not only was the Islamic hardline government attempting to sabotage the site, the reformist movement attempted to ruin the impartiality of the site. With the approaching election in early 2009, supporters of the reformist candidate sought the administrators of Balatarin to launch a new Balatarin-type site for the Reformist candidate, former-president Mohammad Khatami.[34] The administrators declined because they felt if the reformists used Balatarin logos in the launching of the site, it would alienate nonreformist users of the site.[35]

In the postelection crackdown the site transformed ultimately into an information hub for the antigovernment supporters of the Green Movement. Eighty-nine percent of the users were these antigovernment activists.[36] Much attention in the Western media has been given to the role of Twitter and Facebook and their use by antigovernment protesters. But as a Persian-language networking site, Balatarin was much easier to navigate for Green Movement supporters and was a place where links from those Western social-networking sites would be accessible. Activists used the site to announce protest locations and to aggregate material such as YouTube videos of protests and links from Mir-Hossein Mousavi's Facebook page. The site became an information hub for Green Movement activists to circulate information.[37]

In the postelection period, the Green Movement online activists became the unofficial gatekeepers of the site. Nonpolitical posts, some of them comical in nature, for instance, would get negative votes.[38] The site became increasingly under the control of the Green activists who would stifle dissenting views. Any post that was not political and not suited to the Green Movement agenda received negative votes. Pro-government and nonpolitical users of the site thus left the site. Negative votes on anti–Green Movement and nonpolitical posts made those users unmotivated to use the site.[39] Thus non–Green Movement users deserted the site or, worse, exploited the site by creating fake accounts to get positive votes to inflate their popularity on the site. Supporters of the Islamic Marxist opposition group, the MEK, and supporters of the exiled son of the Iran's last monarch, Reza Pahlavi, have been known to use such tactics. Within a matter of weeks, Balatarin moved farther from its ideals of being an experiment in bringing democracy to Iranians through the Internet.[40] As Rahmandad and Mahdian point out, the site became a reflection of polarization in the Iranian online community, a collective undergoing the trauma of political turmoil and seeking ways to make sense of the uncertainty of politics offline.

Yet Balatarin was viewed as a major threat to state security. A major intimidation agenda was unleashed, targeting both users and administrators of the site. Some of the threats targeted administrators with punitive measures if they would travel back to Iran. In one case, the authorities convicted a Balatarin user and issued a two-year prison sentence for inciting discord by posting a link about how to plug in ironing machines collectively to take down electricity during peak hours in the heyday of the summer protests in 2009.[41] More important, as Saeed Golkar explains, the regime also infiltrated the site and posted anti-Islamic posts to destroy cohesion between religious-minded and secular Green Movement users.[42] Religiously controversial posts led to administrators to change the censorship policy to ban blasphemous posts. The change in censorship policy made the administrators realize that there are limits to freedom of speech in the Iranian public sphere, even in cyberspace.[43] While Ashufteh regrets the censorship policy on the site, he acknowledges the importance of such a measure. It was done, he explains, due to the limited resources of the site, and also because offensive posts could alienate a large portion of the Iranian society, which is considerably religious.[44]

State efforts to curtail Balatarin's popularity also involved attempts to frame the activities of the site in terms of association with foreign entities. The state TV, for instance, produced a number of documentaries smearing Balatarin as being funded by the Mossad, the Israeli intelligence agency.[45] The smear campaign by the regime against Balatarin reflects a larger trend of the Revolutionary Guards and the Intelligence Ministry portraying social media as a national security threat.[46] But such policies are contradictory, as the government held its first social media conference in 2011.[47] In addition, hardliners have created a government-sanctioned version of Balatarin called afsarin.ir in an attempt to co-opt the site into a state-approved social site for its supporters.[48]

Besides the public relations smear campaign by the regime and personal intimidation, the regime has threatened the financial solvency of Balatarin by stepping-up its offensive on the site. Balatarin, for instance, is frequently attacked with DDOS (Distributed Denial of Service) attacks. These attacks cost thousands of dollars to perpetrate. These attacks usually have happened during key dates on which the regime anticipated unrest.[49] The site has been forced to switch from physical servers to Amazon's VZ2 virtual servers (also known as Amazon Cloud servers). These servers are quite costly for a site that does not generate profit. They allowed the site to increase the capacity of the servers in anticipation of days the regime would attack the site. But such proactive measures are limited because when the servers face DDOS attacks they will be taken down by Amazon.[50]

The lack of funds the site experienced forced cofounder Balatarin Mehdi Yahyanejad to pitch to Google the launch of Google advertisement services to Balatarin as a way to generate revenue to maintain the site. U.S. sanctions and the fact that most of the Iranian-based users didn't have credit cards made Yahyanejad's pitch initially unattractive to Google.[51] But this offer was a public relations opportunity for Google because the American multinational was making compromises with censorship in China until it decided to cut its operations in the Chinese mainland. To provide funds to a site that was a victim of another authoritarian regime provided Google an attractive venue to renewing its public relations. Thus Google AdSense was allowed access to the site, and gave the site huge revenue to maintain its services.[52]

Numerous attacks on the website by the Iranian state and the realization of the contracted demographics of the users, not entirely representative of the Iranian society and its various political and social views, had already alienated the early enthusiasm of the administrators of the site.[53] As the cofounder of the site and also its leading administrator, Ashufteh left Balatarin in 2012.[54] Ashufteh explains the challenges of the site in terms of both idealism and practicalities of management in relation to finances. While the objective was in the service of the Iranian public sphere, financial gain would keep the site up and running in light of changing demographics of users. For Ashufteh, and many former administrators, there are hardly any profitable Persian websites online. The lack of profit, loss of motivation, and possible government intimidation make it enticing for administrators to abandon work on Persian websites and take on more profitable ecommerce ventures in their new host countries in North America or Europe. Ashufteh is currently working on Norwegian e-commerce websites. He also laments that Balatarin has become similar to Derakshan's collective blog, Sobhana.[55] The site to a certain extent has morphed into Derakshan's collective blog, a place of exclusion and insular discourse. While collective blog membership was open to all, not all were treated equally on the blogosphere. The same can be said of Balatarin. Membership on the site has been closed for a long time. Though he was propagating democratic ideals on the Web, Derakhshan was also perpetuating authoritarian tendencies to promote exclusionary discourse and hence hindering democratic vibrancy online. In contrast to an echo chamber, Balatarin has morphed into a platform exclusive to Green Movement activists, limiting diversity of content and viewpoints. The site is currently a news-gathering source for members of like-minded Green Movement activists.[56]

Ashufteh's frustration with the current status of Balatarin resonates with Homa Katouzian's paradigm of Iran as a short-term society. Long-term development of society, in the form of progress toward collective prosperity, has been neglected in all societal and governmental facets, according to Katouzian, because social actors in the Iranian context pursue short-term interests as they become increasingly dependent on the whims of the state. A viable market economy serves as a necessary institution for a vibrant civil society. However, Iranian websites lack the support of a market economy to develop their endeavors.[57] The Green Movement users on Balatarin have become their own "cyber-dictators," as opposed to allowing a viable civil society to take shape online.[58] Due to the limited infrastructure of Balatarin, ambitious projects to expand the site have been cut, and the earlier visions to create a viable civil society through such social media site have been abandoned. For Ashufteh, developing websites in the Persian-language Internet world as a nonprofit enterprise is an invitation for harassment by the Iranian regime, who could augment the financial instability of an online service to technological challenges with cyber-attacks that could undermine the site's ability to function for its users. Balatarin is now a dystopian failure.

Conclusion

The short history of social media carries stories of successes and epic failures, involving academics, venture capitalists, geeks, and subcultural activists who emerged only to become part of a growing digital mainstream market. With the dotcom bubble in the early 2000s, Silicon Valley saw a need for Internet startup ventures that would span advertising, ecommerce, gaming, and, more important, social networking. Such a participatory model of the Internet became part of a new business model of the online economy. The

Web 2.0 advanced this meme to create the next dot-com bubble, and Google AdSense, which made advertisement recommendations from searches users made, shifted toward a "participatory audience foregrounds labor dynamics" with users and audiences as interchangeable in a new online economic transaction domain.[59] All these features of personalization and social networking existed way before with chat rooms and message boards, but those features became increasingly monetized.[60]

In 2005, social-networking sites such as LinkedIn, Flickr, Reddit, Facebook, and Digg offered a new interactive Internet landscape. These social media sites offered networking features with users on the website; friends shared news stories and photos, and personal information was shared for networking among friends, personal employers, and others. To the CEOs of these startups—soon to be billion dollar industries—options of personalization for the user was exchanged for profit with data mining of the features.[61] By and large, however, the trend in Internet studies has mostly failed to offer studies in variations in development of the Internet on local and contextual factors, which create different trajectories in the development of the Web. The result of this study shows that the Internet is neither the Habermasian public sphere, where critical-debate reigns, nor a free-market domain, where free exchange of commodities is made. For most types of general practices of social media, the Internet is an uneven social domain where such sites serve as distinct public spaces of contestation.[62]

What in the United States and other developed countries was viewed as a market engine to generate profits, in Iran was an idealistic desire to create a dynamic Iranian public sphere. Today, there are thousands of Iranian bloggers, Facebook users, and numerous others who either interact in Persian-language sites or create new ones, despite state regulations. In popular and scholarly accounts, blogging was popularized by Derakshan, who presented a Persian language handbook on how to start blogs for people in Iran. After the closure of a brief season of free press in the early Reformist era (1997–1999), Derakshan called for journalists of the recently closed newspapers and ordinary Iranians to express themselves online. The birth of the Iranian blogosphere was a direct result of the reformist failure to build a free public press.

With the emergence of Reddit and Digg in 2005, the founders of Balatarin and other social networking sites saw that blogs were an out-of-date method of information aggregating.[63] As Ashufteh explains, this new development marked the beginning of Balatarin for redirecting the path Iranian blogosphere was headed and create a more interactive site. By using Web 2.0 to enable users to vote on posts without intervention by a gatekeeper, they sought to counteract the trajectory. Early in its formation, Balatarin would be blocked by Iranian ISPs, hacked by the Iranian government, and some of its users arrested.[64] After the 2009 election, pro-government voices on the website were marginalized and harassed; many left the site for the increasing exclusionary politics of the site. What was supposed to be an open site for all Iranians of various political persuasions soon became an organizing and discussion network for the Iranian opposition alone. This surely was a source of concern for the Iranian state—that the site would be a possible source for organizing offline political activism—but for Balatarin the postelection trend could be described as a radical shift away from its original idealism as an open forum for discussion. To maintain stability, administrators of the site had to act as their own gatekeepers, blocking content and setting algorithms that privileged certain material over other material over the site.[65] Despite the threat it continued to pose to the Iranian regime for the dissemination of alternative news critical of the Islamic Republic, Balatarin then began to reflect an offline everyday life in which politics is factional and legitimacy perpetually contested.

Notes

1. Aziz Ashufteh, personal interview, Oslo, Norway, July 29, 2012.

2. For a brief history of the Internet in Iran, see Cyrus Farivar, *The Internet of Elsewhere: The Emergent Effects of a Wired World* (New Brunswick and London: Rutgers University Press, 2011), 163–166.

3. Niki Akhavan, *Electronic Iran: A Cultural Politics of an Online Evolution* (New Brunswick and London: Rutgers University Press, 2013), 13.

4. For a study of online journalism in Iran, see Chapter 5 in this volume.

5. Nasrin Alavi, *We Are Iran* (London: Portobello Books, 2005), 361.

6. Annabelle Sreberny and Gholam Khiabany, *Blogistan: Internet and Politics in Iran* (New York: I. B. Tauris, 2011), 39–41.

7. For an election-related political blog site, see Parsvote.com.

8. Akhavan, *Electronic Iran*, 13.

9. See http://www.cloob.com/etc/police/report.

10. See also http://facenama.com/home?v=1; http://www.parsiyanchat.com/facebook/; http://i30you.blogfa.com, http://fb.iran.ai.

11. Guobin Yang, *The Power of the Internet in China: Citizen Activism Online* (New York: Columbia University Press, 2009), 21.

12. Ibid.

13. Sreberny and Gholam, *Blogistan*, 51–56.

14. Ibid, 52.

15. Ashufteh interview.

16. Srebrerny and Khiabany, *Blogistan*, 51–56.

17. Matthew Allen, "Tim O'Reilly and Web 2.0: The Economics of Mimetic Liberty and Control," *Communication, Politics & Culture* 42.2 (2009): 6–23.

18. Ashufteh interview.

19. Ibid.

20. Ibid.

21. Ibid.

22. http://balatarin.com/permlink/2007/1/5/1010544.

23. Ashufteh interview.

24. Ibid.

25. Ibid.

26. Ibid.

27. Ibid.

28. Ibid.

29. Ibid.

30. Ibid.

31. Ibid.

32. Ibid.

33. Ibid.

34. Ibid.

35. Ibid.

36. Ibid.

37. Ibid.

38. Ibid.

39. Hazhir Rahmandad and Mohammad Mahdian, "Modeling Polarization in Online Communities," Paper Presentation at the 29th International Conference of the System Dynamics Society, Washington DC, July 24–28, 2011.

40. Ibid.

41. Ibid.

42. Saeid Golkar, "Liberation or Suppression Technology—The Internet: The Green Movement and the State in Iran," *International Journal of Emerging Technologies & Society* 9.1 (2011): 50.

43. Ashufteh interview.

44. Ibid.

45. Ibid.

46. Ibid.

47. Ibid.

48. Ibid.

49. Ibid.

50. Ibid.

51. Ibid.

52. Ibid.

53. Ibid.

54. Ashufteh is currently working for an online advertisement startup in Sweden, which he believes is a long-term sustainable endeavor.

55. Ashufteh interview.

56. Ibid.

57. Homa Katouzian, "Problems of Democracy and the Public Sphere in Modern Iran," *Comparative Studies of South Asia, Africa, and the Middle East 18*.2 (1998): 31–37.

58. Ashufteh interview.

59. Michael Mandiberg, "Introduction," in *The Social Media Reader* (New York and London: New York University Press, 2012), 7.

60. Ibid.

61. Ibid.

62. Yang, *The Power of the Internet in China*, 21.

63. Ibid.

64. Ashufteh interview.

65. Ibid.

Chapter 10

Architectures of Control and Mobilization in Egypt and Iran

David M. Faris

At first glance, the Egyptian uprising of 2011 and the Iranian Green Movement of 2009 would seem to have a great deal in common. They both followed on the heels of a preposterously rigged election—in Egypt, the December 2010 parliamentary charade that increased representation for the National Democratic Party to truly impossible levels, and in Iran, more immediately in the re-election debacle of Mahmoud Ahmadinejad. Both mobilizations appeared superficially to be driven by social media. Iranian protestors were rumored to have used Twitter and Facebook to help organize the protests, and in Egypt, the revolution was openly plotted on the Facebook page dedicated to the murdered young Alexandrian Khaled Said; the Iranian uprising was thus dubbed by many to be the first "Twitter Revolution," whereas Egypt was said to have undergone a "Facebook Revolution." Furthermore, Egyptian activists expressed support for the idea that the Green Movement was an inspiration for their work during the Arab Spring.[1] Both of these ideas obscure more than they illuminate, and lead to unproductive debates about whether social media undermine authoritarian rule. But the reality is that these technologies did contribute to both uprisings, but in different fashions that were structured by their respective political and institutional contexts. Superficial similarities obscure important and ultimately much larger differences in timing, authoritarian structures, and activist networks. The Egyptian and Iranian uprisings were not, therefore, seemingly identical movements that led to different outcomes, but, rather, structurally distinct movements that arose out of different social, economic, and political conditions.

199

This is not a study of the trajectories of the Egyptian and Iranian uprisings. There are existing political science analyses of why elements of the Mubarak regime stepped aside under massive popular pressure,[2] and why the Iranian regime chose to crush its uprising with indiscriminate violence. It should also be clear that if we are interested in explaining the role of social media in generating mass mobilizations, the outcomes of those mobilizations belong to a separate realm of inquiry, since social media are incapable of convincing autocratic military apparatuses to step aside or to refrain from the use of force. The Iranian regime pursued its violent crackdown even in the midst of nearly ubiquitous international press coverage (in spite of kicking nearly every foreign correspondent out of the country at the beginning of the crisis). The absence of democratic change in Iran was not because no one knew what was happening inside the country. In part due to ongoing reports from courageous citizen journalists, the world knew exactly what was happening, just as the Egyptian regime's failed shutdown of the Internet during the height of the protests failed to cut off the supply of information to or from the activists. On the contrary, the Iranian regime emerged from its confrontation with the Green Movement primarily because key figures within the regime maintained the support of the Iranian Revolutionary Guard Corps, and key figures within the IRGC determined that there was more to gain from siding with the regime than with the protestors.

The role of social media in Egypt and Iran should be compared along two primary axes of difference: first, Iran was a considerably more nondemocratic regime than Egypt. To admit this is not to look back at the Mubarak period through rose-tinted glasses—Egyptian internal security services were as ruthless in their applications of torture and detention as any other country—but to take seriously the decade-long project launched by Middle East specialists to understand the functional differences in authoritarian regimes. In that respect, Iran was a far more difficult place to be an activist in the late 2000s than was Egypt, with Iran demonstrating a clear willingness not just to harass or blackmail activists, but to kill them or subject them to long-term imprisonment. These authoritarian structures had a substantial impact on the kinds of activist networks that evolved in the two countries. The second key difference between Egypt and Iran is governance of the Internet, with Egypt maintaining a liberal Internet legal framework that was almost breathtaking in its seeming indifference to what activists were doing online. Iran, on the other hand, even prior to the post–Green Movement crackdown, was much quicker to realize and systematically react to the emergent threat of digital technologies to its ongoing rule. These two institutional differences—authoritarian structures and Internet governance—

would lead the Egyptian and Iranian mobilizations in wildly different directions. Understanding how and why this is so sheds light not only on the two countries, but also on the potentialities of collective mobilization via digital media in authoritarian regimes more generally.

Authoritarian Regimes and the Internet

One goal of this chapter is to advance a three-tiered schema of authoritarian treatment of the Internet. Since activists began using the Internet to advance collective goals against authoritarian governments, those regimes have responded in a variety of distinct ways. The most basic, and certainly the cheapest, reaction was to harass or jail the activists but to leave the sites, applications, and the Internet itself more or less alone. I have termed these governments "response regimes." Some governments, however, were not content with merely responding to activists in piecemeal fashion, and over time, developed extensive architectures of filtering, monitoring, and censorship, all designed to place barriers between ordinary people and politically or culturally sensitive destinations on the shared global Internet.

While such regimes were aware that committed activists under such circumstances were able to deploy software or applications to route themselves around censorship, the goal was control—of information, of mobilization, and of the sites themselves. These are "control regimes." Finally, a third type of regime emerged during the course of the 2000s, similar in goals and behavior to control regimes but featuring also a concerted effort to erect a parallel set of social media and information sites—in effect to close off access to the global Internet and to create a local simulacrum that would meet all of the social and informational needs of the citizens, albeit in a sanitized and deeply monitored fashion. I call these "cordon regimes."[3] For the purposes of this chapter, it is important to note that Mubarak-era Egypt was a response regime, whereas Iran evolved from a control regime into a cordon regime. It is one thing to make claims about the consequences of state policies, and quite another to trace them. To establish that Egypt and Iran differed meaningfully along the axes claimed above, an examination of digital activism in both states is warranted.

Egypt

Egyptian digital activism is commonly dated to the Second Intifada, when the Egyptian government appeared unable to take any concrete action to support Palestinian protests[4] and subsequently increased in scale and importance during the lead-up to the U.S.-led invasion of Iraq in 2003. This convergence took place at the precise moment that free, easy-to-use, and off-the-shelf blogging tools like Blogger were beginning to make self-publishing accessible even to the most technologically averse individuals. Therefore you could say that an increased demand for activism (in the form of popular revulsion at the Mubarak regime's ongoing collusion with Israeli and American security interests) was met conveniently by a suddenly expanded supply of activist tools in the form of free self-publishing software.[5] In 2000–2001, Egypt maintained one of the most closed press environments in the world, directly or indirectly controlling all large-circulation newspapers, and carefully circumscribing what could be said or reported on television. Into this void of critical discussion and dissent stepped independent print newspapers, such as *Al-Dustur* and *Al-Masry Al-Youm*, which were privately owned and carried often devastating criticisms of regime policies.[6] Both newspapers featured functional interaction, and often cooperation and cross-pollination with the emerging Egyptian blogosphere—in other words, many prominent bloggers wrote for, or would later write for, these publications, and reporters at both papers often used the blogosphere as a source of information or ideas for stories. It was this symbiotic relationship between the independent press and the blogosphere that allowed Egypt's most influential bloggers to sometimes perform agenda-setting functions in Egyptian politics.

Egyptian blogging was also distinguished by its substantial cooperation with the primary umbrella opposition group from the 2004–2010 time period, which was called *Kefaya* ("Enough!" in Egyptian Arabic). From the very beginning, entrepreneurial bloggers would publicize and attend *Kefaya*'s protests, write about them, and document them with photographic and video evidence. Many of these same bloggers were also members of the loosely knit organization. The bloggers were led by a pioneering set of activists centered on Manal and Alaa's Bit Bucket, run by Alaa Abd el-Fattah and his wife Manal. This networked core included influential figures such as Hossam el-Hamalawy, Amr Gharbeia, Mahmoud Salem (aka Sandmonkey), Baheyya, Nora Younis, and many others.[7] In this way, the country developed a hardened and battle-tested core of committed political activists who were also skilled in the developing forms of digital protest and coordination. Their skills would be deployed in the most disruptive way in the social battle against the government's deployment of torture. Torture was the issue that brought Egyptian bloggers their first "scalp"—the indictment and prosecution of four police officers for the brutal torture and sodomy of Ehab el-Kabir, a bus driver who was arrested for interfering with the arrest of his cousin.[8] El-Kabir's torture and rape were captured on film by the offending police officers (who were fond of taping and exchanging their various brutalities). That tape found its way into the hands of Egyptian bloggers, most notably the pioneering blogger Wael Abbas, who posted it to his *Misr Digital* homepage, and with the help of a print journalist named Wael Abdel Fatteh at the newspaper *Al-Fagr*, identified El-Kabir and convinced him to cooperate. The ensuing controversy, which was heavily covered in *Al-Dustur* and *Al-Masry Al-Youm*, led the government to reluctantly prosecute the officers responsible and led to prison time. The work of Abbas and others led to an explosion of blogging, thinking, and advocacy around the issue of torture—not just online but also by grassroots organizations like the Egyptian Initiative for Personal Rights, the El Nadeem Center, and the Arab Network for Human Rights Information. Courageous bloggers like the anti-torture activist Noha Atef and the journalist Nora Younis soon joined Abbas.

The years of work by these activists had a number of important effects. First, it created a battle-hardened cadre of hardcore protestors who were skilled in the arts of crowd control, deception, and the seizure of public space, while also linking these activists into other sectors of Egyptian civil society. While in the early 2000s, the digital activists were among a tiny minority of Egyptians who even had access to the Internet at all, by 2011 nearly a quarter of the population was online, vastly increasing the value of the networks themselves, and creating a situation in which key sectors of the country's opinion leadership looked to these digital activist networks for guidance. Together with labor actions involving hundreds of thousands of people during the late 2000s,[9] Egypt's digital activists contributed to a generalized atmosphere of dissent that proved most helpful to activists when the critical juncture arrived in January of 2011. Not only did they now have the experience, but by linking issues like torture, human rights, and economic destitution together, the activists were able to appeal to broad swaths of the Egyptian public that went well beyond the elite activist core in the cities and touched on grievances shared by rich and poor Egyptians, as well as leftist and Islamist constituencies. When Egyptian police murdered Khaled Said in the summer of 2010, then-anonymous activists in the activist community were able to leverage a long history of organizing to create the Facebook group We Are All Khaled Said seemingly out of thin air. But the fact that this group almost instantly had hundreds of thousands of members was no coincidence—it was the legacy of a decade's worth of hard work. The fact that, as Kashani-Sabet argues, the digitally-led opposition was seemingly nonideological actually strengthened their appeal to most

Egyptians.[10] This allowed the activists to build a broad coalition, mounting an unusually strong and unexpected challenge to an entrenched and strong authoritarian regime. As Mona El-Ghobashy argues, "a strong regime faced a strong society versed in the politics of the street."[11]

It also, critically, faced a regime that fatally underestimated the power of digital organizing, and believed, until the end, that its response policies were more than capable of containing whatever dissent did arise. The Egyptian government, of course, was known to imprison and prosecute individual bloggers, like Kareem Amer, who was sentenced to four years in prison in 2007.[12] But trying to generalize from the Egyptian case is challenging, because the Mubarak regime was a genuine outlier in its regulation of the Internet, or lack thereof. Despite being one of the first regimes in the Middle East to experience multiple instances of Internet-driven popular mobilizations against its policies, the Mubarak regime never responded to digital activists except to create architectures of surveillance and punishment, neither of which was undertaken with the ferocity or competence needed to actually deter the activities in question. Egypt is also distinguished by its decision to liberalize its press environment at precisely the moment that social media technologies were emerging as powerful mechanisms of circumvention and dissent, in 2004–2005. The precise motivations behind this liberalization remain opaque, but it is worth noting that the country was under immense pressure from the Bush Administration to pursue democratic reforms, and that there was always an implied conditionality to U.S. economic and military aid that may have prevented the Egyptian regime from pursuing more draconian Internet censorship activities than it did.

Iran

In contrast to Egypt, Iranian bloggers spent much more time squaring off against a state determined not just to perform the occasional spectacular act of punishment, but also to degrade the activists' ability to execute dissent at all. Partially because so many Iranians were blogging about so many disparate subjects, Iran even well before the Green Movement was a global leader in arrests of bloggers (along with Egypt)[13] but also coupled this repression with a broader project. Thus, unlike the Egyptian regime, the Iranian government unveiled its plan to create a "clean" Internet, free from external influence or penetration. Like the Chinese, the Iranian regime aggressively pursued local—and thus co-opted—forms of social media. These sites offered nonpolitical users a similar range of functioning, along with the key networking capabilities of Social Network Sites (SNS) but added a layer of censorship and filtering both to keep tabs on any potential political activities, and of course to deter the marginally political citizen from crossing red lines. Over time, and especially since the failure of the Green Movement to dislodge or alter authoritarian structures, the regime has become even more aggressive in its persecution of activists and its determination to erect a set of parallel sites on an exclusively Iranian Internet.

Of course, the abortive democratic opening of 1997–2005 preceded this period of increasing control of the Iranian Internet, when the reform-ist President Mohammad Khatami was thwarted at seemingly every turn by a conservative establishment determined to undermine the basis of his support, and the program of marginally liberalizing the Islamic Republic.[14] The reformist period saw both a crackdown on opposition media as well as the emergence of the Internet as a vector of dissent and mobilization. As Rahimi argues, "As older spaces of dissent were increasingly choked off by the introduction of a new press law that restricted freedom of expression the new technology appeared as an alternative and safe place to express dis-sent."[15] The use of digital media applications accelerated over the course of the 2000s, and reached its apex with the postelection crisis of 2009, with a plethora of applications and sites, including those explicitly designed to promote the presidential candidacy of Mir-Hossein Mousavi, deployed to maximize network effects and build sustained opposition to policies of the regime. As in Egypt, there was substantial cross-pollination between the worlds of online and offline journalism. As Sreberny and Khiabany detail, ". . . many journalists became bloggers, and many bloggers have become journalists, especially outside Iran."[16] The difference, of course, is that many Iranian digital activists were forced to do their work abroad, and while much of their work has been vital, during the critical juncture of 2009, it proved a less effective vehicle for a sustained on-the-ground challenge to the Iranian regime than the Egyptians were able to mount two years later.

The Iranian blogosphere was, of course, one of the richest in the world, and Farsi one of its top languages. The 2000s saw the emergence not just of tens of thousands of blogs, but of a discourse community committed to the project of reform, linkages between Iranians and Iranian groups in exile, and local actors who sought to carry out projects inside the country. Thus, as of 2005, Egypt and Iran were in somewhat similar structural positions in regards to their relationship with the Internet. This period also represented the high point of the U.S. drive to democratize the Middle East, with sig-nificant rhetorical pressure emanating from Washington to liberalize politics across the region, rhetoric made more menacing and perhaps credible by the presence of an occupying U.S. Army in Iraq. This pressure may have had something to do with the Mubarak regime's relatively tepid response to the threat of Internet activism. From there, however, trajectories diverged. While Egypt focused on harassing, detaining, and occasionally imprisoning digital activists, the Iranian regime, under the presidency of the reactionary Ahmadinejad, set about not just stifling digital dissent but rather bringing the whole panoply of Internet services under the firm control of the government.

The Iranian project of controlling the Internet actually accelerated prior to (and perhaps in anticipation of) the 2009 election crisis. In 2006, the state reduced the Internet speed of all connections to 128 Kbps per second, which as Karagiannopoulos argues, had the effect of "greatly hindering the uploading or downloading of information."[17] With the formation of the Iranian Cyber Army and the strategic unblocking of Facebook in the winter of 2009, which as Rahimi argues, was designed to facilitate intelligence gathering on opposition groups, particularly pro-Mousavi sites,[18] and despite the mobilization mounted by the Green Movement in the summer of 2009, it is easy to see how the Iranian regime's much more aggressive response to Internet activism has dampened the potential of the Iranian Internet to play host to the kind of long-term activist movement that led to the overthrow of the Mubarak regime in Egypt. This is particularly true as the Iranian regime has transitioned from a control regime to a digital siege state. Following the Green Movement crisis, the government moved aggressively to promote a set of parallel, pro-regime social-networking sites, including the since-shuttered Velayatmadaran,[19] a move that signals the state's intention to not just control the Internet, as in prerevolutionary Tunisia, but to create an entirely separate Iranian Internet, as in China. Rahimi argues that this move toward increased vertical control is part and parcel of the Iranian state's militarization:

> . . . since the 2009 elections, the Iranian state has been elevated into a more security-conscious system of governance with the aim of establishing a sophisticated network of surveillance and intelligence-gathering in order to stifle internal dissent.[20]

This increased digital securitization is an outgrowth of the overall drift toward securitization in the Iranian state. This is not to say, however, that digital networks did not play a role in the Green Movement. As Mohammad Sadeghi Esfahlani details in this volume, the architects of the Green Movement leveraged Facebook to their advantage, building a network of committed activists and volunteers who they were able to mobilize when the expected vote-rigging materialized on June 14, 2009. Despite its move toward more authoritarian politics, Iran had played host to a decade's worth of online dissent, and its journalists, bloggers, and activists were skilled in making the Internet a vector of mobilization. The problem was that, whereas in Egypt the 2000s witnessed the proliferation of protest politics explicitly concerned with undoing key aspects of Mubarak-era authoritarianism, in Iran the Green Movement had to overcome the failure of Khatami-era reformism, as well as the state's willingness to deploy nearly limitless deadly violence to maintain power. And some Iranians may have been reluctant to press for a full regime change, with the memory of what became of the 1979 Iranian revolution. The Iranian regime was also willing to risk global approbation in the form of images and stories of repression leaking out to international journalists, if this violence allowed the regime to maintain its grip on the country. Faced with a similar set of options, key elites in the Egyptian military decided that their interests would not ultimately be well-served by the continuation of public and spectacular violence.[21]

Bringing Authoritarianism Back In

Yet the differences go beyond Internet architectures. Iran's more hard-line treatment of political opposition more generally created a climate that was much more difficult to penetrate with traditional organizing. As El-Nawawy and Khamis argue,

> [t]he absence of a domestic Iranian civil society that would lead to the formation of segmented, polycentric and integrated networks of political activism played a critical role in the failure of the 2009 protests.[22]

This absence of civil society groups in Iran was not an accident; it was the direct result of authoritarian politics that brooked little to no dissent, and responded to the heady days of opening in 1997–2005 with a more concerted, and brutal, effort to reestablish the legitimacy and power of the regime by crushing the opposition. In contrast, the Mubarak regime in Egypt, whilst authoritarian by any reasonable standard, nevertheless allowed a limited number of offline civil society groups—such as the Arab Network for Human Rights Information, the Egyptian Personal Rights Initiative, and others—to operate above-ground, and to establish linkages between digital activists, opposition political figures, human rights lawyers, and international organizations. This digitally-mediated activist network was of utmost importance when the activist community decided, in January 2011, to launch a full-fledged challenge to the Egyptian regime. It meant that not only would the digital elite turn out for these protests, but that thousands of activists were able to leverage their offline connections to brick-and-mortar activist groups, and to put together a movement that transcended the limitations of Internet access in a poor, developing country like Egypt.

The Iranian regime and its Internet policies were therefore much more structurally similar to the regime of Zine El-Abadine Ben Ali in Tunisia than they were to those of Hosni Mubarak in Egypt. The critical difference appears to be that, in Tunisia, military elites believed their interests could be more capably protected by a civilian administration established through democratic channels, whereas in Iran the elites of the IRGC saw their interests and those of the Islamic Republic as inextricably tied together.[23] A secondary reason is the different ideological underpinnings of the Egyptian and Iranian regimes. By the 2000s, Egypt's ruling party, the National Democratic Party, had almost no ideological raison d'etre at all, beyond a generalized claim of competence and stability. In its almost total ideational vacuum, the NDP was remarkably similar to the centrist, pan-ideological Institutional Revolutionary Party (IRP) that ruled Mexico for most of the twentieth century. The NDP was the inheritor of the original Nasserist revolution in 1952, which was not a revolution but rather a narrow political coup that initially redistributed benefits more broadly, but that by the time of Mubarak had merely rearranged structural inequalities and gave a new elite access to traditional state rents.[24] By 2011, that neoliberal elite was increasingly threatened by strikes and protests, on the one hand, and by the military's desire to re-establish its commanding position in society. By contrast, the Iranian regime possessed at least the structural façade of an ideological apparatus, and the Islamic Republic maintained some credibility with factions of the public for reasons other than the perceived competence of its economic stewardship. This proved important, as both the Green Movement and the instigators of the Arab Spring played on popular frustration with the corrupt, unequal economic status quo.[25] This is not to say that the regime was popular, but rather that what remained of its popularity could not necessarily be chiseled away by poor economic news or diminished job prospects for its young people and rested at least in part on the mass-based origins of the Iranian revolution itself.

Conclusion

This chapter sought to establish that the success or failure of collective mobilizations through digital media is deeply influenced not only by the potentialities of each individual online or mobile application, but also by the longer-term institutional structures of authoritarianism that are extant in each case of mobilization under authoritarianism. In Egypt, activists squared off against a response regime that made no concerted effort to disrupt the digital architectures of networked organizing and dissent. Meanwhile in Iran, the government pursued the digital policies of a cordon regime, seeking to completely cut Iranians off from most currents on the global Web. These policies resulted in a much denser, more experienced, and battle-hardened cadre of Egyptian digital activists seizing a critical juncture in January 2011, whereas the Iranian Green Movement depended on both information and networks that were at least partially located overseas. Still, the ultimate trajectories of the mobilizations themselves depended also on nondigital variables, largely the repressive will of the coercive apparatus in both states. It should be clear through this analysis that digital media do not confer mystical powers of mobilization and revolutionary vigor on opposition forces in authoritarian societies; authoritarian Internet policies can both alter the utility of networks to function properly, as well as generally clamp down on the density of opposition organization offline. Together the policies of the Iranian regime were able to successfully steward the regime through its period of postelectoral crisis and violence in 2009 in a way that most Arab regimes were not able to do in the aftermath of the Tunisian and Egyptian uprisings in December and January 2010–2011. To say that Iran was successful in preserving its institutional power, however, is not to say that the government, no matter what policies they deploy, can completely shut down the networked activism enabled by digital media technologies. On the contrary, as the Tunisian example demonstrates, even seemingly successful filtering and censorship policies are vulnerable to very simple work-arounds, and that this kind of control has two primary effects: First, dissent is moved out-of-country and becomes located primarily in exile and diaspora networks of activism. Second, and perhaps more important, a committed core of digital activists can therefore become skilled in the complex arts of circumvention, and can build shadow networks even in the face of determined regime interference. Therefore in Iran, if a crisis erupts, we should not be surprised if digital activists once again play key organizational and amplifying roles, even given the seeming success of the Iranian regime in disrupting and controlling the Green Movement.

Notes

1. Charles Kurzman, "The Arab Spring: Ideals of the Iranian Green Movement, Methods of the Iranian Revolution," *International Journal of Middle East Studies* 44 (2012): 162–165.

2. See Erin A. Snider and David M. Faris, "The Arab Spring: U.S. Democracy Promotion in Egypt," *Middle East Policy* 18.3 (Fall 2011): 49–62; Mona El-Ghobashy, "The Praxis of the Egyptian Revolution," *Middle East Report* 41 Spring 2011); Ann M. Lesch, "Egypt's Spring: Causes of the Revolution," *Middle East Policy* 18.3 (Fall 2011): 35–48.

3. I am indebted to my former student Cory Schenn for coining this term.

4. Rania Al-Malky, "Blogging for Reform," *Arab Media and Society* 1 (Spring 2007): 1–31.

5. Courtney Radsch, "Core to Commonplace: The Evolution of Egypt's Blogosphere," *Arab Media and Society* 6 (Fall 2008): n.p.

6. David Faris, *Dissent and Revolution in a Digital Age: Social Media, Blogging and Activism in Egypt* (London: I. B. Tauris, 2013), 55.

7. Ibid., 49–84.

8. Ibid., 69–70.

9. Joel Beinin, "Workers' Struggles under Socialism and Neoliberalism," in *Egypt: The Moment of Change,* ed. Rabab El-Mahadi and Philip Marfleet (London: Zed Books, 2009): 68–86.

10. Firoozeh Kashani-Sabet, "Freedom Springs Eternal," *International Journal of Middle East Studies* 44 (2012): 156–158.

11. Mona El-Ghobashy, "The Praxis of the Egyptian Revolution," *Middle East Report* 41 (Spring 2011): 2–13.

12. "Gloomy Day for Freedom of Expression in Egypt. Tough Sentence for Four Years against Kareem Amer," *Arab Network for Human Rights Information,* February 22, 2007, http://anhri.net/en/reports/2007/pr0222.shtml (accessed June 18, 2013).

13. Annabelle Sreberny and Gholam Khiabany, *Blogistan: The Internet and Politics in Iran* (London: I. B. Tauris, 2010), 62.

14. Trita Parsi, *A Single Roll of the Dice: Obama's Diplomacy with Iran* (New Haven: Yale University Press, 2012).

15. Babak Rahimi, "The Agonistic Social Media: Cyberspace in the Formation of Dissent and Consolidation of State Power in Postelection Iran," *The Communication Review* 14 (2011): 158–178.

16. Sreberny and Khiabany, *Blogistan.*

17. Vasileios Karagiannopolous, "The Role of the Internet in Political Struggles: Some Conclusions from Iran and Egypt," *New Political Science* 34.2 (June 2012): 155.

18. Rahimi, "The Agonistic Social Media," 171.

19. Ibid., 172. Since 2011 the site Velayatmadaran has been closed down.

20. Babak Rahimi, "Iran's Declining Influence in Iraq," *The Washington Quarterly* 35.1 (Winter 2012): 25–40; 32.

21. It is worth nothing that hundreds of Egyptians perished in the eighteen-day uprising, which was in its initial stages substantially bloodier than the Green Movement uprising in June 2009.

22. Mohammed El-Nawawy and Sahar Khamis, "Political Activism 2.0: Comparing the Role of Social Media in Egypt's 'Facebook Revolution' and Iran's 'Twitter Uprising,'" *CyberOrient* 6.1 (2012).

23. Eva R. Bellin, "The Robustness of Authoritarianism Reconsidered: Lessons of the Arab Spring," *Comparative Politics* 44.2 (2012): 127–149.

24. Joshua Stacher, *Adaptable Autocrats: Regime Power in Egypt and Syria* (Stanford: Stanford University Press, 2012), 156.

25. Nikki R. Keddie, "Arab and Iranian Revolts, 1979–2011: Influences or Similar Causes?" *International Journal of Middle East Studies* 44 (2012): 150–152.

Chapter 11

Social Media and the Islamic Republic

Niki Akhavan

The policies of the Iranian state toward social media show similar patterns to how various forms of media have been approached throughout the history of the Islamic Republic, where repressive measures aimed at controlling content are in tension with attempts to expand uses of the same technologies in ways that are favorable to ruling interests. At the same time, official actions vis-à-vis social media have been unique owing both to the specificities of these platforms and the local and global sociopolitical contexts in which they have emerged. Premised on the desirability of ever-growing networks of connections and generally strict word limits, social media heighten the sense that massive amounts of information are being shared with exponentially growing audiences at breakneck speeds. As such, social media have been both credited to varying degrees for facilitating social and political protest[1] and criticized for the opportunities they afford commercial, state, and other interests for surveillance and misuse of personal information.[2]

The rise of social media in Iran can be traced to 2006, but it became a major focus of both Iranian and foreign state attention only after the 2009 presidential election in Iran and its aftermath of massive demonstrations. In addition to the widespread journalistic commentary on the role of social media at the time, scholars have provided multifaceted accounts of how protesters used these platforms.[3] While mainstream and citizen journalists exaggerated the role of new technologies in the protests, both popular and scholarly accounts have shown that social media provided many with the opportunity to expand their protest activities and to spread news in the face of government censorship. What has remained underexamined, however, is the Iranian state's broader strategies vis-à-vis social media, significant aspects of which must indeed be read in relation to the 2009 events.

For independent journalists and activists, as well as for those benefiting from the direct or indirect sponsorship of foreign states, social-media use following the disputed 2009 election indicated that these global platforms could be instrumental in severely wounding the Islamic Republic. Apparently sharing its opponents' take on the power of social media, state actors' responses in the wake of 2009 reflected an urgency captured in the Iranian state's official launch of "soft war" soon thereafter. While explicit references and funding for this policy have waned since 2011, it remains important for assessing the state's approach to social media.

Making sense of soft war is not a straightforward task, primarily because its official articulations and implementations have been prolific but dispersed and often inconsistent. In addition, much of what officials and state supporters have included under the umbrella of soft war is in continuity with previous approaches to media. The soft-war discourse entered official discussions soon after the 2009 election fallout, with the Supreme Leader Ayatollah Khamenei specifically addressing it a number of times and famously stating that "Today, the country's top priority is to fight against the enemy's soft war."[4] While this quote and the context of the speech in which it was delivered put the emphasis on ways that Iran has been the target of largely media focused attempts at undermining the state, official formulations have also framed soft war as something that Iran engages in as a response to said activities of its enemies. As Monroe Price has shown in his overview of sample statements by Iranian officials about soft war, state actors are particularly concerned that Iranian value and belief systems are being targeted by Iran's enemies as part of a larger strategy of overthrowing the current ruling structure.[5] According to these accounts, the main vehicles for this assault are various media forms, from foreign-funded radio and television stations to an increased deployment of digital media technologies.

Unlike "hard" forms of war such as conventional warfare or other militarized operations, these methods are not overtly coercive or destructive. Rather, they aim to attract the target society toward the values of those carrying out the soft war. In this sense, what the Iranian state has called soft war has been a routine part of state discourses and policies since the establishment of the Islamic Republic. In addition, it is similar to definitions of "soft power" as put forth by Joseph Nye. According to Nye, states can use various forms of hard power such as military action or economic coercion to gain an upper hand over their opponents, but states can also use their country's' cultural and policy institutions to draw others into their worldview.[6] In short, these latter methods and aims of exercising "soft power" are very similar to Iranian officials' claims about the intent and effect of foreign organizations and media carrying out soft war against Iran. What further complicates defining the difference between soft war and soft power is that the two terms are sometimes used interchangeably in Iranian discussions.

Despite the connections to the notion of soft power, and despite the continuities with past phases in the Islamic Republic's cultural and media policy, what is called soft war in Iran is distinct in a number of ways. For one, although its main concerns are about soft-power tactics against Iranian values, soft war encompasses broader ideas, policies, and sets of discourses. It is distinct in the intensity of discussions and budgets focused on revealing and combating enemy tactics, with many resources devoted to knowledge production about the soft war itself. It is both a new strategy and policy in the sense that it combines the state's rhetoric on fighting cultural invasion and maneuvers for controlling media content and access with attempts to create state-friendly materials online. In the past, these components did not explicitly overlap, with the state largely pursuing repressive and proactive approaches to media as separate endeavors.

Given that expansions on the soft war intersected—and in part were a response to—the popularity of social media in Iran, it remains an important framework for understanding official stances toward this media form.[7] At the same time, state-linked approaches to social media also include other aspects that require further investigation. In addition to emphasizing vigilance in the face of threats to Iran's cultural and moral fabric, state representatives have also couched concerns about the dangers of the medium in terms of personal and public safety issues. Discourses and institutions that have emerged to variously deal with social media, therefore, provide multiple justifications for state intrusions into citizens' online activities, from protecting individual and public safety to safeguarding the country's cultural and political integrity. State and state supporters' involvement with social media also include strategies for active engagement of the platforms, including both establishing home-grown versions of social media and participating in popular global sites. None of the range of activities and discussions, however, has been without their internal contradictions or gone unchallenged by either state critics or supporters.

Social Media as Sites of Moral and Criminal Transgression

While claims about social media–based assaults on Iran's culture and values make for good political speeches, which have led to a proliferation of state-supported strategies for combatting such attacks, similar emphasis has been placed on how new technologies endanger the personal and moral well-being of individuals. The institution that best exemplifies this is the Iranian cyber police, or FATA, which stands for *Polic-e Fazay-e Toleed va Tabadeel Etellaat* (The Police for the Sphere of the Production and Exchange of Information). FATA was established in 2011 as an official branch of Iran's police forces. Their self-description as outlined in the "About Us" section of their website, which begins with a somewhat philosophical reflection on the relationship between technology and humankind and includes a brief history of computer crimes, justifies FATA's existence by pointing out that ". . . the mushroom-like growth of crimes in the sphere of the production and exchange of information such as Internet scams, the falsification of data and titles, information theft, transgressions on the private spheres of individuals and groups, hacking and infiltration of the Internet and computers, pornography, moral crimes, and organized crime in economic, social, and cultural realms, necessitate a specialized police force with the capacity to address high tech crimes."[8] As such, FATA's activities as reported on their website and via other news outlets emphasize the role they play in safeguarding the moral, economic, and social well-being of the populace in the Internet age. These reports consider digital media writ large as the arena of potential danger, but much of the focus since its establishment has been on social media in particular.

In September of 2012, for example, the Kurdistan branch of the cyber police reported a case of extortion in which a perpetrator had stolen a college student's personal information and created a fake social media account. The police were calling on individuals to refrain from placing personal information and photos on their mobiles and other external storage devices.[9] Privacy violations are also often linked to bigger moral concerns. Again in September, the official Islamic Republic News Agency reported that Major Niknafas of Iran's cyber police had issued warnings against posting any personal pictures on social-media websites. Niknafas argued that such photos may be altered in "inappropriate and obscene" ways and recirculated online, forever damaging the reputation of victims.[10]

The fact that the cyber police takes on the mission of highlighting vulnerabilities online is not by itself worrisome, and indeed, they may be commended for attempts at educating and safeguarding the public against new media dangers. The problem, however, is that potentially legitimate concerns have been used as a pretext for controlling online content and persecuting social-media users they accuse of spreading corruption and obscenity. For example, in August 2012, the cyber police arrested the administrators of a Facebook group called *Dafhay-e Tehran* (which roughly translates as Hot

Girls of Tehran), a page with about thirty thousand members, calling them a gang intent on "deceiving young Iranian youth and Internet users and forming gangs."[11] Pages such as Hot Girls of Tehran and similar sites currently active on Facebook may be subject to a feminist critique and raise ethical questions about privacy online, but the cyber police have taken "moral" concerns as an excuse for criminalizing routine—if objectionable—activities online.[12] Similarly, in December 2012, the head of FATA in Gilan Province called Facebook a "battlefield of criminals," announced that a team of experts from his unit were going to be closely monitoring the activities of those who "target society's morals," and warned ordinary Internet users against becoming Facebook members and keeping their personal photos and videos online.[13]

FATA is not the first law enforcement entity dedicated to Internet crimes. The *Gerdab* Project, which is linked to Iran's Islamic Revolutionary Guards Corps (IRGC) and predates the formation of the FATA police by approximately three years, shares with the latter the tendency to blur the boundaries among "moral crimes," privacy, and public threats to justify its interventions in the online sphere. Unlike FATA, the *Gerdab* Project's "about us" section is relatively brief and emphasizes pursuit of "organized terrorist, espionage, economic, and social crimes in the virtual sphere."[14] Nonetheless, most of the content it houses on its website under the category of "cyber threats" highlights potential harms to individual users with numerous articles devoted to the insidious presence of hackers on social media sites, the dangers these sites pose to children and adolescents, and the vulnerability of one's private information.

Concerns couched in moral terms or in relation to privacy issues also dovetail with broader worries about attacks on Iran's national and cultural identity as well as with assertions about the machinations of foreign intelligence agencies and private corporations. For example, *Gerdab* has claimed that Google misuses the "What's Hot" feature of its social media platform Google+ in "targeted anti-Iran" efforts.[15] *Gerdab* has also accused the "West" of "hosting and spreading pornographic sites in several languages" in order to shake the beliefs of the people of other countries and to weaken their patriotism.[16] The website *Jang-e Narm*, which describes itself as an outlet for providing information about soft war and psychological operations against Iran, also contains numerous original and republished articles that situate a range of concerns about social media in terms of attempts to alter the fabric of Iranian society. For example, social media are described as sites for "promoting the Western lifestyle" and working to "overthrow governments which resist this lifestyle."[17]

Official discourses on social media often assert that the platforms are being used for intelligence gathering and infiltration. Using screen shots to make their case, for example, the *Mehr News Agency* has reported that members of the Mojahadin-e Khalq opposition group have taken to Facebook under the guise of independent journalists and human rights activists to "connect with users inside Iran in order to spy, obtain information, news, and images" for dissemination via their own media platforms.[18] Iranian news outlets and organizations also consistently run stories about various U.S. government projects for mobilizing social media for intelligence gathering and for promoting U.S. policies. The sourcing for many of these stories are themselves U.S. outlets, reflecting some level of engagement—or at minimum, monitoring—of non-Iranian media by pro-government forces in Iran, which are usually vocal in opposing these outlets.

Furthermore, they show the parallels between official Iranian and U.S. positions: though they remain antagonistic and consistently critical of one another's social media policies, both have recognized the intelligence value and threat of the medium, and both have used national security and personal safety threats as justifications for aggressive approaches to emerging media.[19] The increasing push for forms of digital media control under the guise of personal and public safety, of course, is not new; even before the age of social media, a number of scholars outlined the ways that state actors and individuals have called for and enacted various mechanisms of surveillance.[20] Thus, the Iranian state's stance on social media and its attempts to use interlinked concerns about national and individual security as justification for intervention is not unusual; governments of various stripes have used similar claims to justify intrusive Internet policies.

Producing New Spaces and Engaging Popular Platforms

In addition to the above-noted processes of defining the threats of social media and justifying control mechanisms, governmental and pro-government actors have attempted to establish alternate social-media spaces. In so doing, they have often moved in thematically specific directions. That is to say, they have gone beyond the rubric of general networking to introduce specialized sites, most of which revolve around religious themes The idea is not simply to create new platforms but to push for content production in a particular direction. One such site is the Ministry of Culture and Islamic Guidance's sponsored platform, Hadinet.ir, which a Ministry official described as the "first social media site dedicated to the Imams."[21] In turn, the Ministry has asserted the success of Iranian sites to announce support for launching similar platforms.[22] Other specialized social-media sites aimed at drawing the participation of religious and state-friendly populations include *Haya* and *Khakriz,* which is a part of a cyber network for *arzeshees* (a term that roughly translates as "those with values").[23]

The phenomenon of arzeshees deserves a separate analysis, but for the discussion at hand, it will suffice to note their appearance during the first administration of Mahmoud Ahmadinejad. Mostly in their twenties and early thirties, self-described arzeshees identify with hardline elements of the Iranian state and society and are active in various online spaces and on social media in particular. Although initially overwhelmingly in support of Mahmoud Ahmadinejad, identification with him became less pronounced as Ahmadinejad increasingly clashed with other conservatives, including the supreme leader. Whatever their relationship to Ahmadinejad and his faction, arzeshees have had a visible presence on global social media, and it is not surprising that sites inside the country have been set up to build on this participation for the purpose of cultivating native forms of social media.

Other state linked or state supporting organizations have also framed their online presence in terms of independent social media. The website of the governmental *Sazmaan-e Zanan-e Enghelab-e Eslami* (Organization of the Women of the Islamic Revolution), for example, describes itself as a social-media platform, complete with an extensive terms of use document.[24] In addition to having to have their "real identity" confirmed by the administrators, participants must agree to a list of conditions governing their speech and behavior online. Many of these rules, such as not being rude to other users and not ridiculing regional dialects, aim at keeping a generally civil atmosphere that is free from prejudice. However, prohibitions on insulting the previous or current supreme leader narrow the limits of speech in ways that users would not face in non-Iranian social-media sites. While these limits have an explicit basis in Iranian law,[25] the site also sets some odd parameters, including a ban on "giving publicity" to [Iranian] singers from LA or Hollywood or Bollywood stars. Nonmembers can see materials posted by active users of the site and view the public profiles of members, but based on information the site makes available about how many have viewed and commented on materials, it seems minimally interactive, with fewer than a dozen active users accounting for most of the postings. Indeed, based on what is publicly accessible, the site is closer to a typical participatory website of the Web 2.0 era, where several administrators post a range of materials and supervise the supplemental content provided by individual users. The fact that the organization chooses to describe its online presence as a social-media site is in keeping with trends apparent in other official quarters: namely, there is an apparent desire to appear abreast of technological developments and to create autonomous platforms.

At the same time—and claims about the popularity of such websites notwithstanding—state entities and supporters seem to recognize that competing with global sites is no easy feat. In an overview of "pure" social-media sites (as opposed to the corrupting popular platforms), an account on the *Jang-e Narm* website admits the lackluster reception of the former, arguing that,

> "Although lately the efforts of revolutionary bloggers have created social-media sites with an *arzeshee* approach, the relatively weak graphics, inadequate promotion, and the fact that many influential *arzeshee* forces are not familiar with these spaces has meant that these sites have been unable to compete with sites like Twitter and Facebook, which benefit from the financial support of the American government."[26]

While the author does not provide any evidence for the assertion of U.S. government monetary support of these sites, his argument echoes many similar accounts from within Iran which acknowledge the scale of the competition they are taking on. More important, they are an admission that Iranian social-media sites have either failed or—at best—are facing major obstacles in attracting participants.

This difficulty is also sometimes framed in terms of "content production." Numerous forums have been devoted to defining and encouraging proper forms of content production. The gist of these discussions is that producing the right kind and volume of content will bolster the popularity of Iranian social-networking sites, in turn allowing them to compete with services like Facebook and Twitter. For example, in November 2012, the show *Rah-e Sevom* (the Third Way)—broadcast on channel two of the IRIB—was devoted to the topic of content production.[27] That such topics have spilled over to official spaces offline is indicative of their centrality to debates on social media. They also show that unlike independent users of social media, institutions and individuals with state links have an advantage in accessing older forms of media. While this does not seem to be enough to ensure that they make a mark in online spaces, it does show a disparity in resources available to the state, which has the ability to mobilize vast resources as compared to independent users. Yet the state's projects to expand and promote friendly social media as well as the continued active presence of state supporters and officials on popular global platforms indicate that the mass efforts to replace the latter with homegrown sites have not been fruitful.

Individual users predisposed to hardline currents in the ruling establishment have also acknowledged this lack of success in informal spaces. In a well-circulated blog post, Amir-Hossein Mojiri, a self-identified arzeshee, addresses the question of why the "arzeshees are not successful in social networks." In addition to acknowledging the conventions of productive social media presence in a variety of popular sites (e.g, the number of "likes," "followers," "members in circles," etc.), he considers why arzeshee users have not managed to meet another core element of social-media success—namely, the creation of networked connections. Reasons he proposes include lack of personal photos or names and the tendency to lecture others and "act robotically."[28] However, the author does not acknowledge the political dimensions of the issues. Being an arzeshee is about claiming a specific sociopolitical outlook; that alone may explain why other users reject reciprocal connections with them online, no matter how personable and friendly the arzeshee appears. Alternately, non-arzeshee users may not be personally opposed to such connections but may fear being labeled or rejected by their own network of online "friends." The same dynamic may also be at work in the case of well-known figures in the state establishment. The social-media accounts of figures such as the Supreme Leader Khamenei only have followers numbering in the thousands. This is despite the fact that these accounts have attracted much attention, with quotes and pictures from these accounts often showing up in a range of news pieces and online debates. It may be, then, that some readers are checking these accounts without subscribing to them. Thus, while Mojiri does not address all the factors that may be at work, his post and a range of similar discussions indicate a clear recognition on the part of official and individual supporters of the state that their efforts to both participate in existing social-media platforms and create independent spaces have fallen short.

"Enemy" Terrains

In addition to the difficulties they have faced in establishing a secure foothold in social-media spheres, the approaches of pro-state individuals and projects are rife with inconsistencies. The site *Teribon*, for example, which is an online magazine sympathizing with the most conservative elements of the state, regularly runs pieces that are critical of foreign-funded outlets and

call for independence in platforms and content production. At the same
time, *Teribon* also contains content that normalizes participation on popular
social-media sites. In one such case, the site ran an article providing its
readers with a list of guidelines on how to become popular on Facebook.[29]
What makes this example particularly noteworthy is not only the subject
but also the source of the article, which *Teribon* acknowledges as the Persian
language website of the German *Deutsche Welle* (the *Deutsche Welle* piece
was itself a summary of an article originally posted on the American site
The Huffington Post). For an outlet that identifies with the hardline currents
in the ruling establishment, is critical of foreign-funded Persian media and
foreign media in general, and supports the creation of independent platforms and content, the decision to include an article such as this appears
puzzling. Yet it is not rare to find this type of material posted on *Teribon*.

Even the earlier-described *Jang-e Narm* and *Gerdab* projects routinely
post translations of articles from U.S. and other foreign outlets. Examples
include *Jang-e Narm* relying on *Time* magazine to draw attention to Facebook's misuse of users' private information, and *Gerdab*'s various references
to *Computerworld*'s critiques of Facebook.[30] Although most of these articles
highlight various negative aspects of social media, thereby bolstering *Gerdab*'s
and *Jang-e Narm*'s own arguments about such platforms, running pieces
like this implicitly acknowledges the legitimacy of the same sources that are
maligned by government institutions like *Gerdab* itself, pointing to another
contradictory aspect of the ways that official discourses approach social
media as well as foreign media platforms more generally.

Yet such inconsistencies are par for the course when one tracks the
stance of state entities and supporters toward social media. As indicated
by the case of the earlier-mentioned social-media account of the supreme
leader, numerous state-linked individuals, organizations, and news agencies
have accounts on popular platforms in spite of the fact that access to these
sites is filtered inside the country and their insidious consequences are often
discussed in official discourses. This is apparent in the highest echelons of
power in Iran. Ayatollah Khamenei has catalyzed discussions of soft war and
urged all-out mobilizations to combat the media of the perceived enemy at
the same time that he has himself embraced many of these same platforms.
His Twitter account is regularly active in multiple languages, and his decisions to use Instagram and to set up a Facebook page have all attracted
widespread attention, including in the mainstream international press.[31]

Official moves for dealing with social media, including contradictory
aspects such as those noted above, however, have not gone without challenge. One set of responses has come from government critics outside the

country. This is most apparent within social-media spaces themselves, where users in opposition to the ruling system will directly challenge state sympathizers for appearing on the same platforms that they malign. Similarly, given that such sites are usually blocked in Iran and require filter breakers in order to be accessed from within the country, government critics have pointed to the hypocrisy and illegality of state supporters' presence online. Opposition and government critics have also expressed unease about sharing virtual spaces with state supporters in case their identities or whereabouts were compromised, often identifying and blocking other users suspected of being soft-war soldiers.

Perhaps surprisingly, opposition to some of these measures has also come from those identifying themselves as supporters of the ruling system. Some of the strongest and most persistent critiques of state endorsed social-media practices have targeted self-styled soft-war soldiers. In the wake of announcements about the importance of soft war, both opposition and state supporters alike noted a rise in the number of users active on popular social-media platforms who either openly identified with soft-war projects or whose posts strongly suggested affiliation with similar endeavors. As noted above, oppositional voices objected to this increasing presence on social-media sites by pointing out the hypocrisy of state supporters and by expressing concern for their personal safety. One other aspect of their objections—which is unexpectedly shared by many pro-government participants, including those who are sympathetic with the overall tenets of the soft-war project—indicates the one-dimensional and unsubtle nature of the participation of soft-war soldiers.[32] For critics of the government, the uniformity among these users is proof that no authentic support exists for the state and that such participants are paid stooges.[33] Pro-state critics of soft-war activists voice similar concerns from the opposite side of the spectrum: since they assert that genuine support exists for the system, they worry that these "fake" accounts undermine their own attempts to establish a productive presence in social-media spaces. As a result, their hostility and reactions to soft-war soldiers at times rivals that of users identifying with the opposition.[34] Other criticisms from within pro-state ranks include accusations that soft-war funding for new media activism is being misappropriated, either deployed for factional purposes or for self-promotion by "superstars," with "opportunists" using the monies to pursue self-interested gains rather than to thwart the goals of Iran's perceived enemies.[35]

Insider critiques of the soft-war approach echo similar objections that have been raised against other policies affecting social media. Specifically, filtering practices—which have been a part of the state's mechanisms for controlling access to content since the earliest periods of Internet use in Iran—have come under attack by state sympathizers. Many have pointed out the haphazard nature of filtering, noting that religious and/or pro-state sites and activities have been negatively affected by the practice.[36] Criticisms about new and longer-standing digital media policies may explain indications of changes to come in official strategies. In December 2012, for example, the head of the police forces announced that new software was being developed for the "smart" surveillance of social-media sites to allow users to avoid the "harms" of these platforms while benefitting from their positive aspects.[37] The fact that this announcement came from one of the highest law-enforcement officials and was presented as a move to protect individual users underscores earlier outlined trends toward implementing social-media policies under the auspices of law-enforcement agencies and for the ostensible aim of preserving law and order.

The rhetoric of protecting citizens has also been evident in various discussions of a "halal," or "pure" Internet, where what is deemed immoral would be purged and replaced with acceptable content. Proponents of the policy have stressed that this model does not limit access to a national intranet.[38] In practice this translates into improving mechanisms for filtering unwanted content (originating domestically or internationally) and expanding the production of favorable materials. In short, it is an attempt to intensify existing media policies rather than innovating new ones and as such would likely not solve state actors and supporters' conflicting tendencies toward promoting native sites and fixing a foothold in popular platforms. And unlike soft war, which urges soft-war soldiers to expose and analyze what it identifies as media-enabled assaults on Iranian culture and beliefs and thus provides some space for engaging with opposing points of view, the "halal" Internet's aim is focused on keeping offensive material out altogether, and therefore would eliminate even such narrow forms of exposure to differing content.

Conclusion

Mirroring its relationship to past media forms, the Islamic Republic's policies toward social media have been forged at the intersection of two opposing tendencies of engaging and controlling new technologies. Yet both the specificities of these platforms and the prominence they were given during the postelection demonstrations of 2009 have meant that official stances toward social media also include unique elements, the most important of which is its confluence with state-sponsored soft-war projects. It is also noteworthy that officials have increasingly moved toward framing social media in terms of security and criminal concerns, assigning numerous law-enforcement institutions with units devoted to digital media. Concomitantly, officially sanctioned discourses on social media—much of which emerges from the law-enforcement agencies themselves—highlight the dangers of social media in ways that blur the lines between personal, moral, and national threats.

In addition, state entities and supporters have taken a number of steps to increase sympathetic voices on social-media spaces by both creating new platforms and encouraging participation on existing ones. Moves toward the latter further reflect internal tensions in policies: the same sites that are filtered and variously condemned for undermining personal and national security become the loci for state-friendly activities. As noted in the chapter, however, these and other inconsistencies have not gone unnoticed by either insider commentators or state opponents. Indeed, social-media policies overall have been the subject of much internal debate.

Whether and what impact such criticisms will have on future policies remains to be seen. It is likely that the trend toward further employing surveillance methods—both with and without the help of software designed for this purpose—will increase. And while explicit references to soft war have waned since an outpouring of material between late 2009 and early 2011, concerns about cultural assaults and the need for internal production which were a part of the soft-war rhetoric and have long constituted a central element of official arguments about media and cultural policies have continued unabated. As such, state actors' dual strategy of both expanding and controlling new media forms can be expected to frame approaches to existing and emerging digital technologies. At the same time, given Iran's notoriously turbulent and factionalized politics, the chance for a major shift in media policies is not out of the question, especially if the power structure sustains another blow on the scale of the post-2009 election protests.

Notes

1. See Ashraf M. Attia, Nergis Aziz, Barry Friedman, Mahdy F. Elhusseiny, "Commentary: The Impact of Social Networking Tools on Political Change in Egypt's 'Revolution 2.0,' " *Electronic Commerce Research and Applications* 10.4 (July–August 2011): 369–374; Alexandra Segerberg and W. Lance Bennett, "Social Media and the Organization of Collective Action: Using Twitter to Explore the Ecologies of Two Climate Change Protests," *The Communication Review* 14.3 (2011): 197–215;

Susan L. Shirk, "Changing Media, Changing China," in *Changing Media, Changing China,* ed. Susan L. Shirk, 1–37 (London: Oxford University Press, 2011); and Clay Shirkey, "The Political Power of Social Media: Technology, the Public Sphere, and Political Change," *Foreign Affairs* (January/February 2011): http://www.gpia.info/files/u1392/Shirky_Political_Poewr_of_Social_Media.pdf.

2. See Christian Fuchs, Kees Boersma, Anders Albrechtslund, and Marisol Sandoval, eds., *Internet and Surveillance: The Challenges of Web 2.0 and Social Media* (New York: Routledge, 2011).

3. See Kaveh Khonsari Ketabchi, Zahra Amin Nayeri, Ali Fathalian, and Leila Fathalian, "Social Network Analysis of Iran's Green Movement Opposition Groups Using Twitter," International Conference on Advances in Social Network Analysis and Mining, Odense, Denmark, August 9–11, 2010, 414–415; Setrag Manoukian, "Where Is This Place? Crowds, Audio-vision, and Poetry in Postelection Iran," *Public Culture* 22.2 (2010): 237–263; and Babak Rahimi, "The Agonistic Social Media: Cyberspace in the Formation of Dissent and Consolidation of State Power in Post-Election Iran," *The Communication Review* 14 (2011): 158–178.

4. "Emrooz Ooliyat-e Asliy-e Keshvar Mobaraz-e ba Jang-e Narm Ast" (Today, the Country's Top Priority Is to Fight against the Enemy's Soft War), *Fars News,* November 25, 2009, http://www.farsnews.com/newstext.php?nn=8809041385.

5. Monroe Price, "Iran and the Soft War," *International Journal of Communication* 6 (2012): 2397–2415.

6. Joseph Nye, *Soft Power: The Means to Success in World Politics* (New York: Public Affairs, 2004).

7. The decline of discourses and projects referencing soft war deserves a separate analysis that is beyond the scope of this chapter. Iran's constantly splintering political factions and the dissipation and repetition of authority across various offices and institutions should be considered in explaining this decline. The attention, criticism, and, in some cases, ridicule that soft war has received by both government supporters and opponents may also be a factor in why enthusiasm for soft war has waned.

8. http://www.cyberpolice.ir/about, author's translation.

9. "Akhazi ba Ejad-e Profile-Ja'l-e dar Shabak-e Ejtemayee" (Extortion by Creating Fake Profiles on Social Networks), September 9, 2012, http://www.cyberpolice.ir/news/15441, author's translation.

10. "Shahrvand az Enteshar-e Tasaveer-e Khosoosi dar Shabeke Ejtemayee Parhiz Konand" (Citizens Should Refrain from Publishing Private Photos on Social Media), September 29, 2012, IRNA News Agency, http://www.irna.ir/fa/News/397652/%D8%A7%D9%86%D8%AA%D8%B3%D8%A7%D9%85%DB%8C_-_%D8%AD%D9%88%D8%A7%D8%AF%D8%AB/%D8%B4%D9%87%D8%B1%D9%88%D9%86%D8%AF%D8%A7%D9%86_%D8%A7%D8%B2_%D8%A7%D9%86%D8%AA%D8%B4%D8%A7%D8%B1_%D8%AA%D8%B5%D8%A7%D9%88%DB%8C%D8%B1_%D8%AE%D8%B5%D9%88%D8%B5%DB%8C_%D8%AF%D8%B1_%D8%B4%D8%A8%DA%A9%D9%87_%D8%A7%D8%AC%D8%AA%D9%85%D8%A7%D8%B9%DB%8C_%D9%86

BE%D8%B1%D9%87%DB%8C%D8%B2_%DA%A9%D9%86%D9%86%D8%AF, author's translation.

11. "Dovomeen Shabake Tarveej Fesad dar Facebook Mondahem Shod" (The Second Network for Promoting Corruption on Facebook Has Been Destroyed), August 7, 2012, http://www.cyberpolice.ir/news/13841, author's translation.

12. See, for example, Dafhay-e Irani, Dafhay-e Irani 2, and Hot Daf, available, respectively, at https://www.facebook.com/PersianDuff, https://www.facebook.com/hamejori, and www.facebook.com/HotDuff.ir.

13. "Amalkard Karbaran-e Facebook zir-e 'Zarebeen-e' Polic-e FATA ast" (The Activities of Facebook Users Are under the "Microscope" of FATA Police), December 3, 2012, Weblog News, http://weblognews.ir/1391/09/forms/news/24421/, author's translation.

14. http://gerdab.ir/fa/about, author's translation.

15. "Khabarhay-e Dagh-e Google Plus, Jaryan-e hadafmand-e Google Bar Zed-e Iran" (Google Plus's Hot News, Google's Targeted Campaign against Iran), February 25, 2012, http://www.gerdab.ir/fa/news/9761/%D8%AE%D8%A8%D8%B1%D9%87%D8%A7%DB%8C-%D8%AF%D8%A7%D8%BA-%DA%AF%D9%88%DA%AF%D9%84-%D9%BE%D9%84%D8%A7%D8%B3-%D8%AC%D8%B1%DB%8C%D8%A7%D9%86-%D9%87%D8%AF%D9%81%D9%85%D9%86%D8%AF-%DA%AF%D9%88%DA%AF%D9%84-%D8%A8%D8%B1-%D8%B6%D8%AF-%D8%A7%DB%8C%D8%B1%D8%A7%D9%86, author's translation. Gerdab seems particularly concerned with Google, often pointing out the technology giant's latest "espionage instruments." See, for example, "Tashkhees Chehre ham be Abzar Jasoosi Google Ezafe Shod" (Face Recognition Has Been Added to Google's Instruments of Espionage), October 3, 2012, http://gerdab.ir/fa/news/12187/%DA%AF%D8%B1%D8%AF%D8%A7%D8%A8-%D8%AA%D8%B4%D8%AE%DB%8C%D8%B5%E2%80%8C%DA%86%D9%87%D8%B1%D9%87-%D9%87%D9%85-%D8%A8%D9%87-%D8%A7%D8%A8%D8%B2%D8%A7%D8%B1-%D8%AC%D8%A7%D8%B3%D9%88%D8%B3%DB%8C-%DA%AF%D9%88%DA%AF%D9%84-%D8%A7%D9%81%D8%B2%D9%88%D8%AF%D9%87-%D8%B4%D8%AF.

16. "Ahdaf-e Keshvarhay-e Gharbi Baray-e Gostaresh-e Sitehay-e Mostajan" (The Aims of the West for Expanding Obscene Sites), December 24, 2012, http://www.gerdab.ir/fa/news/12467, author's translation.

17. "Shabakehay-e Ejtemayee Cyberi va Zendegi Gharbi" (Cyber Social Networks and Western Lifestyles), August 8, 2011, http://www.psyop.ir/?p=8129, author's translation.

18. "Kameen-e Monafegheen dar Facebook Baray-e Karbaran-e Iran" (The Mujahedin's Ambush of Iranian Users on Facebook), January 5, 2003, http://www.mehrnews.com/fa/newsdetail.aspx?NewsID=1783637, author's translation.

19. The FBI, for example, has been at the forefront of calls for new Internet surveillance laws that would allow law enforcement more flexibility in accessing private digital communications. See Declan McCullagh, "FBI Renews Broad Internet Surveillance

Push," September 22, 2012, http://news.cnet.com/8301-13578_3-57518265-38/
fbi-renews-broad-Internet-surveillance-push/. In Europe, the German government's
acquisition of surveillance software has raised concerns about infringements on citizens' rights. See Claudia Bracholdt, "German Government's Surveillance Software
Unsettles a Nation That Prizes Privacy," January 17, 2013, http://qz.com/44208/
german-governments-surveillance-software-unsettles-a-nation-that-prizes-privacy/.

   20. Mark Andrejevic, *iSpy: Surveillance and Power in the Interactive Era* (St.
Lawrence: University Press of Kansas, 2007); Ronald Deibert, "Black Code Redux:
Censorship, Surveillance, and the Militarization of Cyberspace," in *Digital Media
and Democracy: New Tactics in Hard Times,* ed. Megan Boler, 137–164 (Cambridge:
MIT Press, 2008); Shirk, "Changing Media, Changing China"; Daniel J. Solove,
The Digital Person: Technology and Privacy in the Information Age (New York: New
York University Press, 2004).

   21. "Shabake Ejtemayee Mojazee Vizhe ome Rahandazi Mishavad" (The Virtual Social Network Dedicated to the Imam Will Be Launched), May 12, 2012,
http://www.irna.ir/fa/News/198283/%D8%B9%D9%84%D9%85%DB%8C/%D
8%B4%D8%A8%DA%A9%D9%87_%D8%A7%D8%AC%D8%AA%D9%85%
D8%A7%D8%B9%DB%8C_%D9%85%D8%AC%D8%A7%D8%B2%DB%8
C_%D9%88%DB%8C%DA%98%D9%87_%D8%A7%D8%A6%D9%85%D9
%87_%D8%B1%D8%A7%D9%87_%D8%A7%D9%86%D8%AF%D8%A7%
D8%B2%DB%8C_%D9%85%DB%8C_%D8%B4%D9%88%D8%AF, author's
translation. For direct access to the site, see Hadinet.ir.

   22. "Vazeer-e Ershad Khabar Dad: Rah Andazi Shabake Mehdi Yavaran"
(The Minister of Culture and Islamic Guidance Announced the Companions
of Mehdi Social Network), July 9, 2012, http://www.jamejamonline.ir/newstext.
aspx?newsnum=100816809889.

   23. http://sn.hijabportal.com/home; http://khakriz.arzeshiha.ir/group.
php?group_id=1.

   24. http://saznaa.ir/help/terms.

   25. Specifically, Iran's Islamic Penal Code (Articles 513 and 514 in particular) forbids insults directed at any of the "Islamic sanctities" or at past or present
supreme leaders.

   26. "Gashti dar Shabakehay-e Ejtemayee Pak" (A Stroll through Pure Social
Media Sites), March 27, 2011, http://www.psyop.ir/?p=5354, author's translation.

   27. http://www.rahesevomtv.ir/fa/content/%D8%A8%D8%B1%D8%
B1%D8%B3%DB%8C%C2%AB%D8%AA%D9%88%D9%84%DB
%8C%D8%AF-%D9%85%D8%AD%D8%AA%D9%88%D8%A7-
%D8%AF%D8%B1-%D9%81%D8%B6%D8%A7%DB%8C-
%D9%85%D8%AC%D8%A7%D8%B2%DB%8C%C2%BB-%D8%
AF%D8%B1-%D8%B1%D8%A7%D9%87-%D8%B3%D9%88%D9%85.

   28. http://divane83-2.persianblog.ir/post/270, author's translation.

   29. "Chegoone dar Facebook Mahboob Shaveem" (How We Can Become
Beloved on Facebook), November 26, 2012, http://www.teribon.ir/archives/13
8572/%DA%86%D8%B1%D8%A7-%D9%81%D8%B9%D8%A7%D9%84

%DB%8C%D8%AA%E2%80%8C%D9%87%D8%A7%DB%8C-%D8%B4
%D8%A8%DA%A9%D9%87%E2%80%8C%D9%87%D8%A7%DB%8C-
%D8%A7%D8%AC%D8%AA%D9%85%D8%A7%D8%B9%DB%8C-
%D8%B4%D9%85%D8%A7.html.

30. For examples, see http://www.psyop.ir/?p=5947 and http://www.gerdab.
ir/fa/news/12176.

31. See, for example, "Iran's Supreme Leader Joined Instagram—Here's His
First Photo," August 1, 2012, *The Atlantic,* http://www.theatlantic.com/interna-
tional/archive/2012/08/irans-supreme-leader-joined-instagram-heres-his-first-pho-
to/260607/; "Like? Iran's Supreme Leader Ayatollah Ali Khamenei Joins Facebook,"
December 18, 2012, The Guardian, http://www.guardian.co.uk/world/2012/dec/18/
iran-ayatollah-khamenei-joins-facebook.

32. It should be noted that the term "soft war soldiers" is not only used by
critics but is a self-description as well. The self-identified social-media site called
Afsaran (Soldiers), which clearly aligns itself with Ayatollah Khamenei, includes
posts addressing fellow "soft war soldiers." See, for example, the post entitled "Dark-
hast-e Hakfekri va Hamkari baray-e Barpaye-e Namayeshgah dar Ayam-e Moharram
az Shoma Afsar-e Jang-e Narm" (Request for Collaboration from You, the Soldier
of Soft War, for Setting up an Exhibition during the Days of Muharaam), http://
www.afsaran.ir/link/139119.

33. Many posts of oppositional and critical social-media users about soft war
sites and participants speculate on the budgets allotted for such projects. Twitter user
@nimarod, for example, claimed to know on October 1, 2012, that soft-war types
receive budgets of forty to fifty million tomans (in dollars) for working on one site.

34. See, for example, the following public post on Friendfeed from well-
known state supporter and active social-media user Mohammad Saleh Meftah, where
he identifies a soft-war soldier with a screen shot and notes in the comments that
he is coming up with a new list of such users to block: http://friendfeed.com/
meftah/a3573abb.

35. See, for example, the blog post at http://maniraniam-mosalmana.
blogfa.com/cat-63.aspx and "boodje Jang-e narm ra be superstarh-a dadeand"
(They Have Given the Soft War Budget to Superstars), http://www.javanonline.ir/
vdcd5k0kkyt0zo6.2a2y.html.

36. See, for example, Naqd-e Jedi: Meyar Filtering Cheest, www.netiran.net/
sosan/blog/9568/.

37. "Ahmadi-Moghaddam Khabar Dad: Tahiye Narmafzari Jadid baray-e con-
trol-e Hooshmand-e Shabkahehay-e Ejtemayee" (Ahmadi-Moghaddam Announced:
The Creation of New Software for the Smart Control of Social Media," December
23, 2012, http://isna.ir/fa/news/91101308210/%D8%A7%D8%AD%D9%85%D
8%AF%DB%8C-%D9%85%D9%82%D8%AF%D9%85-%D8%AE%D8%A8%
D8%B1%D8%AF%D8%A7%D8%AF-%D8%AA%D9%87%DB%8C%D9%87-
%D9%86%D8%B1%D9%85-%D8%A7%D9%81%D8%B2%D8%
A7%D8%B1%DB%8C-%D8%AC%D8%AF%DB%8C%D8%AF-
%D8%A8%D8%B1%D8%A7%DB%8C.

38. "Shabak-e Internet halal dar Iran rah andazi mishavad" (A Halal Internet Network Will Be Established in Iran), April 16, 2011, Tabnak, http://www.tabnak.ir/fa/news/158720.

Chapter 12

Political Memory and Social Media

The Case of Neda

Samira Rajabi

It is the summer of 2009, and the Western media is inundated by grainy images of the hot smog of the Tehran summer hanging over hordes of silent protestors. A flurry of cell phone images and videos flood the Internet and would come to serve as a window into the political expression of a nation divided. On June 12, 2009, Iranians came out in droves for elections held between Mir-Hossein Mousavi and incumbent president, Mahmoud Ahmadinejad. The results of this election, as reported by the Ministry of the Interior, showed a "clear victory" for Ahmadinejad with 64 percent of the popular vote.[1] Mousavi contested those results on June 14, 2009, leading to street protests that hearken back to modes of representation familiar from the 1979 revolution.[2] While the tactics and tools of protest may have mimicked a historical protest, the goals were far from the same. This was the Green Movement. It was a peaceful movement that used the tools of social media and the digital arena to facilitate engagement with the global infosphere.[3] It was in this context that the story of Neda Agha-Soltan emerged. Neda was a participant, not just a bystander as was often the story told in the media, in what were largely nonviolent protests on the part of the Green Movement. She walked down the street with her music teacher that day, her *hejab* wrapped around her ponytail, a visor shielding her eyes from the sun. She was shot directly through the heart, and the world soon bore witness to her death in a forty-seven-second mobile phone

231

video that was posted to YouTube,[4] filtered through various social-media networks, including Facebook, and then aired by news stations throughout the world.[5] It is through acts such as the murder of Neda that the Basij military is implicated in killing the "beauty" of the Green Movement that evolved in the days following the election.[6] Neda's death became one of the most-searched YouTube videos at that time, and her image captivated the world. President Obama cited her death as heartbreaking, calling her a rallying cry for the revolution in Iran.[7] Neda instantaneously had become an important symbol to Iranian social, collective,[8] and political memory.[9] Neda mobilized the wired people of Iran and supporters of Iran around the world. The Iranian diaspora took to the metaphorical streets of the Internet to join the national struggle. Neda's image, through the visual, social, and digital nature of her death, gave face to a movement that would leave an enduring mark on the conceptualization of what it means to be an Iranian national in a time of technological convergence and social media.

Postelection Protest in Iran:
The First Real Digital Martyr of Our Time

Prior to the election of Ahmadinejad in 2005, Iran's political landscape was one in which three main factions operated in a "precarious equilibrium" between religious conservatism and Islamic reform.[10] Until the 2005 election, the three factions more or less balanced themselves out, resulting in maintenance of the status quo over time. Leading up to the 2005 elections, reformists proved themselves "too weak to overcome the entrenched resistance of conservative elements spread across most of the sensitive positions within the State who repeatedly blocked and frustrated their policies"; thus a disillusioned electorate brought the conservative Principalist Ahmadinejad to power.[11] Ahmadinejad led in a manner that brought the Islamic Revolutionary Guard Corps (IRGC) to the forefront of political power. Therefore, in 2009, when elections brought protests that threatened the new privilege of the IRGC and the authority of the supreme leader, the IRGC was instrumental in suppressing demonstrations and maintaining the power of Ahmadinejad and what had become the status quo.[12] Supreme Leader Khamenei warned protestors during Friday prayer, the day before Neda was shot, that their protests would result in "dire consequences."[13] The contested elections and response to them shattered the perception shared by Mousavi supporters of a relatively free election. The voting public's understanding of its own government's electoral process transformed from a system with certain freedoms and potential for reform to a closed political order that was undemocratic, unaccountable, and largely repressive.[14]

The religious context of the remembrance and public memorialization of martyrdom, which dates back to Khomeini's Iran–Iraq war, is central in understanding Neda's significance to the overall political and memorial context of Iran. In Khomeini's Iran, "the idea of martyrdom came to represent and conflate the ultimate union of citizen and nation, lover and beloved, and servant of God and God. Martyrdom became state policy."[15] As Roxanne Varzi explains, it is not the martyr himself (or in this case herself) who is important, rather it is the way the memorialization of that martyr, the symbol of that person, and the role he/she plays comes to represent the needs, fears, and desires of all survivors.[16] In turn, this creates a culture of individuals bound by the blood of their brothers and sisters to their nation. The most common type of martyr in the Iranian imaginary cultivated by the Islamic Republic is the *shahid*, or war dead, a title typically reserved for men who fought in the Iran–Iraq war.[17] Varzi indicates that "the ideal for an Islamic Basij was to die for the nation, which took on the role of an object of love and . . . was ultimately inscribed in the names of the dead—young virgin martyrs."[18] While this discussion pertains specifically to male martyrdom in conflict, the principal of the young virgin martyr provides an insightful dimension to Neda's story. Of additional importance to the understanding of Iranian martyrdom is the way the cultivation of public memory around the image of the martyr becomes magnified through photography and, by extension, the mass proliferation of photography and images made possible by the Internet. Varzi explains: "martyrdom is meaningless without memorialization, and memorialization is not possible without the photograph."[19] The Internet, then, in adding immediacy and access to these images, acting within and on behalf of a culture and a diaspora that firmly understands and fosters this process of cultivating memory, provides the ability to create more than just a martyr—it allows for the creation of an icon.

From this brief overview of the political and cultural context of Iran, we can begin to understand how a striking visual of a young woman dying on the street in the midst of a protest came to find the significance it did, on such a global scale. A simple Google search of the name "Neda" will result in graphic images of this young woman bleeding to death on the street, her gaze locking with the camera lens, as though to invoke our attention and our emotion.[20] The response to this powerful imagery was immediate. In the days following her death, in various media, Neda took on many forms and labels. "We are Neda," it was said in solidarity across YouTube videos, on protest banners, and in re-mediated images of her death online. Elsewhere she was called "Martyr," "Angel of Freedom," "Pillar of the Movement," "Symbol of Struggle," "Symbol of Goodness," "the YouTube Martyr," and "Our Angel."[21] As a *New York Times* article explained just two days after her murder, "the very public adulation of Ms. Agha-Soltan could create a religious symbol for the opposition and sap support for the government among the faithful who believe Islam abhors killing innocent civilians."[22] It was Neda's death, though not a conscious sacrifice on her part, which would lead to freedom and salvation for the young protestors in Iran, their voice, their *Neda* would lead them to freedom. Freedom would, in turn, lead to salvation. The power of what had been witnessed was almost immediately articulated and understood. A woman participating in a protest for her political freedoms and human rights could now be a symbol evoking prayer, faith, and hope. She became an angel, a voice, and a potent symbol of a movement that used the digital, particularly for those outside of Iran, unable to give voice to the Green Movement struggle, to signify her importance.[23]

In examining why Neda, over many others who died in that period and on video in Iran, was catapulted to instant iconic status, we have to consider notions of gender and sexuality, religion and martyrdom, the impact of the digital in collective memory creation, as well as Neda's power-ful gaze that implicates us all as witnesses to her death. Through assessing the way Neda's image was mediated and re-mediated in the days, weeks, and months after her death we find that Neda went from being a "referential image to an iconic image symbolizing a greater cause and struggle."[24] Gender norms and representations are important here as postrevolutionary Iranian women "saw their legal status and social positions dramatically decline in the name of religious revival."[25] While many women push back against reli-gious norms, others don't seek a secular transformation of Iran, but rather a religious reinterpretation.[26] Transnational Iranian secular feminists argue that enthusiasm about Islamic feminisms "obscures the fact that in a country like Iran, Islam is not a matter of personal spiritual choice, but rather a legal and political system,"[27] and gains women make within the structural constraints of the Islamic Republic have not liberated women, but rather silenced them based on minor concessions that "strengthen the legitimacy of the Islamic system in Iran."[28] Despite this complex context, initial press coverage surrounding Neda's death framed her as the innocent victim of a cruel regime, a further demonization of the Islamic regime in the Western press. The false characterization of Neda as innocent bystander, as opposed to active agent, played into a comfortable gender representation of passive, blameless women, thus constructing her as a pawn in a world of men who seek to debase and devalue purportedly helpless women. This representative frame diminishes Iranian women's agency and operates through Orientalist framings of the Other to elicit action from Western audiences in opposition to so-called backward cultures and regimes of power.[29]

Though Iranian women actually navigate a precarious boundary of marginalized ethnic status, they are often mistakenly attributed white privilege that their ethnicity would not allow for, which, in the case of Neda caused her to be a more sympathetic victim in Western eyes.[30] The way she wore her *hejab* wrapped around her head under a quintessentially Western visor made her seem liberated. Furthermore, her way of dress, her Adidas-style shoes, her blue jeans, and the aesthetic formations of the people in and around her highlighted the secular nature of those individuals. She subverted the images of Iranian women so often portrayed in the media; her ability to act as symbol of a more Western Iranian woman made her relatable to Western audiences. The very reasons Neda and other women were dismissed, their secular Western norms of beauty, are the reasons Neda became such an apt symbol for The Green Movement. Sabety correctly relates Neda's representation to her gender, "That Saturday, Neda, who symbolized the failure of coercive Islam in Iran, died. Her death gave the struggle for civil rights and freedom a face. It is befitting that the struggle should have a female face: women, whose civil rights have been the most damaged by the Islamic Revolution of 1979, gave the reformist campaign its soul, its zeal, and feminized the uprising."[31] Neda is representative of a deeply ingrained Iranian conflict between modernity and tradition. It is her in-betweeness that makes Neda and her story attractive; she balanced (and continues to do so in death) marginal identities across boundaries that are typical of contemporary Iranian women.[32]

The way that Neda was constructed into a martyr extends beyond the modern memorialization of martyrdom in Iran that found dominance in the period of the Iran–Iraq war. Neda's online manifestations as a martyr for the Green Movement in social media exist outside of the confines of traditional salvational religion. In various re-mediations of Neda's image that appear on YouTube, it is clear that the manifestations of the Green Movement online were part of a larger movement that, according to Varzi, was not a cry to return to a prerevolutionary Iran but rather to reclaim Islam and operate under a regime that allows for the separation of church and state.[33] This was not a revolutionary movement toward democracy; it was a revolutionary movement that sought to make sense of the unjust conditions in the Iranian state, which are entrenched in religious and political doctrines. Neda's image and iconic status are deeply steeped in the religious. She is contrasted with pre-Abrahamic images and symbols as well as framed in much the same tradition as Marian devotions. Of particular importance here is the fact that it was specifically social media and the various tools made possible by online encounters that allowed and created a space for these re-mediations to take place. It is through these digital tools that Neda was transformed from a victim of a cruel regime to an icon and symbol of a revolutionary movement.

Neda can be seen as simulacra in the way that Baudrillard conceptualizes the notion.[34] As simulacra of an icon, Neda gained power by becoming an authentic representation and simulation of what is sacrilized in the Iranian context for the Iranian people and for all those who engaged with them via social media. This process of simulation transformed Neda's image into spectacle; the context of her re-mediation can be seen as mass, social, detached, and unifying.[35] Images here are not restricted to one type of image, nor are they dependent on the exact format of the message (video, still photograph, or montage); rather, what is significant is how each image is taken up and the way it operates as part of memory. Each image has the potential to facilitate the creation of narratives that shift the locus of a collective's consciousness. Images such as the ones taken of Neda and created in her memory function effectively as part of memory in the way that they are contingent, emotional, and imaginative. These images, which seem to contain moments in time that are no longer spatially and temporally relegated to their original environment, become effective though their "as if" qualities.[36] Barbie Zelizer argues that images of Neda, like many other images, gain their power through the process of repetition, a process made possible through their subjunctive qualities. The repetition and re-mediation is arguably facilitated and enabled by social media—recall the sheer volume of hits Neda's dying moments received on YouTube. This underscores that repetition and consistent engagement with material are constitutive elements in social media. Zelizer argues, "at some point, the picture's recycled contexts became equally important, if not more so, to the original setting in which it was taken."[37] Neda's death does more than just represent death in Iran; "the image of Agha-Soltan not only denotes a dying woman and connotes state repression, but acts as a relay for community building, the expression of women's rights, recognition of amateur videography, and a new tweaking of this relationship between old and new media."[38] Many tout this process as a byproduct of social media. Gaffney describes the dimensions of online activism as awareness and advocacy, organization and mobilization, as well as action and reaction.[39] These components work as part of a process that allows activism to continue as traditional media breaks down, as was the case in Iran in 2009.[40] The traditional media then engage social media, expanding its reach, leading to a cycle of information sharing that propels political opposition and activism forward.

With foreign reporters expelled from Iran, "Web 2.0" audiences bore witness to political turmoil in new ways that are dislocated, contested, and resistive.[41] This can be seen very clearly in the context of the election: "the 2009 Iranian presidential election and its aftermath illustrated the power of social media to help generate political opposition, shape political discourse, and facilitate action in the face of a powerful regime. Iran is a vivid example of the new role social media can now play in authoritarian countries where freedom of expression is limited."[42] While many see the power that social media carried to keep activism alive and transform it in a new realm, others disagreed. Morosov argues that the excitement behind the so-called "Twitter Revolution" and its connections to social-media technology had little basis in reality.[43] For Morosov, marking what happened in 2009 as revolutionary was a means to justify hours wasted on social media. Instead he contends that errors accumulate through the transmission process and the final message loses meaning and power. It seems, according to Morosov, that this disconnection from reality and inability to provide accurate and timely information simply amplifies the noise.[44] Contrary to Morosov's assertion, it seems clear that in the case of Neda, that grassroots accumulation of information and viral sharing of images served to interrupt messages the Iranian government sought to make dominant. Official agencies, the same that backed the election results, cracked down on journalists and sought to reframe the story of election protest through traditional and social media, but Neda's story, the visuality of it, the instantaneity of it, made it hard to reframe, even by the Iranian regime.[45] Despite the best efforts of the Iranian government to pin the murder on anyone but themselves (including assertions that the bullet that shot Neda could not be found in Iran or pinning her murder on the CIA),[46] the way that social media bypassed the frameworks of traditional and state media made the legacy media's efforts ineffective. Neda's dying moments "became caught up in a recursive process of saliency reinforcement by both networks and traditional media. Here, as in other cases, traditional media signaled the existence of networked content, while network content fed traditional media."[47] Neda signals a shift from traditional to social media that has changed the process of news gathering and communication for even veteran news agencies.

Neda can be seen as a rallying point for a movement that continues to have traction in the online realm. She held her power through the ease with which anonymous mourners and activists could re-mediate and re-interpret her story, contributing their own voice and thus changing the landscape of meaning and the collective meaning-making process. The following discussion of social and collective memory and the digital will illuminate why Neda's story is a prime example of the way nationalism, memory, and social media go hand in hand in contexts of political strife and violence.

Collective Memory: Creating Political Memories Online, and Remediation as Commemoration

Downing, Ford, Gil, and Stein, in a discussion of radical Internet use, demonstrate that "people who participate in posting and debating information on the Internet occupy a discursive realm outside of mainstream media. They may speak freely and still enjoy a wide audience, a remarkable opportunity in a world in which information and its means of distribution are so closely guarded by politicians."[48] This is magnified in settings like that of Iran and, coupled with discourses on social and collective memory, allows us to understand why, for Iranians, this ability to circumvent traditional avenues of political discourse allows for redefinition of a populaces' collective memory and national consciousness. Building from the work of Assmann and Czaplicka, we conceptualize cultural identity as "the specific character that a person derives from belonging to a distinct society and culture," which is a result of socialization and customs.[49] Cultural memory is then understood as the relation between memory, culture, and the group. This interrelation of concepts speaks to the individual's need for collective identity, which is reconstructed through group dynamics. "Cultural memory works by reconstructing, that is, it always relates its knowledge to an actual and contemporary situation. True, it is fixed in immovable figures of memory and stores of knowledge, but every contemporary context relates to these differently, sometimes by appropriation, sometimes by criticism, sometimes by preservation or by transformation."[50] This is what Neda's story did for the Green Movement and young Iranians: it recaptured and reconstructed the revolutionary mentality and history in Iran as well as notions of Ashura and a reframing of Islam through the lens of a changing, young Iranian populace.[51] Cultural memory, as a facet of collective memory, highlights the importance of the cultural practice of group remembrance, and acknowledgment of national histories. It is through the past that current values emerge and shape overall political and social tendencies of a nation.

Further examination of how memory is culturally constituted leads us to the distinction between memory and myth. Bell highlights the way personal and collective identity are intertwined through the concept of nationalism: "To recognize oneself as a member of a particular nation—indeed to feel a powerful sense of belonging—and to be recognized by others as such is a prerequisite for the formation of the inside/outside, self/other, us/ them, boundaries that define the topography of nationalist sentiment and rhetoric."[52] Thus it would be reasonable to assert, using the 2009 election protests in Iran as a case study, that nationalism is fueled by a desire for individuals to feel connected to a greater calling. Nationalism is part of a type of collective/social memory that is framed and propelled forward through myth that simplifies and dramatizes specific memories, allowing for the formation and construction of social groups for the sheer purpose of remembrance.[53] These groups that come together to remember are groups that have the ability, through the repetitious acts Zelizer identified, to give new spatial and temporal dimensions to an event, making that event itself politics. Memory exists within a framework of social interaction; we remember socially.[54] In Halbwach's view, memory is not individually conceived; rather it is part of a shared cognitive structure of frames of memory that are socially held and constructed. These frames are often culturally contingent and rooted in cultural practices, traditions, and narratives.[55] These culturally framed notions of memory that fuel national and social consciousness become increasingly relevant as social media enables a space through which individuals can shift and transform the way they (as users) conceive of themselves within a larger community that is no longer delimited by territorial boundaries. Before fully indulging in this analysis, it is important to push the notion of social, cultural, collective memory—and thus political memory—into the visual realm.

Memories within a society cannot be seen outside of the context of collective memory and cultural practice. Collective memories, though often not a reflection of direct experience or political reality, foster the creation of communities that are necessary precursors to political action. As Confino argues in a discussion of collective memory and method, "National memory, for example, is constituted by different, often opposing, memories that, in spite of their rivalries, construct common denominators that overcome on the symbolic level real social and political differences to create and imagined community."[56] Tragedy, however, can shift the cultivation of national or collective (for collectivities outside of those confined by the borders of the nation-state) memories and thus can shift the narratives that go with them. Bourdon notes that tragedy "opens a fault in the landscape."[57] In viewing her near death, viewers of Neda's image assimilate her image with experience and cultural narratives and make her an intractable part of the growing, shifting collective political memory. This is different from a politics of memory that would indicate the story of Neda that was manifested online somehow functioned to cement a political ideology or coerce a certain interpretation of historical experience.[58] While political memory *can* function to legitimate a social arrangement it constitutes something much larger, especially online. Political memories are events that dictate understandings of the past and desires for the future and are remembered specifically for the way they harbor power—in this case, the counter-hegemonic power to create an icon outside of spatial, temporal, and territorial boundaries. Conversely, political memory functions much in the way a physical memorial does: imposing "meaning and order beyond the temporal and chaotic experiences of life"[59] and cultivating a space through which mourners can bear witness.[60] In an environment where Neda could not be physically mourned in public, the space online assisted the testimony of her mourners, but even more significantly, those acts of bearing witness caused her narrative to take on a significance, within the collective memory of her mourners, that has a spatial and temporal dimension all its own. When collective memory gives way to political memory, the act of memorializing functions in such a way that the political significance of the event becomes inextricable from the event itself. The event thus becomes the politics that drives it.

Zelizer examines the way that the visual interacts with memory. Images serve as vehicles of memory, making memory concrete and external, representable. Through this process "visual memory's texture becomes a facilitator for memory's endurance."[61] Images, photos, and videos enhance our experiences of the real; they can shape a collective past despite their arbitrary nature.[62] They can be re-represented and re-interpreted in order to keep with a "particular conception of the world."[63] This ability to understand and reinvent a collective past and, by extension, a cultural identity is enhanced by technology. Technology allows for the cultural contingency of visual memory. Zelizer explains, "By playing to the contingent aspect of a depicted event or issue, the image's capacity to speak for the past changes in its relation to the events it depicts. And when dealing with events of a tragic nature, contingency may be the best interpretive stance for which we can hope."[64] Olick and Robbins point to revolutions in technology as being revolutionary in changing the way we remember as societies. This progression of technology creates a way to think and rethink the confines and boundaries of what was possible for a nation.[65] Digital technology transforms temporality in a way that is critical to understanding the case of Neda, as a means of defining and redefining the Iranian social, collective, and cultural memory and thus the political memories and consciousness of a nation.

Neda was seemingly silenced the day she was shot and killed. Her voice, like that of many other Iranian women, became frozen in time. To the dismay of the Iranian government, however, her silence was transformative. Through the images of her death and the reconceptualizations of her narrative through social media, Neda became an icon that shifted the political consciousness of Iranians by conjuring images of the past that spoke to possibilities for the future. The historical narrative of martyrdom, the legacy of the Iran–Iraq war, was a deeply seeded aspect of Iranian's collective identity that in turn informs how they turn events into important political memories. This, in combination with Neda's framing as innocent victim, gave her a power that spoke to other historical images of protest from Tiananmen Square to the Vietnam War.[66] It is here that social media becomes central. Being that Neda was not allowed to be publicly mourned in Iran, as a rising symbol of Iran's prodemocracy and anticorruption protestors, Neda had to find a space online through which to exist posthumously.[67] The Internet enabled the formation of a third space in which conceptual truths could be challenged and through which a martyr was created.[68] Even more important, it gave a platform for many transnational mourners to express themselves. These mourners displayed new forms of religious devotions, a newly minted and continuously progressing national and cultural identity, and a collective political consciousness that was deeply rooted in pre-Islamic Iranian history, Islamic frameworks for understanding death, and modern and postmodern ways of knowing and reimagining the dead.

The outcry of support and the re-mediation of Neda's image from "secondary witnesses" of her death were fostered by the safe, relative anonymity of the online space.[69] The images ranged from images of a living, vibrant Neda to her tragic gaze in the final moments before her death, beckoning the viewer to take a degree of responsibility for what they had borne witness to. Assmann and Assmann explain: "Together with its commentary, the image was turned into a symbol and was read within a certain cultural tradition. The cultural symbol is an augmented image; it invests experiences with emotions and values that are drawn from traditional patterns of meaning."[70] What happened to Neda's image online highlights that what seemingly began as a political struggle for change in Iran was much more than that. Iran exists in a tense dialectic between modernity and tradition. Often the Iranian regime takes pride in elements of the secular achievements of ancient Persians, yet simultaneously denounces the popular uses of science, technology, and their advances, all of which is steeped in a much deeper struggle for freedom of religious expression.[71] New spaces of expression and creations of a new collective memory, as facilitated by the Internet and mobile technology, give Iranians a place to consistently contest the difficult juxtapositions of ideas that dominate their reality and gives voice to the silence that emanates from the country. The discursive conditions of the third space of contestation and commemoration allow for the possibilities of supplementary sites of resistance, negotiation, and agency.

Conclusion

Neda, and her remembrance online, is but one example of the way social media allows space for the reconceptualization of cultural identity. Through the facilitation of new forms, frames, and spaces for commemoration, the online sphere—specifically, tools such as YouTube that allow for viewing of contingent moments that invoke the viewer to become the producer and engage directly with the materials seen—has a great power in redefining national consciousness. This re-memory is no longer based on the traditional nationalistic myth. Rather, the myth becomes redefined outside of the structural confines of territorial boundaries. After Neda's death in 2009, protestors around the world took to the street chanting, "We are all Neda!" On their faces were commemorative representational masks of Neda. These masks were not invoking the Neda that her friends and family knew. Rather, the masks, and in fact the act of carrying the mask, invoked images of Neda, the icon. The Neda that had been created through the process of re-mediations could not have taken place anywhere but in the digital realm.[72] As Assmann and Assmann describe, "this striking aesthetic performance acted out the nightmare of the Iranian state: for one that had been killed, hundreds have arisen. Her images assumed the character of avatars marching in the demonstrations in an uncanny and ghostlike way. The power of images lies in this resurrection, not of the dead person but of her memory, which returns with the universal claim to human rights in public acts of performed cosmopolitanism."[73]

Neda was not born to be a martyr. She was turned into a martyr by the supporters of her homeland across borders. Hers is an image that will live on, not on the streets in Iran or in some notion of paradise, but in a realm of creation fostered and developed through her YouTube video and the various YouTube re-mediations of her image. The violent nature of her death and the way it was visualized online contributed to many different parties claiming her as a martyr for their side. While the Iranian government seeks to argue to this day that Neda was either killed by protestors or by the Western powers that be, the truth of her murder as well as justice for it was determined via a collective memory of a transnational community online. The truth becomes less important than that which is constructed as truth. Neda's authenticity lies not in her truth, but in her power to reframe national, political, and cultural consciousness. She is the manifestation of immortality as created by the Internet. Her image, her name, and her story live on far beyond her earthly years. Millions of people watched the last forty-seven seconds of this young woman's life and shed tears for her innocence.[74] Now, they bear witness to new meanings conferred on her that are arguably just as important to the world as her original dying image.[75] As articulated by one Iranian blogger: "Neda symbolizes innocence of a large group of people that are seeking justice from these oppressive groups. Neda's blood will one day hunt these tyrannical groups down. For me, Neda is a symbol of peace, serenity and denial of violence."[76] The act of bearing witness and re-memorialization in social media shifted the way Iranians remembered a political moment but also shifted the fabric of that political memory and, thus, to an extent, their cultural identity as well. The memory of her is prominent because social media made it so. She was fashioned into and manifested as a martyr, angel, and icon through discursive frames created and cemented by the digital space. She is perhaps the first real digital martyr of our time.

Notes

1. Emile Sahliyeh, "The Presidential Eelection in Iran, June 2009," *Electoral Studies* 29.1 (2010): 183.

2. Ibid., 182–183.

3. Yahya R. Kamalipour, ed., *Media, Power, and Politics in the Digital Age: The 2009 Presidential Election Uprising in Iran* (Plymouth: Rowman & Littlefield, 2010), 105–118.

4. Neda was in fact featured in two separate videos that capture her death. The original video has 1,331,006 views; another video of the shooting has 1,138,897 views. Including the views on YouTube, there are additional views of her death as it was picked up by most major Western news networks including CNN, BBC, and BBC Persia.

5. Arash Hejazi, *The Gaze of the Gazelle: The Story of a Generation* (London: Seagull Books, 2011), xiii–xvii; Megan Knight, "Journalism as Usual: The Use of Social Media as a Newsgathering Tool in the Coverage of the Iranian Elections in 2009," *Journal of Media Practice* 13.1 (2012): 62.

6. Anthony Thomas, *For Neda* (HBO Documentary Films, 2010).

7. Barbie Zelizer, *About to Die: How News Images Move the Public*, (New York: Oxford University Press, 2010).

8. Collective memory here is borrowed from scholarly work such as Zelizer's "The Voice of the Visual in Memory" (157–180) and Bell's "Mythscapes: Memory, Mythology, and National Identity." Here collective memory is taken to indicate the various mediations that provide collectives, such as those members of a nation or a diaspora, a sense of their past. Collective memory contributes to myth production as well as constructions of nationality, diasporic identity, and transnational solidarity. Representational practices are inherent to collective memory, as understood here. Collective memory is built from a social imaginary fostered through shared experience, history, and cultural memory, which relates the past, culture, and society to one another.

9. Political memory cannot exist without collective memory and occurs at the juncture where the politics of a certain memory shift the temporal and spatial understanding of an event, in a way that the event can no longer be understood outside of its political significance. In this way, political memories that are a part of a society's collective memories exist outside of the historical chronology of a nation and take on a certain power of their own. For more on politics of memory and how that differs from political memory, see Javier Auyero, "Re-membering Peronism: An Ethnographic Account of the Relational Character of Political Memory," *Qualitative Sociology* 22.4 (1999): 331–351; the introduction to the volume on politics and memory in Daniel J. Walkowitz and Lisa Maya Knauer, *Memory and the Impact of Political Transformation in Public Space* (Durham: Duke University Press, 2004); Jan Assmann and John Czaplicka, "Collective Memory and Cultural Identity," *New German Critique* 65 (1995): 130; Duncan S. A. Bell, "Mythscapes: Memory, Mythology, and National Identity," *The British Journal of Sociology* 54.1 (2003): 65.

10. Mehran Kamrava, "The 2009 Elections and Iran's Changing Political Landscape," *Orbis* 54.3 (2010): 401–402.

11. Ibid.

12. Ibid., 404.

13. Setareh Sabety, "Graphic Content: The Semiotics of a YouTube Uprising," in *Media, Power and Politics in the Digital Age: The 2009 Presidential Election Uprising in Iran*, ed. Yahya R. Kamalipour, 119–124 (Plymouth: Rowman & Littlefield, 2010).

14. Ibid., 409.

15. Roxanne Varzi, *Warring Souls: Youth, Media, and Martyrdom in Post-Revolution Iran* (Durham: Duke University Press, 2006), 47.

16. Ibid.

17. Amber Hildebrandt, "An Unintentional Martyr: Neda Becomes 'Symbol of Goodness,'" CBC News, 2009, http://www.cbc.ca/news/world/story/2009/06/22/f-neda-iran.html.

18. Varzi, *Warring Souls*, 47.

19. Varzi, *Warring Souls*, 62.

20. Anonymous, "Wounded Girl Dying in Front of Camera, Her Name was Neda," YouTube, 2009. https://www.youtube.com/watch?v=bbdEf0QRsLM

21. mikemcpd, "Neda Agha-Soltan," YouTube, 2009; Alex Burns and Ben Eltham, "Twitter Free Iran: An Evaluation of Twitter's Role in Public Diplomacy and Information Operations in Iran's 2009 Election Crisis," Record of the Communications Policy and Research Forum 2009 (2009): 12, http://youtube/DjGF1TD1HE4.

22. Nazila Fathi, "In a Death Seen Around the World, a Symbol of Iranian Protests," New York Times, June, 22, 2009, accessed December 17, 2011, http://www.nytimes.com/2009/06/23/world/middleeast/23neda.html?_r=0.

23. Maryam Aghvami, "Persian Bloggers: Exile, Nostalgia, and Diasporic Nationalism," Theses and Dissertations (2009): paper 505.

24. Carsten Stage, "Thingifying Neda: The Construction of Commemorative and Affective Thingification of Neda Agha-Soltan," Culture Unbound 3 (2011): 19.

25. Valentine Moghadam, "Women in the Islamic Republic of Iran: Legal Status, Social Positions, and Collective Action," paper presented at the Woodrow Wilson International Center for Scholars Conference, November 16–17, 2004, 1.

26. Valentine Moghadam, "Transnational Feminist Networks Collective Action in an Era of Globalization," International Sociology 15.1 (2000): 60; Valentine M. Moghadam, "Islamic Feminism and Its Discontents: Toward a Resolution of the Debate," Signs 27.4 (2002): 1135–1171.

27. Moghadam, "Islamic Feminism and Its Discontents," 1148.

28. Ibid.

29. Nandita Dogra, Representations of Global Poverty: Aid, Development, and International NGOs (London: Palgrave Macmillan, 2012).

30. Kamalipour, Media, Power, and Politics in the Digital Age, 235–250.

31. Ibid., 119–124.

32. Janet Afary, Sexual Politics in Modern Iran (Cambridge, UK: Cambridge University Press, 2009), 233.

33. Roxanne Varzi, "Iran's French Revolution," The Annals of the American Academy of Political and Social Science 637.1 (2011): 60.

34. Jean Baudrillard, "The Precision of Simulacra," in Images: A Reader, ed. Arthur Piper Sunil Manghani and John Simons (London: Sage, 2006), 70–74.

35. Guy Debord, "Society of the Spectacle," in Images: A Reader, ed. Arthur Piper Sunil Manghani and John Simons (London: Sage, 2006), 69–70.

36. Zelizer argues that when looking at images in the subjunctive or images that prioritize the "as-if" the visual contains voice: "Voice makes an image's completion dependent on features beyong its own parameters." Zelizer goes on to argue that the voice of the visual is wholly subjunctive in character and "suggests rethinking how images work when they come into contact across time and space with other people, events, contexts, and images. Voice helps explain why a single image can be recycled to multiple contexts . . ." This is clear in the case of Neda. The notion that Neda somehow exists outside of her death online is what makes her iconic and is also what makes her central to the cultivation of political memory. Looking at

political memory as an extention of collective memory shifts the politics of memories to make the event itself a significant political moment with its own spatial and temporal markers. Barbie Zelizer, *About to Die: How News Images Move the Public* (New York: Oxford University Press, 2010), 13–14.

37. Ibid., 24.

38. Ibid., 13.

39. Devin Gaffney, "#IranElection: Quantifying Online Activism," Web Science Conference, http://journal.webscience.org/295/2/websci10_submission_6.pdf.

40. Kamalipour, *Media, Power, and Politics in the Digital Age.*

41. C. W. Anderson, "From Indymedia to Demand Media: Journalism's Visions of Its Audience and the Horizons of Democracy," in *The Social Media Reader*, ed. Michael Mandiberg (New York: New York University Press, 2011), Kindle edition.

42. Sara Beth Elson, Douglas Yeung, Parisa Roshan, S. R. Bohandy, Alireza Nader, *Using Social Media to Gauge Iranian Public Opinion and Mood after the 2009 Election* (Santa Monica: Rand, 2012), 1.

43. Evgeny Morosov, "Iran: Downside to the 'Twitter Revolution,'" *Dissent* (Fall 2009): 10–14.

44. Morosov, "Iran: Downside to the 'Twitter Revolution,'" 10–13.

45. Morosov, "Iran: Downside to the 'Twitter Revolution,'" 10–14; Knight, "Journalism as Usual," 64.

46. Andrew Malcolm, "Iran Ambassador Suggests CIA Could Have killed Neda Agha-Soltan," Los Angeles Times, June 25, 2009, latimesblogs.latimes.com/washington/2009/06/neda-cia-cnn-killing.html.

47. Steven Livingston and Gregory Asmolov, "Networks and the Future of Foreign Affairs Reporting," *Journalism Studies* 11.5 (2010): 753.

48. John D. H. Downing, Ramara Villarreal Ford, Geneve Gil, and Laura Stein, *Radical Media: Rebellious Communication and Social Movements* (Thousand Oaks, CA: Sage, 2001), 223.

49. Jan Assmann and John Czaplicka, "Collective Memory and Cultural Identity," *New German Critique* 65 (1995): 125.

50. Ibid.,130.

51. Ashura is an important day for Iranian Shia Muslims in which the importance of martyrdom is exemplified. It is the reenactment and mourning of Imam Hossein's martyrdom. Observed on the tenth day of Muharram, the day marks the death of Hossein, the grandson of the prophet Mohammad and the second of the twelve imams. The day is commemorated publicly in Iran as a national day of mourning.

52. Bell, "Mythscapes," 63.

53. Ibid., 72–75.

54. Jens Brockmeier, "Remembering and Forgetting: Narrative as Cultural Memory," *Culture & Psychology* 8.1 (2002): 18.

55. Ibid., 23.

56. Alon Confino, "Collective Memory and Cultural History: Problems of Method," *The American Historical Review* (1997): 1399–1400.

57. Jérôme Bourdon, "Television and Political Memory," *Media, Culture, and Society* 14.4 (1992): 548.

58. Auyero, "Re-membering Peronism," 333.

59. James M. Mayo, "War Memorials as Political Memory," *Geographical Review* (1988): 62.

60. Walkowitz and Knauer, *Memory and the Impact of Political Transformation in Public Space.* 1.

61. Barbie Zelizer, "The Voice of the Visual in Memory," in *Framing Public Memory*, ed. Kendall R. Phillips (Tuscaloosa: University of Alabama Press, 2004), 160.

62. Again, here we refer not to one specific type of image or a particular medium of images but take images on the Internet, particularly those of "as if" traumatic moments, to be contingent, emotional, and imaginative. The types of images are not as significant as the way they are shared via vehicles such as Facebook and YouTube. What is significant is the subjunctive nature of the images and the way they become contingent in new ways as they are mediated and remediated or recycled via social media.

63. Zelizer, "The Voice of the Visual in Memory," 160–161.

64. Ibid., 161.

65. Jeffrey K. Olick and Joyce Robbins, "Social Memory Studies: From 'Collective Memory' to the Historical Sociology of Mnemonic Practices," *Annual Review of Sociology* 24 (1998): 115–116.

66. Aleida Assmann and Corrina Assmann, "Neda: The Career of a Global Icon," in *Memory in a Global Age: Discourses, Practices, and Trajectories*, ed. Aleida Assmann and Sebastian Conrad (Houndsmills and New York: Palgrave Macmillan, 2010), 237.

67. Melissa Tabatabai, "Neda Soltan, Young Woman Hailed as Martyr in Iran, Becomes Face of Protests," Fox News June 22, 2009, accessed December 17, 2011, http://www.foxnews.com/story/2009/06/22/neda-soltan-young-woman-hailed-as-martyr-in-iran-becomes-face-protests/. The online space that allows for this type of expression is a "third space" that sits "in-between" online and offline and also balances notions of authenticity, truth, experience, and expression. The Internet itself is not a third space; rather, it enables the cultivation of third spaces when issues arise that cannot be wholly addressed in either the online or offline spaces exclusively. For more information on the way the practices in third spaces can be transfigurative and facilitate expression, see Stewart Hoover and Neda Agha-Soltan, *The 'Third Spaces' of Digital Religion* (Boulder: The Center for Media, Religion, and Culture), in press, http://cmrc.colorado.edu/wp-content/uploads/2012/03/Third-Spaces-Essay-Draft-Final.pdf.

68. The third space is a conceptual space in which patterns of meaning and cultural understanding are challenged through new discursive forms; often this is

facilitated by the Internet and mobile technologies. See Kim Knott, *The Location of Religion: A Spatial Analysis* (London: Equinox, 2005); Shahnaz Khan, "Muslim Women: Negotiations in the Third Space," *Signs* 23.2 (1998): 463–494.

69. Assmann and Assmann, "Neda: The Career of a Global Icon," 236.

70. Ibid.

71. Hejazi, *The Gaze of the Gazelle.*

72. Reza Deghati, "We Are All One Neda." www.payvand.com/news/09/sep/1241.htm.

73. Assmann and Assmann, "Neda: The Career of a Global Icon," 239.

74. Anonymous, "Wounded Girl Dying in Front of Camera, Her Name Was Neda," YouTube, 2009, https://www.youtube.com/watch?v=bbdEf0QRsLM.

75. Hejazi, *The Gaze of the Gazelle;* Zelizer, *About to Die.*

76. Aghvami, "Persian bloggers," 11.

Part III

CULTURE

Chapter 13

Iranian Cinema and Social Media

Michelle Langford

Across the globe, new media technologies are rendering cinema less a discrete medium and more a part of much larger convergent systems of entertainment, information, economics, cultures, and ideologies. Where a small number of vertically integrated Hollywood film studios once dominated the world's film markets, now monolithic multinational, although still mostly American, media conglomerates maintain an even greater stranglehold over film production, distribution, and exhibition. As they do so, many such media corporations have embraced the enhanced interactivity offered by Web 2.0 technologies and the possibilities of connecting with potential viewers, or rather "end-users" almost anywhere mobile data service is available.[1]

At the same time, the increased potential for interactivity provided by the same Web 2.0 has seen an increase in user-led production and distribution of film and media content. As Henry Jenkins has argued, no longer can consumers be considered passive, predictable, and isolated; now they are "migratory," "more socially connected," "resistant," "noisy and public."[2] As we have seen with the wealth of scholarly literature on the use of social media by participants in and commentators on the Iranian Green Wave and during the Arab Spring, social media has provided ample opportunities for the enhancement of extant forms of noisy, socially connected resistance, making such movements and actions even more internationally visible and "migratory" than ever before; even and in spite of the various kinds of media blackouts imposed during such times of sociopolitical crisis.

In postrevolutionary Iran, cinema has long been a site of contestation between the Islamic government and filmmakers attempting to resist socio-political and religious censorship of film form and content. In the wake of the Iranian revolution in 1979, strict censorship guidelines were introduced to ensure that films conform to revolutionary values and codes of modesty in line with Islamic law. Between 1979 and the present day, these censorship rules have shifted slightly with the ebbs and flows of Iranian politics, with a perceptible loosening of codes during the presidency of reformist Moham-mad Khatami (1997–2005) and a gradual tightening of restrictions again following the election of Mahmoud Ahmadinejad (2005–2013). Under the presidency of Hasan Rouhani there has been little evidence of a loosen-ing of censorship, despite the new president's more moderate political pro-file. It was, however, under Ahmadinejad's presidency that the most severe restrictions were placed on Iran's film community as the country entered into political crisis in 2009 following President Mahmoud Ahmadinejad's contested re-election and the rise of the Green Wave protest movements.

These restrictions, which have seen travel bans placed on various film-makers and actors, the arrest of numerous filmmakers, actors, and producers and a twenty-year filmmaking ban imposed on prominent director Jafar Panahi, are increasingly designed to control the people with the means and expertise to produce meaningful content, rather than the content itself. Arguably, this is in part a result of the sophisticated practices of allegori-cal encoding that Iranian filmmakers have developed over more than three decades of censorship and political scrutiny.[3] Authorities have become increasingly aware of and sensitive to the openness and critical potential of such "texts" and the attendant capacity of audiences to read into them. At the same time, digital and Web 2.0 technologies are enabling filmmakers to connect much more directly with viewers, bypassing the many layers of censorship imposed at all stages of the filmmaking process: production, distribution, and exhibition.

To talk about cinema and social media in Iran, therefore, is to talk about a very particular kind of media convergence and entails a consider-ation of complex and often highly politicized interactions between diverse media. This chapter will take the concept of media convergence as prof-fered by cultural theorist Henry Jenkins as a point of departure for discuss-ing some of the intersections emerging between cinema and social media in Iran (and beyond) as Iranian filmmakers embrace new technologies to both resist censorship and engage active participatory audiences in Iran and around the globe. The chapter will then turn to examine Panahi's *This is*

Not a Film, showing how the film highlights the now inextricable relationship between and interdependence of various media, old and new. This is evidenced both by the sociopolitical and contextual parameters the film's production, distribution, and exhibition as well as in the very content and structure of the film itself.

In his book *Convergence Culture: Where Old and New Media Collide*, Henry Jenkins defines media convergence as a place "where old and new media collide, where grassroots and corporate media intersect, where the power of the media producer and the power of the media consumer interact in unpredictable ways."[4] He continues:

> By convergence, I mean the flow of content across multiple media platforms, the cooperation between multiple media industries, and the migratory behaviour of media audiences who will go almost anywhere in search of the kinds of entertainment experiences they want. Convergence is a word that manages to describe technological, industrial, cultural, and social changes depending on who's speaking and what they think they are talking about.[5]

As the terms of Jenkins's definition of media convergence suggest, discussions of this phenomenon pivot primarily around the embrace of convergent media practices by media institutions and corporations on the one hand and their use by consumers or end users on the other. Furthermore, in cultural studies, research into convergence has focused predominantly on its relationship to global capitalism and the way convergent media facilitate the circulation and consumption of commodities, brands and franchises, such as the oft-cited example of the multiplatform *Matrix* franchise. Thus much of the scholarship looking at the place of cinema within cultures of convergence places emphasis on film as commodity and the economic value-adding potential of new media and the growth of participatory audience cultures. To this definition, however, Jenkins adds that media convergence also provides opportunities to bring into play new forms of what cyber theorist Pierre Lévy called "collective intelligence." Jenkins writes: "Right now, we are mostly using this collective power through our recreational life, but soon we will be deploying those skills for more 'serious' purposes."[6] Recent years have seen a significant move toward socially mediated collective intelligence and this, as I shall outline below, is having an impact on Iranian cinema in terms of production, distribution, and exhibition and is also figuring heavily in international actions in support of Iran's oppressed filmmakers.

As noted above, the heavy government regulation of Iran's film industry, combined with highly protectionist policies governing film imports that
limit the number and types of internationally produced films in official
circulation, tend to render Iran's film industry far more ideological than
commercial, yet also at times critical and allegorical. In effect, the government, or more specifically the Ministry of Culture and Islamic Guidance
and Farabi Cinema Foundation, stand in place of multinational corporations to control production, distribution, and exhibition of film in Iran
at a national level. This situation has led to longstanding and widespread
traditions of movie piracy in Iran. Over the last thirty years alternate, illicit
modes of distribution have emerged and evolved along with technology:
from videotape to VCD and DVD. Furthermore, as Hamid Naficy has
discussed, despite the prohibition of satellite dishes, satellite television, much
of which is beamed from the diasporic communities in Southern California
and Europe, provides, along with the more recent phenomenon of Internet
TV, yet further means of accessing a broader selection of film, music, news,
and media content than that which is officially sanctioned by the Iranian
government.[7] The heavy policing of these illicit modes of distribution and
exhibition along with periodic confiscation of satellite dishes has inspired
viewers to become both agile and resourceful.[8]

However, uptake of Web-based distribution still remains limited. Compared with the widespread uptake of text-based social media in Iran—blogging, tweeting, social networking—video-based Internet activity has been
hindered by the Iranian government's strict filtering and speed limiting
of the Internet. Although VPNs and other methods of circumvention can
enable users to work around government restriction of forbidden sites, the
relatively large size of feature-length video files can make downloading or
streaming a slow and painstaking process. Indeed, as Negar Esfandiari has
written, "[t]o upload five minutes of footage on YouTube could take 50
minutes."[9] Even so, according to Alexa.com, a number of Persian-language
video-enabled social-networking sites are among some of Iran's most visited.
According to the authors of "Finding a Way," however, the penetration and
use of social-networking sites in Iran among the general population is minimal, and while an online survey of technologically savvy youth revealed that
they are much more adept than the wider population at using circumvention tools to access filtered and restricted sites, social-networking sites were,
according to the report, not among the most visited. Furthermore, a general
population survey revealed that while 35 percent of respondents reported
recording video on mobile phones, only 5 percent of those uploaded content to the Internet.[10] This suggests that while Iranians possess the means
and know-how to record and distribute video content, this practice remains

limited in scale and is practiced mainly by the technology savvy and politically motivated youth.

Access to YouTube remains restricted in Iran, however, in addition to the various forms of governmental filtering and surveillance of Internet usage that limit user-led uptake of the participatory advantages of media convergence, the government is also embracing Web 2.0 technology as a way of attempting to engage users and audiences. In late 2012, the Iranian national television broadcaster IRIB launched its own video-sharing website mehr.ir, which has been described as an "Islamic YouTube," reportedly one of the first steps in establishing an Iranian national or "halal" Internet in the country, and an attempt to impose even greater control over access to the World Wide Web.[11] Three years on, however, this initiative has gained little traction, and Iran's Internet remains more or less open.

In the area of film production, the increasing availability of affordable high-end digital video equipment and editing software has enabled almost anyone to become a filmmaker, and in the main to slip under the censor's radar. An extension of this is the rise of the citizen video journalist. During the 2009 postelection protests, masses of amateur video footage, including the now iconic images of the final moments of Neda Agha-Soltan's life, was posted on video-enabled social-networking sites in defiance of the media blackout that was imposed by the government. According to Nazanine Moshiri, at the height of the unrest the BBC reported receiving around eight videos a minute.[12] The majority of this footage was filmed on the protesters' own smart phones or small, easily hidden video cameras with links shared on social-networking sites such as Facebook, or via email due to the blocking of YouTube. More recently, in May 2014, a group of young Iranians were arrested for posting a video of themselves dancing to Pharell William's hit song "Happy" on YouTube. The arrests inspired others across the globe to create their own videos in support of the Iranian youths. Even President Rouhani appeared to enter the conversation, tweeting "#Happiness is our people's right. We shouldn't be too hard on behaviors caused by joy" (29/6/2013).[13] Although arguably these clips do not qualify as "films," they do evidence the proliferation of technologies for producing and distributing moving images both in Iran and internationally. Furthermore, presented with sufficient motivation, Iran's youth are certainly proficient, agile, noisy, and mobile enough to embrace the advantages of social media for political purposes, bringing it into play to form highly converged forms of collective intelligence.

Such practices also highlight the important role convergent media plays in facilitating the flow of moving image content into and out of the country. While much of the content produced by the 2009 demonstrators

was disseminated in a highly dispersed, disconnected, and often uncon-
textualized fashion on social-networking and news sites, this material has
also recirculated back into filmmaking proper. This is reflected in Hana
Makhmalbaf's use of the Neda footage along with other hand-held and
low-resolution videography in her 2009 documentary *Green Days*. In 2010,
the German-Iranian filmmaker Ali Samadi Ahadi took this strategy further
with his eighty-minute documentary entitled *The Green Wave*, in which
he pieced together hundreds of fragments of blog posts voiced by actors,
mobile phone video footage, interviews, photographs, and animation both
to provide a record of the events and examine the significant role played by
social media in the postelection protests. Interestingly, the film also features
sequences involving an important but somewhat older, uniquely Iranian
form of "social media": conversations in a shared taxi punctuate the film,
bringing the more technologically mediatized into contact with traditional
forms of collective, and arguably, "mobile" intelligence. The film premiered
on German television in June 2010 and subsequently travelled to a variety
of international film festivals, including Sundance in the United States. It
is a good example of how social media is beginning to inform film aesthetics, as most of the footage is shaky, hand-held, and extremely low quality.

Ahadi cleverly mitigates the low quality of the footage through the
addition of digital filters, which at times grant the pixelated footage an
animated effect that some critics have compared to the Israeli animated film
Waltz with Bashir (Ari Folman, 2008) and *Persepolis* (2007), an animated
film co-directed by French-Iranian author and filmmaker Marjane Satrapi.
Films like *The Green Wave*, which uses animation to tie the disparate pieces
together, provide a platform, context and aesthetic mediation for technically
imperfect footage to reach a wider audience. Other short and documentary
films such as *Juste une femme* (*Just a Woman,* Mitra Farahani, Sonbol B.
Y., 2002), the first of numerous films by diasporic filmmakers to examine
the practice of sex change operations in Iran, was filmed by its French-
Iranian director on a small, easily hidden video camera, but it circulated on
the international film festival circuit despite its technical limitations. While
developments in technology enable such films to be produced, and in some
cases may be the only way certain stories can be told, this trend also arguably results in the diminution of the overall quality of films from and about
Iran in international circulation. Aside from the Academy Award–winning
A Separation (*Jodaeiye Nader az Simin,* Asghar Farhadi, 2011), many of the
most internationally prominent Iranian films of the last few years, such as
Green Days (Hana Makhmalbaf, 2009), *No One Knows About Persian Cats*
(Bahman Ghobadi, 2009), and *This is Not a Film* (Jafar Panahi, 2011) have

either by choice or necessity been technically flawed. These have arguably been stylistically influenced by the aesthetics of social media and mobile videography.

The Internet is also beginning to play a crucial role in the promotion and distribution of Iranian films, particularly those that have been officially banned by the government, or the so-called "underground" films for which no production permission was obtained. In early 2012, news reports emerged about two films, *Zendegi-e Khosusi* (*Private Life,* Mohammad Hossei Farahbakhsh, 2012) and *Gasht-e Ershad* (Saeed Soheili, 2012), that were pulled from cinemas in Iran after being described as "obscene" by a hardline cleric at a Friday prayer service shortly after their theatrical release. *Gasht-e Ershad* was also reportedly removed from video stores just days after going on sale. Arash Karami and Negar Mortazavi also reported that social media users had been "speculating about whether the criticism of the two movies and their subsequent disappearance from cinemas was intended to eliminate competition for *Golden Collars*, a pro-government film about the 2009 postelection protests.[14] In response, a Facebook page urging viewers to boycott *Golden Collars* was established, although with fewer than seventy-five hundred "likes," it is unlikely this had any significant impact on audience opinion. However, despite their removal from cinemas, both films were quickly made available for online viewing and download, albeit in significantly diminished quality. While online distribution serves as an important avenue for filmmakers to ensure their films do not disappear into oblivion, like movie piracy it provides little opportunity for producers to recoup costs.

One site that is attempting to provide socially conscious filmmakers from around the world, including Iran, with the opportunity to have their films viewed internationally and to receive financial contributions from viewers is Culture Unplugged. Launched in 2008 with their first online film festival, Culture Unplugged brings an emphasis on global consciousness, humanitarianism, and community to the arena of online film exhibition, which is dominated on the one hand by large media corporations and on the other by film piracy. Through their website, viewers can submit financial contributions to specific filmmakers, with Culture Unplugged committed to pass on 100 percent of monies raised. Interestingly, while the organization also provides apps for the iPhone and iPad and membership login via Facebook, they do not actively engage in promotion of their website via mass or social media. Rather, they aspire to grow primarily by mobilizing the collective intelligence of their viewers who use email, social media, and word of mouth to promote the website. To date, Culture Unplugged has screened more than one hundred short, feature, and documentary films by Iranian and diasporic Iranian filmmakers and in doing so has made a significant contribution to the online presence of Iranian cinema.

In 2009, prominent Kurdish-Iranian filmmaker Bahman Ghobadi made strategic use of both the Internet and the international film festival circuit with what might be described as a hybrid distribution strategy. Knowing that his film about Tehran's alternative music scene, *No One Knows About Persian Cats* (*Kasi az gorbehaye irani khabar nadareh*), which was made on the sly without government approval, would never be given exhibition approval in Iran, Ghobadi made a low-resolution version of his film available as a free download to Iranian audiences. This occurred around the same time the film was due to premiere at the Cannes Film Festival, where it won the Un Certain Regard Special Jury Prize. Although a highly competent director known for his aesthetically sophisticated cinematic works such as *Turtles Can Fly* (2004), Ghobadi adopted a very low-budget, grunge aesthetic for *No One Knows About Persian Cats*, which arguably attempts to mimic the style of Iran's thriving underground, amateur, and semiprofessional music video industry. The film is only one of numerous examples of the recent convergence of film, music, and social media.

The London-based Bar-ax promotions is one diasporic multimedia company that evidences such convergence. Their mission is to provide advocacy and advice to Iranian musicians and to promote contemporary "alternative" music in Iran and abroad. They also produce music videos and promote Iranian music, art, and film on their website bar-ax.com, which includes news about Iranian and diasporic entertainment industries, promotes events, and streams short films and music videos. It also contains a "backstage" section where members can connect with each other or contact their favorite artists. Aside from Ghobadi, the alternative or underground music scene, which encompasses a variety of musical styles from fusion and rock to heavy metal and rap, has inspired several other fictional feature films and documentaries, which also evidence varying degrees of media convergence. These include *My Tehran for Sale* (Granaz Moussavi, 2009) and the feature documentary *Not an Illusion* (Torang Abedian, 2009). Although Moussavi obtained permission to film much of *My Tehran for Sale* in Tehran, she did not seek an exhibition permit for the film, knowing that the completed film, which was postproduced in Australia, might cause problems for her Iranian cast and crew, a concern that unfortunately came to pass only after bootleg copies of the DVD began to circulate on Iran's black market.

In 2011, actress Marziyeh Vafamehr, who portrayed the film's central female character was arrested on charges that her appearance in the film contravened Iran's strict Islamic morality codes by, among other accusations, appearing unveiled with a shaved head.[15] While the film itself had seen a rather conventional "old media" distribution pattern through the international film festival circuit, limited commercial release, and DVD distribution, the dark afterlife of the film played out across both traditional media as well as social-networking sites such as Facebook and Twitter, as well as the numerous online petitions that quickly sprang up to protest the severity and inhumanity of Vafamer's sentence, which was to include punishment by ninety lashes.[16] Although it is difficult to tell the extent to which international online petitions might have contributed to the eventual reduction of Vafamer's punishment and sentence, this is just one example of how mediatized social networking has played an important part in promoting international awareness of Iran's strict film censorship laws and the inherent dangers involved in producing films that test the limits of these laws.

A much earlier example of such online activism in support of an Iranian filmmaker came in 2001 with the arrest of one of Iran's most prominent female filmmakers Tahmineh Milani. Upon news breaking of Milani's arrest, French filmmaker Catherine Breillat established an online petition with the assistance of Chicago-based film distributor Facets Multimedia. The petition was quickly distributed via email, online discussion boards, and through news reports in the traditional media. Within hours, electronic signatures flowed in from across the world and included prominent names from Hollywood and World cinema, including Martin Scorsese, Frances Ford Coppola, Agnieszka Holland, and Ang Lee.[17] More recently, similar online activism was initiated following the arrest of Panahi in 2009.

As mentioned above, the outbreak of street protests following the hotly contested 2009 Iranian elections has brought with it an intensified climate of film and media censorship. In this highly sensitive situation, an unprecedented number of filmmakers and other film professionals—actors and producers among them—have been arrested on a variety of charges, and others have either been prevented from leaving the country or have gone into voluntarily exile. Among the most prominent directors who have faced arrest and censure are Mohammad Rasoulof and Panahi. On July 30, 2009, the pair were arrested and detained for several days after attending Tehran's Behesht-e Zahra Cemetery along with thousands of mourners paying respect to Neda Agha-Soltan, who had been shot during the postelection protests. Authorities alleged that they were taking video footage at the event without approval, deeming this "assembly and collusion and propagation against the regime."[18] Panahi was arrested again on March 1, 2010, along with several friends and members of his family, and held in custody for almost three months. In December 2010, both directors were sentenced to six-year jail terms, a twenty-year filmmaking ban, and prohibited from giving interviews or leaving the country. International media coverage of the arrests was initially minimal and details sketchy, however, upon announcement of their sentencing, reports intensified among international news agencies and media outlets. Social media, including Facebook and Twitter, was also awash with expressions of outrage. In March 2010, a Panahi Facebook page was established and has to date received more than 176,000 likes.[19] This is the most active of several "Jafar Panahi" Facebook pages. Similarly, @Jafar_Panahi on Twitter posts and reposts news of Panahi and related stories, such as the imprisonment of human rights lawyer Nasrin Sotoudeh.

Thanks to mediatized and traditional social networking, a range of tribute screenings were arranged to bring awareness to the harsh sentences faced by Panahi and Rasoulof. A consortium of Australian film festival directors and film critics were among the first to respond. On December 23, prominent Australian film critic Julie Rigg was instrumental in mobilizing the Sydney, Melbourne, and Adelaide film festivals in conjunction with Australian film distributor Madman Entertainment to organize screenings of Panahi's film *Offside* (2006) in early March 2011.[20] In February and March 2011, the Asia Society in New York City hosted an extensive Panahi tribute film series organized by Senior Program Officer at the Asia Society, La Frances Hui, along with prominent Iranian studies scholars Hamid Dabashi and Negar Mottahedeh.[21] The film screenings were augmented by introductions, Q & A sessions, and a panel discussion that were subsequently uploaded to the Asia Society website, granting them a persistent afterlife in the world of convergent media. Other events were held at the YBCA in San Francisco (March 2011), the Pacific Cinémathèque in Vancouver (June 2011), and the BFI in London (August 2012). In January 2011, the Metropolis Association in Beirut, Lebanon, screened three Panahi films alongside a retrospective of films by fellow Iranian filmmaker Abbas Kiarostami, and in November and December 2012 the Harvard Film Archive in Boston held an event titled "This is Not a Retrospective." A host of other screenings organized by small student societies and cultural collectives as far afield as the University of Alberta, Canada (February 2011), and maraa media collective in Bangalore, India (September 2012), were also held. While these and the many other events not mentioned here evidence the convergence of cinema and new media only in small ways, the speed with which they could be organized and promoted was certainly assisted by the ease of communication facilitated by the Internet, through websites, email, and various social-media networks.

Aside from screenings of Panahi's and Rasoulof's films, awareness has also been generated through the production and online dissemination of short films. Not only has Panahi's own short film *The Accordion* (2010) been widely distributed via video-sharing websites, including YouTube, a range of other films have been produced in response, including *Iranian Cinema Under Siege* (2012), made by the New York–based not-for-profit International Campaign for Human Rights in Iran. The most socially mediatized online action in support of Panahi and Rasoulof was mounted by Cine Foundation International (CFI), a not-for-profit organization established in early December 2010 by a collective of independent filmmakers. Their goal was to promote an "open cinema society that empowers minority and third-world cultures through the technologic voice of the cinema."[22] Inspired by the Occupy movement and embracing the potential of convergent media, they also aimed to take film screenings into unexpected public places. Coinciding so closely with the handing down of Panahi's and Rasoulof's sentences, CFI was well placed to mount a highly original action in support of the filmmakers. Their response was threefold. First, they called for filmmakers to submit "protest" films. Several films, including one by an anonymous Iranian director, were subsequently screened at a range of public events, uploaded to the CFI website, and shared by followers through various social-media sites. Second, CFI was developing an innovative computer and smartphone application, entitled the "White Meadows" project that would enable users to record and post a video message in support of the embattled filmmakers. Even more ambitiously, CFI planned to commission several features and short films. Unfortunately, the collective has become dormant since late 2011 due to the immense challenge of raising finances for their ambitious projects. Adding further to the collective's attempts to mobilize social media, several attempts to raise project funding through crowd-sourcing sites such as Indiegogo and Kickstarter were not ultimately successful. One of the founders, Jesse Richards, explained that several more conventional funding applications were rejected on the grounds that their projects were considered "too political" or "too radical."[23] This example speaks to the considerable limitations facing independent filmmakers and activists attempting to make the most of the possibilities offered by convergent media, not just in heavily policed media environments like Iran, but also in the West, where competition for funding is fierce.

International film festivals are also important sites where cinema and social media collide and have in recent years become particularly active in highlighting the struggles of Iran's persecuted and incarcerated filmmakers.

Long before this age of new media convergence, film festivals have been about much more than the films themselves. Since the establishment of the earliest postwar European festivals like Venice, Cannes, and Berlin, these have been constructed as high-profile media events. In recent years they have become loci of intensified intermediality; concentrated sites where "films" are processed into a myriad of other mediatized "products," including stars, images, reviews, interviews, news items, awards, tweets, likes, pins, blog posts, mobile video uploads, and of course signifiers of national identity, controversies, and political actions. Film festivals are sites where a range of interconnected media industries, producers, and users converge. As Naficy has written, following Marshall McLuhan, in this new age of media convergence, old media like film has become the "contents of newer media."[24]

Numerous major international film festivals have taken part in protesting Panahi's arrest and sentence, thereby registering a high degree of convergence between cinema, politics, and social media. In 2010 the Cannes film festival left an empty chair on its jury to mark Panahi's absence. This act was subsequently mirrored at the 2010 Venice and 2011 Berlin film festivals. At the opening ceremony, prominent actress and filmmaker Isabella Rossellini read an impassioned open letter from Panahi, which expressed both his frustration and defiance. Once again, Panahi was virtually present, listening to Rossellini and the reactions of the audience via mobile telephone. The text was quickly disseminated via the Internet, initially on the Berlinale website in English and Farsi, and while short excerpts made it into the traditional news media, the video footage of the entire speech was made available on YouTube within hours of the event, ensuring it would quickly reach a worldwide audience far beyond the honored guests at the Berlinalepalast in Berlin.[25] Additionally, throughout the festival, a truck mounted with an advertising billboard asked "Wo ist Jafar Panahi?" ("Where is Jafar Panahi?"), providing plenty of photo opportunities for visitors and journalists alike; and, in an unprecedented move, five of Panahi's films were inserted into various sections of the program, including his last feature *Offside* (2006), which screened in the competition section usually reserved for film premieres. In 2013, the Berlinale demonstrated its continued commitment to promoting Panahi's cause. On January 11, 2013, the Berlinale announced in a press release that a new film entitled *Closed Curtain* (*Parde*), co-directed by Panahi and prominent Iranian screenwriter and director Kambuzia Partovi would premiere in competition at the 2013 Berlinale.[26] The film subsequently went on to win a Silver Bear for best screenplay. At the opening ceremony, German Minister for Culture and Media Bernd Naumann appealed to the Iranian government to allow Panahi to travel to Berlin to present his film, an appeal echoed by Berlinale director Dieter Kosslick.[27] Shortly after the festival, Iran's deputy minister of culture Javad Shamaqdari censured the Berlinale organizers for screening a film that had not received production or distribution approval from the Iranian government.[28] And, further, upon returning to Iran, Partovi and the film's star, actress Maryam Moqadam were punished by having their passports seized.[29]

Further evidence of Panahi's presence in social media appeared in early January 2013. A short clip posted on YouTube showed Panahi "blessing" and "directing" the camera and actors via Skype, purportedly part of a new film entitled *Cancel* by prominent Iranian theatre director Mohammad Rahmanian.[30] This news is evidence that Panahi remains active, defiant, virtually mobile, and resistant despite the twenty-year filmmaking ban imposed on him, with social media becoming a vital and necessary part of the filmmaking process.

Indeed, in 2011, less than six months after his sentence was handed down Panahi surprised the international film world with the release of *This is Not a Film*, which premiered at the Cannes film festival on May 19, 2011. Apparently smuggled out of Iran on a USB stick hidden in a cake, *This is Not a Film* is a good example of how digital filmmaking technology is enabling not only clandestine production to take place but is also helping to make strictly controlled export barriers more porous. Although barred from international travel and giving interviews, Panahi "attended" the press conference via Skype while his co-creator Mojtaba Mirtahmasb responded to questions.[31] Within a day of the screening, a trailer appeared on YouTube and (inaccurate) rumors had begun to spread that it had been filmed entirely on a mobile phone. While the film does contain footage shot on an iPhone, such rumors may reflect the important role mobile videography had played in producing and exporting footage of the 2009 postelection protests, as it was such devices that provided the protesters with the sense that they maintained at least a modicum of free speech and could produce a record of events from their own perspective. Throughout the film, Panahi builds on this idea of the video-enabled mobile phone being used as a vehicle for free speech and visual evidence in a climate of heavily controlled audiovisual media. The release of *This is Not a Film* at such a high-profile "media event" as the Cannes Film Festival certainly ensured that it would not be just a "film." Thanks to the intensified forms of media convergence that occur at such events, the "film" could become, as Naficy suggests, the content of newer media. In effect, it functioned as a major contribution to what might be understood as the Panahi "brand"—that is, the set of "products" and interactive "actions" that circulate thanks to intensified forms of media convergence and draw attention not just to the plight of Panahi but also to the more general lack of free speech in Iran today.

This is Not a Film is also worthy of more extended analysis, as it is a film that quite consciously registers a vital sense of intermediality and convergence within its very structural, textual, and signifying strategies. Shot entirely in Panahi's high-rise Tehran apartment with the assistance of his colleague Mojtaba Mirtahmasb (who was later arrested for his involvement in a documentary screened on BBC Persian), *This is Not a Film* unfolds in seemingly chronological fashion as a kind of day-in-the-life documentary, although it was reportedly made over a period of four days in the lead-up to fireworks Wednesday (*chaharshanbe-soori*) 2011, the last Tuesday evening before Persian New Year (*nowruz*). This ancient ceremonial day, which symbolizes collapse before the renewal of the New Year provides a highly symbolic frame of reference for the film. The film begins with Panahi performing his morning routine alone in front of the camera: eating breakfast, drinking tea, getting dressed, feeding the pet iguana, Iggy, and speaking on the phone with his lawyer, eager to hear news of his pending legal appeal. With the arrival of Mirtahmasb, who takes over the filming, a more distinct thematic element is introduced: the theme of Iranian filmmakers not making films. A significant portion of *This is Not a Film* is devoted to Panahi attempting to "tell" a film he had been planning to make about a girl whose family keep her locked up at home. This act of "telling" a film that to some extent mirrors Panahi's own situation ultimately anguishes the frustrated director. Toward the end of the film, a third and final element is added. Just as Mirtahmasb is leaving, a young man arrives at Panahi's door, the brother-in-law of the building's caretaker, who has come to collect the garbage. Panahi proceeds to follow him, at first filming with his iPhone and then switching to the DV camera, which Mirtahmasb has purposefully left running in the kitchen, just as he had found it earlier in the day. Panahi follows the young man as he makes his way down in the lift, collecting the building's refuse at each floor. As they descend, Panahi, ever the filmmaker, prompts him to talk about himself, his studies, his life, and the day that police came to arrest Panahi in his home. Even the simple act of filming this quotidian moment becomes, in Panahi's hands, an act of filmmaking and thereby an act of defiance, regardless of the dissemblance suggested by the title.

Structurally and conceptually, *This is Not a Film* is organized around a series of analogies, doubles, and mirrors that turn the space of Panahi's home into a veritable *mise en scène* of media convergence and the film itself into a meditation on the limits of cinematic representation. On a literal level this is a space into, through, and ultimately out of which a range of old and new mediatized images, ideas, and products flow. The voices of Panahi's wife, son, lawyer, and colleagues emanate from his iPhone as well as the older hard-wired phone/fax machine. Panahi accesses the Internet wirelessly via his Mac laptop, watches news on his wide-screen Sony TV, and uses it to screen clips of his films *The Mirror* (1997), *The Circle* (2000), and *Crimson Gold* (2003) on internationally produced DVDs bearing English subtitles: the non-Iranian origins of these DVDs pointing perhaps to the fact that all three films were banned in Iran. Indeed, many of the DVDs on his shelf are banned Hollywood films, which can be purchased in Iran cheaply and easily from unlicensed vendors. Then there is the digital video camera with which most of the footage is shot along with the sequences shot by Panahi with his iPhone, which are incorporated into the final film. These relatively new media are brought together with a range of older media, including a printed script for the film Panahi had been planning to make and a roll of masking tape that helps Panahi sketch out the setting for this same film on his living room rug, as he attempts in vain to describe the film it was to become. Panahi screens locations he had filmed on his iPhone and displays photos of the actresses he had tested for key roles in the film. We might even think of the intricately decorated Persian carpet on which he creates this makeshift *mise en scène* as a mediatized image, a combination of intricately interlaced geometry and stylized nature, the coils of vines, leaves, and flowers "digitized" as it were by each colored thread. Even the history and prehistory of cinema is registered here. Photographs of film stars including Charlie Chaplin and James Dean adorn the walls of Panahi's kitchen and living room, and an old bellows photographic camera stands sullen and lifeless on its tripod in the corner. This and the antique telephone mounted on his kitchen wall serve as monuments to older technologies (camera and phone) that remain ever-present in the life of newer technologies. Amidst this proliferation of screens, frames, and representational and communication media, even the large picture window of Panahi's apartment takes on the semblance of a cinema screen as it frames a view of the Tehran skyline as a huge crane swings its load just beyond Panahi's balcony, adding movement to what might otherwise be a rather static image. Later, as darkness falls, this window becomes a kind of mirror screening Panahi's and our view of the fireworks exploding somewhere in the distance. Like so many of Panahi's films before it, this off-screen sound registers a world beyond the frame, beyond representation.

As noted above, this meditation on the nature of representation becomes a key theme throughout the film. Indeed Panahi himself draws our attention to this quite early. After discussing his pending legal appeal on the phone with his lawyer, Panahi, who has become quite visibly upset looks directly at the camera, saying, "I think I should remove this cast and throw it away." Now registering the presence of someone off screen, he asks, "Do you remember the film *The Mirror*?" He then provides a brief synopsis of the film, and as he continues speaking the image cuts from Panahi seated in his kitchen talking to the camera to a television screen on which a moment from *The Mirror* is playing. It is the moment when his central protagonist, Mina, suddenly refuses to continue acting. She rips the cast from her arm and the *hejab* from her head, and demands to be let off the bus on which they were shooting, demanding to go home. As this occurs, the film cuts to hand-held video footage, revealing Panahi first trying to placate the little girl and then positioned behind the 35mm film camera, rearranging the shot and calling "action," asking his crew to ensure they are also recording sound. In *This is Not a Film*, Panahi then uses his remote to pause the film at this moment as his mediatized profile is shown in close-up on the right of the TV screen. If *The Mirror* is already an example of meta-cinema, then *This is Not a Film* becomes perhaps a form of meta-meta-cinema. Looking directly at the camera, Panahi explains, "I think right now I'm in exactly a similar position as Mina. Somehow I must remove my cast and throw it away." Despite seeing his own, slightly younger mirror image on screen, it is not with his on-screen self that he identifies, but with the little girl. He explains that after reviewing the footage he had shot earlier, he felt that it seemed like pretending, that he was capturing a lie rather than his authentic self. It is at this point that he asks Mirtahmasb, who we now realize has assumed the role of cameraman, about an idea he had for a film: "Behind the scenes of Iranian filmmakers not making films." This leads into the next movement of the film during which Panahi attempts, not to make a film, but to explain the film he had been planning to make before the twenty-year ban was imposed on him.

It is arguable, however, whether Panahi ever really manages to throw off his cast during *This is Not a Film*, for as much as he is able to quite genuinely express his frustrations, this will quite literally "not" be a film in the sense he is used to making; rather, it will serve more as a vehicle for communicating his plight to the outside world, a fact that Panahi acknowledges in a phone conversation with fellow Iranian filmmaker Rakhsahn Bani-Etemad. Just as in this scene *The Mirror* becomes, as Naficy might say, the content of a new film, so too, *This is Not a Film* will be not so much a film, but the content for newer media, an intermedial vehicle for spreading a crucial message. It was, as I have indicated, to become an important way of ensuring the Panahi "brand" remains present and not forgotten at international festivals; that his name continues to be posted, tweeted, blogged, liked, and pinned; and that the issues facing not only himself, but other embattled Iranian filmmakers remain at the forefront of a collective intelligence, connected by little more than heavily mediated social networking and the haphazardly territorialized spaces we know as international film festivals.

Conclusion

In this chapter I have aimed to provide an overview of some of the ways in which Iranian cinema and social media are converging. While restrictive measures by the Iranian government control and limit the scale of this convergence in Iran itself, social media has played a crucial role in connecting Iranian filmmakers with fellow Iranians, the Iranian diaspora, and the rest of the world. Further evidence of this convergence may be found in the development of new aesthetic approaches, as well as in production and distribution practices. More important, the enhancement of "collective intelligence" enabled by Web 2.0 technologies offers vital ways of connecting disparate communities and highlighting the ongoing pressures and restrictions facing Iranian filmmakers today.

Notes

1. Web 2.0 refers to the second generation of the World Wide Web. More specifically, it refers to the enhancement of online experience via interactive interfaces such as blogs, wikis, social-networking sites, and other online applications.

2. Henry Jenkins, *Convergence Culture: Where Old and New Media Collide* (New York and London: New York University Press, 2006), 37–38.

3. For a discussion of the use of allegory in Iranian cinema, see Negar Mottahedeh, *Displaced Allegories: Post-Revolutionary Iranian Cinema* (Durham: Duke University Press, 2009); Michelle Langford, "Allegory and the Aesthetics of Becoming-Woman in Marziyeh Meshkini's The Day I Became a Woman," *Camera Obscura* 22.64 (2007): 1–41.

4. Jenkins, *Convergence Culture*, 2.

5. Ibid., 2–3.

6. Ibid., 4.

7. See Hamid Naficy, *A Social History of Iranian Cinema: Volume 4: The Globalizing Era 1984–2000* (Durham: Duke University Press, 2012), 295–306.

8. See Small Media, "Satellite Wars: Why Iran Keeps Jamming," *Frontline* (online) November 20, 2012, http://www.pbs.org/wgbh/pages/frontline/tehranbureau/2012/11/briefing-satellite-wars-why-iran-keeps-jamming.html (accessed April 8, 2013).

9. Negar Esfandiari, "Censorship," in Iran Human Rights Review: Access to Information, ed. Tahirih Danesh and Nazenin Ansari (London: Foreign Policy Centre, 2011), 25, http://fpc.org.uk/publications/ (accessed December 10, 2012).

10. Magdalena Wojcieszak, Briar Smith, and Mahmood Enayat, "Finding a Way: How Iranians Reach for News and Information," Iran Media Program, Annenberg School for Communication, University of Pennsylvania, 2011–2012, 21, www.global.asc.upenn.edu/fileLibrary/PDFs/FindingaWay.pdf (accessed December 10, 2012).

11. Anonymous, "Iran Launches a Google Rival Video-Sharing Website," mehrnews.com, December 13, 2012, http://www.mehrnews.com/en/newsdetail.aspx?NewsID=1765232 (accessed December 15, 2012).

12. Nazanine Moshiri, "New Media Technology and the Uprisings in Iran and Tunisia," in *Iran Human Rights Review: Access to Information,* ed. Tahirih Danesh and Nazenin Ansari (London: Foreign Policy Centre, 2011), http://fpc.org.uk/fsblob/1369.pdf (accessed December 10, 2012).

13. Hasan Rouhani, Twitter post, May 21, 2014, https://twitter.com/Hassan Rouhani.

14. Arash Karami and Negar Mortazavi, "Two Popular Movies Pulled from Screens after Protests," *Frontline,* April 4, 2012, http://www.pbs.org/wgbh/pages/frontline/tehranbureau/2012/04/behind-the-curtain-two-popular-movies-pulled-from-screens-after-protests.html (accessed December 16, 2012). See also Yassmin Manauchehri, "The Golden Collars: A Cinematic Retelling of Iran's Green Movement," *Iran Media Program,* Annenberg School of Communication, University of Pennsylvania, April 19, 2012, http://iranmediaresearch.com/en/blog/65/12/04/19/914 (accessed February 13, 2013).

15. It is important to note that Iranian actresses have previously appeared unveiled with a shaved head without penalty, for example, in Abbas Kiarostami's *Ten* (2002). Vafamehr's conviction is evidence of the unpredictable application of censorship guidelines.

16. Dewi Cook, "Actor in Australian Film Sentenced to 90 Lashes," *The Age,* October 11, 2011, http://www.theage.com.au/entertainment/movies/actor-in-australian-film-sentenced-to-90-lashes-20111010-1lhkw.html (accessed April 8, 2013). Petitions were launched on numerous online sites including change.org, activism.com, gopetition.com, and petitionbuzz.com. The sentence of ninety lashes and a prison term was ultimately overturned on appeal.

17. http://www.facets.org/petition.html (no longer available).

18. Anonymous, "Panahi's Lawyer Concerned about Severe, Disproportionate Sentence," International Campaign for Human Rights in Iran, December 21, 2010, http://www.iranhumanrights.org/2010/12/panahi_lawyer/ (accessed December 16, 2012).

19. See https://www.facebook.com/#!/jafarpanahi?fref=ts (accessed June 16, 2014).

20. Anonymous, "Australian Festivals Unite for Human Rights Campaign," http://mumbrella.com.au/australian-festivals-united-for-human-rights-protest-6613 (accessed December 10, 2012).

21. Anonymous, "Film Series: A Tribute to Iranian Filmmaker Jafar Panahi," http://asiasociety.org/arts/film/film-series-tribute-iranian-filmmaker-jafar-panahi (accessed December 10, 2012).

22. Jose-Luis Moctezuma, "Cine Foundation International & White Meadows," *Hydra Magazine*, February 27, 2011, http://www.hydramag.com/2011/02/27/cine-foundation-international-white-meadows/ (accessed January 9, 2013).

23. Personal communication, January 16, 2013. A selection of the short films may still be viewed on the CFI website. http://cfi.posterous.com/ (accessed January 18, 2013).

24. Hamid Naficy, "From Accented Cinema to Multiplex Cinema," in *Convergence Media History*, ed. Janet Staiger and Sabine Hake (New York: Routledge, 2009), 3.

25. The text and video may be accessed here: "Open Letter from Jafar Panahi: On the Occasion of the Opening of the 61st Berlinale," 2011, http://www.berlinale.de/en/archiv/jahresarchive/2011/06b_berlinale_themen_2011/openletterpanahi.html (accessed February 15, 2013).

26. Anonymous, "Berlinale Competition 2013: Another Nine Films Confirmed," Berlinale Press Release, January 11, 2013, http://www.berlinale.de/en/presse/pressemitteilungen/alle/Alle-Detail_16404.html (accessed January 12, 2013).

27. Excerpts of the speeches may be viewed on YouTube, http://www.youtube.com/watch?v=iQz9Bs6UFv0 (accessed February 10, 2013).

28. Anonymous, "Iran Responds to 'Closed Curtain' Win at Berlinale," *Tehran Times* (online), February 19, 2013, http://tehrantimes.com/arts-and-culture/105763-iran-responds-to-closed-curtain-win-at-berlinale (accessed March 21, 2013).

29. Ben Child, "Jafar Panahi's Closed Curtain Collaborators Grounded in Iran," *The Guardian* (online), February 28, 2013, http://www.guardian.co.uk/film/2013/feb/28/jafar-panahi-closed-curtain-iran (accessed March 6, 2013).

30. The clip was uploaded on January 5, 2013, http://www.youtube.com/watch?v=Bwt8nzLKPQU&feature=share (accessed January 10, 2013).

31. Anonymous, "Mojtaba Mirtahmasb: 'We prefer being free men than imprisoned heroes,'" May, 20, 2011, http://www.festival-cannes.fr/en/theDailyArticle/58652.html (accessed January 10, 2013).

Chapter 14

The Online Avant-Garde

Iranian Video Art and Its Technological Rebellion

Staci Gem Scheiwiller

To see the newest and best video art made in Iran, all one has to do is go to www.vimeo.com and search various names: Pooya Aryanpour (b. 1971), Samira Eskandarfar (b. 1980), Amirali Ghasemi (b. 1980), Neda Razavipour (b. 1969), Farideh Shahsavarani (b. 1955), and the list continues. Even Eskandarfar's *A Dowry for Mahrou* (2006), which was purchased by the Tate in 2010, can be viewed online (although not currently on display at the museum itself).[1] Having all these avant-garde videos at one's fingertips offers one an opportunity to view cutting-edge artwork on a platform like a virtual museum, making Vimeo an invaluable scholarly and pedagogical tool at home and in the classroom, gallery, or museum. An entire university course or exhibition could be taught on Iranian Video Art using only the films posted on Vimeo.

Strikingly, however, Vimeo, Facebook, YouTube, and Twitter have not been accessible through public Internet usage in Iran since the Green Revolts of 2009–2010, after the country and world viewed the political upheaval that occurred after the contested 2009 elections.[2] At the outset, the situation of video art in Iran might appear subversive, evading censorship and governmental restrictions. Perhaps this type of digital maneuvering is subversive, posting on and using websites that are forbidden by the government. Yet there is another area of concern that is political in a different way that does not *directly* engage the Islamic Republic or its policies. I argue that

the target, so to speak, is the global art institutions that privilege more reified, commodified artistic media, such as painting and sculpture, and that
generate millions of dollars per year on contemporary art from the Middle
East.[3] In this regard, there are parallel art scenes occurring—those in the
virtual world and those in the auction houses, galleries, and museums in
the ontological world. Furthermore, I suggest that Iranian Video Art shown
online is where the genuine avant-garde in Iranian art scenes lies in relation
to more conservative trends in the art market and galleries.

My argument, though, does not mean that all Iranian Video Art is
posted on the Internet, or that this cultural production is specifically meant
as a jab at major art institutions; in fact, there is, at times, overlap—Eskandarfar being one of them. My main point is that there is more than just
one Contemporary Iranian Art scene at play. As art critic Bavand Behpoor
has noted that Iranian public spaces are heterotopias, I extend his argument
to public virtual ones.[4] Moreover, as art institutions promote canonized,
"famous" Iranian artists and their artwork, alternative digital spaces might
be where the most experimental work lies, because it is not heavily contingent on sales and market dictates but on expressing diverse visions and
voices, thus pushing the boundaries of what is considered "Contemporary
Iranian Art."[5]

My thesis is not novel; scholars on video art have already proclaimed
its inherent radical nature and snub toward the institution and the com-
modification of art. As early as 1936, Frankfurt School philosopher Walter
Benjamin argued in "The Work of Art in the Age of Mechanical Reproduction" for the subversive nature of technologically (re)produced images, which
liberated art from its elitist and enshrined venues, thus declaring photography and film's potential for political action and revolution. Since the 1960s,
the neo-avant-garde has been using video as an artistic medium, challenging
prominent artists and styles, such as American Abstract Expressionism, and
making cultural critiques (i.e., mass-produced television culture) and institutional critiques (i.e., the White Cube). But "Contemporary Iranian Art"
as a subgenre since the 1970s has had its own crises that are in need of
cultural and institutional critiques, though not in the same ways as in the
past. In the postmodern and digimodernist eras that have produced many
exhibitions on Contemporary Iranian Art, the older methods of exhibiting
and selling the Other remain within their (neo)colonial framings, reflecting
the antiquated attitudes of the global art world. Furthermore, my goals in
this essay include delineating a history of video art in Iran and how Iranian
Video Art, specifically on the Internet and in social media, acts as an alternative to the conservative art scenes in Tehran, Dubai, and elsewhere, thus

providing more nuanced and integrated venues of exhibition that allow for heterogeneous expressions and visions.

Iranian Video Art: A Long(er) History and a Technological Rebirth

The concept of video art in Iran was around long before 2009, the year of the Green Revolts and the framing of this book, and there is no major indication that 2009 was a milestone year in Iranian Video Art—it has continued to grow and thrive since the end of the Iran–Iraq War in 1988. During the Green Revolts, it was the world *outside* Iran that realized how tech-savvy Iranians were[6]—a condition already well known inside Iran for at least two decades! But as for video art, one has to be careful not to conflate it with short and feature films, since they are not the same artistic genre. Usually, video art does not have a narrative (or at least not a complete one) and focuses more on visuality than on plot. Pakistani video artist Bani Abidi (b. 1971) explains that video art provides a variety of ways of storytelling in conjunction with the type of equipment used, so that the medium itself is a field of potentials and possibilities for a multitude of expressions in a globalized art scene.[7] Video art can and does tell stories and messages but not in the commercial or standard ways a plot unravels and develops in film, regardless of the length. Usually, the demographic of video art is smaller than for film, even smaller than for independent films. Both this overlap and divergence make for a diverse group of artists who create video art.

The second qualification is the technology used and how the work is displayed. In general, video art is viewed through a monitor or projected in a museum, gallery, theater, or other art space, including online platforms. Currently, animation, computer graphics, and photographs can make up video art sequences. In fact, with the increased sophistication of computer graphics, the physicality of the body has become more virtual and digital, adding a dimension that was not available to earlier video artwork.[8] These changes in technology have caused angst about the future and definition of video art—if it has remediated into something different under the aegis of multimedia and new media. Indeed, video art is a form of new media and time-based art, but this short chapter is not concerned with video art's identity crisis in the face of newer technologies. My aim is to discuss Iranian video artwork viewed online, whether shot on 16mm and transferred digitally or with an iPhone—not computerized graphic design, installation art, and other art forms that also fall under "New Media" and "Time-Based" rubrics.

As mentioned earlier, another key feature of video art is its potential
to subvert hegemonic artistic attitudes in gallery and museum spaces, as
well as in mass-produced visual culture prevalent in film and television,[9]
thus aligning video art and its artists with the neo-avant-garde. In 1965, the
invention of the hand-held, portable video camera, the Sony Portapak and
other versions by Norelco and Concord, which did not require a camera
crew or sophisticated technology, liberated visual artists (as well as filmmakers) to make art, in particular women and people of color, at a time of
global unrest and change,[10] although as early as 1963, avant-garde artists,
such as Andy Warhol and Carolee Schneemann, were using the windup
16-mm Bolex, a slower, silent hand-held camera.[11] Furthermore, by not
having institutional training in cinema, painting, sculpture, or architecture,
and/or by not being able to travel to major art centers of the world, usually women and people of color were at a disadvantage from expressing
their visions and from promoting themselves in artistic venues. With the
advent of the Portapak, many who were not artists became ones; already
working artists also quickly adopted the medium, and exhibitions of video
art immediately formed.[12]

Although this history is quite Americentric, as noted by art director
Michael Rush,[13] curator Babak Tavassoli has also suggested that video art
was an indigenous, natural phenomenon in Iran,[14] seen in the continuum
of photography and cinema in Iran, which were both adopted quickly after
their inceptions. Indeed, art director and curator Sylvia Martin has asserted
that generations already exposed to photography and cinema were prepared
to appreciate and to read moving images, thus paving the way globally
for video art as a major artistic medium.[15] However, associating specific
technology with video art has caused a rift between its proliferation in
Iran as compared to the rest of the world. According to art critic Helia
Darabi and architect Susan Habib, although television came to Iran in the
1950s, personal video filmmaking was not possible until the late 1970s, but
the Iranian Revolution (1978–1979) and the Iran–Iraq War (1980–1988)
temporarily halted the creation of personal, experimental, avant-garde video
art.[16] Anthropologist Shahram Khosravi also cites that during the 1980s,
"[p]ossessing, renting, selling, or buying them [video recorders] was punishable."[17] Yet during the Pahlavi Dynasty (1925–1979) it was also very difficult
for persons not associated with the government to own private, personal
video cameras. But despite this ban during the 1980s, many short, artistic
films continued to be made, though most of them were produced by state
agencies.[18] Then by the 1990s, the *majles* (parliament) was pressured to
legalize video cameras, as satellite television and VCRs began inundating

homes, thus creating an overflow of media and equipment that seemed impossible to control and regulate.[19]

Although I agree that Iranian Video Art could not follow the same trajectory as in other countries, communications scholar Marita Sturken observes that critiquing television was not always the prerequisite for video art, and setting certain technologies as the standard by which video art is written on and measured is quite flawed and deterministic.[20] For example, Andy Warhol's *Sleep* (1963) was filmed on a Bolex and first shown in a movie theater. So video art in Iran could possess a different origin story, perhaps more connected to cinematic history, since Iranian filmmakers have been receiving global recognition as early as the 1950s.[21] One could argue that the first Iranian video artwork includes Forough Farrokhzad's *The House is Black* (1962) and Manouchehr Tayyab's *The Rhythm (Hossein Tehrani and His Drum)* (1971). Both short films are creative and experimental, focus more on modernist form and poetic abstraction rather than a coherent narrative by transcribing poetry and music onto the screen, and were shot on 16mm film.[22] Yet even if these earlier films are closer to cinema than bonafide "Video Art," some of these films are now seen on the Internet, including on a Google+ group website, Mooweex, devoted to Iranian cinema,[23] and on YouTube,[24] thus re-mediating them into video art online.

The 1990s became a flourishing decade in relation to Contemporary Iranian Art, including the end of the war, new technological developments, such as the globalization and commercialization of the Internet and digital camera, and the directorship of Alireza Sami Azar (1999–2005) of the Tehran Museum of Contemporary Art.[25] Currently, Darabi and art historian Elahe Helbig state that new media art, such as performance art and video art, are an accepted and appropriate means of artistic expression in Iran;[26] however, artist/curator Sohrab Kashani (b. 1989) has stated otherwise,[27] considering that in 2004 the Tehran Museum of Contemporary Art exported the first Iranian Video Art exhibition *Beams of Blue* to the Apeejay Media Gallery in New Delhi, India, but has never held one domestically.

There are two noncommercial art project spaces in Tehran that use the Internet and social media as major platforms and have become very successful: the Parkinggallery and the Sazmanab Center for Contemporary Art.[28] In 1998, the Parkinggallery began in the garage of artist/curator Amirali Ghasemi's parents' home[29] and was initially an exhibition space and graphic design studio, but its scope and activity increased by 2002 to include experimental new media artwork, which also encompassed video art.[30] It was the first of its kind, introducing new media art to an unfamiliar

Iranian public.[31] Presently, the Parkinggallery is in collaboration with several art groups and projects, including the *International Roaming Biennial of Tehran*, an "independent, low-budget exhibition [that] started out both as a critique of the situation in Tehran, and of the international 'biennialization' and 'gentrification' process."[32] The biennials utilize major city venues but are organized and networked via the Internet, showcasing new media art in inexpensive and mobile ways. An exciting aspect of these roaming biennials is the inclusion of artists from any country, producing a transnational spirit that does not homogenize participating Iranian artists by showing all artists together without pigeonholing them.

Initially an open studio in 2008, Sazmanab was founded by Kashani in 2009 and created to support a broader range of new media art, as well as to engage Iranian artists with other international artists, thus providing, events, residencies, exhibitions, screenings, and discussion panels, among other services.[33] Several workshops have included teaching local artists how to use technology, the Internet, and social media in their artistic practices.[34] Moreover, in describing the work generated and promoted at Sazmanab, Kashani emphasizes the importance of the Internet: "A lot of our projects start as collaborations between us and artists groups or project spaces elsewhere, and . . . that contact comes, exclusively, from the Internet."[35] One of Sazmanab's innovative works-in-progress is "Sazmanab TV," which will be an Internet TV Channel "where anyone can make a program to be streamed [online]."[36]

What is critical about both these project spaces is their archiving of new media artwork, which has posed problems for art institutions and one of the many reasons why they steer away from capitalizing on it. Both centers' websites provide extensive documentation on past shows, links, videos, and other vital information that help one construct the new media art scene in Tehran; their Twitter accounts also remain active, unlike the laxity shown by other Tehran galleries, which invest more on Facebook postings. Furthermore, since the opening of these two spaces, other Iranian art scenes, such as in Isfahan, Sanandaj, and Mashhad, have organized new media collectives and exhibitions.[37] The expansion of these project spaces also reaches globally via the Internet "to be in touch with other galleries, institutions, and project spaces to open up . . . for alternatives,"[38] and this global outreach is one way to diminish the ghettoizing and homogenizing of "Contemporary Iranian Art."

In terms of technology, the Islamic Republic of Iran was one of the first countries to use the Internet, and the government has always encouraged technological innovation, which has caused concern and debate in relation to computer and Internet technologies being regulated and censored.[39] This governmental attraction/repulsion to advanced technology has had an impact on framing consumer desire for electronic goods. As globalization expands in its insatiability to commodify everyone and everything, virtual worlds—places also colonized and commodified—can also be framed as alternative spaces to explore expression, as *nasl-e sevom* (the third generation) and *nasl-e chaharom* (the fourth generation) learn, acculturate, and adapt digital articulation as the basic, prevalent, consistent forms of communication (e.g., social media, email, blogging, and texting).[40]

Even though Vimeo (founded 2004) and YouTube (founded 2005), two of the most popular video sites, are blocked on the public Internet in Iran, citizens have found various ways to circumvent the system in order to upload and view video art. For example, they can utilize smartphone applications, such as Open Door or Puffin, or the videos can be embedded within other acceptable websites. Other avenues include purchasing Virtual Private Networks (VPNs) or using anonymous browsers, such as Tor Browser. In addition, there are Internet service providers (ISPs) providing Internet access outside Iran and are thus less controllable.[41] Finally, there are filter breakers that access forbidden sites.[42] Moreover, Internet users in Iran can find other avenues to bypass censored websites, thus enabling them to continue to participate in larger virtual communities and virtual art scenes. Online platforms allow for a global audience to view artists' artwork, and prominent video artists working in Iran, such as Eskandarfar, have posted their work online, both in the past and recently, for free and easy viewing. In diaspora, however, video art by highly reputable artists, such as Shirin Neshat (b. 1957) and Mitra Tabrizian, cannot be found online, except for Neshat's *Turbulent* (1998);[43] generally, their films have to be purchased or negotiated to view through their represented galleries. In this regard, there are several issues in play, such as copyright law (or lack thereof) and the accessibility to art venues beyond geopolitical borders.

Vimeo as a platform is usually more suitable for and used by video artists in general, including artists in Iran. It is commonly accepted by artists, filmmakers, and graphic designers that Vimeo is the preferred platform for uploading high-quality, sophisticated artwork. While YouTube seems like an unwieldy menagerie of various videos strung together, uploaded by a diverse, motley group of users, and driven by advertisements and popularity determined by the number of clicks, Vimeo users are typically of a higher caliber, being artists and professionals themselves.[44] In fact, Vimeo has fewer

followers and requires payment for more sophisticated usage, whereas You-
Tube is free for users but also a money-making enterprise based on number
of views of a video.

Another issue with using YouTube as a platform to upload and to view
Iranian Video Art is that technological mediation becomes the only act of
curating. For instance, the hypertextual nature of recommendations, especially on YouTube, becomes problematic in that a computer program gener-
ates a series of suggestions for a viewer based on assumed interests. These
hypertexts create another narrative and thus associate the videos together,
also very willy-nilly. Although some recommendations can be useful and
relevant, others are not and are even harmful to uneducated viewers. For
example, on YouTube in the United States, I searched for *Hushhh!* (2011)
by Razavipour and Rambod Vala (b. 1985), part of the *Tehran Monoxide
Project*.[45] Instead of other "similar" videos by these artists or the project
itself, unrelated, bizarre recommendations appeared, such as Rick Steves's
documentary on Iran (2010)[46] and "Search for Solutions: Nuclear Fusion"
from a University of Maryland course, which actually does not discuss Iran,
but the implication is that American audiences will ideologically connect this
lecture on nuclear fusion to the struggle between Iran, the United States,
and Israel over Iran's sovereignty to develop domestic nuclear energy.[47] In
searching for *Cura*, a recorded (secular) performance by Barbad Golshiri (b.
1982) in Moscow,[48] Jafer Qureshi, who recites Sunni prayers and preaches,
was also suggested.[49] Furthermore, these extraneous suggested videos are
impractical in understanding the artwork and only belie political codings.
The technological "innocence" and neutrality become dispelled in what
seems an ideological playground in a web of images. When searching for
Razavipour's work on Vimeo, however, eight of her videos appear with only
one suggested video that is a highlighted video, featured by an advertisement or a Vimeo Staff Pick. The featured video is not meant as a hypertext
and understood not to be related to the content of artists' work, as it may
appear with other unrelated searches, although it never loses the potential
to be related. A similar process happened when I searched for other artists,
including Shahsavarani and Golshiri.

Yet YouTube is not necessarily shunned by artists, either. In 2010,
Kashani co-curated with American artist Jon Rubin a show of video art
specifically for YouTube as part of a larger series entitled *Conflict Kitchen*,
which serves food from countries that the United States has "conflict" with.[50]
One event included people attending Sazmanab and the Conflict Kitchen
in Pittsburgh to eat *kubideh* over Skype together. But in the next related
event, Kashani in Tehran and Rubin in Pittsburgh streamed YouTube vid-

eos live between the two countries, followed up by a Skype Q&A.[51] This type of use of YouTube videos was curated and part of a larger context of events—directed and guided by two professional artists to create a broader understanding between Iranian and American artists; hence, the haphazard nature of YouTube was channeled willfully into a more meaningful platform.

Parallel Worlds

What makes Iranian Video Art avant-garde? Why are art institutions a target for rebellion? And how do the virtual spaces of the Internet help achieve artistic goals? I am reticent, however, to use the term "avant-garde" in order to describe Iranian Video Art and its artists because the label is European—stemming from a French military term—and has a particular European modernist context. Delineating its specifications in this article is time consuming and historically complicated. I have argued elsewhere that this terminology has Eurocentric implications that cannot be applied globally, implying that Europe is the norm and standard, and everything else is below and behind it.[52] So I invoke this term to describe Iranian video artists who use new, innovative media, as well as experimentation, that go against the status quo and the expectations of art institutions and of wealthy patrons who invest in "Contemporary Iranian Art," which is also difficult to define in this short article.[53] But Habib and Darabi have likewise described the works of Iranian Video Art as "address[ing] diverse concerns and issues like cultural identity, questioning imposed codes, everyday life, and the contradictions of a contemporary society, intellectual contemplation as well as most personal experiences and narrations."[54]

According to Michael Rush, video art in general is quite prominent in the international art venues,[55] and video artist Shalom Gorewitz has declared that video art was finally canon, omnipresent, and mainstream in the art world.[56] However, Martin maintains that although video art is "an accepted part of the art world," it still has not gained similar prestige as other older media, despite artists using limited editions and installations to raise the financial value of their artwork.[57] On contemporary Middle Eastern art markets, video art is not a major player at all; when it rarely shows up, it is mostly in singular film stills that can be bought as photographs and hanged in institutional and private spaces.[58] If one peruses the catalogues of Christie's, Sotheby's, or Bonhams, who are all based in London but showcase in Dubai—the main playground for selling Contemporary Middle Eastern Art—most prominent are paintings and sculpture from the modern period to contemporary times. From these catalogues, one can develop a sense of what and who are marketable, and these institutions play a large role in determining what is viable and profitable—what is "good art."

The domestic art auction in Tehran is also problematic, creating controversy and upheaval. On May 31, 2014, Tehran held its third annual art auction, grossing over four million dollars.[59] Soon thereafter, many of my colleagues were dismayed by what had taken place, all of them reiterating similar concerns: most of the artwork sold was not high quality; the work was overpriced, it was unknown who the buyers or what their purposes were (a concern for archival reasons); and the artists and galleries received no commissions from the sales.[60] Many buyers might have also been speculators—they pay lower prices in the domestic market, only to make larger profits in the international one, particularly in Dubai. And the most famous names whose work sold (such as poet and painter Sohrab Sepehri [1928–1980] and painter Mohammad Ehsai [b. 1939]) are also some of the most well-known names flooding the international art markets, thus demonstrating a link between the Tehran art scene, Dubai, and London—part of the economic stronghold of the UAE, dubbed the "Dubai-Effect," permeating Iran and the world.[61]

This economic situation has produced vociferous dialogues that include self-Orientalization critiques; competition for the resources generated by the millions of dollars from the art market on the rubric "Contemporary Iranian Art"; and the artists chosen, groomed, and promoted on the art market as "Contemporary Iranian Artists" who come under scrutiny and criticism, as that label may seem disingenuous, dishonest, essentialist, or arbitrary. In 2009, Golshiri even refused to have his artwork auctioned at Christie's and denounced the Magic of Persia Art Prize in London, for which he was nominated, due to their dictating interests in sales, essentialism, and ideological exoticism.[62]

Another concern entails auction houses outside Iran promoting "Contemporary Iranian Art" to uninformed, elite, rich audiences, such as artwork by Neshat and Tabrizian in diaspora. This is not a criticism toward Neshat or Tabrizian but toward auction houses. Invariably, Neshat's and Tabrizian's positionalities are different from artists working full-time in Iran, whether the auction houses or their buyers want to admit this. Although these artists have depicted Iranian motifs, they are transnational artists more engaged with the New York and London art scenes, respectively, possessing varying sets of factors that determine their visibility, privilege, and accessibility in the global art world.

Art historian Hamid Severi has noted that exhibitions outside Iran tend to focus on ethnicity and identity as opposed to serious investigation of the artwork's meaning, and this conflation has limited serious inquiry into Contemporary Iranian Art.[63] As Kashani explains, "The work that gets sold, the work that gets made, is about meeting . . . the expectations of the West," and that Iranian artists are pressured to use perceived "Iranian" elements in their artwork in order to be successful and accepted by major art institutions.[64] Moreover, as the showing of European and North American artwork in museums and galleries has changed and gone through several phases since the early modern period,[65] exhibitions of non-European artists and their artwork have remained Othered and segregated, still mimicking the 1851 exhibition style of the Crystal Palace in London. These international expositions categorized and separated artwork and objects by geography and culture, thus allowing colonial apparatuses to compose narratives of racial superiority and to justify military occupation (i.e., highlighting surgical instruments and weapons in several French rooms while displaying "traditional" Persian carpets in the sole "Persia" room).[66] Even recently, the photography show *She Who Tells a Story* (2013–2014) at the Museum of Fine Arts in Boston, repeated the same motifs of chador, oppression, war, violence, and revolution with its inclusion of Middle Eastern and diasporic artists side by side, thus fortifying ideological constructs that continue to "hide," for example, how colonial war, poverty, and violence have also had ruinous impacts on American lives.

Overall, the spaces online, although also ideologically reconstructed and often mimicking the ontological world (humans make virtual spaces), provide alternate ones for Iranian video artists to subvert art venues that continually position their work in flat, one-dimensional ways. Online platforms, such as Vimeo, allow for a sense of equality among artists, and the Internet in general permits artists from all over to communicate and show their artwork together without the contrived artifices of art institutions that continue to operate on colonial paradigms in exhibiting and selling non-European art. However, on one level, it may be fair to categorize "Contemporary Iranian Art" as a subgenre, since every art scene has its own nuances. For instance, video art produced in Iran, Turkey, China, and India all look startlingly different from one another, employing their own forms of aesthetics. But who is the one to determine these cultural deviations created with the same medium—old colonial paradigms, or thriving art spaces, such as the Parkinggallery, Sazmanab, or Apeejay? Participating within the global art community online demonstrates that art produced in Iran is global, technological, innovative, diverse, and cannot be framed within the limited categorizations set solely by neocolonial and monetary standards.

Notes

Many thanks to Sohrab Kashani, Hamid Severi, and Helia Darabi for their patience, kindness, and assistance in composing this chapter. I would also like to thank Babak Rahimi for being a supportive, helpful colleague who always offers valuable insights and values scholarship on the Arts.

1. Tate, "Samira Eskandarfar: A Dowry for Mahrou 2007," http://www.tate.org.uk/art/artworks/eskandarfar-a-dowry-for-mahrou-t13198 (accessed July 26, 2014). See also Samira Eskandarfar, *A Dowry for Mahrou,* 2006, https://vimeo.com/17704006.

2. Annabelle Sreberny and Gholam Khiabany, *Blogistan: The Internet and Politics in Iran* (New York: I. B. Tauris, 2010), 170–174.

3. Barbad Golshiri, "For They Know What They Do," *Journal #3* 1.3 (2011): 83.

4. Bavand Behpoor, "Public Spaces and the Politics of State Experience in Iranian Cities," paper presented at the Literary and Cultural Perspective International Conference, Krakow, Poland, May 21, 2009, http://www.behpoor.com/?p=285 (accessed July 30, 2014).

5. This term is unwieldy and complicated because what is considered "Contemporary Iranian Art" is not clear, especially in relation to the artwork of the Iranian diaspora. I examine this term more closely in "(Neo)Orientalism: Alive and Well in Contemporary Art—A Case Study of Contemporary Iranian Art," *Neo-Orientalism, American Hegemony, and Academia after September 11,* ed. Tugrul Keskin, Gary Wood, and Mohamed Bamyeh, forthcoming.

6. Leili S. Mohammadi, "Sohrab M. Kashani: 'The Distance is Only Geographical,'" *Journal #3* 1.3 (2011): 59.

7. Bani Abidi, "Everything You Ever Wanted to Know about Video Art but Were Afraid to Ask," *Tehelka Magazine* 6.32 (August 15, 2009), http://archive.tehelka.com/story_main42.asp?filename=hub150809everything_you.asp (accessed July 26, 2014). See also Michael Rush, *Video Art* (New York: Thames & Hudson, 2007 [2003]), 9–10.

8. Rush, *Video Art,* 11.

9. Ibid., 16, 20.

10. Ibid., 7, 9, 13–14; Deidre Boyle, "From Portapak to Camcorder: A Brief History of Guerilla Television," *Journal of Film and Video* 44.1/2 (Spring/Summer 1992): 67.

11. Roy Grundmann, Andy Warhol's "Blowjob" (Philadelphia: Temple University Press, 2003), 5; M. M. Serra and Kathyrn Ramey, "Eye/Body: The Cinematic

Paintings of Carolee Schneemann," in *Women's Experimental Cinema: Experimental Frameworks, ed. Robin Blaetz* (Durham: Duke University Press, 2007), 109.

12. Rush, *Video Art,* 7.

13. Ibid., 38.

14. Babak Tavassoli, "Beams of Blue," *Beams of Blue;* Iranian Video Art (Tehran: Tehran Museum of Contemporary Art, 2004), 1.

15. Sylvia Martin, *Video Art* (Cologne: Taschen, 2006), 6.

16. Helia Darabi and Susan Habib, "Silent Messages," *Silent Messages: Iranian Video Art* (Tehran: International Association of Aesthetics 2007), 1.

17. Shahram Khosravi, *Young and Defiant in Tehran* (Philadelphia: University of Pennsylvania Press, 2008), 22. This ban extended to video entertainment between 1983 and 1993. Mahmood Shahabi, "The Iranian Moral Panic over Video: A Brief History and a Policy Analysis," in *Media, Culture, and Society in Iran: Living with Globalization and the Islamic State,* ed. Mehdi Semati (New York: Routledge, 2008), 114–116.

18. Bahram Reipour and Jamal Omid, eds., *Iranian Cinema (1985–1988)* (Tehran: Fardin Press House, 1988), 320–345.

19. Khosravi, *Young and Defiant in Tehran,* 22–23. Babak Rahimi has also noted that technological media, such as the satellite and the Internet, have been more than unwieldy to control and to regulate. See "The Politics of the Internet in Iran," *Media, Culture and Society in Iran: Living with Globalization and the Islamic State,* ed. Mehdi Semati (New York: Routledge, 2008), 51.

20. Marita Sturken, "Paradox in the Evolution of an Art Form: Great Expectations and the Making of a History," *in Illuminating Video: An Essential Guide to Video Art,* ed. Doug Hall and Sally Jo Fifer (New York: Aperture, 1990), 115–116.

21. Asia Society New York, "International Short Film Festival: Independent Films on Iran," http://www.nyisff.com/awardwinners.htm (accessed July 26, 2014).

22. Hamid Naficy, *A Social History of Iranian Cinema, Volume 4: The Globalizing Era, 1984–2010* (Durham, NC: Duke University Press, 2012), 521.

23. "Mooweex.com: Iranian Film Makers Showcased," https://plus.google.com/+Mooweex/posts (accessed July 26, 2014). For the exhibition curated by Mooweex, see "Documentary Screening," Parkinggallery Projects, Tehran, http://www.parkingallery.com/?page_id=1268 (accessed July 26, 2014).

24. Forough Farrokhzad, Khaneh Siyah Ast (The House Is Black), 1962, https://www.youtube.com/watch?v=5WL4w5ceO7w (accessed July 29, 2014).

25. Susan Habib and Helia Darabi, "Video Art as a Rising Medium in Iranian Contemporary Art," paper presented at 17th conference of International Association of Aesthetics, Ankara, Turkey, July 9–13, 2007.

26. Helia Darabi and Elahe Helbig, "Foreword," *Unanonymously Condemned: Video Art and Performance Documentary from Iran* (Bonn: Bonner Kunstverein, 2012), 3.

27. Mohammadi, "Sohrab M. Kashani," 60.

28. Ibid.

29. Sohrab Kashani, interview with the author, Tehran, June 9, 2014.

30. "About," Parkinggallery Projects, Tehran, http://www.parkingallery.com/?page_id=2 (accessed July 26, 2014).

31. Amirali Ghasemi, "Iran: Making Space for New Media," paper presented at the Centre of Contemporary Art Ujazdowski Castle, Warsaw, Poland, June 25, 2014, http://www.parkingallery.com/?p=1925 (accessed July 26, 2014).

32. International Roaming Biennial of Tehran, http://www.biennialtehran.com/ (accessed July 28, 2014).

33. Mohammadi, "Sohrab M. Kashani," 60; "Mission," Sazmanab Center for Contemporary Art, http://www.sazmanab.org/about/mission/mission/ (accessed July 26, 2014).

34. "Education," Sazmanab Center for Contemporary Art, http://www.sazmanab.org/education/ (accessed July 28, 2014).

35. Mohammadi, "Sohrab M. Kashani," 62.

36. Ibid. Currently, Sazmanab TV is active but only streaming the center's programming for now. Sohrab Kashani, email message to the author, September 12, 2014.

37. Ghasemi, "Iran."

38. Mohammadi, "Sohrab M. Kashani," 63.

39. Rahimi, "The Politics of the Internet in Iran," 38; Sreberny and Khiabany, *Blogistan*, 73.

40. Abidi, "Everything You Ever Wanted to Know about Video Art but Were Afraid to Ask."

41. Rahimi, "The Politics of the Internet in Iran," 51.

42. Sreberny and Khiabany, *Blogistan*, 82–83.

43. Shirin Neshat, *Turbulent*, 1998, http://www.youtube.com/watch?v=VCAssCuOGls&index=3&list=PLAZqOwbH-FQkQb_m2Nzx7YdJKXyxDiDoD (accessed July 27, 2014).

44. Scott Olster, "How Vimeo Became Hipster YouTube," *Fortune*, February 23, 2011, http://fortune.com/2011/02/23/how-vimeo-became-hipster-youtube/ (accessed July 28, 2014); Richard Tiland, "Things You Should Know about YouTube, Vimeo, Vine, and Instagram," *Forbes*, May 4, 2014, http://www.forbes.com/sites/womensmedia/2014/05/04/things-you-should-know-about-youtube-vimeo-vine-and-instagram/ (accessed July 28, 2014).

45. Neda Razavipour and Rambod Vala, Hushhh! Tehran Monoxide Project, 2011, http://www.youtube.com/watch?v=U7AJ6RJO7YQ (accessed July 27, 2014).

46. Rick Steves, *Rick Steves' Iran* (Edmonds: Back Door Productions, 2010), http://www.youtube.com/watch?v=D61uriEGsIM (accessed July 27, 2014).

47. UMCP College Park Scholars Research Project, "Search for Solutions: Nuclear Fusion," University of Maryland, accessed July 27, 2014, http://www.youtube.com/watch?v=_kEOea0Zano.

48. Barbad Golshiri, *Cura: The Rise and Fall of Aplasticism*, 2011, http://www.youtube.com/watch?v=YIobXT7Wunk (accessed July 27, 2014).

49. Jafer Qureshi, "Jafer Qureshi Hum Barbad Q Hain Part 1 Mansoor 03006038378.flv," http://www.youtube.com/watch?v=4hKzkq_iuHQ (accessed July 27, 2014).

50. Ashpazkhaneh-ye Keshmakesh (Conflict Kitchen), 2010, http://conflict-kitchen.org/past/iran/ (accessed July 29, 2014); Mohammadi, "Sohrab M. Kashani," 61–62.

51. Mohammadi, "Sohrab M. Kashani," 62.

52. See Staci Gem Scheiwiller, "Reframing the Rise of Modernism in Iran," in *Modernism beyond the West: A History of Art from Emerging Markets,* ed. Majella Munro (London: Enzo Arts and Publishing, 2012), 11–32.

53. See Scheiwiller, "(Neo)Orientalism."

54. Habib and Darabi, "Video Art as a Rising Medium in Iranian Contemporary Art."

55. Rush, *Video Art,* 7–8.

56. Shalom Gorewitz, "Video Art Is Dead, Long Live Video Art," *Journal of Religion and Health* 41.1 (Spring 2002): 95–97.

57. Martin, *Video Art,* 24.

58. This assessment was made through looking at all the catalogues of Christie's and Sotheby's (2007–present) on Contemporary Middle Eastern Art and confirmed by Kashani, personal conversation with the author, Tehran, June 9, 2014.

59. "2014 Tehran Auction Grosses over $4 Million," *Tehran Times,* May 31, 2014, http://www.tehrantimes.com/arts-and-culture/116042-2014-tehran-auction-grosses-over-4-million (accessed July 27, 2014).

60. This evidence is anecdotal. All conversations took place in Tehran, June 1–9, 2014, with nine different colleagues on different occasions. I have kept their names anonymous, as these were not official interviews but passing or dinner table conversations.

61. Michael J. Totten, "The Dubai Effect," *Commentary,* November 29, 2009, http://www.commentarymagazine.com/2009/11/29/the-dubai-effect/ (accessed July 29, 2014).

62. Golshiri, "For They Know What They Do," 83.

63. Hamid Severi, "Contemporary Iranian Art: A Golden Age or Time of Crisis?" paper presented at Contemporary Iranian Art: Searching for Identity? Bonn, Germany, March 2012.

64. Mohammadi, "Sohrab M. Kashani," 63. See also Golshiri, "For They Know What They Do," 83.

65. Yuliya Vyazhlinskaya, "The Global Virtual Museum: Collaboration and Cooperation of Museums via the Internet," master's thesis, San Francisco State University, 2001, 63.

66. Tony Bennett, *The Birth of the Museum: History, Theory, Politics* (London: Routledge, 1995), 83–84.

Bibliography

"2009–2010 Iranian Election Protests." *Wikipedia, the Free Encyclopedia*, 2012: http://en.wikipedia.org/w/index.php?title=2009%E2%80%932010_Iranian_election_protests&oldid=523144897.

Abidi, Bani. "Everything You Ever Wanted to Know about Video Art but Were Afraid to Ask." *Tehelka Magazine 6.32 (August 15, 2009):* http://archive.tehelka.com/story_main42.asp?filename=hub150809everything_you.asp.

Abrahamian, Ervand. *Tortured Confessions: Prisons and Public Recantations in Modern Iran.* Berkeley: University of California Press, 1999.

Acevedo, Manuel. "Network Cooperation: Development Cooperation in the Network Society." *International Journal of Information Communication Technologies and Human Development (IJICTHD)* 1.1 (2009): 1–21.

———. "Network Capital: An Expression of Social Capital in the Network Society." *The Journal of Community Informatics* 3.2 (2007): http://www.cijournal.net/index.php/ciej/article/viewArticle/267/317. Accessed November 11, 2014.

Aday, Sean, Henry Farrell, Marc Lynch, John Sides, and Deen Freelon. "Blogs and Bullets II: New Media and Conflict after the Arab Spring." *United States Institute of Peace* (2012): 1–24.

Adler, Paul. S., and Seok-Woo Kwon. "Social Capital: Prospects for a New Concept." *Academy of Management Review* 27.1 (2002): 17–40.

Afary, Janet. *Sexual Politics of Modern Iran.* Cambridge: Cambridge University Press, 2009.

Afary, Janet, and Kevin Anderson. *Foucault and the Iranian Revolution: Gender and the Seductions of Islamism.* Chicago: University of Chicago Press, 2005.

Afshari, Ali, and H. Graham Underwood. "The Green Wave." *Journal of Democracy* 20.4 (2009): 6–10.

Aghvami, Maryam. "Persian Bloggers: Exile, Nostalgia, and Diasporic Nationalism." *Theses and Dissertations* (2009): paper 505.

Ahmadi, K., and A. Saghafi "Psychosocial Profile of Iranian Adolescents' Internet Addiction." *Cyberpsychology, Behavior, and Social Networking*, April 24, 2013: http://www.ncbi.nlm.nih.gov/pubmed/23614793. Accessed July 19, 2013.

Akhavan, Niki. *Electronic Iran: A Cultural Politics of an Online Evolution.* New Brunswick and London: Rutgers University Press, 2013.

Alasuutari, Pertii. "Theorizing in Qualitative Research: A Cultural Studies Perspective." *Qualitative Inquiry* 24 (1996): 371.

Alavi, Nasrin. *We Are Iran*. London: Portobello Books, 2005.

Allen, Matthew. "What Was Web 2.0? Versions and the Politics of Internet History." *New Media and Society* 15.2 (2012): 260–275.

———. "Tim O'Reilly and Web 2.0: The Economics of Mimetic Liberty and Control." *Communication, Politics & Culture* 42.2 (2009): 6–23.

Al-Malky, Rania. "Blogging for Reform." *Arab Media and Society* 1 (Spring 2007): 1–31.

Altman, L., and D. A. Taylor. *Social Penetration: The Development of Interpersonal Relationship*. New York: Holt, Rinehart, and Winston, 1973.

Ameli, Said Reza. "Web Log: House of Identity and Imagining Personhood." Hamshahrionline, September 4, 2006: http://hamshahrionline.ir/details/3233. Accessed June 4, 2010.

Amir Abbas Momenan, Maryam Delshad, Parvin Mirmiran, Arash Ghanbarian, and Fereidoun Azizi. "Leisure Time Physical Activity and Its Determinants among Adults in Tehran: Tehran Lipid and Glucose Study." *International Journal of Preventive Medicine* 2.4 (October–December 2011): 243–251.

Amir-Ebrahimi, Masserat. "Weblogistan: The Emergence of a New Public Sphere in Iran." In *Publics, Politics, and Participation*, ed. Seteney Shami, 325–358. New York: Social Science Research Council, 2009.

Anderson, Chris. W. "From Indymedia to Demand Media: Journalism's Visions of Its Audience and the Horizons of Democracy." In *The Social Media Reader*, ed. Michael Mandiberg, 77–96. New York: New York University Press, 2011.

Andrejevic, Mark. *iSpy: Surveillance and Power in the Interactive Era*. St. Lawrence: University Press of Kansas, 2007.

Anonymous. "Iran Responds to 'Closed Curtain' Win at Berlinale." *Tehran Times* online, February 19, 2013: http://tehrantimes.com/arts-and-culture/105763-iran-responds-to-closed-curtain-win-at-berlinale. Accessed March 21, 2013.

———. "Berlinale Competition 2013: Another Nine Films Confirmed." Berlinale Press Release, January 11, 2013: http://www.berlinale.de/en/presse/pressemitteilungen/alle/Alle-Detail_16404.html. Accessed January 12, 2013.

———. "Iran Launches a Google Rival Video-Sharing Website." mehrnews. com, 13 December 13, 2012: http://www.mehrnews.com/en/newsdetail. aspx?NewsID=1765232. Accessed December 15, 2012.

———. "Australian Festivals Unite for Human Rights Campaign." Last updated January 25, 2011: http://mumbrella.com.au/australian-festivals-united-for-human-rights-protest-6613. Accessed December 10, 2012.

———. "Mojtaba Mirtahmasb: 'We prefer being free men than imprisoned heroes.'" May 20, 2011: http://www.festival-cannes.fr/en/theDailyArticle/58652.html. Accessed January 10, 2013.

———. "Panahi's Lawyer Concerned about Severe, Disproportionate Sentence." International Campaign for Human Rights in Iran, December 21, 2010: http://www.iranhumanrights.org/2010/12/panahi_lawyer/. Accessed December 16, 2012.

————. "Film Series: A Tribute to Iranian Filmmaker Jafar Panahi": http://asiaso-ciety.org/arts/film/film-series-tribute-iranian-filmmaker-jafar-panahi. Accessed December 10, 2012.

————. "Wounded Girl Dying in Front of Camera, Her Name Was Neda." YouTube, 2009. http://www.youtube.com/watch?v=bbdEf0QRslm. Accessed January 15, 2013.

Ansari, Ali M. *Crisis of Authority: Iran's 2009 Presidential Elections*. London: Royal Institute of International Affairs, 2010.

Ansari, Mahin Shaykh. "Tahlil-e rabeti-ye hambastegi karbari dar shabake-ye ejte-mai-ye Facebook va sarmay-i ejtemai." PhD dissertation, Tehran, University of Tehran, 2013.

Antias, Floya. "The Concept of 'Social Division' and Theorizing Social Stratification: Looking at Class and Ethnicities." *Sociology* 35.4 (2001): 835–854.

Appadurai, Arjun. "Disjuncture and Difference in the Global Cultural Economy." *Theory, Culture & Society* 7.2–3 (1990): 279–293.

Arendt, Hannah. *Denktagebuch*. München: Piper, 2002.

————. *The Human Condition*. Chicago: University of Chicago Press, 1958.

Arjomand, Said Amir. *After Khomeini: Iran under His Successors*. New York: Oxford University Press, 2009.

Assmann, Aleida, and Corrina Assmann. "Neda: The Career of a Global Icon." In *Memory in a Global Age: Discourses, Practices, and Trajectories*, ed. Aleida Assmann and Sebastian Conrad, 225–242. Houndsmills and New York: Palgrave Macmillan, 2010.

Assmann, Jan, and John Czaplicka. "Collective Memory and Cultural Identity." *New German Critique* 65 (1995): 125–133.

Attia, Ashraf M., Nergis Aziz, Barry Friedman, and Mahdy F. Elhusseiny. "Commentary: The Impact of Social Networking Tools on Political Change in Egypt's 'Revolution 2.0,'" *Electronic Commerce Research and Applications* 10.4 (July–August 2011): 369–374.

Auyero, Javier. "Re-membering Peronism: An Ethnographic Account of the Relational Character of Political Memory." *Qualitative Sociology* 22.4 (1999): 331–351.

Babaie, Susan. *Isfahan and Its Palaces: Statecraft, Shi'ism, and the Architecture of Conviviality in Early Modern Iran*. Edinburgh: Edinburgh University Press, 2008.

Bakardjieva, Maria. "Virtual Togetherness: An Everyday-Life Perspective." *Media, Culture, and Society* 25.3 (2003): 291.

Ballard, Roger. "The Dynamics of Translocal and Transjurisdictional Networks: A Diasporic Perspective." *South Asian Diaspora* 1.2 (2009): 141–166.

Barabasi, Albert-Laszlo. *Linked: How Everything Is Connected to Everything Else and What It Means for Business, Society, and Everyday Life*. New York: Penguin Books, 2003.

Barak, Azy, and Yael Sadovsky. "Internet Use and Personal Empowerment of Hearing-Impaired Adolescents." *Computers in Human Behavior* 24.5 (2008): 1802.

Bargh, John A., and Katelyn Y. A. McKenna. "The Internet and Social Life." *Annual Review of Psychology* 55 (February 2004): 573–590.

Barnes, Susan B. "A Privacy Paradox: Social Networking in the United States." *First Monday* 11.9 (2009): http://www.firstmonday.org/issues/issue11_9/ barnes/ index.html. Accessed September 8, 2008.

Bastani, Susan. "Middle Class Community in Tehran: Social Networks, Social Support and Marital Relationship." PhD dissertation, Toronto, University of Toronto, 2001.

Baudrillard, Jean. "The Precision of Simulacra." In *Images: A Reader*, ed. Arthur Piper Sunil Manghani and John Simons, 70–74. London: Sage, 2006.

Bauman, Zygmunt. *Wasted Lives: Modernity and Its Outcasts*. London: Polity Press, 2003.

Baym, Nancy. "The Emergence of On-Line Community." In *Cyber-Society 2.0: Revisiting Computer-Mediated Communication and Community*, ed. S. G. Jones, 35–68. Thousand Oaks, CA: Sage, 1998.

Beall, Jo, and Laure-Hélène Piron. "DFID Social Exclusion Review." Overseas Development Institute. London: The London School of Economics and Political Sciences, May 2005: http://dspace.cigilibrary.org/jspui/ bitstream/123456789/22869/1/DFID%20Social%20Exclusion%20Review. pdf?1. Accessed June 7, 2010.

Beinin, Joel. "Workers' Struggles under Socialism and Neoliberalism." In *Egypt: The Moment of Change*, ed. Rabab el Mahdi and Philip Marfleet, 68–86. London: Zed Books, 2009.

Béland D. "The Social Exclusion Discourse: Ideas and Policy Change." *Policy and Politics* 35.1 (2007): 123.

Bell, Duncan S. A. "Mythscapes: Memory, Mythology, and National Identity." *The British Journal of Sociology* 54.1 (2003): 63–81.

Bellin, Eva R. "The Robustness of Authoritarianism Reconsidered: Lessons of the Arab Spring." *Comparative Politics* 44.2 (2012): 127–149.

Benford, Robert D., and David A. Snow. "Framing Processes and Social Movements: An Overview and Assessment." *Annual Review of Sociology* 26 (2000): 611–639.

Bennett, Tony. *The Birth of the Museum: History, Theory, Politics*. London: Routledge, 1995.

Bikchandani, Sushi, David Hirshleifer, and Ivo Welch. "A Theory of Fads, Fashion, Custom and Cultural Change as Informational Cascades." *Journal of Political Economy* 100.5 (1992): 991–1026.

Bimber, Bruce, Andrew Flanagin, and Cynthia Stohl. "Reconceptualizing Collective Action in the Contemporary Media Environment." *Communication Theory* 15.4 (November 2005): 365–388.

Bjornskov, C. "The Multiple Facets of Social Capital." *European Journal of Political Economy* 22.1 (2006): 22–40.

Boeder, Pieter. "Habermas' Heritage: The Future of the Public Sphere in the Network Society." *First Monday* 10.9 (September 2005): n.p. http://firstmonday. org/ojs/index.php/fm/article/view/1280/1200. Accessed December 16, 2014.

Boggs, C. "Social Capital and Political Fantasy: Robert Putnam's *Bowling Alone.*" *Theory and Society* 30.2 (2001): 281–297.

Bohman, James. "Expanding Dialogue: The Internet, the Public Sphere, and Prospects for Transnational Democracy." In *After Habermas: New Perspectives on the Public Sphere*, ed. Nick Crossley and John Michael Roberts, 131–155. Oxford: Blackwell Publishing: Sociological Review, 2004.

Bourdieu, Pierre, and Loïc JD Wacquant, eds. *An Invitation to Reflexive Sociology.* Chicago: University of Chicago Press, 1992.

Bourdon, Jérôme. "Television and Political Memory." *Media, Culture, and Society* 14.4 (1992): 541–560.

boyd, danah m. "Why Youth (heart) Social Network Sites: The Role of Networked Publics in Teenage Social Life." In *MacArthur Foundation Series on Digital Learning: Youth, Identity, and Digital Media Volume*, ed. David Buckingham, 119–142. Cambridge: MIT Press, 2007.

boyd, danah, and Nicole B. Ellison. "Social Network Sites: Definition, History, and Scholarship." *Journal of Computer-Mediated Communication* 13.1 (2007): 210–230. http://www.jcmc.indiana.edu/vol13/issue1/boyd.ellison.html. Accessed September 6, 2008.

———. "Social Network Sites: Definition, History, and Scholarship." *Engineering Management Review* 38.3 (2010): 16–31.

boyd, danah, and Jeffrey Heer. "Profiles as Conversation: Networked Identity Performance on Friendster." *Proceedings of the Hawai'i International Conference on System Sciences* (HICSS-39), Persistent Conversation Track, Kauai, Hawai'i; IEEE Computer Society, January 4–7, 2006.

Boyle, Deidre. "From Portapak to Camcorder: A Brief History of Guerilla Television." *Journal of Film and Video* 44.1/2 (Spring/Summer 1992): 67–79.

Boyte, Harry C., and Kathryn Stoff Hogg. *Doing Politics: An Owner's Manual for Public Life.* Minneapolis: Project Public Life, University of Minnesota, 1992.

Bozorgmehr, Mehdi. "From Iranian Studies to Studies of Iranians in the United States." *Iranian Studies* 31.1 (1998): 4–30.

Brah, Avtar. *Cartographies of Diaspora: Contesting Identities.* London: Routledge, 1996.

Brickell, Katherine, and Ayona Datta. 2011. *Translocal Geographies: Spaces, Places, Connections.* Burlington, VT: Ashgate, 2011.

Brinkerhoff, Jennifer. *Digital Diasporas: Identity and Transnational Engagement.* Cambridge: Cambridge University Press, 2009.

Brockmeier, Jens. "Remembering and Forgetting: Narrative as Cultural Memory." *Culture & Psychology* 8.1 (March 1, 2002): 15–43.

Brubaker, Rogers. "The 'diaspora' Diaspora." *Ethnic and Racial Studies* 28.1 (2005): 1–19.

Burchart, Tania, et al. "Social Exclusion in Britain 1991–1995." *Social Policy & Administration* 33.3 (1999): 227.

Burns, Alex, and Ben Eltham. "Twitter Free Iran: An Evaluation of Twitter's Role in Public Diplomacy and Information Operations in Iran's 2009 Election Crisis." *Record of the Communications Policy and Research Forum* (2009): 12.

Busumtwi-Sam, Jamse, and Robert Anderson. "Trans-Local Diaspora and Development: A Concept and Research Note." Simon Fraser University, 2010: http://www.sfu.ca/diasporas/research.htm.

Butler, Kim D. "Defining Diaspora, Refining a Discourse." *Diaspora: A Journal of Transnational Studies* 10.2 (2001): 189–219.

Castells, Manuel. *Networks of Outrage and Hope: Social Movements in the Internet Age.* Cambridge: Polity Press, 2012.

———. "Communication, Power, and Counter-Power in the Network Society." *International Journal of Communication* 1 (2007): 238–266.

———. *The Rise of the Network Society,* Volume 1. Oxford: Blackwell, 1996.

Chamberlain, K. "A Working Definition of Empowerment." *Psychiatric Rehabilitation Journal* 20:46 (1994): 43–46.

Chaves, Elisabeth. "The Internet as a Global Platform? Grounding the Magically Levitating Public Sphere." *New Political Science* 32.1 (March 2010): 23–41.

Chehabi, Houchang E. "The Political Regime of the Islamic Republic of Iran in Comparative Perspective." *Government and Opposition* 36.1 (2003): 48–70.

Child, Ben. "Jafar Panahi's Closed Curtain Collaborators Grounded in Iran." *The Guardian* online, February 28, 2013: http://www.guardian.co.uk/film/2013/feb/28/jafar-panahi-closed-curtain-iran. Accessed March 6, 2013.

Christensen, Christian. "Iran: Networked Dissent." *Le Monde Diplomatique,* July 2009: http://mondediplo.com/blogs/iran-networked-dissent.

Cochrane, Paul, "BBC Persian Television Launches." *Arab Media & Society* (Spring 2009): http://www.arabmediasociety.com/?article=716.

Cohen, Robin. *Global Diasporas: An Introduction.* London: UCL Press, 1997.

Coleman, J. S. "Social Capital in the Creation of Human Capital." *American Journal of Sociology* (1988): 95–120.

Confino, Alon. "Collective Memory and Cultural History: Problems of Method." *The American Historical Review* (1997): 1386–1403.

Cook, Dewi. "Actor in Australian Film Sentenced to 90 Lashes." *The Age,* October 11, 2011: http://www.theage.com.au/entertainment/movies/actor-in-australian-film-sentenced-to-90-lashes-20111010-1lhkw.html. Accessed April 8, 2013.

Crossley, Nick, and John Michael Roberts. *After Habermas: New Perspectives on the Public Sphere.* Oxford: Blackwell, 2004.

Cunningham, Michael R., and Anita P. Barbee. "Social Support." In *Close Relationship,* ed. Clyde Hendrik and Susan S. Hendrik, 273–285. Thousand Oaks, CA: Sage, 2000.

Curran, Claire, et al. "Challenges in Multidisciplinary Systematic Reviewing: A Study on Social Exclusion and Mental Policy." *Social Policy and Administration* 41.3 (2007): 289.

Dabashi, Hamid. 2011. *The Green Movement in Iran*. Ed. Navid Nikzadfar. New Brunswick and London: AldineTransaction, 2011.

Dahlberg, Lincoln. "Rethinking the Fragmentation of the Cyberpublic: From Consensus to Contestation." *New Media and Society* 9.5 (2007): 827–847.

Dahlgren, Peter. "The Internet, Public Spheres and Political Communication." *Political Communication* 22 (2005): 147–162.

Darabi, Helia, and Susan Habib. *Silent Messages: Iranian Video Art*. Tehran: International Association of Aesthetics, 2007.

Darabi, Helia, and Elahe Helbig. *Unanonymously Condemned: Video Art and Performance Documentary from Iran* (Bonn: Bonner Kunstverein, 2012).

Debord, Guy. "Society of the Spectacle." In *Images: A Reader*, ed. Arthur Piper, Sunil Manghani, and John Simons, 69–70. London: Sage, 2006.

Deghati, Reza. "We Are All One Neda." www.payvand.com/news/09/sep/1241.htm. Accessed December 17, 2014.

Deibert, Ronald. "Black Code Redux: Censorship, Surveillance, and the Militarization of Cyberspace." In *Digital Media and Democracy: New Tactics in Hard Times*, ed. Megan Boler, 137–164. Cambridge: MIT Press, 2008.

Delio, Michelle, "Blogs Opening Iranian Society?" *Wired*, May 28, 2003: http://www.wired.com/culture/lifestyle/news/2003/05/58976?currentPage=all. Accessed August 13, 2012.

Dogra, Nandita. *Representations of Global Poverty: Aid, Development, and International NGOs*. London: Palgrave Macmillan, 2012.

Dolfsma, Wilfred, and Charlie Dannreuther. "Subjects and Boundaries: Contesting Social Capital–Based Policies." *Journal of Economic Issues* 37 (2003): 405–413.

Doucet, Lyse. "#BreakingNews: Can TV Journalism Survive the Social Media Revolution?" Presented at the RTS Huw Wheldon Lecture 2012: http://www.bbc.co.uk/programmes/b01nd97f.

Downey, John, and Natalie Fenton. "New Media, Counter Publicity, and the Public Sphere." *New Media and Society* 5.2 (2003): 185–202.

Downing, John D. H., Ramara Villarreal Ford, Geneve Gil, and Laura Stein. *Radical Media: Rebellious Communication and Social Movements*. Thousand Oaks, CA: Sage, 2001.

Driscoll, Catherine. "This Is Not a Blog: Gender, Intimacy, and Community." *Feminist Media Studies* 8 (2008): 198–202.

Durieux, Dorothée. *ICT and Social Inclusion in the Everyday Life of Less Abled People*. Liege and Amsterdam: University of Liege and ASCOR, 2003.

Edwards, B., and M. W. Foley. "Civil Society and Social Capital beyond Putnam." *American Behavioral Scientist* 42.1 (1998): 124–139.

Ehteshami, Anoushiravan, and Mahjoob Zweiri. *Iran and the Rise of Its Neoconservatives: The Politics of Tehran's Silent Revolution*. London and New York: I. B. Tauris, 2007.

El-Ghobashy, Mona. "The Praxis of the Egyptian Revolution." *Middle East Report* 41 (Spring 2011): 2–13.

Ellison, Nicole B., Charles Steinfield, and Cliff Lampe. "The Benefits of Facebook "Friends": Social Capital and College Students' Use of Online Social Network Sites." *Journal of Computer-Mediated Communication* 12.4 (2007): 1143–1168.

El-Nawawy, Mohammed, and Sahar Khamis. "Political Activism 2.0: Comparing the Role of Social Media in Egypt's 'Facebook Revolution' and Iran's 'Twitter Uprising.'" *CyberOrient* 6.1 (2012): n.p.

Eloranta, J., J. Ojala, and H. Valtonen. "Quantitative Methods in Business History: An Impossible Equation?" *Management & Organizational History* 5.1 (2010): 79–107.

Elson, Sara Beth, Douglas Yeung, Parisa Roshan, S. R. Bohandy, and Alireza Nader. *Using Social Media to Gauge Iranian Public Opinion and Mood after the 2009 Election.* Santa Monica: Rand, 2012.

Emerson, Robert. *Writing Ethnographic Fieldnotes.* Chicago: University of Chicago Press, 2005.

Entman, Robert M. "Framing: Toward Clarification of a Fractured Paradigm." *Journal of Communication* 43 (1993): 51–58.

Esfandiari, Halleh. *Reconstructed Lives: Women and Iran's Islamic Revolution.* Washington, DC: The Woodrow Wilson Press, 1997.

Esfandiari, Negar. "Censorship." In *Iran Human Rights Review: Access to Information*, ed. Tahirih Danesh and Nazenin Ansari. London: Foreign Policy Centre, 2011: http://fpc.org.uk/publications/. Accessed December 10, 2012.

Eslaminassab, Ali. *A Clinical Approach to the Psychology of the Disabled and Disabled War Veterans.* Tehran: Safi Ali Shahi Publications, 1994.

Etzioni, Amitai, and Oren Etzioni. "Face-to-Face and Computer-Mediated Communities, a Comparative Analysis." *The Information Society* 15.14 (October–December 1999): 241–248.

Facebook Factsheet. http://www.facebook.com/press/info.php?factsheet. Retrieved March 30, 2010.

Facebook group. Facebook Users against Section 4.3. http://www.facebook.com/group.php?gid=75954597333&ref=share.

Faist, Thomas. *The Volume and Dynamics of International Migration and Transnational Social Spaces.* Oxford: Clarendon Press, 2000.

Farhi, Farideh. "Improvising in Public: Transgressive Politics of the Reform Press in Postrevolutionary Iran." In *Twentieth-Century Iran: A Critical Survey*, ed. Negin Nabavi, 147–179. Gainesville: University Press of Florida, 2003.

Faris, David. *Dissent and Revolution in a Digital Age: Social Media, Blogging and Activism in Egypt.* London: I. B. Tauris, 2013.

Faris, David, and Patrick Meier. "Digital Activism in Authoritarian Countries." *The Routledge Participatory Cultures Handbook*, ed. Aaron Delwich and Jennifer Jacobs Henderson, 195–205. New York: Routledge, 2012.

Farivar, Cyrus. *The Internet of Elsewhere: The Emergent Effects of a Wired World.* New Brunswick and London: Rutgers University Press, 2011.

Fathi, Nazila. "In a Death Seen around the World, a Symbol of Iranian Protests." *New York Times* (June 23, 2009). http://www.nytimes.com/2009/06/23/world/middleeast/23neda.html. Accessed December 16, 2014.

Foucault, Michel. *The History of Sexuality, Volume 1: An Introduction.* New York: Knopf Doubleday, 1990.

Fraser, Nancy. "Transnationalizing the Public Sphere: On the Legitimacy and Efficacy of Public Opinion in a Post-Westphalian World." *Theory, Culture & Society* 24.4 (2007): 7–30.

———. "Rethinking the Public Sphere: A Contribution to the Critique of Actually Existing Democracies." In *Habermas and the Public Sphere*, ed. Craig Calhoun, 56–80. Cambridge: MIT Press, 1992.

———. "Rethinking the Public Sphere: A Contribution to the Critique of Actually Existing Democracy." *Social Text* 25.26 (1990): 56–80.

Freitag, Ulrike, Achim Von Oppen, and Elisabeth Boesen. *Translocality: The Study of Globalising Processes from a Southern Perspective.* Leiden; Boston: Brill, 2009.

Fried-Amivilia, Gabriela. "Remembering Trauma in Society: Forced Disappearance and Familial Transmissions after Uruguay's Era of State Terror (1973–2001)." In *Sociology of Memory: Papers from the Spectrum*, ed. Noel Packard, 135–139. Newcastle upon Tyne: Cambridge Scholars, 2009.

Fuchs, Christian, Kees Boersma, Anders Albrechtslund, and Marisol Sandoval, eds. *Internet and Surveillance: The Challenges of Web 2.0 and Social Media.* New York: Routledge, 2011.

Fukuyama, Francis. *Trust: The Social Virtues and the Creation of Prosperity.* New York: Free Press, 1995.

Gaffney, Devin. "#Iranelection: Quantifying Online Activism." *Web Science Conference* (2010): http://journal.webscience.org/295/2/websci10_submission_6.pdf.

Ganley, Gladys D. "Power to the People via Personal Electronic Media." *The Washington Quarterly* 14.2 (1991): 5–22.

Gardelli, Assa. "ICT as a Tool for Empowerment with People with Disabilities." *From Violence to Caring: Gendered and Sexualized Violence as the Challenge on the Life Span.* Oulu, Finland: Kasvatustieteiden tiedekunnan elektronisia julkaisuja 8, 2008.

Garland-Thompson, Rosemarie. "Feminist Disability Studies." *Signs* 30.2 (2005): 1557–1587.

Geidner, Nicholas. W., Christopher. A. Flook, and Mark. W. Bell. Masculinity and Online Social Networks: Male Self-Identification on Facebook.com. Paper presented at Eastern Communication Association 98th Annual Meeting, Providence, Rhode Island, April 2007.

Ghafouri, Arash. "Setad 88: Iran's Greatest Campaign in Support of Mir Hossein Moussavi." In *Election Fallout: Iran's Exiled Journalists on Their Struggle for Democratic Change*, ed. Marcus Michaelsen, 50–61. Berlin: Hans Schiler Verlag, 2011.

Gheissari, Ali, and Kaveh-Cyrus Sanandaji. "New Conservative Politics and Electoral Behavior in Iran." In *Contemporary Iran: Economy, Society, Politics*, ed. Ali Gheissari, 275–298. New York: Oxford University Press, 2009.

Gillies, V., and R. Edwards. "A Qualitative Analysis of Parenting and Social Capital: Comparing the Work of Coleman and Bourdieu." *Qualitative Sociology Review* 2.2 (2006): 42–60.

Gillmor, Dan. *We the Media: Grassroots Journalism by the People, for the People.* Sebastopol: O'Reilly, 2004.

Gladwell, Malcolm. "Small Change: Why the Revolution Will Not Be Tweeted." *The New Yorker*, October 4, 2010.

"Gloomy Day for Freedom of Expression in Egypt. Tough Sentence for Four Years against Kareem Amer." Arab Network for Human Rights Information, February 22, 2007: http://anhri.net/en/reports/2007/pr0222.shtml. Accessed June 18, 2013.

Godwin-Jones, R. "Emerging Technologies: Blogs and Wikis, Environments for Online Collaboration." *Language Learning and Technology* 7.2 (2003): 12.

Goffman, Erving. *Stigma: Notes on the Management of Spoiled Identity.* New York: Simon and Schuster, 1963.

Goggin, Gerard, and Christopher Newell. *Digital Disability: The Social Construction of Disability in New Media.* Lanham: Rowman & Littlefield, 2003.

Golkar, Saeid. "Liberation or Suppression Technology—The Internet: The Green Movement and the State in Iran." *International Journal of Emerging Technologies & Society* 9.1 (2011): 50–70.

Golshiri, Barbad. "For They Know What They Do." *Journal #3* 1.3 (2011): 82–91.

Gorewitz, Shalom. "Video Art Is Dead, Long Live Video Art." *Journal of Religion and Health* 41.1 (Spring 2002): 95–97.

Gould, Roger V. "Collective Action and Network Structure." *American Sociological Review* (1993): 182–196.

Graham, Mark, and Shahram Khosravi. "Reordering Public and Private in Iranian Cyberspace: Identity, Politics, and Mobilization." *Identities* 9.2 (2002): 219–246.

Granovetter, Mark. "The Impact of Social Structure on Economic Outcomes." *The Journal of Economic Perspectives* 19.1 (2005): 33–50.

———. "The Strength of Weak Ties." *American Journal of Sociology* 78 (1973): 1360–1380.

Grossman, Lev. "Iran Protests: Twitter, the Medium of the Movement." *Time*, June 17, 2009: http://www.time.com/time/world/article/0,8599,1905125,00.html.

Habermas, Jürgen. *The Structural Transformation of the Public Sphere.* Cambridge: MIT Press, 1989.

———. *The Theory of Communicative Action.* Boston: Beacon Press, 1984.

Hafez, Kai. "Globalization, Regionalization, and Democratization: The Interaction of Three Paradigms in the Field of Mass Communication." In *Democratizing Global Media*, ed. Robert A. Hackett and Yuezhi Zhao, 145–161. London and New York: Rowman & Littlefield, 2005.

Hammer, T. "Transitions and Mobility in the Youth Labor Market." TIY workshop. Oslo: NOVA, 2000.

Hejazi, Arash. *The Gaze of the Gazelle: The Story of a Generation.* London: Seagull Books, 2011.

Hendelman-Baavur, Liora. "Promises and Perils of Weblogistan: Online Personal Journals and the Islamic Republic of Iran." *The Middle East Review of International Affairs* 11.2 (2007): 77–93.

Hindman, Matthew. *The Myth of Digital Democracy.* Princeton: Princeton University Press, 2008.

Hoover, Stewart, and Nabil Echchaibi. "The 'Third Spaces' of Digital Religion." (in press), *The Center for Media, Religion, and Culture. Boulder* (2012). http://cmrc.colorado.edu/wp-content/uploads/2012/03/Third-Spaces-Essay-Draft-Final.pdf. Accessed December 18, 2014.

Howard, Philip N., Sheetal D. Agarwal, and Muzammil N. Hussain. "When Do States Disconnect Their Digital Networks? Regime Responses to the Political Uses of Social Media." *Communication Review* 14.3 (2011): 216–232.

Howard, Philip N., and Muzammil M. Hussain. "The Role of Digital Media," *Journal of Democracy* 22.3 (2011): 35–36.

Human Rights Watch. *We Are a Buried Generation: Discrimination and Violence against Sexual Minorities in Iran.* New York: Human Rights Watch, 2010.

Hur, Mann Hyung. "Empowerment in Terms of Theoretical Perspectives: Exploring a Typology of Process and Components across Disciplines." *Journal of Community Psychology* (2006): 523.

Hynes, Deirdre, et al. *Articulating ICT Use Narratives in Everyday Life.* Hershey: Ideas Publishing Group, 2006.

Internet World Stats. "Internet Users in the Middle East 2012." http://www.Internetworldstats.com/stats5.htm. Accessed October 11, 2012.

Iran Human Rights Documentation Center. "Ctrl+Alt+Delete: Iran's Response to the Internet." New Haven, 2009: http://www.iranhrdc.org/english/publications/reports/3157-ctrl-alt-delete-iran-039-s-response-to-the-internet.html.

———. "Forced Confessions: Targeting Iran's Cyber-Journalists." New Haven, 2009: http://www.iranhrdc.org/english/publications/reports/3159-forced-confessions-targeting-iran-s-cyber-journalists.html.

———. "Violent Aftermath: The 2009 Election and Repression of Dissent in Iran." New Haven, 2010: http://www.iranhrdc.org/english/publications/reports/3161-violent-aftermath-the-2009-election-and-suppression-of-dissent-in-iran.html.

Iranian Internet Infrastructure and Policy Report, June–July 2013: http://www.smallmedia.org.uk/sites/default/files/u8/iiipjune.pdf. (This work is licensed under a Creative Commons Attribution-Noncommercial 3.0 Unported License.)

Iran Media Program at the Annenberg School for Communication, University of Pennsylvania. *Liking Facebook in Tehran: Social Networking in Iran,* 2013: http://www.iranmediaresearch.org/en/research/download/1609. Accessed November 11, 2013.

Islamic Republic News Agency. "Four Thousand Accessible Automobiles Trans-
    ferred to the Ministry of Work and Social Service." http://www.irna.ir/fa/
    News/80646760/. Accessed May 8, 2013.

Jaghatayee, Behzad. "The Condition of People with Disability in Iran." Rahman
    NGO, rahman.org. 2007, rahman.org.ir/sportal/.../uploads/Dr.%20Jogha-
    taee%2001.pdf. Accessed June 7, 2010.

Jalaeipour, Hamidreza. "Dowlat-e penhan. Barresi-ye jamehshenakhti avamel-e tahdid-
    konandeh-ye jonbeshe eslahat" (The Hidden State: A Sociological Analysis of
    the Elements Menacing the Reform Movement). Tehran: Tarh-e Now, 2000.

Jenkins, Henry. Convergence Culture: Where Old and New Media Collide. New York
    and London: New York University Press, 2006.

Jenkins, Henry, Ravi Purushotma, Katherine Clinton, Margaret Weigel, and Alice J.
    Robison. "Confronting the Challenges of Participatory Culture: Media Edu-
    cation for the 21st Century." http://www.newmedialiteracies.org/wp-content/
    uploads/pdfs/NMLWhitePaper.pdf. Accessed June 15, 2014.

Johns, Alessa. Women's Utopias of the Eighteenth Century. Urbana: University of
    Illinois Press, 2003.

Kafi, Helene. "Tehran, Dangerous Love." In Sexuality and Eroticism among Males
    in Moslem Societies, ed. Arno Shmitt and Jehoda Sofer, 67–79. New York:
    Haworth Press, 1992.

Kaid, Lynda Lee, and Christina Holtz-Bacha. Encyclopedia of Political Communica-
    tion, Volume 1. Thousand Oaks, CA: Sage, 2007.

Kalathil, Shanthi, and Taylor C. Boas. Open Networks, Closed Regimes: The Impact
    of the Internet on Authoritarian Rule. Washington, DC: Carnegie Endowment
    for International Peace, 2003.

Kallians, Virginia, and Phyllis Rubenfeld. "Disabled Women and Reproductive
    Rights." Disability and Society 12.2 (1997): 203.

Kamali Dehghan, Saeed. "We Are Everywhere: Gay and Lesbian Iranians Come
    Out on Facebook." The Guardian, September 11, 2011. http://www.guard-
    ian.co.uk/world/2011/sep/11/gay-iranians-facebook-defiance. Accessed Octo-
    ber 2, 2012.

Kamali, Masoud. Revolutionary Iran: Civil Society and State in the Modernization
    Process. Aldershot and Brookfield: Ashgate, 1998.

Kamalipour, Yahya R., ed. Media, Power, and Politics in the Digital Age: The 2009
    Presidential Election Uprising in Iran. Plymouth: Rowman & Littlefield, 2010.

Kamrava, Mehran. "The 2009 Elections and Iran's Changing Political Landscape."
    Orbis 54.3 (2010): 400–412.

Kaplan, Andreas M., and Michael Haenlein. "Users of the World, Unite! The Chal-
    lenges and Opportunities of Social Media." Business Horizons 53.1 (2010):
    59–68.

Karagiannopolous, Vasileios. "The Role of the Internet in Political Struggles: Some
    Conclusions from Iran and Egypt." New Political Science 34.2 (June 2012):
    151–171.

Karami, Arash, and Negar Mortazavi. "Two Popular Movies Pulled from Screens after Protests." *Frontline*, April 4, 2012: http://www.pbs.org/wgbh/pages/frontline/tehranbureau/2012/04/behind-the-curtain-two-popular-movies-pulled-from-screens-after-protests.html. Accessed December 16, 2012.

Karpf, David. "Online Political Mobilization from the Advocacy Group's Perspective." *Policy and the Internet* 2.4 (December 2010): 7–41.

———. "Understanding Blogspace." *Journal of Information Technology and Politics* 5.4 (December 2008): 369–395.

Kashani, Majid, and Somayih Zarih. "Motaleay-e jameyat shenakht-e shabakehay-e ejtima-ye-e majazi ba takd bar karbaran Facebook dar Iran." *Ulum-e Ejtemae-ye* 56 (1391/2012): 78–84.

Kashani-Sabet, Firoozeh. "Freedom Springs Eternal." *International Journal of Middle East Studies* 44 (2012): 156–158.

Katouzian, Homa. "Problems of Democracy and the Public Sphere in Modern Iran." *Comparative Studies of South Asia, Africa, and the Middle East* 18.2 (1998): 31–37.

Kazemi, Abbas. "Jamehshenasi rowshanfekri-ye dini dar Iran" (Sociology of Religious Intellectualism in Iran). Teheran: Tarh-e Now, 2004.

Keddie, Nikki R. "Arab and Iranian Revolts, 1979–2011: Influences or Similar Causes?" *International Journal of Middle East Studies* 44 (2012): 150–152.

Keele, Luke. "Social Capital and the Dynamics of Trust in Government." *American Journal of Political Science* 51.2 (2007): 241–254.

Kelly, John, and Bruce Etling. *Mapping Iran's Online Public: Politics and Culture in the Persian Blogosphere*. Cambridge: Harvard University, Berkman Center for Internet and Society, 2008.

Kermani, Hossein. "Sanjesh-e sarmay-e ejtema-e dar shabakehay-e ejtemai va majazi." PhD dissertation, Tehran, University of Tehran, 2012.

Keshavarzian, Arang. "Contestation without Democracy: Elite Fragmentation in Iran." In *Authoritarianism in the Middle East: Regimes and Resistance*, ed. Marsha P. Posusney and Michelle P. Angrist, 63–88. Boulder, CO: Lynne Rienner, 2005.

Ketabchi, Kaveh Khonsari, Zahra Amin Nayeri, Ali Fathalian, and Leila Fathalian. "Social Network Analysis of Iran's Green Movement Opposition Groups Using Twitter." International Conference on Advances in Social Network Analysis and Mining. Odense, Denmark, August 9–10, 2010, 414–415.

Khalaji, Mehdi. *Through the Veil: The Role of Broadcasting in U.S. Public Diplomacy toward Iranians*. Washington, DC: The Washington Institute for Near East Policy, 2007.

Khamis, Sahar, and Katherine Vaughn. "Cyberactivism in the Egyptian Revolution: How Civic Engagement and Citizen Journalism Tilted the Balance." *Arab Media and Society* 13 (Summer 2011): http://www.arabmediasociety.com/?article=769.

Khan, Shahnaz. "Muslim Women: Negotiations in the Third Space." *Signs* 23.2 (1998): 463–494.

Khiabany, Gholam, and Annabelle Sreberny. "The Iranian Press and the Continuing Struggle over Civil Society 1998–2000." *Gazette* 63 (2001): 203–223.

Khosravi, Shahram. *Young and Defiant in Tehran*. Philadelphia: University of Pennsylvania Press, 2008.

Kia, Ali Asghar, and Yonis Nori Murad Abadai. "Avamal-e murtabet ba gherayish-e daneshjoyan bi shabake-ye ejtema-ye 'Facebook': Barresi-ye tatbighi-yeh daneshjoyan-e Iran va America." *Motaleat-e Farhang-Ertebatat* 13.17 (1391/2012): 181–212.

Knight, Megan. "Journalism as Usual: The Use of Social Media as a Newsgathering Tool in the Coverage of the Iranian Elections in 2009." *Journal of Media Practice* 13.1 (2012): 61–74.

Knott, Kim. *The Location of Religion: A Spatial Analysis*. Sheffield, UK: Equinox, 2005.

Korycki, Katarzyna, and Abouzar Nasirzadeh. "Desire Recast: Production of Gay Identities in Iran." *Journal of Gender Studies*. doi:10.1080/09589236.2014.889599.

Kowsari, Masoud. *Jahan-e farhang-e karbaran-e Irani Orkut*. Tehran: Vezarat-e Farhang va Ershad Eslami, Pajoheshgha-he farhang, honar va ertebatat, 1386 (2007).

Kuran, Timur. "Now Out of Never: The Element of Surprise in the East European Revolution of 1989." *World Politics* 44.1 (October 1991): 7–48.

Kurzman, Charles. "The Arab Spring: Ideals of the Iranian Green Movement, Methods of the Iranian Revolution." *International Journal of Middle East Studies* 44 (2012): 162–165.

Labelle, Micheline, and Franklin Midy. "Rereading Citizenship and the Transnational Practices of Immigrants." *Journal of Ethnic and Migration Studies* 25.2 (1999): 213–232.

Laclau, Ernesto, and Chantal Mouffe. *Hegemony and Socialist Strategy: Towards a Radical Democratic Politics*. London: Verso, 1985.

Lambert, Alex. *Intimacy and Friendship on Facebook*. New York: Palgrave Macmillan, 2013.

Langford, Michelle. "Allegory and the Aesthetics of Becoming-Woman in Marziyeh Meshkini's *The Day I Became a Woman*." *Camera Obscura* 22.64 (2007): 1–41.

Lenard, David J. *Enforcing Normalcy: Disability, Deafness, and the Body*. London: Verso, 1995.

Lesch, Ann M. "Egypt's Spring: Causes of the Revolution." *Middle East Policy* 18.3 (Fall 2011): 35–48.

Lesser, Eric L., ed. *Knowledge and Social Capital*. Boston: Butterworth-Heinemann, 2000.

Lévy, Pierre. *Collective Intelligence: Mankind's Emerging World in Cyberspace*. Trans. Robert Bononno. New York: Plenum, 1997.

Lie, Merete, and Knut Holtan Sørenson. *Making Technology Our Own: Domesticating Technology into Everyday Life.* Oslo: Scandinavian University Press, 1996.

Lievrouw, Leah A. *Alternative and Activist New Media.* Cambridge: Polity, 2011.

Lim, Merlyna. "Clicks, Cabs and Coffee Houses: Social Media and Oppositional Movements in Egypt, 2004–2011." *Journal of Communication* 62.2 (April 2012): 231–248.

Lin, J., W. Peng, M. Kim, S. Kim, and R. LaRose. 2012. "Social Networking and Adjustments among International Students." *New Media and Society* 14 (2012): 421–440.

Lin, N. "Building a Network Theory of Social Capital." *Connections* 22.1 (1999): 28–51.

Lindlof, Thomas R., and Bryan C. Taylor. *Qualitative Communication Research Methods.* London: Sage, 2002.

Lindström, M. "Ethnic Differences in Social Participation and Social Capital in Malmö, Sweden: A Population-Based Study." *Social Science & Medicine* 60.7 (2006): 1527–1546.

Ling, R. *New Tech, New Ties: How Mobile Communication Is Reshaping Social Cohesion.* Cambridge: MIT Press, 2008.

Livingston, Steven, and Gregory Asmolov. "Networks and the Future of Foreign Affairs Reporting." *Journalism Studies* 11.5 (2010): 745–760.

Loewenstein, Antony. *The Blogging Revolution.* Carlton: Melbourne University Press, 2008.

Lupia, Arthur, and Gisela Sin. "Which Public Goods Are Endangered? How Evolving Communication Technologies Affect the Logic of Collective Action." *Public Choice* 117.3–4 (2003): 315–331.

MacKenzie, Donald, and Judy Wajcman, eds. *The Social Shaping of Technology, 2nd ed.* Buckingham, England, and Philadelphia: Open University Press, 1999.

MacKinnon, Rebecca. *Consent of the Networked: The Worldwide Struggle for Internet Freedom.* New York: Basic Books, 2012.

Madden, Mary, Susannah Fox, Aaron Smith, and Jessica Vitak. *Digital Footprints: Online Identity Management and Search in the Age of Transparency.* Pew Internet and American Life Project, December 16, 2007: http://www.pewinternet.org/pdfs/PIP_Digital_Footprints.pdf. Accessed December 12, 2007.

Malcolm, Andrew. "Iran Ambassador Suggests CIA Could Have Killed Neda Agha-Soltan." *Los Angeles Times*, June 25, 2009: latimesblogs.latimes.com/washington/2009/06/neda-cia-cnn-killing.html.

Manauchehri, Yassmin. "The Golden Collars: A Cinematic Retelling of Iran's Green Movement." Iran Media Program, Annenberg School of Communication, University of Pennsylvania, April 19, 2012: http://iranmediaresearch.com/en/blog/65/12/04/19/914. Accessed February 13, 2013.

Mandiberg, Michael. "Introduction." In *The Social Media Reader.* New York and London: New York University Press, 2012.

Manoukian, Setrag. "Where Is This Place? Crowds, Audio-Vision, and Poetry in Postelection Iran." *Public Culture* 22.2 (2010): 237–263.

Maps of World. Social Networking Websites Popularity Map. http://www.mapsofworld.com/world-top-ten/social-networking-websites-popularity-map.html.

Martin, Sylvia. *Video Art*. Cologne: Taschen, 2006.

Mayo, James M. "War Memorials as Political Memory." *Geographical Review* 78.1 (1988): 62–75.

McAdam, Doug. "Conceptual Origins, Current Problems, Future Directions." In *Comparative Perspectives on Social Movements: Political Opportunities, Mobilizing Structures, and Cultural Framings*, ed. Doug McAdam, Jackie McCarthy, and Mayer Zald, 23–40. New York: Cambridge University Press, 1996.

McAdam, Doug, and Ronnelle Paulsen. "Specifying the Relationship between Social Ties and Activism." *American Journal of Sociology* (1993): 640–667.

McClurg, Scott D. "Social Networks and Political Participation: The Role of Social Interaction in Explaining Political Participation." *Political Research Quarterly* 56.4 (2003): 449–464.

McKenna, Katelyn Y. A., and John A. Bargh. "Plan 9 from Cyberspace: The Implications of the Internet for Personality and Social Psychology." *Personality and Social Psychology Review* 4.1 (2000): 57–75.

Mehdi, Montazerghaem, and Kobra Elahifar. "Bloggers with Disabilities: Blog Use and Its Implications on the Social Presence of People with Disabilities." *Letter of Sociological Studies* 89.4 (Winter 2012): 319–355.

Mehra, Bharat, et al. "The Internet for Empowerment of Minority and Marginalized Users." *New Media and Society* 6.6 (2004): 781–802.

Metzgar, Emily, and Albert Maruggi. "Social Media and the 2008 US Presidential Election." *Journal of New Communications Research* 4.1 (2009): 141–165.

Michaelsen, Marcus, ed. *Election Fallout: Iran's Exiled Journalists on Their Struggle for Democratic Change*. Berlin: Hans Schiler Verlag, 2011.

mikemcpd. "Neda Agha-Soltan." 3:36. YouTube, 2009. http://youtube/DjGF1T-D1HE4. Accessed December 13, 2014.

Mitra, Ananda. "Using Blogs to Create Cybernetic Space, Convergence." *The International Journal of Research into New Media Technologies* 14.4 (2008): 457–472.

Moctezuma, Jose-Luis. "Cine Foundation International & White Meadows." *Hydra Magazine*, February 27, 2011: http://www.hydramag.com/2011/02/27/cine-foundation-international-white-meadows/. Accessed January 9, 2013.

Moghadam, Valentine. "Women in the Islamic Republic of Iran: Legal Status, Social Positions, and Collective Action." Conference on "Iran after 25 Years of Revolution: A Retrospective and a Look Ahead," organized by the Woodrow Wilson International Center for Scholars and the National Defense University, Washington, DC, November 16–17. 2004.

———. "Islamic Feminism and Its Discontents: Toward a Resolution of the Debate." *Signs* 27.4 (2002): 1135–1171.

——. "Transnational Feminist Networks Collective Action in an Era of Global-ization." *International Sociology* 15.1 (2000): 57–85.

Mohammadi, Leili S. "Sohrab M. Kashani: 'The Distance Is Only Geographical.'" *Journal #3* 1.3 (2011): 58–65.

Mohammadi, Majid. "The Iranian Disabled Legal Struggle." Radio Farda, May 27, 2010: http://www.radiofarda.com/content/f35_Disability_Rights_Com/2036120.html. Accessed June 7, 2010.

Morgenthau, Hans J., Hartmut Behr, Felix Rösch, and Maeva Vidal. *The Concept of the Political.* New York: Palgrave Macmillan, 2012.

Morozov, Evgeny. *The Net Delusion: The Dark Side of Internet Freedom.* New York: PublicAffairs, 2012.

——. *The Net Delusion: How Not to Liberate the World.* London: Allen Lane, 2011.

——. "Iran: Downside to the 'Twitter Revolution.'" *Dissent* (Fall 2009): 10–14.

Moshiri, Nazanine. "New Media Technology and the Uprisings in Iran and Tuni-sia." In *Iran Human Rights Review: Access to Information,* ed. Tahirih Danesh and Nazenin Ansari. London: Foreign Policy Centre, 2011: http://fpc.org.uk/fsblob/1369.pdf. Accessed December 10, 2012.

Moslem, Mehdi. *Factional Politics in Post-Khomeini Iran.* Syracuse: Syracuse University Press, 2002.

Mottahedeh, Negar. *Displaced Allegories: Post-Revolutionary Iranian Cinema.* Durham, NC: Duke University Press, 2009.

Mousavi, Mir-Hossein. "The Agenda of Hope Administration for Better Future [Persian]." Presidential Campaign Manifesto published in June 2009: http://www.4shared.com/account/document/EbUsEAgM/Ketabe_Dolate_omid.htmlAccessed June 15, 2013.

——. "Statement #17: 'Ways Out of the Crisis,'" trans. Khordaad 88 blog, January 1, 2010: http://khordaad88.com/?p=925. Accessed June 15, 2013.

——. "The Green Movement Is Standing Firm on Its Rightful Demands." Trans-lated transcript from an interview with *Kaleme* website published on Mousa-vi's Facebook page on February 27, 2010: http://www.facebook.com/note.php?note_id=330992387605&id=45061919453. Accessed June 15, 2013.

——. "Statement #18: The Green Charter." Translated transcript published on Mousavi's Facebook page on June 15, 2010: http://www.facebook.com/note.php?note_id=400395637605.

Murugesan, San. "Understanding Web 2.0." *IT Professional* 9.4 (2007): 34–41.

Naficy, Hamid. *A Social History of Iranian Cinema: Volume 4: The Globalizing Era 1984–2000.* Durham, NC: Duke University Press, 2012.

——. "From Accented Cinema to Multiplex Cinema." In *Convergence Media History,* ed. Janet Staiger and Sabine Hake. New York: Routledge, 2009.

Nahuis, Roel, and Harro Van Lente. "Where Are the Politics? Perspectives on Democracy and Technology." *Science, Technology & Human Values* 33.5 (2008): 559–581.

Najmabadi, Afsaneh. *Women with Mustaches and Men without Beards: Gender and Sexual Anxieties of Iranian Modernity.* Berkeley: University of California Press, 2005.

Newton, K. "Mass Media Effects: Mobilization or Media Malaise?" *British Journal of Political Science* 27 (1999): 577–599.

———. "Social Capital and Democracy." *American Behavioral Scientist* 40.5 (1997): 575–586.

Norris, P. "Does Television Erode Social Capital? A Reply to Putnam." *PS: Political Science and Politics* 29 (1996): 474–480.

Nye, Joseph. *Soft Power: The Means to Success in World Politics.* New York: Public Affairs, 2004.

Olick, Jeffrey K., and Joyce Robbins. "Social Memory Studies: From 'Collective Memory' to the Historical Sociology of Mnemonic Practices." *Annual Review of Sociology* 24 (1998): 105–140.

OpenNet Initiative. "After the Green Movement: Internet Controls in Iran 2009–2012." 2013: www.opennet.net/iranreport2013. Accessed December 20, 2014.

———. "Internet Filtering in Iran in 2004–2005: A Country Study." https://opennet.net/studies/iran. Accessed October 1, 2012.

———. "Internet Filtering in Iran 2009. http://opennet.net/sites/opennet.net/files/ONI_Iran_2009.pdf. Accessed October 10, 2012.

O'Reilly, Tim. *What Is Web 2.0?* Beijing, Cambridge, Farnham, Köln, Sebastopol, Tokyo: O'Reilly Media, 2009.

———. "Web 2.0: Compact Definition." http://radar.oreilly.com/archives/2005/10/web_20_compact_definition.html. Accessed December 15, 2014.

Oswald, A. J. "Happiness and Economic Performance." *The Economic Journal* 107.445 (1997): 1815–1831.

Panahi, Jafar. "Open Letter from Jafar Panahi: On the Occasion of the Opening of the 61st Berlinale," 2011: http://www.berlinale.de/en/archiv/jahresarchive/2011/06b_berlinale_themen_2011/openletterpanahi.html. Accessed February 15, 2013.

Papacharissi, Zizi. *A Private Sphere: Democracy in a Digital Age.* Cambridge: Polity, 2010.

Pariser, Eli. *The Filter Bubble: What the Internet Is Hiding from You.* New York: Penguin, 2011.

Parsi, Trita. *A Single Roll of the Dice: Obama's Diplomacy with Iran.* New Haven, CT: Yale University Press, 2012.

Paxton, P. "Is Social Capital Declining in the United States? A Multiple Indicator Assessment 1." *American Journal of Sociology* 105.1 (1999): 88–127.

Pénard, T., and N. Poussing. "Internet Use and Social Capital: The Strength of Virtual Ties." *Journal of Economic Issues* 44.3 (2010): 569–595.

Pfeifle, Mark. "A Nobel Peace Prize for Twitter?" *Christian Science Monitor*, July 6, 2009: http://www.csmonitor.com/Commentary/Opinion/2009/0706/p09s02-coop.html.

Phipps, Linda. "New Communications Technologies: A Conduit for Social Inclusion." *Information, Communication, and Society* 3.1 (2000): 39.

Pilkington, Ed. "Evgeny Morozov: How Democracy Slipped through the Net." *The Guardian*, January 13, 2011: http://www.guardian.co.uk/technology/2011/jan/13/evgeny-morozov-the-net-delusion.

Pink News. "Ahmadinejad's Gay Comments Lost in Translation." October, 30, 2010: http://www.pinknews.co.uk/news/articles/2005-5566.html/. Accessed October 20, 2012.

Pleace, N. "Single Homelessness as Social Exclusion: The Unique and the Extreme." *Social Policy and Administration* 32.1 (1998): 46.

Polletta, Francesca, and James M. Jasper. "Collective Identity and Social Movements." *Annual Review of Sociology* (2001): 283–305.

Portes, A. "Social Capital: Its Origins and Applications in Modern Sociology." *Annual Review of Sociology* 24.1 (1998): 1–24.

Poster, Mark. *Information Please: Culture and Politics in the Age of Digital Machines.* Durham, NC: Duke University Press, 2006.

Price, Monroe. "Iran and the Soft War." *International Journal of Communication* 6 (2012): 2397–2415.

Putnam, Robert D. *Bowling Alone: The Collapse and Revival of American Community.* New York: Simon and Schuster, 2000.

———. "Bowling Alone: America's Declining Social Capital." *Journal of Democracy* 6 (1995): 65–78.

———. *Making Democracy Work: Civic Traditions in Modern Italy.* Princeton: Princeton University Press, 1993.

———. "The Prosperous Community: Social Capital and Public Life." *The American Prospect* 13 (Spring 1993): 35–42.

Radsch, Courtney. "Core to Commonplace: The Evolution of Egypt's Blogosphere." *Arab Media and Society* 6 (Fall 2008). n.p.

Rahimi, Babak. "Iran's Declining Influence in Iraq." *The Washington Quarterly* 35.1 (Winter 2012): 25–40; 32.

———. *Theater State and the Formation of the Early Modern Public Sphere in Iran: Studies on Safavid Muharram Rituals, 1590–1641 CE.* Leiden and Boston: Brill, 2012.

———. "The Agonistic Social Media: Cyberspace in the Formation of Dissent and Consolidation of State Power in Postelection Iran." *The Communication Review* 14 (2011): 158–178.

———. "The Politics of the Internet in Iran." In *Media, Culture, and Society in Iran: Living with Globalization and the Islamic State*, ed. Mehdi Semati, 37–56. London and New York: Routledge, 2008.

———. "The Rebound Theater State: The Politics of the Safavid Camel Sacrifice Rituals, 1598–1695 C.E." *International Journal of Iranian Studies* 3 (2004): 451–478.

Rahimi, Babak, and Elham Gheytanchi. "Iran's Reformists and Activists: Internet Exploiters." *Middle East Policy* 15.1 (2008): 46.

Rahmandad, Hazhir, and Mohammad Mahdian. "Modeling Polarization in Online Communities." Proceedings of the 29th International Conference of the System Dynamics Society, 2011.

Rainie, Lee, and Barry Wellman. *Networked: The New Social Operating System*. Cambridge, MA, and London: MIT Press, 2012.

Rambod, M., and F. Rafii. "Perceived Social Support and Quality of Life in Iranian Hemodialysis Patients." *Journal of Nursing Scholarship* 42.3 (2010): 242–249.

Rappaport, Julian. "Terms of Empowerment/Exemplars of Prevention: Toward a Theory of Community Psychology," *American Journal of Community Psychology* 15 (1987): 121.

Rassooli, Mohammad Reza, and Maryam Moradi. "Avamil-e moasir bar towlid-e muhtava dar shabakiha-ye ejtemai." *Ulum-e Ejtemae-ye* 56 (1391/2012): 57–66.

Rivetti, Paola. "The Role of the Iranian Diaspora in Shaping Iranian Activisim." 2012: http://www.academia.edu/1800365/THE_ROLE_OF_THE_IRANIAN_DIASPORA_IN_SHAPING_IRANIAN_ACTIVISM.

———. "The Role of Diasporas in Establishing Transnational Activism: The Case of Iran." 2012: http://www.iranianalliances.org/?p=659&option=com_wordpress&Itemid=458.

Room, G. J. "Social Exclusion, Solidarity, and the Challenge of Globalization." *International Journal of Social Welfare* 8.3 (1999): 166.

Rosenberg, Scott. *Say Everything: How Blogging Began, What It's Becoming, and Why It Matters*. New York: Broadway Books, 2010.

Rouhani, Hassan. Twitter post. May 21, 2014: https://twitter.com/HassanRouhani.

Rutten, Rosanne, and Michiel Baud. "Concluding Remarks: Framing Protest in Asia, Africa, and Latin America." In *Popular Intellectuals and Social Movements: Framing Protest in Asia, Africa, and Latin America*, ed. Rosanne Rutten and Michiel Baud, 197–217. Amsterdam: International Review of Social History, 2004, Supplement.

Sabety, Setareh. "Graphic Content: The Semiotics of a YouTube Uprising." In *Media, Power, and Politics in the Digital Age: The 2009 Presidential Election Uprising in Iran*, ed. Yahya R. Kamalipour, 119–124. Plymouth: Rowman & Littlefield, 2010.

Sahliyeh, Emile. "The Presidential Election in Iran, June 2009." *Electoral Studies* 29.1 (2010): 182–185.

Saraji, G. N., and H. Dargahi. "Study of Quality of Work Life (Qwl)." *Iranian Journal of Public Health* 35.4 (2006): 8–14.

Schectman, Joel. "Iran's Twitter Revolution? Maybe Not Yet." *BusinessWeek: Technology*, June 17, 2009: http://www.businessweek.com/technology/content/jun2009/tc20090617_803990.htm.

Scholte, Jan Aart. *Globalization: A Critical Introduction*. Basingstoke: Palgrave, 2000.

Scheiwiller, Staci Gem. "(Neo)Orientalism: Alive and Well in Contemporary Art—A Case Study of Contemporary Iranian Art." In *Neo-Orientalism, American Hegemony, and Academia after September 11th*, ed. Tugrul Keskin and Mohamed Bamyeh, in press.

————. "Reframing the Rise of Modernism in Iran." In *Modernism beyond the West: A History of Art from Emerging Markets*, ed. Majella Munro, 11–32. London: Enzo Arts and Publishing, 2012.

Schmitt, Carl. *The Concept of the Political*. Chicago: University of Chicago Press, 2007.

Schuller, T., S. Baron, and J. Field. "Social Capital: A Review and Critique." *Social Capital: Critical Perspectives* (2000): 1–38.

Schwering, Markus. "Internet and the Public Sphere: What the Web Can't Do." July 24, 2014: www.resetdoc.org.

Segerberg, Alexandra, and W. Lance Bennett. "Social Media and the Organization of Collective Action: Using Twitter to Explore the Ecologies of Two Climate Change Protests." *The Communication Review* 14.3 (2011): 474–490.

Shahabi, Mahmood. "The Iranian Moral Panic over Video: A Brief History and a Policy Analysis." In *Media, Culture, and Society in Iran: Living with Globalization and the Islamic State*, ed. Mehdi Semati, 111–129. New York: Routledge, 2008.

Shahidi, Hossein. *Journalism in Iran: From Mission to Profession*. London and New York: Routledge, 2007.

Sheffer, Gabriel. *Diaspora Politics: At Home Abroad*. New York: Cambridge University Press, 2006.

Shirk, Susan L. "Changing Media, Changing China." In *Changing Media, Changing China*, ed. Susan L. Shirk, 1–37. London: Oxford University Press, 2011.

Shirkey, Clay. "The Political Power of Social Media: Technology, the Public Sphere, and Political Change." *Foreign Affairs* (January/February 2011): http://www.gpia.info/files/u1392/Shirky_Political_Poewr_of_Social_Media.pdf.

Shuter, Robert. "Intercultural New Media Studies: The Next Frontier in Intercultural Communication." *Journal of Intercultural Communication* 41.3 (2012): 219–237.

Small Media. "LGBT Republic of Iran: An Online Reality?" http://smallmediafoundation.com/files/LGBTRepublicofIran.pdf. Accessed September 29, 2012.

Small Media. "Satellite Wars: Why Iran Keeps Jamming." *Frontline* (online), November, 20, 2012: http://www.pbs.org/wgbh/pages/frontline/tehranbureau/2012/11/briefing-satellite-wars-why-iran-keeps-jamming.html. Accessed April 8, 2013.

Smith, Michael P., and Luis Guarnizo, eds. *Transnationalism from Below*. New Brunswick, Canada: Transaction, 1998.

Snider, Erin A., and David M. Faris. "The Arab Spring: U.S. Democracy Promotion in Egypt." *Middle East Policy* 18.3 (Fall 2011): 49–62.

Söderström, Sylvia. "Offline Social Ties and Online Use of Computers: A Study of Disabled Youth and Their Use of ICT Advance." *New Media & Society* 11.5 (2009): 709.

Solomon, Barbara Bryant. *Black Empowerment: Social Work in Oppressed Communities*. New York: Columbia University Press, 1976.

Solove, Daniel J. *The Digital Person: Technology and Privacy in the Information Age.* New York: New York University Press, 2004.

Solow-Niederman, Alicia Grae. "The Power of 140 Characters? #IranElection and Social Movements in Web 2.0." *Intersect: The Stanford Journal of Science, Technology, and Society* 3.1 (2010): 30–39.

Spilker, Hendrik Storstein, and Knut Holtan Sørenson. "A Room of One's Own or a Home for Sharing." *New Media and Society* 2. 3 (2000): 268–285.

Sreberny, Annabelle, Ali Mohammadi. *Small Media, Big Revolution: Communication, Culture, and the Iranian Revolution.* Minneapolis: University of Minnesota Press, 1994.

Sreberny, Annabelle, and Gholam Khiabany. *Blogistan: The Internet and Politics in Iran.* London and New York: I. B. Tauris, 2010.

Stacher, Joshua. *Adaptable Autocrats: Regime Power in Egypt and Syria.* Stanford, CA: Stanford University Press, 2012.

Stage, Carsten. "Thingifying Neda: The Construction of Commemorative and Affective Thingification of Neda Agha-Soltan." *Culture Unbound* 3 (2011): 19.

Staples, Lee H. "Power Ideas about Empowerment." *Administration in Social Work* 14.2 (1990): 29.

Stone, Brad. "New Tool from Facebook Extends Its Web Presence." *New York Times*, July 24, 2008: http://www.nytimes.com/2008/07/24/technology/24facebook. html?ex=1374638400&en=005f9a606dcd42f2&ei=5124&partner=permalink &exprod=permalink. Accessed July 24, 2008.

Sturken, Marita. "Paradox in the Evolution of an Art Form: Great Expectations and the Making of a History." In *Illuminating Video: An Essential Guide to Video Art*, ed. Doug Hall and Sally Jo Fifer, 101–121. New York: Aperture, 1990.

Sundbo, Jon. "Three Paradigms in Innovation Theory." *Science and Public Policy* 22.6 (1995): 399–410.

Tazmini, Ghoncheh. *Khatami's Iran: The Islamic Republic and the Turbulent Path to Reform.* London: I. B. Tauris, 2009.

Tehranian, Majid. "Global Communication and International Relations: Changing Paradigms and Policies." *The International Journal of Peace Studies* 2.1 (1997): n.p. http://www.gmu.edu/programs/icar/ijps/vol2_1/cover2_1.htm. Accessed December 15, 2014.

———. "Iran: Communication, Alienation, Revolution." *InterMedia* 7.2 (March 1979): 6–12.

Temple, J. "Initial Conditions, Social Capital, and Growth in Africa." *Journal of African Economies* 7.3 (1998): 309–347.

Thevenot, Guillaume. "Blogging as a Social Media." *Tourism and Hospitality Research* 7.3–4 (2007): 287.

Thomas, Anthony. *For Neda.* HBO Documentary Films, 2010. 68 minutes.

Tilly, Charles. *Trust and Rule.* Cambridge and New York: Cambridge University Press, 2005.

Totten, Michael J. "The Dubai Effect." *Commentary*, November 29, 2009: http://www.commentarymagazine.com/2009/11/29/the-dubai-effect/.

Tufekci, Zeynep, and Christopher Wilson. "Social Media and the Decision to Participate in Political Protest: Observations from Tahrir Square." *Journal of Communication* 62.2 (April 2012): 363–379.

United Nations. *Disabilities: A Guide to Adaptation and Effective Implementation of the International Covenant of the Rights of People with Disabilities*, trans. Faghih Abolhassan, Nazmdeh Kazem, and Hamrangi Yousefi, Mohammadtaghi. Tehran: State Welfare Organization, 2007.

Uslaner, E. M. "Social Capital, Television, and the 'Mean World': Trust, Optimism, and Civic Participation." *Political Psychology* 19 (1998): 441–467.

Valkenberg, P. M., and J. Peter. "Pre-Adolescents' and Adolescents' Online Communication and Their Closeness to Friends." *Developmental Psychology* 43.2 (2007): 267.

Van Doorn, Neils, Sally Wyatt, and Liesbet Van Zoomer. "A Body of Text: Revising Textual Performances of Gender and Sexuality on the Internet." In *The Gender and Media Reader*, ed. Mary Celeste Kearney, 423–437. New York: Routledge, 2012.

Varzi, Roxanne. "Iran's French Revolution." *The Annals of the American Academy of Political and Social Science* 637.1 (September 1, 2011): 53–63.

———. *Warring Souls: Youth, Media, and Martyrdom in Post-Revolution Iran*. Durham, NC: Duke University Press, 2006.

Veisi, Reza. "From 'Guerrilla Journalism' in Tehran to Exile Journalism in Prague." In *Election Fallout: Iran's Exiled Journalists on Their Struggle for Democratic Change*, ed. Marcus Michaelsen, 174–189. Berlin: Hans Schiler, 2011.

Vertovec, Steven. "Super-Diversity and Its Implications." *Ethnic and Racial Studies* 30.6 (2007): 1024–1054.

Viegas, Fernanda B. "Bloggers' Expectations of Privacy and Accountability: An Initial Survey." *Journal of Computer-Mediated Communication* 10.3 (2005): http://jcmc.indiana.edu/vol10/issue3/viegas.html.

Vyazhlinskaya, Yuliya. "The Global Virtual Museum: Collaboration and Cooperation of Museums via the Internet." Master's thesis, San Francisco State University, 2001.

Wacjman, Judy. "Feminist Theories of Technology." *Cambridge Journal of Economics* (2009): http://wiki.medialabprado.es/images/4/4b/Wajcman_Feminist_theories_of_technology.pdf.

Walkowitz, Daniel J., and Lisa Maya Knauer. *Memory and the Impact of Political Transformation in Public Space*. Durham, NC: Duke University Press, 2004.

Walther, Joseph B. "Computer-Mediated Communication: Impersonal, Interpersonal, and Hyper-Personal Interaction." *Human Communication Research* 23.1 (1996): 3–43.

Walther, Joseph B., and Judee K. Burgoon. "Relational Communication in Computer-Mediated Interaction." *Human Communication Research* 19.1 (1992): 50–88.

Waltz, Mitzi. *Alternative and Activist Media*. Edinburgh: Edinburgh University Press, 2005.

Wattal, Sunil, David Schuff, Munir Mandviwalla, and Christine B. Williams. "Web 2.0 and Politics: The 2008 US Presidential Election and an e-Politics Research Agenda." *MIS Quarterly* 34.4 (2010): 669–688.

Watts, Duncan. *Six Degrees: The Science of a Connected Age.* New York: W.W. Norton, 2003.

Weaver, Matthew. "Iran's 'Twitter Revolution' Was Exaggerated, Says Editor." *The Guardian*, June 9, 2010: http://www.guardian.co.uk/world/2010/jun/09/iran-twitter-revolution-protests.

Welzel, Christian, Ronald F. Inglehart, and Franziska Deutsch. "Social Capital, Voluntary Associations, and Collective Action: Which Aspects of Social Capital Have the Greatest 'Civic' Payoff?" *Journal of Civil Society* 1.2 (2005): 121–146.

West, Mark. "Is the Internet an Emerging Public Sphere?" *Journal of Mass Media Ethics* 28.3 (2013): 155–159.

Wilson, Christopher, and Alexandra Dunn. "Digital Media in the Egyptian Revolution: Descriptive Analysis from the Tahrir Datasets." *International Journal of Communication* 5 (2011): 1248–1272.

Winner, Langdon. *Autonomous Technology: Technics-out-of-Control as a Theme in Political Thought.* Cambridge: MIT Press, 1978.

———. "Do Artifacts Have Politics?" *Daedalus* 109.1 (1980): 121–136.

Wojcieszak, Magdalena, Briar Smith, and Mahmood Enayat. "Finding a Way: How Iranians Reach for News and Information." Iran Media Program, Annenberg School for Communication, University of Pennsylvania, 2011–2012, 21: www.global.asc.upenn.edu/fileLibrary/PDFs/FindingaWay.pdf. Accessed December 10, 2012.

Wolfsfeld, Gadi. "Social Media and the Arab Spring: Politics Comes First." *The International Journal of Press/Politics* 18.2 (2013): 115–137.

———. *Media and Political Conflict: News from the Middle East.* Cambridge, New York: Cambridge University Press, 1997.

Woolcock, Michael. "Social Capital and Economic Development: Towards a Theoretical Synthesis and Policy Framework." *Theory and Society* 27 (1998): 151–208.

Yang, Goubin. *The Power of the Internet in China: Citizen Activism in China.* New York: Columbia University Press, 2009.

Yeung, Douglas, Sara Beth Elson, Parisa Roshan, S. R. Bohandy, Alireza Nader. *Using Social Media to Gauge Iranian Public Opinion and Mood after the 2009 Election.* Santa Monica: Rand, 2012.

Youmans, William Lafi, and Jillian York. "Social Media and the Activist Toolkit: User Agreements, Corporate Interests, and the Information Infrastructure of Modern Social Movements." *Journal of Communication* 62.2 (2012): 315–329.

Zavella, Patricia. "Feminist Insider Dilemmas: Constructing Ethnic Identity with 'Chicana' Informants." In *Frontiers: A Journal of Women Studies* 13.3 (1993): 53–76.

Zelizer, Barbie. *About to Die: How News Images Move the Public.* New York: Oxford University Press, 2010.

———. "The Voice of the Visual in Memory." In *Framing Public Memory*, ed. Kendall R. Phillips, 157–186. Tuscaloosa: University of Alabama Press, 2004.

Zimmerman, Marc A. "Empowerment Theory: Psychological, Organizational, and Community Levels of Analysis." In *Handbook of Community Psychology*, ed. Julian Rappaport and Edward Seidman, 43–63. New York: Spring Press, 2000.

Zuckerman, Ethan. "International Reporting in the Age of Participatory Media." *Daedalus* 139.2 (2010): 66–75.

Contributors

Niki Akhavan is an assistant professor of media studies at the Catholic University of America. Her research examines relationships between New Media technologies and Iranian transnational political and cultural production, with a specific interest in how state actors have participated in and reacted to New Media landscapes. She is the author of *Electronic Iran: The Cultural Politics of an Online Evolution.*

Kobra Elahifar is a PhD candidate in the communication and culture department at the University of Calgary. She pursues her research on the discursive politics of food marketing to children, with a focus on the socio-cognitive aspects of new brand marketing practices. She is interested in the transformative aspects of cultural practices of consumption.

Jari Eloranta is professor of history at Appalachian State University. He received his PhD in history from the European University Institute in Florence, Italy. He is also an adjunct professor at the University of Jyvaskyla, department of history and ethnology. His research focuses mainly on government spending patterns and trade in Europe from the eighteenth to the twenty-first centuries. In addition, he has worked on social cohesion in certain groups, such as seamen who deserted their ships in the eighteenth and nineteenth centuries.

Arash Falasiri has received a national prize for best journalist in Iran and has been published internationally for more than a decade. He studied political philosophy at Sydney University in Australia and is a PhD candidate in social and political thought at York University in Canada. His research, a critique of democratic reason, a double definition of democracy, which mainly focuses on the relationship of and dialectics of truth in the political sphere, won the Joseph-Armand Bombardier scholarship from the Social Sciences and Humanities Research Council of Canada (SSHRC).

David M. Faris is chair of the department of political science and public administration at Roosevelt University in Chicago. He earned his PhD in political science at the University of Pennsylvania in Philadelphia in 2010. His book *Dissent and Revolution in a Digital Age: Social Media, Blogging and Activism in Egypt*, published in 2013, focuses on the use of digital media by Egyptian opposition movements. His academic work has been published in *Middle East Policy, Arab Media & Society*, and *Politique Etrangère*. He has published op-eds in *NPR.org*, the *Christian Science Monitor*, the *Daily News Egypt*, the *Philadelphia Citypaper, the Philadelphia Inquirer*, and other publications.

Nazanin Ghanavizi has studied sociology at Sydney University and political theory at the University of Toronto. Her main area of expertise, in which she has published internationally, is the role of the Internet on public reasoning and social movements. She is currently pursuing her PhD in social and political thought at York University in Canada, where she focuses on critical theory and political sociology.

Elham Gheytanchi teaches sociology at Santa Monica College. Her research focuses on media, online activism, and civic engagement. Her scholarly articles, opinion columns, essays, and book reviews on the impact of digital media on women's rights movements in the Middle East and North Africa have appeared in academic journals and in online and print media such as *CNN 360, The Huffington Post, Ms. Magazine*, the *Boston Globe*, and the *San Francisco Chronicle*. She has collaborated on programming for "To the Point," a popular show on National Public Radio as an associate producer (2001–2002). She is a mother of two and lives in California.

Hossein Kermani is an independent scholar based in Tehran, Iran. He has studied social communication science at the University of Tehran, where he achieved first rank at the Iranian MA examination. He has published numerous articles in Persian on digital technology and social networking sites in Iran. His research interests include the study of information communication technologies, discourse analysis, and cultural studies.

Michelle Langford, PhD, lectures in film studies at UNSW in Australia. Her current research spans the cinemas of Iran and Germany. She is the author of *Allegorical Images: Tableau, Time and Gesture in the Cinema of Werner Schroeter* and editor of *The Directory of World Cinema: Germany*. Her work on Iranian cinema has appeared in leading film studies journals, including *Camera Obscura, Screen,* and *Screening the Past.* Her current research looks at allegory in Iranian cinema.

Reza Masoudi Nejad is an Alexander von Humboldt fellow at the Centre for Modern Oriental Studies (ZMO) in Berlin and affiliated with SOAS at the University of London. He was a Research Fellow at the Max Planck Institute for the Study of Religious and Ethnic Diversity, where he completed a two-year research project (2009–2011) on the Muharram rituals in public spaces in Mumbai, India. He is an architect and urban morphologist interested in the spatial organization of rituals, the interaction between society and space, and urban transformation. Masoudi Nejad received his PhD from the Bartlett Faculty of the Built Environment, University College London (UCL) in 2009.

Marcus Michaelsen is a postdoctoral researcher in the political science department at the University of Amsterdam. He received his PhD in media and communication studies from the University of Erfurt (Germany) in 2012. His thesis examined the role of the Internet in Iran's political transformation. Michaelsen holds an MA in Middle Eastern studies from the Université de Provence (France) and was a research fellow at the Institut Français de Recherche en Iran in Tehran from 2004 to 2006. His main research interests are media in political transitions as well as Iranian politics and society.

Abouzar Nasirzadeh is a doctoral student in the department of political science at the University of Toronto. He holds an MA in international relations from the London School of Economics and Political Science in London. His research interests include civil–military relations, modern Iranian politics, Middle Eastern politics, U.S. foreign policy in the Muslim world, Queer politics in Islamic countries, and HIV/AIDS policy.

Babak Rahimi is an associate professor of communication, culture, and religion and the director of Third World Studies at the University of California at San Diego. He has been a visiting scholar at the Internet Institute, University of Oxford, Berlin Graduate School Muslim Cultures and Societies, Freie Universität Berlin, and the Annenberg School for Communication at the University of Pennsylvania. He is the author of *Theater State and the Formation of Early modern Public Sphere in Iran: Studies on Safavid Muharram Rituals, 1590–1641 C.E.* His work has also appeared in *Thesis Eleven: Critical Theory and Historical Sociology, International Political Science*

Review, The Communication Review, and *Journal of the International Society for Iranian Studies.* His current research focuses on relationships among culture, religion, and technology.

Samira Rajabi is a doctoral candidate in media studies at the University of Colorado at Boulder. She has her MA in International and Intercultural Communications from the University of Denver School of Mass Communications and the Josef Korbel School of International Studies. Her undergraduate degree is a BS in entrepreneurship from the University of Colorado at Boulder. Her research focuses on representations and interventions to violence against women through the media as well as the use of online tools and social media in the wake of traumatic experiences. Using a strong focus on meaning-making online, she interrogates multiple levels of trauma in diverse communities. She focuses on mediations and re-mediations of trauma as they relate to identity, race, ethnicity, and gender. She has a strong grounding in feminist and gender studies as well as development as it relates to women. Her regional interests include Iran, the Middle East, and Central and East Africa.

Nima Rassooli is a PhD student in the literature department at the University of California at San Diego. He has a BA in political science from the University of California, San Diego, and an MA in political science from San Francisco State University. His current research is on relationships among digital technology, cyber-capitalism, and state power.

Mohammad Sadeghi Esfahlani is a PhD student at the Department of Communications at the University of Calgary in Canada. He graduated in International Business and Economics from the RWTH Aachen University in Germany. His thesis project presented a sociological critique of the concept of identity in a game theoretical model in neo-classic economics, substantiated with a case study of sociopolitical developments in Iran in 2009. He founded and administered the Facebook campaign for Mir Husyan Mousavi during the Iranian 2009 presidential elections and engaged as an activist throughout the subsequent Iranian Green Movement. He has published on the politics of social media in the Iranian context in academic and journalistic venues.

Staci Gem Scheiwiller is an assistant professor of Modern Art History at California State University in Stanislaus. She received her PhD in the History of Art from the University of California, Santa Barbara, in 2009. Her field is Modern and Contemporary Art, with an emphasis on Iranian Art and photography and a minor field in Islamic Art. She also specializes in theories of postcolonialism and gender. Currently, she is focused on issues of modernity and modernism in Iran during the nineteenth and twentieth centuries and finishing a manuscript on constructions of gender and beauty in nineteenth-century Iranian photography. Among several publications, her most recent includes an edited volume entitled *Performing the Iranian State: Visual Culture and Representations of Iranian Identity* (2013).

Index

Abbas, Wael, 203
Abd El-Fattah, Alaa, 202
Abdel Fatteh, Wael, 203
Abdi, Ali, 170–71, 173
Abedian, Torang, 258
Abidi, Bani, 273
addiction, online, 38n59
afsaran.ir website, 186, 192
Afshari, Ali, 169, 176
Agha-Soltan, Neda, 104, 152, 231–43, 255–56, 259
Ahadi, Ali Samadi, 256
Ahmadinejad, Mahmoud, 26, 144, 148, 206, 252; election of, 101–4, 113–14, 131, 145, 150, 199; on homosexuality, 57, 68, 75n57; website of, 133–34, 136n23
Akhavan, Niki, 11, 35n12, 213–25, 313
Alavi, Nasrin, 185
Allen, Matthew, 4
Altman, Irwin, 88
Amazon Corporation, 193
Ameli, Said Reza, 81
Amer, Kareem, 204
Anderson, Chris, 2
"anti-politics," 143, 156–57
Apeejay Media Gallery, 275, 281
Appadurai, Arjun, 167
Arab Network for Human Rights Information, 203, 207–8
Arab Spring (2011), 5, 35n13, 138, 199–200, 208–9, 251; in Egypt, 3,

11, 138, 199–205, 207–9; Iranian support of, 154; in Tunisia, 138, 206, 209
Arendt, Hannah, 9, 123–25
Argentina, 50
Aryanpour, Pooya, 271
arzeshees ("those with values"), 219–21, 224
Ashouri, Darius, 188
Ashufteh, Aziz, 183, 188–90, 192–94
Assad, Bashar al-, 5
Assmann, Jan, 238, 240, 242
asylum seekers, 63, 66
Atef, Noha, 203
avant-garde art, 271–82
Azar, Alireza Sami, 275

Baavar Organization, 82–83, 85
Balatarin website, 10, 72n7, 133, 183–84, 187–96; advertising on, 193; founding of, 183, 188; Green Movement and, 173, 174, 183–84, 191–94
Bani-Etemad, Rakhsahn, 266
Banisadr, Abolhassan, 118n23
Bar-ax.com website, 258
Basiji Organization of the Iranian Society, 51, 52, 131; blogs of, 132; cyber attacks by, 191; gay entrapment by, 65, 74n41
Bastani, Susan, 25
Baudrillard, Jean, 236
Bauman, Zygmunt, 20–21